A NEW and CORRECT
SEA CHART OF THE
World,

WRIGHT'S, COMMONLY
called

... PROJECTION

... humbly INSCRIBED to the
...rs Commissioners of the
...RALTY.

be a part of the Continent or not

EMPIRE
OF
CHINA

S
...IA

LEOTUNG
Peking

XANTUN
NANKING
CHEKIANG
FOCHIEU
CANTON

COREA

JAPON

TONSA
CICOKO

YEDSO

Companys
Land

North Cape

C.Patience

BENGALA
ARACAN
PEGU
SIAM
BENGALL
ANDAMINE
CEYLAN
de Galle

FORMOSA

PHILIPPINE
ILUCON

LADRON
ISLES

los Hermanos

BORNEO

GILOLO
MOLUCCA ISLES

TERRA DE PAPOS NOVA GUINEA

HOLLANDIA
NOVA

P. Nuyts Land

Land Discovered
Anno 1622

Van Diemens Land

THE WORLD OF DEFOE

BOOKS BY PETER EARLE

THE WORLD OF

DEFOE

•

PETER EARLE

ATHENEUM NEW YORK
1977

Library of Congress Cataloging in Publication Data

Earle, Peter, 1937–
    The world of Defoe.

    Includes bibliographical references and index
    1.   Defoe, Daniel, 1661?–1731.   I.   Title.
PR3406.E2   1977   823'.5 [B]   76–40310
ISBN 0–689–10772–2

CONTENTS

INTRODUCTION

My original motive in writing this book was to force myself to find out something about the social and economic history of England in the late seventeenth and early eighteenth centuries in preparation for a course which I had agreed to teach at the London School of Economics. This is a period about which remarkably little has been written by social and economic historians, but one thing struck me as I began my reading. This was the fact that nearly all those historians who do write about this period rely heavily on quotations from Defoe. It was at this stage that I thought it might be possible to do what they were doing on a larger scale, to base a study of English society in the early eighteenth century almost entirely on the writings of this one extraordinary man. I drew up an ambitious synopsis and approached Weidenfeld and Nicolson, who trustingly commissioned me to go ahead with my ideas. The result is *The World of Defoe*.

It was only then, with the contract signed, that I began to realize just what I had let myself in for. I should perhaps have been a little more cautious. The fact that one man could be the author of such well-known and well-loved books as *Robinson Crusoe* and *Moll Flanders* and at the same time the author of a number of pieces of economic journalism widely quoted by academic historians should have warned me that I was dealing with an unusual writer. I soon found out that these quotations and the books from which they had been drawn were only the tip of an enormous iceberg. To my horror I discovered that Defoe was probably the most prolific writer in the English language, a writer moreover who wrote on every conceivable topic from angels to annuities and from adultery to agriculture. But it was too late to back out. This turned out to be fortunate, since the study of Defoe has been doubly rewarding. I have acquired an

enormous respect for this strange and remarkable man who wrote
the great majority of his full-length books in the last decade of his
life, when he was in his sixties. And my original hypothesis was
correct, in spite of the lack of information on which I based it. It is
possible to base a study of English society in the early eighteenth
century almost entirely on the writings of Daniel Defoe.

How much exactly Defoe did write is impossible to say. For
almost everything he wrote was written anonymously. It has been
left to the devotion and ingenuity of a long line of editors and
bibliographers to decide what does and does not belong to the opus
of Defoe.[1] Their methods fall outside the scope of a mere historian
who knows a little about internal and external evidence, but feels
somewhat lost in admiration at that instinctive, almost extrasensi-
tory, conviction that leads one bibliographer to absolute certainty
that the work which he has before him on his desk was written by
Defoe and the next critic to total scorn at his predecessor's credulity.
Works are attributed to Defoe because of their style, their vocabu-
lary, their ideas, sometimes simply because of their subject-matter.
As time passes some works are deleted from the canon, some added,
but still the list grows. Every now and then Professor Moore, Defoe's
most devoted bibliographer, adds a few more titles to the British
Library copy of his *Checklist of the Writings of Daniel Defoe*.[2] The total
number in this most authoritative work has long passed five hundred,
varying in length from pamphlets of a few pages to the *Review*, one
title covering nine years of journalism and totalling 5,610 pages
nearly all written by Defoe,[3] the 900-plus pages of the *Complete
English Tradesman*[4] or the letter-press of the *Atlas Maritimus*,[5] with
its total of well over half a million words. And all this, we must
remember, was written without such modern aids as typewriter,
dictaphone and electric light, just a quill and a candle and gallons
and gallons of ink.

Writers in Defoe's day were often paid by the sheet, and he was
guilty of some outrageous padding as his theme flagged and he
laboured to make up his required total.[6] Anecdotes, repetition,
massive quotations from his previous works were all grist to the mill
of this king of wordsmiths. But this padding is not all loss to the
reader. Some of Defoe's best comment on the contemporary scene
comes in anecdotes which have virtually no relevance to the main
theme of the particular work. But it must be admitted that the last
hundred pages of some of Defoe's books are as boring to the modern

reader as they clearly were to Defoe himself. Four hundred pages
was a common length and Defoe made sure he received four hundred
pages' worth of cash for his efforts. Indeed, according to a later
editor, it was necessary to give him so much per sheet to write a
book in his own way and 'half as much afterwards to lop off its
excrescences, or abstract it'.[7] Still a writer must live, and being paid
to do something does not necessarily make a man mercenary, as
Defoe himself pointed out. A beggar begs for money, a judge judges
for money, and a writer writes for money, but he does at least try to
do some good in the world in return for the meagre living with
which the world rewards him, which is more than can be said of a
judge or a beggar, or so Defoe claimed.[8]

The works of Defoe might well be described in the same words
that he used to describe *Mist's Journal*, the popular Tory weekly for
which he wrote some of his best journalism – 'an agreeable miscel-
lany of subjects, out of which every person may pick something
wherewith to entertain himself'.[9] Not everything in this bran-tub
has been of interest to me. I wanted to generalize about Defoe's
society and the people who lived in it and, as a result, I have for the
most part avoided discussion of particular historical events and
particular people, even though a considerable amount of Defoe's
enormous output consists of polemical comment on them. I have
also resisted the temptation of using too much description, mainly
in order to keep the book to a reasonable length. Defoe had an
extremely fine eye for the detail which makes a description come to
life, but it is chiefly as an analyst, rather than simply as a recorder of
his world, that I have discussed him.

To call a book *The World of Defoe* is perhaps somewhat ambitious.
No one, not even Defoe, could pin down for ever the whole of his
world in a few hundred pages. What the book tries to do is to summarize Defoe's view of the world and the relationships of the people
who lived in that world with each other, with the world itself and
with God who created it and them. This is obviously a difficult thing
to do. One writer has said that no generalization about Defoe is
quite true.[10] I would be inclined to take this a little further and say
that no generalization about anything is quite true. For all that,
Defoe clearly had a mental image of his world and the way in
which it worked. This image is remarkably consistent for a man
who wrote so much. It is obvious that a writer who tries to impose
an analytical order on the multifarious works of another, extremely

prolific, writer who flourished two and a half centuries previously is likely to do much injustice. I am sure that I am guilty of imposing order where Defoe never meant it to exist. But I do have one advantage over Defoe himself. I read through most of his works in a single year, which I am sure he never did. As I read, I naturally selected what seemed significant for the book I was writing and ignored or skimmed through what did not. This may seem a hazardous way of working, but speed has its advantages. By the time I had finished I was able to see Defoe's works and his world as a whole, a fact which has enabled me to make generalizations about his ideas which, even if not completely true, are unlikely to be completely false.

The world which Defoe had in his mind was not necessarily the same as the world of any of his contemporaries. Indeed it was often very different. Defoe had few really original ideas. He relied for the most part on the very considerable pool of ideas that already existed, but the somewhat eclectic mix which he created from them was his own. I have not attempted to determine the original source of Defoe's ideas, but I have tried to compare his analysis of the problems of his world with other contemporary analyses and with the findings of modern historiography.

The world which Defoe wrote about was also selective. No one else wrote about so many things as Defoe, but even Defoe could not write exhaustively about everything. This book reflects the emphasis of its subject-matter. There is little here, except abuse, on the world of the wits and the coffee-houses which seems in the mind of some historians to be all that matters in the England of Queen Anne. The reader will also find very little about those great men who were the period's glory. The fact that Defoe was a contemporary of such men as Swift and Pope, Handel and Bach, had little effect on his view of his world. Defoe read widely and he enjoyed good music. He even played the lute himself, but he has not much of interest to say on the arts. Even within the more modest scope of English society there are many gaps. There is little here on the world of the farmer or peasant. Defoe was not very interested in rural life. What he was interested in was the life of middle-class Londoners and much of this book is an analysis of the conditions of that life. But Defoe's world was much wider than that and I hope my book will do justice to the width of his interests. There is something, if not much, on both China and Patagonia, on both the very rich and the very poor, on both Heaven and Hell. There are sections on profanity, piracy, the poor law and prostitution. None of these sections are very long; some are only a couple of sentences or a paragraph. With such a variety of subject-matter, it was sometimes difficult to devise a satisfactory structure, though I have tried my best to weld them all together into a coherent and acceptable whole.

The World of Defoe is divided into four parts. The first consists of a discussion of the biography of Defoe. I have drawn very heavily on his previous biographers for this, and have attempted to suggest in what ways his own background and experiences might have affected the way he thought and wrote. This is not easy, since remarkably little is known of Defoe, and both his biographers and myself often find themselves forced into the position of deducing his biography from the sort of thing he wrote, an unsatisfactory situation which is almost bound to lead to circular arguments. The second part looks at the general background of the world of Defoe. 'The Inner World' discusses his religious, moral and philosophical view of the world and of nature. 'The Wider World' considers his ideas on geography and exploration and his view of the racial, social and economic peculiarities of those people who lived in the wider world beyond Europe. This part ends with a chapter called 'The Inheritors', which consists mainly of a comparison of the very different societies which existed in France and England, the two nations which were threatening to dominate not only Europe but the whole world of Defoe.

The third part of the book concentrates on England, with one chapter on the economy and one on the social structure of this newcomer who was to become a world power within Defoe's lifetime. Finally, the fourth part of the book discusses the life-cycle of the individual within English society, his role in that society, his ambitions, and the failures and successes which he was likely to undergo, if he behaved in various different ways.

My chief debt is, of course, to Defoe. Even when I finished writing this book I found that I did not know him as a person too well. He exists far more positively in his writings than in his own biography, but I am grateful that he did exist. I feel that I now know far more about the world in which he lived, even if I still know too little about the man himself. My next debt is to those who have written about Defoe. I trust that they will forgive me for trespassing on their territory and pinching a few of their ideas and hope that I have given due acknowledgement in the notes. Finally I would like to thank my colleagues, Jack Fisher, Dudley Baines and Malcolm Falkus, for reading the manuscript and pointing out some of the worst of my howlers, and Joan Lynas for typing it so accurately and so quickly.

PART I

THE OBSERVER

DANIEL DEFOE

WHAT sort of a man was Daniel Defoe? Did he in fact exist at all? Modern biographers and critics often seem to be more interested in what he stood for than what he was. He emerges as the embodiment of their interpretation of his ideas, a man of paper put together from the tens of thousands of pages that he covered with his writing. He is the father of the novel, the founder of modern journalism, the apostle of the middle class, the triumphant herald of the all-conquering bourgeoisie, but rarely a man. The fact that patient research has established that he was born in 1660, the very year of the Restoration, helps to sustain his symbolic role. He is seen as the harbinger of a new world, the symbol of modernity, individualism and the bourgeois spirit. *1660*

There was of course a man behind the ideas. Someone wielded the bourgeois pen. Someone stirred up the non-stop stream of abuse that greeted its labour. Sometimes we may even think we can see him, riding on horseback along a muddy road or enjoying the good, strong ale of northern England after a tiring day. But always there is that nagging doubt at the back of our mind. Is it Defoe we see or some figment of that still shadowy Defoe's imagination? We are never able to see him as we see Swift, sitting in bed in his night-cap, writing letters to Stella and moaning about the cost of coal and candles. When we do see Defoe we tend to see him in very bizarre settings. We see him in Newgate, writing hopeful, self-demeaning letters in a bid to secure his release. We see him dying alone in Cripplegate, hiding from a creditor. We see him best of all standing far above the street in the pillory, his trapped, wigless, disembodied head watching quizzically and somewhat apprehensively as the soldiers hold the crowd back, a crowd who are straining to pelt him, not with rotten eggs but with flowers.[1] What sort of a man was that?

To do them justice, his biographers have done their best to tell us. But their task is a hard one. It is always difficult to write a convincing biography of a man of letters, to distil the reality of the man from the torrent of words. For Defoe the lack of good evidence makes the task particularly difficult. References to him bob up here and there throughout his lifetime, but strung together they hardly add up to creating a convincing picture of a real man. The best portrait of Defoe stares at us from the frontispiece of *Jure Divino*.[2] The face is memorable, impressive, but it is very difficult to animate it, to make the great periwigged head with its high forehead, thoughtful dominating eyes, hooked nose and fleshy chin come to life. One feels one knows Robinson Crusoe considerably better. But then there is an extremely good contemporary biography of Robinson Crusoe.

The available evidence for a biography of Defoe is limited, and what there is presents problems of interpretation which have meant that many different Defoes have been presented to the public. Defoe himself lets drop a string of autobiographical hints throughout his writing career. But no biographer is under any compulsion to believe such hints. After all, Defoe was a creative artist praised by all critics for his realism and his ability to get into the minds of other people. He was a chameleon. He could turn himself with ease into a Quaker, a High-Churchman or a shipwrecked mariner. Why should he tell the truth about himself? His most sustained autobiographical piece was written as a defence against his political enemies,[3] a genre which has rarely carried the banner of truth through the ages. So the biographer has to select. He decides to believe this and disregard that. But on what criteria? Too often, he has a preconceived idea of the sort of man Defoe must have been if he wrote the sort of books that he is reputed to have written. Indeed these books themselves are mined for facts about the life of their author. Surely much of the material must have been autobiographical. No man could have made up so much. Certainly, if some of Defoe's works were not illustrations of his own life, the biography is going to be rather thin. But what does one select? And from which books? From the novels or from the didactic works? Was Defoe like Robinson Crusoe or the Complete English Tradesman, like Moll Flanders or like the repentant father in the first volume of *The Family Instructor*? Was he an adventurer or was he a rational economic man, was he obsessed with sex or with salvation; was he all of them or none of them? The scope is wide.

Having exhausted what Defoe himself wrote, the biographer can then move into another vein of evidence, perhaps even harder to interpret, the comments of his contemporaries. Was the fact that so much of this was hostile a sign of Defoe's errors or the blindness of his fellow-countrymen? The latter was, of course, what Defoe thought. He always saw himself as a reasonable, moderate man, the victim of a continuous stream of unfair attacks on his character, his ideas and his political honesty. But could so many people have been wrong? Modern critics are far more charitable to him than were the men of his own time. After all, they did not know that he was going to write *Robinson Crusoe* and when he did they abused him for it. Modern writers start off with the preconception that to write *Robinson Crusoe* was a good thing, though they may disagree on what the book is about or what sort of a man wrote it. Once one admires a man as a writer of fiction, a deceiver, then one is likely to take a more favourable view of other kinds of deceit which he has practised in his life.

Faced with such a mass of nebulous or conflicting evidence about their subject, biographers naturally feel a sense of relief when they find what seems a real fact about Defoe, even if it is only the date of publication of one of his books. It does help to pin the man down a bit. Much hard work has unearthed several facts of the sort that historians feel happiest about, nice objective things like wills, marriage licences or documents from the Chancery archives in the Public Record Office. There is nothing like a legal document for persuading the researcher that the man he is interested in really did exist. But even in this field Defoe is elusive. The discovery of no less than eight law-suits in which Defoe was the defendant, between 1688 and 1694, clearly throws much light on a formerly little known period of his life. But the evidence is not complete and tells us more about the plaintiff's view of the case than it does about Defoe.[4] Other legal documents have been discovered which provide hitherto unknown details of the lives of Defoe's relatives, but tell us little about Defoe himself. We do not even know exactly when he was born. Records of the birth of both his sisters have been discovered but there is no record of the birth or christening of Daniel.[5]

As is true of so many great men who rose to fame from comparative obscurity, it is the early years of Defoe's life which are the most poorly documented. Indeed, there is very little hard factual evidence at all for the first forty years of his life. This lack of evidence has

offered his numerous biographers ample opportunity to embroider
the little that is known and to select real or imaginary events as the
basis on which to build up an analysis of Defoe's complicated
psychology. Brian Fitzgerald, in his attractive and amusingly
written, if largely fictional, biography, wants Defoe to be, amongst
other things, a radical obsessed by sex. The young Defoe wanders
from his puritanical home and sees a grandee pass by in a coach and
six. But the gentleman is not alone. 'Beside him sits a lady, a pretty
girl with curls and bright red lips and pointed little breasts.'[6] Where
Fitzgerald discovered this fact we are not told, but the thought of
the girl becomes an obsession with Defoe. He is still seeking 'the
pretty girl, with the million curls and bright dancing eyes', forty
pages further on in the book.[7] Radicalism is added to sex in the
young Defoe's make-up by a reference to Monmouth's rebellion in
1685. Thirty years later Defoe himself claimed to have 'been in arms
under the Duke of Monmouth'.[8] Fitzgerald correctly points out that
we do not know what he actually did, but cannot resist giving a
dramatic description of the battle of Sedgemoor in the assumption
that Defoe was there. He introduces his account with the stirring
lines: 'Certainly Defoe rode with the rebels. Certainly he fought to
realise the Levellers' dreams.'[9] Well, perhaps he did.

All of Defoe's biographers stress his childhood in a Dissenting
household as an important factor in his psychological development.
What sort of a child grew up in such a home? What sort of people
were these latter-day puritans who had in so short a time sunk from
being the rulers of the country to become a persecuted and usually
despised minority? Defoe's father was a tallow-chandler, probably
descended from Flemish immigrants of Elizabethan times, who
followed his minister, Dr Samuel Annesley, into the underground
world of Dissent after the passage of the Act of Uniformity in 1662.
There is no evidence that Defoe's family were particularly strict,
but it is obvious that they were not prepared to compromise on
matters of conscience. Indeed, it is generally assumed that persecution made the puritan die-hards even more earnest and godly than
they had been before.

The puritan conscience was a piece of mental baggage that Defoe
was to carry all his days, but no biographer has been prepared to
allow him to leave home with that baggage alone. No one as ener-
getic and inquiring as Defoe could have been a good boy all the
time. But to determine what he got up to as a boy it is necessary

once more to resort to speculation. Not that there is much problem about that. Nearly all writers on Defoe assume that at least some of the early part of *Colonel Jack* is autobiographical. And so the young Defoe is made to wander about the city and talk to old soldiers and sailors, storing up information which he will be able to use to advantage fifty years later. Dottin has him visit the glass-houses in Rosemary Lane, looking 'curiously at the little piles of warm coal-ashes heaped in corners' where the young vagabonds sleep at night.[10] Fitzgerald even has him sleeping there himself, strange behaviour for the respectable son of a respectable tallow-chandler.[11] Nearly everyone has him wistfully observing the exciting panorama of Restoration London, worldly ambition struggling successfully to overcome the pangs of the puritan conscience in the mind of a boy being educated for the Nonconformist ministry.[12] It is in terms of this conflict that Defoe is seen to have made the important decision to renounce the ministry, the career that his parents had chosen for him. Since much of Defoe's fiction and many of his didactic works are dominated by the conflicts between morality, vice and the pursuit of wealth, this seems an acceptable psychological position to take, especially since Defoe himself stresses the reign of Charles 11 as a time of enormous increase in both the vice and the wealth of the nation. It would have been difficult for an imaginative and ambitious child not to have been affected by it.

Another subject which plays an important role in Defoe's writings is that of marriage. Naturally his biographers and critics have been interested in Defoe's own marriage, an event which in any case would seem to have some importance in everybody's psychological make-up. Was it a happy union? The charitable Moore thinks that a modern man should have a modern marriage based on love. 'Theirs was certainly a love match', he confidently declares, adding for our benefit a word picture of the dashing young bridegroom who was fortunate enough to be sunburned in the middle of the coldest winter in living memory.[13] The love match turned into a happy marriage: 'For nearly fifty years Daniel and Mary lived together in a censorious age, without public scandal and (as far as we can learn now) with no private recrimination.'[14] Dottin, however, decided that such a rational man would not marry for love: 'He disregarded so dangerous and impractical a passion, to be ruled instead by the dictates of cool reason, mature reflection, and sound judgment.'[15] Sutherland, cautious and rarely enthusiastic about

Defoe's personal life, comments drily that 'there is some reason for
supposing that his marriage was not one of the more romantic
unions of the seventeenth century'.[16] Finally Fitzgerald, obsessed
by Defoe's obsession with sex, finds it possible that Defoe married
Mary for a kiss, but then was disappointed at her failure to conjure
up the pretty girl of his dreams: 'They were married nearly fifty
years and produced eight children, but a great part of their married
life they lived under different roofs. Even when together they were
frequently not on speaking terms . . . It was a bungle of a marriage –
that was all there was to it.'[17] Who is right? The truth is that there
is really no evidence to support any of these views. All we do know
is that Mary Defoe bore eight children, six of whom survived to
adulthood, that she put up stoically with her husband's long absences
from home, his imprisonments, his almost fraudulent misuse and
waste of her dowry,[18] and that she stood by him in his most difficult
times. Few men could hope for more.

While Defoe's biographers choose to disagree on the amount of
love involved in his marriage, they all take it as a sign of his youthful
promise that the son of a tallow-chandler could catch the daughter
of a wealthy Dissenting merchant with a dowry of £3,700. This was
a very big dowry indeed. How much money had Defoe himself
acquired by 1683 to match it? We do not know. What we do know
is that only eight years after his marriage he was to go bankrupt,
owing £17,000, which was a small fortune. But once again we only
have hints as to how Defoe got into a position to be able to get so
far in debt. A man had to have a good business reputation to be
given so much credit in the first place. The evidence we have
suggests that Defoe earned his living as a merchant throughout the
1680s only to go bankrupt, like so many others, when he over-
reached himself in the early years of King William's War. Economic
historians know little about the 1680s but, from the little evidence
we have, this decade seems to have incorporated much of the
commercial expansion of the whole period from 1620 to 1700.
English overseas commerce had been dogged by one difficulty after
another for most of the seventeenth century and it was only in the
1670s and 1680s that it broke through to a new plateau of achievement, particularly in the Spanish and American trades.[19] It is in
these trades that Defoe seems to have sought his fortune, riding on
the crest of a wave until the vulnerability of these trading routes to
the attacks of French privateers sank him in 1692. He seems to have

dealt as a general import–export merchant, his main business being the shipment of hosiery to Spain in exchange for wine and brandy, and general cargoes to the American plantations in exchange for tobacco. It was during his early business career that he made his first great travels in England and also obtained most of his first-hand experience of the continent. A very wide knowledge of business is clear in all of Defoe's works, though one often gets the impression that it is knowledge of business acquired in the 1680s which he is using to interpret the very different conditions of the 1720s.

What seems clear is that the young man who had declined the Nonconformist ministry, with its unworldly salary, was a young man in a hurry to make a fortune, and that he was prepared to behave in a not too honest way to do so.[20] Why such a hurry? Once again the critics disagree. Sutherland, who distinguishes Defoe's energy and love of adventure as his most striking characteristics, felt that 'the impulse that drove him along through a quite extraordinary career was not so much the desire for riches as an incurable love of excitement'.[21] Other writers stress the end rather than the means. They feel that Defoe wanted to be rich in order to enjoy the benefits of wealth rather than because getting rich itself was such good fun. Michael Shinagel has developed this thesis into a whole book. Defoe wanted to be rich in order to be a gentleman and this was the guiding instinct of his whole career.[22]

Although Shinagel overdoes his thesis of Defoe's drive to gentility, building him up as dandy, wit and social climber on the basis of some rather thin, mainly circumstantial evidence, there seems no doubt that this was an important strand in Defoe's psychological make-up. The urge to be a gentleman or at least to rise in the social scale was a vital element in Defoe's whole view of society[23] and that he too shared this urge is clear from much of the material which Shinagel incorporates in his book. But Defoe never made it. Just when he seems to be reaching that position of financial ease which would have allowed him to adopt the rentier attitude to life, essential to the station of a gentleman, something always seemed to go wrong, like his bankruptcy in 1692. As he was to put it in 1711:[24]

> No man has tasted differing fortunes more,
> And thirteen times I have been rich and poor.

The nearest he got to gentility was probably in the early 1720s. Then, as a successful author living in a large house set in four acres in Stoke Newington, complete with stables, coach and horses and the rest of the trappings of at least 'middle-class gentility,' he might seem to be justified in styling himself gentleman, as indeed he did. But no real gentleman would have written the books that Defoe wrote. Nor could any real gentleman have had the biography of Defoe. By the late seventeenth century it was acceptable for a gentleman to dabble in trade, but no gentleman would remain one if he had gone bankrupt twice, been in prison half a dozen times, stood in the pillory, and earned his living for half his adult life swapping abuse with hack journalists and giving tendentious advice to the middle classes.

If it was important to have a good biography to be accepted as a gentleman, it was equally important to have a good biography to be accepted in the political world of the early eighteenth century. Everyone liked to know where everyone else stood in the divided society of the day. Moderation was a dirty word to the committed men who fought for power, patronage and political advantage on both sides, to the High Tory churchman and the Jacobite on the right as to the Whig and the Dissenter on the left. Defoe liked to think of himself as a moderate, a man of no party, but a moderate with Whig political ideals who believed in the principles of the Revolution of 1688. These were the early days of party politics and Defoe was not alone in distrusting and disliking the party men of both sides who seemed to be pursuing their private advantage rather than the public interest.[25] For all that, he had no doubt that the public interest was a Whig interest, as we can see from a *Review* of 1710 where he summed up what he saw to be the difference between Whig and Tory in words which somewhat simplify the subtle political reality of his day:[26]

> A *Tory* is a plunderer of his country, a persecutor for religion, a bloody destroyer without law, a betrayer of liberties and one that will give up his nation to popery and arbitrary power, under the pretence of a passive obedience and non-resistance. A *Whig* is one that blesses God from the bottom of his heart for the legal provisions made against popery in a parliamentary succession; that vigorously withstood popery and arbitrary power at the Revolution.

Despite the vigour of this denunciation Defoe was to become tainted with Toryism in the years that followed its publication.[27] When the

Tory party collapsed at the death of Queen Anne he found himself
in a dangerous political wilderness and felt the need to prove the
purity of his ideals by writing himself a Whig biography.[28] Not that
he had to lie too much to do so. As far as we can tell, Defoe had led
an impeccable political life on the radical, dissenting wing of the
Whigs up to 1703. One could hardly fault his parents, fine upstand-
ing Presbyterians, untainted with the more disreputable aspects of
Civil War politics, such as association with regicides. As a young man
he underwent just the right amount of religious suffering at the hands
of the High Tories in the reign of Charles II. When the moments
of crisis came he was ready to do his bit, copying out the Pentateuch
in shorthand lest bibles be banned at the time of the Popish Plot,[29]
turning out with the lads to beat up Catholics in the heady days
following its exposure. Over thirty years later he was to recall
the effectiveness of the 'Protestant flail' at this time. 'Arm'd with
this scourge for a Papist, I remember I fear'd nothing.'[30] Then
when the worst happened and a Catholic prince became King of
England he was ready to risk all in the rebellion of Monmouth, as
we have seen, though not so foolish as to be captured and subjected
to the fury of Judge Jefferys' Bloody Assizes.[31] Monmouth was not
really worth dying for.[32] But William of Orange was quite a different
matter, especially once he had been seen to have been successful in
his bid to oust the hated King James. Who was there to welcome
him; who rode in the great Lord Mayor's procession of 1689,
'gallantly mounted and richly accoutred' in a Royal Regiment of
volunteer horse? No other than 'Daniel Foe, at that time a hosier in
Freeman's Yard; the same who afterwards was pilloried'.[33]

In the Williamite world of the 1690s Defoe was rewarded for his
good biography. It was then that he obtained the only official posts
of his life, as accountant to the commissioners of the Glass Duty and
manager-trustee for the royal lotteries. His unofficial bounty also
appears to have been considerable, enabling him to rise again from
the misfortunes of his bankruptcy and acquire sufficient capital to
invest in a flourishing brick and tile works at Tilbury in Essex.
Indeed, he seems to have done extremely well financially between
1692 and 1703, paying off his debts at a rate of between £1,000 and
£2,000 a year, whilst at the same time living in a very handsome
fashion.[34] It was during this period, too, that he came nearest to the
central management of public affairs, advising not only the king's
ministers but, if he is to be believed, advising and acting as a secret

agent to the king himself. But here again there is a problem of
evidence. Defoe was always to stress the close relations, indeed the
intimate friendship, that he had enjoyed with his hero, King William,
and the important role that he played in his reign, but we have to
rely, once more, mainly on his own unsupported testimony. Biographers have, for the most part, accepted Defoe's boasts at their
face value, making the most of the contrast in his fortunes that
Defoe himself was later to emphasize in suitably dramatic terms. In
the preface to volume eight of *The Review* he writes, 'I have seen the
rough side of the world as well as the smooth, and have in less than
half a year tasted the difference between the closet of a king and
the dungeon of Newgate.'

We are on surer ground when we look at what Defoe wrote during
the reign of King William. It was during this time that his reputation
as pamphleteer and writer was firmly established. Three main
strands can be distinguished in these early works. First, he wrote a
number of very able pamphlets in the Whig and Williamite interest
defending and interpreting the Revolution settlement and supporting William's foreign policy after the Peace of Ryswick in 1697.[35]
In this year he made his rather belated contribution to the great
outburst of economic literature which marked the economic and
financial crisis of the mid-1690s with the publication of *An Essay
upon Projects*. This, his first full-length book, advocated a number of
economic and social reforms, many of them derived from the flow
of new ideas which emerged from the extraordinary output of
pamphlet literature during the Civil War and interregnum. Nevertheless, the *Essay upon Projects* is an impressive book, illustrating
Defoe's love of detail and his advocacy of better conditions for the
underprivileged – the lunatic, the female and the poor.

But the most interesting writings of this period are a series of
works of an extremely radical nature, attacking the misuse of privilege and questioning many of the contemporary assumptions of the
nature and responsibilities of political power. It is between 1698 and
1703 that Defoe really earns the soubriquet of 'the hard-headed
tribune of the people' that one writer has honoured him with.[36]
Starting with the *Poor Man's Plea*,[37] a savage attack on the double
standards, hypocrisy and vice of the rich, he continued the theme in
The True-born Englishman[38] and *Reformation of Manners*.[39] These are
all hard-hitting pieces in which individuals, thinly disguised by the
use of initials, as well as the collective body of the well-born and

wealthy, are shown up for their failure to justify by their behaviour
the privileges accorded to them by society. Such attacks on the
establishment were supported by a series of radical political pamphlets in the Whig interest, following the Tory gains in the election of
February 1701. Here Defoe stresses the ultimate power of the people
over their representatives in Parliament, warning his audience in the
justly famous *Legion's Memorial* that 'they that made you members,
may reduce you to the same rank from whence they chose you; and
may give you a taste of their abused kindness, in terms you may not
be pleased with'.[40] This petition, which Defoe triumphantly delivered
in person to the Speaker of the Tory House of Commons, marks at
the same time the high point of his personal involvement in politics
and of his impeccable Whig biography.

So radical was Defoe and such a nuisance that he was a marked
man when King William died in 1702 and a resurgent Toryism
sought its victims in the early years of the reign of Queen Anne.
Characteristically, Defoe stuck his head into the noose with the
publication of *The Shortest-Way with the Dissenters*, an attack on the
Tories' renewed persecution of the Dissenters.[41] Defoe ironically
advised the Church and the queen to get rid of the hated Dissenters
once and for all by banishing all or some of its conventicles and hanging the preachers. The example would so turn the rest back into
the Church in a way that small fines and ostracised attendance would
never do.

The pamphlet seems harmless enough today but, unfortunately,
both High Tories and Dissenters took it seriously and were furious
when they found out who had written it. For the first of many times
Defoe found himself attacked by both sides and forced to take up the
stance of the injured man in the middle. In 1713, in one of the last
numbers of the *Review*, he was to reflect again on his misfortune in
being the object of attack from both sides, by Dissenter and high
churchman. 'I have been like a man that runs in between two duel-
lers to part them, and who to prevent them losing their lives, loses his
own; the furious gladiators run both their swords into him that would
part them, and he falls a sacrifice to his own zeal.'[42] Defoe's zeal in
1702 led to the loss of much of his political liberty, if not his life.
A warrant for his arrest was issued by the Secretary of State, the
Tory Earl of Nottingham, and in July 1703, after a long period
hiding from the law, he was brought to trial on a charge of seditious
libel. Defoe, after unwisely[43] pleading guilty in a bid for mercy, was

sentenced to a heavy fine, to stand three times in the pillory and to remain in prison during the queen's pleasure. The sentence was savage and reflected the hatred felt for the man who had spent the last five years attacking the most precious institutions of the Tory establishment.

Defoe was to have his revenge. While waiting in prison, he dashed off the defiant *Hymn to the Pillory*, a poem declaring the inability of such a punishment to injure an honest man and giving a long list of those who should stand there in his place. And when the dreaded time came his pillory was a triumph. The crowd eagerly bought copies of his poem and hailed him as a popular hero. But, although Defoe was a brave man, his imprisonment was to mark him for ever. He was to attack the behaviour of the upper classes all his life and was never to waver from his support of the Revolution settlement and his belief that ultimate sovereignty lay in the people. Nevertheless, fear of further imprisonment or of another sentence to the pillory was to keep his future exuberance within bounds. No longer was he to be the tribune of the people. Indeed, by the 1720s, he was ready to attack the behaviour of the poor in language as violent as he had used to attack the behaviour of the rich in the pamphlets written before his imprisonment.

Defoe's release from Newgate was secured by Robert Harley, the very man to whom as Speaker of the House of Commons he had presented *Legion's Memorial*. Harley, the rising man and a moderate Tory, was to replace the Earl of Nottingham as Secretary of State in 1704.[44] Defoe had petitioned him for help before his arrest[45] and Harley was quick to see the advantage of helping such a talented writer. Defoe's situation was pitiable. He had no idea how long he might remain in prison, he was despised by all except the fickle mob and he was once again broke, neglect of his tile business during his tribulations having led to a second bankruptcy. Harley could rely on such a man being loyal, and indeed to Defoe gratitude was the greatest of all virtues. Harley need be in no hurry. Defoe's fear and his gratitude to the man who effected his release would be the greater the longer he was kept in suspense. Not till November was he released and not till July of 1704 did he receive his official pardon. Harley's tactics paid off well. With the exception of the years 1708–10 when Harley was out of office and Defoe served Godolphin, the Lord Treasurer, in his place, Defoe was to remain his loyal though not humble servant till Harley, now Earl of Oxford, was dismissed in the very last days of Queen Anne. When the Whigs were baying for Harley's blood after the queen's death, Defoe published *The Secret History of the White-Staff*, an anonymous defence of Harley's conduct during the last years of the queen's reign.[46] For, as he wrote in his own *Appeal to Honour and Justice*, 'gratitude and fidelity are inseparable from an honest man'.[47]

The years of Defoe's association with Harley are the best-known years of his life. The publication of *The Review* from 1704 till 1713 kept Defoe firmly in the public eye. This newspaper's main function was to promote Harley's foreign and domestic policies, but Defoe also used it as a forum for discussing every conceivable subject and it serves as an essential source for his ideas on society, as well as providing some interesting biographical details.[48] Even more useful to the biographer is the fact that Harley was an inveterate collector of documents and over three-quarters of all Defoe's surviving correspondence consists of letters and reports written to Harley between 1703 and 1714.[49]

The relationship was a very strange one. Both men took an almost pathological delight in secrecy, in the use of pseudonyms[50] and in the very necessary task of concealing from the public what role Defoe played in Harley's political schemes. Harley never acknowledged Defoe's service and, if we can believe Defoe's continuous pleas for more money, never adequately rewarded his valuable agent, not even on many occasions providing enough cash for what were state services. But Defoe's constant reminders to his paymaster and his pathetic descriptions of the condition of his family probably need to be taken with a pinch of salt, especially after he had made a composition with his creditors under the new Bankrupts' Act of 1706.[51] Defoe was engaged in business,[52] as well as writing for profit, while he was serving Harley and by 1709 he had acquired sufficient cash to buy an expensive lease on a large property in Stoke Newington.[53] During the period of Tory ascendancy between 1710 and 1714 he certainly had the reputation of being extremely well-paid, both as journalist and political agent.[54] Defoe's main financial worry was the fact that despite his composition with his creditors he was constantly harassed by the ghosts of his dubious financial past. Political enemies could always buy up and present old debts or simply present fraudulent ones to embarrass and, if possible, cripple such an irritating opponent.

To keep Defoe on financial tenterhooks was of course part of

Harley's tactics to ensure the continuation of his agent's loyalty. More serious, from the point of view of Defoe's effectiveness, was Harley's slackness as a letter-writer and his failure to give precise, sometimes any, instructions as to what Defoe should do. Constantly we find Defoe ready to set off on a journey for his master and begging for some instructions. But, as we might expect, even if he received none, Defoe was quite ready to go ahead on his own initiative and in his reports ask for his master's approval. Indeed he became increasingly plain-speaking and man-to-man in his correspondence with Harley. The somewhat cringing, over-grateful Defoe of the earlier letters soon disappears and, though he never loses the formal tone one would expect in letters from servant to master, he is often very forthright in his advice.

During the early years of his relationship with Harley his main function was to collect political information and to convince individuals all over the country of the wisdom of his master's policies. The immediate efficiency that he displayed in this role as spy and political agent argues for the truth of Defoe's claim to have done similar work for King William in the 1690s. In a long letter written in the summer of 1704 he outlined the methods by which Harley could attain both popularity and effective political power in the country.[55] Defoe's part in the scheme was to set up an intelligence service. Here Defoe compares England very unfavourably with absolutist France. In order to know who was who Harley should have a list of all the gentry and families of rank in England, together with their residence, characters and political interest in their respective counties; similar lists should be drawn up for the clergy and the leading men of the boroughs. Such information should be kept up to date by regular correspondence with a chain of agents all over the country.

In 1704 and 1705 Defoe went on two tours for Harley to collect political information and to set up a correspondence service of the sort he had outlined in the letter discussed above, the first to the eastern counties and the second to the West Country and the North. Everywhere he went he reported on the political leanings of the gentry and other notables and organized a correspondence, mainly with nonconformist ministers, but also with other contacts such as merchants, clothiers and booksellers. Such people could also be used as a distribution network for pamphlets in the government interest. In 1706 Defoe sent his master a list of sixty-four people all over the country to whom a pamphlet defending Marlborough and Harley had been sent.[56]

During his journeys Defoe often had trouble with the local worthies who thought that he must be some sort of rebel or spy, especially as the first person he normally sought out in any town was the Dissenting minister. In Devon a warrant was taken out for his arrest and he was forced to show a pass which he had extracted with some difficulty from Harley, who was of course reluctant to admit the official nature of Defoe's duties.

Such journeys naturally helped to build up his knowledge of his own country and to give him an idea of the extent of the changes that had occurred since his previous travels in the 1680s and 1690s. This information was often fed into *The Review* and was to remain in Defoe's head when he wrote his great *Tour* and his other full-length economic works in the 1720s. One has to remember, too, that all the time that Defoe was riding round England on horseback he was issuing *The Review* three times a week,[57] as well as turning out a flood of pamphlets, poetry and full-length books.

Defoe's next journey for Harley was to Scotland to promote the Union. Once again he had no instructions and he outlined in a letter of 13 September 1706 what he considered his duties to be. He intended to discover who opposed the Union and to 'applye my self to prevent them'.[58] He set out on the same day and his journey was attended by almost continuous rain. By the time he reached Newcastle, one horse was spent and he had to draw money from Harley's agent, Mr Bell, to buy another. Bell was at first somewhat suspicious of the gentleman called Alexander Goldsmith who said that he was 'so publiccly knowne that it would not be prudence' to travel under his own name. But after drinking a bottle with him and a few days' conversation he found him to be 'a very engenious man and fit for that busness I guess he is goeing about'.[59] This seems to have been a sound assessment.

Defoe's position in Scotland was ambiguous, to say the least. Simply as an Englishman he was suspect at this delicate time in the relations between the two countries. Defoe managed to allay the natural suspicions of the Scots by the convincing claim that he had fled north to escape his creditors and was hoping to repair his fortunes in the northern kingdom. He did in fact engage in business in Scotland and this story enabled him to move about with reasonable safety. If it had been known that he was Harley's spy he could

well have been lynched by the suspicious Scots. On more than one
occasion he refers to the fate of De Witt, who had been torn to
pieces by a Dutch mob in 1672. 'I can not say to you I had no
apprehensions, nor was Monsr. de Witt quite out of my thoughts,
and perticularly when a part of this mob fell upon a gentleman who
had discretion little enough to say something that displeased them
just undr my window.'[60] Apparently, however, Defoe was never
recognized as an agent of Harley. He spent his time profitably lobby-
ing, talking and arguing, particularly over the complex issues of the
customs and excise changes necessary to create this early forerunner
of the Common Market.

For there was very considerable opposition to the Union in
Scotland. The Jacobites opposed the Union because, amongst other
things, it would commit them to the Hanoverian Succession, which
they had never accepted. Defoe was often worried by the large
number of Highlanders appearing in the streets of Edinburgh,
though this did not prevent him amusing his master with a description of the Highland gentleman, 'a man in his mountain habit with
a broad sword, targett, pistol or perhaps two at his girdle, a dagger
and staff, walking down the street as upright and haughty as if he
were a lord – and withall driving a cow'.[61] Further opposition came
from the members of the Kirk, who felt that the Union was a threat
to their hard-won establishment position in Scotland. Indeed many
people found it difficult to understand how a union between two
countries could be effective in which one had an established church
which was presbyterian and the other episcopalian. Much of Defoe's
time was therefore spent talking to ministers in an attempt to persuade them that union would not be followed by English attempts
to reappoint the hated bishops in the Scots church. As it turned
out the Scots were right to be suspicious. With the High Tory
domination of English politics after 1710 many inroads were made
into the Kirk's established position and Defoe's tongue and his pen
were kept even busier. Political and religious opponents were joined
by those who doubted the economic wisdom of the Union. Ironically,
these were strongest in Glasgow and the west generally, the region
which in the long run was to make its fortune on the basis of their
new freedom of trade within England's American empire.[62] All these
interests had no trouble in raising a mob and 'a Scots rabble is the
worst of its kind'.[63] But, in fact, God seemed to be on the side of the
Union. It was generally accepted that the very bad weather of the

winter of 1706–7 made the assembly of people opposed to the Union very difficult to organize. Physical opposition died down and was replaced by an attempt to force so many amendments in the Scots Parliament that the English would never accept the amended version of the Bill. All this gave Defoe a long winter's work. Up till the first of May when the Union was finally achieved he spent most of his time in Edinburgh, and much of his future career as a servant both of Harley and Godolphin was to be spent on the affairs of North Britain. The English were guilty of many breaches of both the spirit and the letter of the Act of Union, whilst opposition remained strong in Scotland. It was not till the Jacobite Rebellion of 1715 forced the Lowlanders to a full realization of the alternatives to partnership with England that the Union was safe.

Defoe's activities in Scotland were successful because Harley's policy in promoting the Union coincided with Defoe's own inclinations. He himself fervently believed in the importance of the Union to both countries and his arguments for both the economic and political benefits are very convincing.[64] Indeed a very good case can be made out for a general community of interest between Harley and Defoe. In many ways they were very similar people. They were about the same age and both had been brought up in Dissenting homes, though Harley of course had since conformed to the Church of England. Harley was a genuine moderate who tried successfully to fill all his administrations with men of both parties and to dampen down the political infighting which was so characteristic of the reign of Queen Anne. Defoe, as Harley's man, naturally supported his policies, but it can be argued that he need have suffered no qualms of conscience in doing so. Harley was in many ways the best advocate of the continuation of the policies of Defoe's hero, King William. To support the administration of such a man was therefore no great strain and on non-political subjects Defoe appears to have been given total freedom.

This sort of analysis can, however, be taken too far. From 1710, when Harley emerged as the leader of triumphant and vindictive Toryism, even if he was a leader who tried his hardest to muzzle the more extreme demands of his supporters, Defoe was often forced to write in a vein quite counter to his own beliefs. He tried hard to defend himself against the many shouts of turncoat, urging changed circumstances to explain his apparent turnabout on policy or claiming to have never changed his policy at all.[65] He also salved his

conscience by writing anonymous articles in support of those things
he really believed in, even attacking articles written by himself in
the semi-official *Review* and *Mercator*.[66] And, indeed, he never was
forced into writing in support of really extreme measures. Unlike
his master, Harley, he never wavered from the Hanoverian Succession and much of the last two volumes of *The Review* is composed of
attacks on the Jacobites and the High Churchmen. Later, in the
Appeal to Honour and Justice of 1715, Defoe was to claim that, even
where he appeared to have been inconsistent, he was very sensibly
making the best of a bad job. Shouting could not get rid of the Tory
majority in Parliament but Tory policies could be watered down.
Referring to the Peace of Utrecht, which was very unpopular with
the Whigs, he wrote that 'when it was made, and could not be
otherwise, I thought our business was to make the best of it, and
rather to enquire what improvements were to be made of it, than to
be continually exclaiming at those who made it'.[67]

But these ex-post-facto justifications of his conduct are not very
convincing, nor are they entirely true. The fact is that Defoe was
becoming increasingly alarmed at the ambiguous position which he
had been forced into. In August 1712 he wrote a strange letter to
Harley in which he seemed to be trying to convince himself that he
had always been a free agent. 'Your Lordship has allways acted
with me on such foundations of meer abstracted bounty and goodness, that it has not so much as suggested the least expectation on
your part that I should act this way or that, leaving me at full
liberty to persue my own reason and principle; and above all enable-
ing me to declare my innocence in the black charge of bribery.'[68]
No doubt at this juncture Defoe was desperate to try and persuade
himself of the truth of this nonsense. Only three months earlier, in
May, he had been forced into betraying his own people, following
the passage of the Schism Act which abolished the Dissenting
Academies. Defoe had himself been educated at such an institution
and was proud of it, but the best he can do now is to offer some
mealy-mouthed advice to the Dissenters to stick to their religion
now that politics has treated them so badly. Less politics and more
religion would make them better men.[69] It was in May, too, that he
wrote to Harley with some amazement that it was the talk of the
town that the British general in Flanders had received orders not to
fight. Could this be true? If it was, of course he would write to
justify it.[70] It was true.[71] Dutifully, the man who had often lambasted

the failure of soldiers to fight in the early years of the war defended the orders of the British army not to fight. With peace at hand why should young men be 'kill'd to make a little sport'?[72] Why, indeed?

Once again, as in 1702, Defoe had successfully managed to antagonize all parties. He was not Tory enough to satisfy the Tories and far too Tory to satisfy the Whigs. And, once again, he offered himself to his enemies. He never learned. In 1713 he published three pamphlets, one a straightforward warning to his readers of the queen's mortality and the need to make up their minds what they were going to do about the succession,[73] and the other two transparently ironical pieces proclaiming the supposed advantages of an absolutist Jacobite king.[74] To think that Defoe was a Jacobite supporter was absurd, as he was to point out himself.[75] But he had in fact a certain admiration for the benefits of absolutism[76] and, despite his irony, some of these advantages may have seemed rather too cunningly described to a thick-headed supporter of Hanover. He may well have given the other side too many ideas for his own good. In any case the Whigs saw their chance to take their revenge on the turncoat and Defoe was arrested at his home in Stoke Newington for publishing such scandalous, wicked and treasonable libels. This time his powerful patron Harley, now the Earl of Oxford, was able to get him off the hook, but there was more trouble to come.

There is an ironic symmetry in Defoe's career as a journalist and pamphleteer. In 1703 Harley got him out of prison and obliged him to write in his support for the rest of his political career. In 1714 there appears to have been an almost exact parallel. The occasion was a rather strange one which foreshadows the next stage of Defoe's surprising career. Some of the most virulent opponents of Harley's ministry were the contributors to the Whig newspaper, the *Flying-Post*, 'these devils of Grubstreet rogues', Swift called them in a letter to Stella.[77] Defoe had for some time been 'endeavouring to take off the virulence' of this incendiary newspaper.[78] A quarrel within the management of the paper gave him his chance and for some weeks Defoe found himself in the ambiguous position of supplying foreign news, no doubt doctored, to the Whig paper, whilst still working for the Tory ministry.

But then, on 1 August 1714, occurred the event which everyone had been waiting for but had hardly dared to mention. Queen Anne died. The Whigs had long made their preparations and their machine moved swiftly and efficiently into action. George of Hanover was proclaimed King of England and, by the provisions of an Act of 1708,[79] the immediate government of the country was entrusted to regents selected in advance by the new king. It must, then, have been mildly embarrassing when a letter arrived at the offices of the *Flying-Post* accusing one of these regents, the Earl of Anglesey, of being a Jacobite.[80] The publisher decided to print the letter but asked Defoe to 'soften' it before publication. Defoe claims that he 'left out indeed a great deal of scandalous stuff that was in it but added nothing and sent it back'.[81] But even 'softened', the letter could not be ignored and of course the fair copy was in Defoe's hand. Now that the Whigs were in power they could nail at last the man who for the last four years had betrayed the cause by writing in support of Tory policies.

Defoe was arrested but released on bail. A strange delay followed. It was nearly a year before, in July 1715, he was brought to trial to answer for his libel. He was found guilty but sentence was deferred. It was never passed. The reason is made clear to the historian in a letter written by Defoe nearly three years later. He had made his peace with the Whigs, a wise move since they were to remain in power for the rest of his life. 'Notwithstanding some mistakes which I was the first to acknowlege,' he wrote, 'I was so happy as to be believd in the professions I made of a sincere attachment to the interest of the present government.' His past faults were forgiven. And the price? 'It was proposed by my Lord Townshend [Whig Secretary of State] that I should still appear as if I were as before under the displeasure of the government; and seperated from the Whiggs; and that I might be more servicable in a kind of disguise, than if I appeard openly.'[82] In fact what Defoe was required to do was a task for which he was clearly well qualified. He was to write for the Tory press, to take the sting out of it, 'to prevent the mischievous part', in other words to 'soften' it, just as he had previously tried to soften the Whig *Flying-Post*.[83] Defoe had once again taken up the thread of his good Whig biography, somewhat in abeyance since 1703.

The last sixteen years of Defoe's life, from 1715 till his death in 1731, whilst hiding from yet another ghost of his financial past,[84] are dominated for his biographers by commentary on his writings. Now is the time that the psychological insights about his youth can be brought to play in critical studies of his books. Now is the time to search through the literature of the past fifty years, with special reference to the catalogue of Defoe's own library, to discover where he got it all from.[85] Very few letters survive for this period[86] and there is remarkably little other information about a man who, even in his own lifetime, must have been extremely well known, especially after the publication of *Robinson Crusoe* in 1719. Most of what we know comes, as for the first forty years of his life, from hints and allusions in his own works. There is plenty to choose from. Defoe must have been writing almost non-stop from 1715 till his death in 1731. The great majority of all his full-length books was written in this period, between the age of fifty-five and seventy. All his novels and travel-books, all his books on marriage and the family, all his books on the occult and nearly all his books on history and economics were crammed into this short period. Indeed, most of them were written in the even shorter period between 1719 and 1728. He really was an incredibly hard-working man. We can, if we like, imagine the old man writing away in his study, pained by gout and a stone in the kidney and by that ever-present anguish of old men, the unfilial behaviour of his family. But we will find that it is still difficult to bring him to life, even if we allow the 'hermit of Stoke Newington'[87] an occasional visit to his much-loved garden. And he did not just write books. All this time he continued to write vast numbers of pamphlets on the political and economic affairs of the moment. And, until the mid-1720s, he carried out his task of censoring the Tory press from within.

His most famous collaboration, if that is the right word, was with the *Weekly Journal, or Saturday's Post* owned by Nathaniel Mist. Defoe was not too successful in softening Mist's Toryism and Mist was to be arrested several times, imprisoned, fined and pilloried. On the other hand, it is in this paper and in *Applebee's Original Weekly Journal* for which he wrote between 1720 and 1726 that we can find some of the most attractive examples of Defoe's journalism. So effective was the partnership of Defoe and Mist that their paper became the most popular in England, with a circulation of about 10,000 copies a week.[88] It seems unlikely that Mist never realized Defoe's official role and it is probable that Professor Sutherland's suggestion that he did not mind too much is correct.[89] Defoe as Whig agent provided some sort of safeguard for Mist's continued liberty. Defoe as writer sold his paper.

Defoe as writer. That is the man we know. All the rest is shadowy, though not without at least some substance as we have seen. But what is one to make of the writings of such a man? Defoe's chequered career as a political pamphleteer and journalist has led many writers to doubt whether they can believe Defoe at all. A man who could lie and deceive, as Defoe lied and deceived, cannot be trusted. This is giving up too soon. In fact, such an attitude to historical evidence would end with no history being written at all. One has to be a little careful with Defoe, of course. But we know enough about the stormiest parts of his career to make reasonable assumptions about what to believe and what to doubt. It would be unwise, for example, to generalize about Defoe's ideas on the basis of his political journalism in the last three years of Tory rule, 1712–14.[90] But it is not necessary to do so. He wrote plenty of other things. As I hope to show in the remainder of this book Defoe was, in fact, surprisingly consistent for a man who wrote so much. He was often weak on fact and on chronology and he usually exaggerated when he mentioned figures, but he was nearly always consistent at the level of generalization of ideas. His main trouble lies where his generalizations in one field clash with his generalizations in another. This in fact leads to a dualism in his ideas which often causes confusion and anomaly. But this dualism is itself consistent. In other words we find the same clashes of ideas occurring over and over again in his works; what is good for salvation is rarely good for success; what is good for the individual may well not be good for society and so on. But, with this important qualification, Defoe is consistent, developing a body of ideas which are nearly all fully formed in his mind by the time he starts writing in earnest. The emphasis may change a little over his lifetime. He is more optimistic in his thirties, more pessimistic in his sixties. Such changes in emphasis reflect not only the often observed swing towards authority and paternalism that one expects as a man grows older, but also a change in the society he described.

For a man of Defoe's views and instincts the 1690s were a brave new world in which the possibilities of progress seemed endless. The world of the 1720s was quite different. It was a world where the Revolution of 1688 was quite safe but one where those ideals which Defoe saw as its greatest glory had been tarnished by political realities. It was a world of economic stagnation in which Defoe's hopes of continuing economic development appeared to diminish as the decade went on.[91] It was also a world in which English society seemed to have rejected the desirability, indeed the very possibility, of social reform. Both at home and at school Defoe had been influenced by the astonishing range of ideas for social progress which had developed in the heady days of the Civil War and Inter-regnum and had then been carried forward into Restoration England by the Dissenters. Young men like him had hoped that such ideas would be realized once the absolutist government of the Stuarts had been destroyed by the Revolution of 1688. They were to be disappointed. Few periods of history can have been so sterile in this respect as the first half of the eighteenth century. This was at least in part because of the contemporary concentration on the improve-ment of the individual rather than of society. Society would be reformed through the moral reform of individuals.[92] Defoe shared this view. But he could also see that life was loaded against those not fortunate enough to live in the comfortable world of the moralists, and he tried all his life to do something to improve the legal as well as the economic conditions of their existence. His achievements were very limited. But we who come later are lucky. Defoe's brave attempt gives us the best picture of the world we have left behind that we shall ever have.

PART II

THE WORLD OF DEFOE

THE INNER WORLD

THE world which Defoe wrote about was one which really existed only in his own mind. This is not to say that he simply invented it, but that what he saw, heard and read was translated inside his head into something which squared with his preconceived ideas of the way things were. His world is not like the objective modern world, buttressed by statistics and indigestible facts, which geography teachers expound to us at school. It is a personal world, so personal indeed that there are few aspects of either the world itself or of the relationships between those who lived in it which tally exactly with the views of the majority of his contemporaries, let alone with those of modern research.

The fact that Defoe's world was personal does not make it any the less interesting, but it does make it necessary for us to try and understand just what his preconceived ideas were. Otherwise we are likely to get lost. Such an understanding is necessary if we are to appreciate any writer, as Virginia Woolf points out in her essay on *Robinson Crusoe*.[1] 'All alone we must climb upon the novelist's shoulders and gaze through his eyes until we, too, understand in what order he ranges the large common objects upon which novelists are fated to gaze: man and men; behind them Nature; and above them that Power which for convenience and brevity we may call God.' It is hardly surprising that Defoe's preconceptions on such subjects were not the same as those of Virginia Woolf and were even further removed from those of today. Many assumptions which he and his contemporaries took for granted have disappeared or have been seriously undermined in the quarter of a millennium that separates us from the early decades of the eighteenth century. This is important to remember because it was in just this period that many modern views were springing to the fore. A scepticism in religion leading to the denial of the very existence of God, a belief in the power of science to solve all problems and a constant urge towards material aggrandizement were all attitudes which, while not invented in Defoe's lifetime, yet became very much more commonplace in that period. Defoe, as a very intelligent and well-educated man of his times, was clearly influenced by the impact of such modern ideas. But this is only part of the story. Defoe often seems to be a very modern man and much criticism and appreciation of him depends on an analysis which stresses his modernity. But such an analysis only tells us about one side of Defoe. For, although he was certainly modern in some ways, in others he held strictly to traditional ideas and could be on occasion deliberately archaic. This combination of the old and the new sometimes makes him difficult to interpret, particularly as Defoe liked to think of himself as a man in the middle who could weigh up all problems and take the sensible, moderate course. 'All the confusions, all the oppressions, persecutions, and national mischiefs in the world, owe their birth to the want of this healing, heavenly temper of moderation', he wrote in *The Review*.[2] If one had to use one word to describe his message to mankind it would be moderation, whether he was talking about politics, economics or morals. But the philosophy of the man in the middle can be deceptive. We, who live in an age which glorifies statistics, love to talk of the average man. Sometimes this makes sense, but often it is meaningless. The average of two extremes bears none of the characteristics of either. Defoe was at the same time modern and traditional, rational and irrational, optimistic and pessimistic about the future of mankind. But he was certainly not an average man, even if the ideas of his society lay halfway between these poles.

One of the most interesting aspects of Defoe's dualism was his view of the relationship between God and the world. In very simple terms he was at the same time very worldly and very religious and was not really prepared to compromise between these two extremes. Such an attitude was bound to lead to many problems, particularly on the many occasions when Defoe set himself up as a moralist, a favourite role which he sustained throughout his writing career and which led him to write several full-length books of pious moral instruction, as well as ostensibly providing the motivation of much of his journalism and his novels.

Moralizing was a favourite pastime of nearly all the writers of the early eighteenth century, but Defoe felt that their efforts, though witty, too often missed their mark. He prided himself on his plain speaking and on the directness of the attacks which he launched on the vices of his age. Not for him that 'air of odious school-ma'amish benevolence' which a modern critic has justly discerned in the moral essays of the *Tatler* and *Spectator*.[3] Defoe, like nearly all his contemporaries, welcomed these two extremely successful innovations in literary journalism, the happy favourites of the times, as he called them, but he felt that his own readers required sterner stuff than was handed out by Addison and Steele. 'Are we to be laugh'd out of our follies?', he wrote in *The Review*, 'will we be rally'd out of our dear brutallity? Our vices are too deep rooted to be weeded out with a light hand.'[4] Defoe's hand was often heavy and his speaking undoubtedly plain, but he was unable to avoid the temptation to laugh his readers out of their follies. His moral message was nearly always wrapped up in an attractive parcel of worldliness. He saw no reason why a pious book should not be entertaining, so long as the message was not obliterated by the entertainment. His public obviously agreed with him. If the earnest and godly of the early eighteenth century and later had to read pious books, and it is obvious from the sales that they did have to, how much more fun to read Defoe than his competitors.[5] Defoe devised an attractive technique of writing such books which clearly foreshadowed his later use of the novel or adventure story as a literary form. A convincing real-life background was quickly built up and then the moral was delivered in lively dialogues between characters who could present to the public both sides of the particular point at issue. The message itself is often rather mawkish for modern taste, but the method is very effective. The only trouble with such a technique was that Defoe found, as others have before and after him, that the Devil tended to get all the best lines. The dialogue between the brother and sister who defy Sabbath observance and parental authority in the first volume of *The Family Instructor* is to modern ears the best thing in the book, and some of the remarks of the ungodly apprentice run it a fairly close second, whereas Defoe's attempts to convey religious emotion are unconvincing to say the least.

This was a problem which was to run through all Defoe's works. As he saw it, a writer had a dual obligation to entertain and to instruct, but of the two instruction was the most important. In 1704 he compared the responsibilities of the writer and the preacher. 'Preaching of sermons is speaking to a few of mankind: printing of

books is talking to the whole world.'[6] There is no doubt that Defoe
often thought of himself as a preacher in print and many critics
have made the point that much of his writing has the flavour of a
spoken sermon, as if it was written to be read aloud. The preacher,
like the writer, has to hold his audience, to entertain them, if he
wishes to instruct them and convey his moral in a convincing way.
Defoe's problem was that he was better at the entertainment than
he was at conveying the moral. His habit of illustrating the vice
which he was condemning gradually took over from the condemnation itself so that by the 1720s it is the vice which catches our attention, while the moral seems little more than lip-service to the pious
expectations of his middle-class readers.

Many critics see this development reaching its peak in *Roxana*,
Defoe's last novel describing social relationships.[7] 'In the case of
Roxana', wrote Rudolf G. Stamm, '[the moralistic clothes were]
nothing more than a veil, a veil, besides, that had slid down from
the incorrigible sinner it was supposed to envelop, and barely
covered her feet.'[8] Michael Shinagel has suggested that Defoe felt
that after writing *Roxana* he no longer had full control of his imagination and decided to write no more imaginative biographies.[9] Not
that this stopped him using his imagination to illustrate vice in a
way which, if hardly an incitement to sin, was certainly entertaining.
In the introduction to his fascinating moral work on marriage,
Conjugal Lewdness, he is at pains to excuse himself from the possible
charge of obscenity. No one can write on vice without mentioning it.
If the imagination of the vicious is stimulated by such a work, that is
not the fault of the moralist and reformer.[10] This seems acceptable,
though contemporary readers may well have doubted his sincerity
when they noticed that the book was given the none too pious sub-
title of *The Use and Abuse of the Marriage Bed*. Such doubts could well
have been sustained. For, by the end of the book, Defoe has fallen
into his old trap several times. Entertainment is increasingly tending
to push morals aside, even if the moral itself is made far more
convincingly than in *Moll Flanders* or *Roxana*.

It is tempting to dismiss Defoe's pious books as the work of a
mercenary writer well aware of the vast potential market for such
books[11] and, because of his Dissenting background, familiar with
the sort of moral their readers expected, but himself alienated by his
worldliness from a real understanding of what religious experience
was all about.[12] It is always hard to judge a man's sincerity in

religion, but it seems probable that such a criticism does little justice to Defoe. He was certainly worldly, but there seems little reason to doubt that he was at the same time sincerely religious. This may seem a difficult position to understand, but probably only because we are so far removed from the sort of society in which Defoe lived. Perhaps the best modern analogy to the dualism implicit in Defoe's attitude to God and the world is provided by the fairly common type of the rich socialist. He sincerely works towards a revolution, one of whose aims appears to be to disinherit the rich, and at the same time enjoys the worldly benefits of his wealth. He too, like Defoe, is likely to be called a hypocrite whose socialism is an attempt to climb on to a trendy bandwagon. But such criticism, although inevitable, is often unjust.

If Defoe was not a sincerely religious man it is difficult to see why he should have remained a Dissenter. In the late seventeenth and eighteenth centuries such a decision to dissent from the doctrine of the established church imposed many civil disabilities on a man and implied a reluctance to compromise on matters of religion. It was a decision to be made by all those who came from the sort of religious background that Defoe did.[13] Some good men were prepared to compromise, but what is striking is the numbers who held true to their principles despite the secular problems involved in Dissent. Defoe appears to have belonged to this considerable minority of Englishmen. One could of course argue that the decision was the product of inertia. He was brought up in a nonconformist home and he was given a sound religious education in one of the best Dissenting academies in England.[14] Was it then too late to change his view of religion? There might be some truth in this, although it should be obvious that in Defoe's day as in ours a religious education was no guarantee of a religious life. According to a recent biographer, Bolingbroke had a similar education, but he hardly ended up puritanical, being notorious even in the lax world of the early eighteenth century as a rake and a deist.[15] Some men might dissent for social reasons. Just as today, a man who belonged to a religious minority holding strict views was likely to find his family and friends in the same group and to leave it would be to court social ostracism. But a man who could irritate his fellow Dissenters so often in his writings as Defoe did does not sound like a person who remained a Dissenter to keep his friends. What seems likely is that Defoe was a Dissenter for the most obvious reason, because his conscience told him that a

Dissenter had a better chance of salvation than an Anglican and he wanted to be saved.

When the Dissenter read his Bible and searched his conscience he found that there were 'some things in the establish'd way of worship which do not seem to correspond with the rule he has found out in the Scripture'.[16] But there were only 'some things' which did not correspond. Defoe often stressed the closeness of the two positions and did not hold that a man adhering to the Church of England could not be saved.[17] He just had a slightly smaller chance. Defoe was in fact exceptionally tolerant on matters of religion, holding that the most important distinction was between those who believed in God and those who denied Him.[18] He could even be tolerant towards Catholics. In *Robinson Crusoe* he created a French priest who 'was a grave, sober, pious, and most religious person; exact in his life, extensive in his charity, and exemplar in almost every thing he did'.[19] Crusoe and the priest discover that 'there are some general principles in which we both agree, viz. first, that there is a God; and that this God having given us some stated general rules for our service and obedience, we ought not willingly and knowingly to offend Him'.[20] This was an unusually tolerant position and not surprisingly Defoe was attacked for it.[21] But Defoe who, on his own admission, had been a Papist-basher in his youth,[22] realized that most people did not really know what popery was:

> 'Tis the universal scare-crow, the hobgoblin, the spectre with which the nurses fright the children and entertain the old women all over the country, by which means such horror possesses the minds of the common people about it, that I believe there are 100,000 stout fellows, who would spend the last drop of their blood against popery, that do not know whether it be a man or a horse.[23]

By the 1720s indifference seemed to be a far more dangerous enemy than the Catholic Church.

Such indifference was the product of the intellectual revolution that was taking place in Defoe's lifetime. Everywhere traditional authority was under fire.[24] That triumphant march of empiricism and confidence in the power of reason to solve all mysteries, which had toppled Aristotelean physics and had ushered in the scientific revolution, was equally busy challenging the long accepted tenets of revealed religion. Nothing was sacred. Nothing was safe from the searching probe of the sceptic determined to accept no belief of the past which was not amenable to empirical proof. The scientists, who had believed that their discoveries would lead to the greater glory of God by demonstrating the immense cleverness of His creation, soon found that their methods could lead to His belittlement as well as to the enhancement of His reputation. Few men denied God completely. They accepted that there must be a first cause, a supreme being, a creator who had made this beautiful machine whose secrets were daily becoming more accessible to that marvel of His creation, rational thinking man. But many felt that, with the universe created, God had done His job and refused to accept the need for any further interference in the working of the machine. God had created Nature; but now Nature had taken over from her creator and God Himself was obliged to conform to the natural laws of His own creation. As for revelation, for scripture and miracles, angels and devils, and the rest of the supernatural paraphernalia that cluttered up the minds of simple folk, what evidence was there for all that? How could modern man believe in a miracle that directly contravened the laws of nature, the laws of God's own creation? How could one accept the word of a Bible which so signally failed to stand up to the tests of modern criticism? Revealed religion had its defenders of course. But many who set out to defend it asked the very questions which led to the destruction of the bastion which they were so valiantly trying to protect from the godless and the sceptic. Soon it was necessary to resort to subterfuge to protect the scriptures. Ingenious attempts were made to invent new number systems which could square Old Testament chronology with the far longer history of man discovered by a study of Chinese or Egyptian historiography. Miracles were declared to be allegories, not factual descriptions of a real event. Devils and evil spirits were simply evil men dressed up in metaphor to suit the simple-minded audience for whom the Bible was originally written.

Defoe's position in this debate illustrates once more his dualism, combining as he did a stubborn defence of the literal truth of the Bible with a very modern faith in the power of reason, 'first monarch of the world . . . hereditary director of mankind . . . the almighty's representative and resident in the souls of men'.[25] Sometimes his reasoning led him into dubious moral positions which hardly tallied with the ethical tenets of the Dissenter or indeed any Christian. This can best be seen by a consideration of Defoe's view of the nature of man, a subject of immense interest to most thinking men of his time.[26]

Man in nature was characterized for Defoe by two main traits. He was evil and he was motivated by an unbounded self-love. The evil nature of man was of course sound theology, even though Defoe's contemporaries were becoming increasingly sure that man was good-natured and benevolent.[27] Most writers would also have accepted a certain amount of self-love in their natural man. But few went as far as Defoe who made it the predominant motivating force in man's conduct, 'the ground of all the things we do', as he put it in *Jure Divino*.[28] Man's immense self-love meant that he would do anything to keep himself alive. No one would observe the moral law if such behaviour would result in his own death. This natural right of self-defence is stated categorically in *Jure Divino* and is a fundamental part of Defoe's concept of human psychology.[29] Indeed it is extended to excuse the behaviour not only of those who are directly threatened with death, such as a drowning man,[30] but also of those who may be threatened with it at some unspecified time in the future. Time and again, in his journalism and in his novels, Defoe excuses the sins of the poor simply because they are poor and hence might starve if they did not sin.

Defoe does not deny that the sin committed as a result of necessity is still a sin but he argues that the necessity which caused it is sufficient grounds for tolerance and forgiveness on the part of society. He often goes farther than this, blaming society for the poverty which led to the sin in the first place. The sins of the poor are thus explained by the sins of the rich, sins of omission in that the rich have done nothing to promote the social and economic reforms which would remove the poor from the state of necessity, sins of commission in that it is often the rich who provide both the temptation and the means for the poor to sin. Who is most guilty – Moll Flanders or her customer, Colonel Jack or the man who left his wallet hanging in plain view from his pocket? Defoe leaves us in little doubt. Indeed he takes this sociological view of crime a stage further in some of his pious works. Since the poor have an excuse for their sins and the rich do not, can the rich be saved? The implication is certainly that they are likely to have a hard job of it. In *Religious Courtship*, the poor labourer who manages to convert his irreligious landlord quotes from the scriptures, 'not many rich, not many noble, are called' and 'it is the poor of this world that are rich in faith'.[31]

If self-love was the guiding instinct in man's psychology, self-help was the means by which he got on in the world. Man himself was the architect of his own destiny. Defoe occasionally paid lip-service to the strict doctrine of predestination[32] but it is clear that for him, as for most of his contemporaries, the concept was dangerously close to denying man free-will. Predestination seemed to most people to be little different from the oriental idea of fate. In the *Journal of the Plague Year* the saddler's brother scorns the Turks who in a time of plague, 'presuming upon their profess'd predestinating notions, and of every man's end being predetermin'd and unalterably before-hand decreed, they would go unconcern'd into infected places, and converse with infected persons, by which means they died at the rate of ten or fifteen thousand a week'. The Christian merchants looked after themselves and survived.[33]

Self-help was an attractive philosophy for the successful, since the assumption was that their success was the product of their own efforts. Defoe shared this view to a certain extent, but he did not take its implications to the callous limits of many of his contemporaries. An idle man who was poor had received his just deserts. But poverty itself was not necessarily the product of idleness, as many held. In a *Review* of 1707 he distinguished between two sorts of poverty, the poverty of disaster caused by misfortune or mismanagement, or both, and the poverty of inheritance in which a man was born poor.[34] Neither sort of poverty carried any moral opprobrium, so long as the individual set out to help himself to escape from his wretched situation. Only those who wallowed in despair were condemned.

So far we have seen Defoe as the exponent of an extremely rational, humanistic view of man and his role in the world. But to leave it at that would be to give entirely the wrong impression. For such a view ignores the most important part of Defoe's explanation of the varied fortunes of man, the role of God. Defoe was not one who thought that God had finished His job at the Creation. At its simplest he thought that God would help those who helped themselves. But God's role was very much greater than that. Defoe believed that God interfered continuously in the affairs of man. For, although quite happy to dedicate a book to Reason,[35] he was equally a defender of traditional Christian doctrines, even though these might be directly counter to the ideas of the Age of Reason. We have seen already that he clung to the concept of original sin,

despite the confidence of so many writers of his time in man's good
nature. He demonstrated his traditionalism even more by his continued acceptance and defence of the concept of divine providence
and indeed by his view of the supernatural generally.

Traditional Protestant theology placed great significance on the
concept of divine providence. At its most extreme it was held that
nothing at all could happen without the direct intervention of God:

> The Providence of God governs the world, and extends it self to
> all times, and places, and persons upon the face of the earth;
> interposes in all events, has the supremacy in all affairs, so that
> nothing upon any pretense is remote or exempt from his
> jurisdiction.[36]

Everything that happened was part of God's purpose and plan for the
world and everything that happened, whether good or bad, had
some reason which it was the individual's duty to try to discover.
But, as the seventeenth century progressed, such beliefs came increasingly under fire as more was discovered of the natural causes of
physical phenomena. By the time of Defoe most intelligent men
accepted that practically everything that happened could be explained by natural causes and thus, although the work of God the
creator, had no special significance. Christians still believed that
God occasionally intervened in the affairs of men. If they had not
there would have been little point in prayer. But they no longer
felt it necessary to see the immediate hand of God in all the trivial
events of everyday life, tending to confine their attention to the
more remarkable manifestations of God's omnipotence, such as
plagues and earthquakes. These served as occasional reminders 'to
make us know that we are but men, and that the reins of the world
are not in our hands'.[37] It was accepted that even such disasters as
these had a natural cause and that God, though directly intervening,
usually, though not necessarily, used nature to make His point.
Meanwhile sceptics had gone further, denying the possibility of
miracles or of any providential interference at all with the working
of nature.[38] Even the great catastrophes of man which nearly everyone still accepted as direct evidence of God's displeasure could be
explained by the sceptic who held that God had built a series of
disasters into His creation, programmed to give intelligent but sinning
man a shock every now and then.[39]

Defoe, as a continuing believer in the existence and importance of the supernatural in the daily life of man, was one of an increasingly desperate rearguard which struggled to combat the tide of incredulity.[40] He saw the 'invisible hand'[41] of providence in everything from a military victory or a plague to the most ordinary occurrences of everyday life.[42] Providence could reward or punish; it could act on a whole nation or an individual; but Defoe found its most frequent intervention in a stick and carrot operation to bring corrupt man to repentance and salvation. It could work through fear, as a warning to bring the sinner to heel, such as when the storm strikes Robinson Crusoe on his first voyage. Or it could work through gratitude by providing the means of delivery from danger, such as when he, 'directed by Heaven, no doubt', opens his chest and finds tobacco to cure his fever and a Bible to save his soul.[43] Punishment, too, could work in different ways. A man might be punished by God so that he would behave better in the future. But he was not always given the chance. A character in *The Family Instructor* thought that 'many fathers are removed from their families, either by death or disaster, by the direction of providence, that the children may fall into better hands'.[44] This might seem a rather harsh way of ensuring a child's salvation, but at least the father had done something wrong in neglecting the child's religious education. Often, however, when providence operated on a big scale it was unable to separate the good from the bad. Both had to suffer, in a plague for example, and it became a little difficult for the believer to convince the sceptic of the rationale behind the apparently random distribution of death.[45] Charles Gildon, in his attack on *Robinson Crusoe*, makes this point.

> I cannot pass in silence his coining of providences; that is, of his making providence raise a storm, cast away some ships, and damage many more, meerly to fright him from going to sea . . . why should he imagine that the storm was sent to hinder him from going to sea, more than any other that were in it, and suffer'd more by it?

If storms are sent by providence to deter men from following the vocation of seaman, the trade of the world would soon come to a halt.[46]

Defoe, of course, was aware of this problem which was conventionally solved by pointing out that God knew best.[47] In the *Farther Adventures* Crusoe upbraids his crew for the massacre of some natives

in Madagascar in revenge for the killing of one of their shipmates
who had asked for all he got. Later, when five of the crew were
surrounded by Arabs in the Persian Gulf and either killed or enslaved
Crusoe claims that it was the just retribution of Heaven. He is
rebuked by the boatswain who refers him to St Luke, 'where our
Saviour intimates that those men, on whom the tower of Siloam
fell, were not sinners above all the Galileans'.[48] It turns out that the
well-read boatswain has made a rather good point, since the five
men had in fact never gone ashore in Madagascar. God moves in a
mysterious way. Man can only try to understand His providence.

How did providence work? What was the technique by which
God imposed his will on the world? Normally he simply operated
through natural causes. Something happened which could be
explained rationally but, in the particular instance, God was
making it happen for some good reason of his own. Such an
explanation was quite acceptable, though it occasionally did scant
honour to the men who were God's agents. In a *Review* of 1706
Defoe tells his readers that he has been criticized for ascribing
England's military successes to the immediate finger of providence,
thus grudging due honour to the generals and soldiers. It was, of
course, 'the concurrence of their valour with the design of providence' which made our victories peculiarly glorious.[49]

Providence did not always work through natural causes. It was
quite possible for God to work a miracle, though nowadays he rarely
felt it necessary to do so.[50] There were also areas of the working of
nature itself which God had kept hidden from man. Such were the
winds whose causes philosophers had long attempted to discover
without success. Defoe thought that there was more of God in the
winds 'than in any other part of operating nature', which might
explain why storms tended to be quoted so often as examples of
divine providence.[51]

God did not need to influence man in such a roundabout way.
For he could contact man direct through the medium of his angels.
'God does not want agents; he has apparently posted an army of
ministring spirits, call them angels if you will, or what else you
please; I say, posted them round this convex, this globe the earth,
to be ready at all events to execute his orders and to do his will.'[52]
Defoe believed all his life in some form of angelic ministration.[53]
'From whence else come all those private notices, strong impulses,
pressings of spirit, involuntary joy, sadness and foreboding apprehen-

sions and the like, of, and about things immediately and really attending us, and this in the most momentous articles of our lives.'[54] Men ignored such ministration to their cost. Defoe himself stated that he 'had never any considerable mischief or disaster attending me, but sleeping or waking I have had notice of it before-hand, and had I listned to these notices, I believe might have shunnd the evil . . .'[55] The details of Defoe's angelology tend to be somewhat ambiguous, if only because the existence and particular location of angels was somewhat tricky to prove to the sceptics of the Age of Reason. He was inclined to believe that the direct ministry of the angels of Heaven belonged to the biblical past, thinking them too distinguished to demean themselves by interfering directly in the trivial affairs of the modern world.[56] Instead, he hypothesized a spirit living in space, not perfect like the angels of Heaven, but benevolent, whose main function was to warn and advise man. Such spirits seem usually to have had freedom of action, though they could also act as messengers from God. Their main means of communication with man was through dreams.[57]

Not all dreams were the result of angelic ministration. Defoe accepted the power of the imagination to conjure up any sort of fancy or trifle in the human mind. It was therefore up to men to determine when a dream was brought about by the visitation of an angel and when it was not. But that was not the end of the problem. For the Devil, too, had his host of angels ready to appear in the dreams of man, in order to tempt him and lead him off into evil. And the Devil, of course, was quite clever enough to pretend to be doing good in order to do evil.

The Devil was just as real as God to Defoe. Indeed the evidence for his existence lay in the existence of God. If you believed in one you must believe in both.[58] Fortunately for man the power of the Devil was limited. He could not foretell the future, though he was so clever that he was able to make more rational predictions from what he saw than could most men. Nor did the Devil have power to destroy or touch. 'He can only bark, but cannot bite.'[59] Man was so easily tempted that he would long since have been destroyed, had this not been the case. The Devil therefore was forced to confine himself to 'mischief, seducing and deluding mankind, and drawing him in to be a rebel like himself.'[60]

Defoe normally insists on the dignity of the Devil, a fallen angel, who personally engages only in matters worthy of him, such as causing wars, leaving little tricks such as tumbling chairs and upsetting pots to his underlings.[61] He pictures him sitting in great state 'with all his legions about him, in the height of the atmosphere', watching the world as it revolves and dispatching his emissaries to stir up trouble.[62] These agents in turn made contact with the representatives of the Devil on earth, magicians, witches and 'his particular modern privy-counsellors call'd wits and fools'.[63]

The rational and modern Daniel Defoe accepted the reality of witches, just as he did that of the Devil and angels. Here, too, his ideas run counter to the views of the educated men of his age who were becoming increasingly sceptical of the existence of witches.[64] But, for Defoe, witchcraft was not only supported by biblical evidence but from the testimony of the witches themselves.

> That there are and ever have been such people in the world who converse familiarly with the Devil, enter into compact with him, and receive powers from him, both to hurt and deceive, and these have been in all ages call'd witches, and it is these, that our law and God's law condemn'd as such; and I think there can be no more debate of the matter.[65]

To do him justice he did not think that all supposed witches were real witches just as he did not think that all dreams were the result of angelic ministration. He could indeed be just as sceptical as the next man, remarking that if all tales of witches were true, 'I know not how any one could be easy to live near a widow after she was five-and-fifty.'[66] But that witches existed he had no doubt, though sometimes he is surprised that such a magnificent creature as the Devil should stoop to conniving in their shabby tricks.

Defoe continued to defend the traditional Protestant concepts of the supernatural even though these were directly contrary to the rational trend of belief in his day.[67] The struggle between good and evil was played out in men's minds, not simply as the workings of human psychology but in a real battleground where good and bad angels fought for control.[68] But where the supernatural did not have the sanction of revelation or Protestant theology, Defoe was normally much nearer the position of the rational men of his day. Fairies, for instance, were contemptuously dismissed. 'There never were such beings in any place, but the empty heads of old women and in penny story-books.'[69] About ghosts, however, he was to change his mind in the course of his lifetime. In his occult writings of the 1720s he denied the possibility of the reappearance of disembodied souls. This was good Protestant theology which held that the soul goes straight to Heaven or Hell at death. Defoe thought it would spoil the future state of bliss to be interrupted by the problems of the world. Equally, it would not be much of a state of everlasting misery where the damned could get loose of their chains and come hither and thither on trifles.[70] Earlier in his life Defoe had not been so sure. The idea of ghosts was of course very popular because it was the best available evidence of immortality.[71] In 1706 he published what was to become 'the most famous ghost story of the eighteenth century',[72] in which the recently deceased Mrs Veal appeared to her former friend Mrs Bargrave and had a pious talk about death with her. Defoe's book includes an advertisement for Drelincourt's *Book of the Consolations against the Fears of Death* which the ghost of Mrs Veal pronounced 'the best on that subject was ever written'.[73] As a result it was popularly thought that Defoe wrote his piece simply to boost the sales of Drelincourt's book and in the later eighteenth century it was assumed that the whole thing was a fiction. But in fact there seems no doubt that Defoe took the whole affair completely seriously and it is one of his best early pieces of *reportage*. Later, however, he was to adopt a more orthodox position.

But even when he had rejected ghosts he did not reject the reality of apparitions. He accepted that these could be the result of grief or a guilty conscience playing on the imagination. But some apparitions were genuine. However, they were not ghosts but spirits assuming a shape of flesh and blood for their own purposes.[74] These could be bad or good like the spirits who appeared in dreams. Defoe illustrates his theme with a number of stories, which formed the basis of collections of ghost stories for a long time into the future. One of the best tells of a girl going to meet her lover who was persuaded to go back home by her minister, whom she met on the way. Later she discovered that the minister had been in London at the time and realized that what she had met had really been an apparition of a good spirit determined to deter her from the path of fornication.[75]

It can be seen that man in the world of Defoe was in a rather confused state. On the one hand stood worldly rational man, the student of natural law, the survivor at all costs who must succeed here and now on earth. But man, too, was the pilgrim seeking salvation, subject to divine providence and bombarded in his dreams and even on the highway by the apparitions of good and bad spirits. Since we have been creditably informed by the great seventeenth-century astrologer William Lilly that when angels speak 'it's like the Irish, much in the throat', the life of man must have been at times somewhat alarming.[76] Defoe thus stands at the cross-roads in the great debate between reason and revelation, sometimes looking backward to a world where the influence of the supernatural on mankind was still unchallenged and sometimes looking forward to a world where men were not prepared to believe anything that they could not see for themselves. Not surprisingly there was a continuous clash between these two views in the writings of Defoe, as indeed there clearly was in the character of Defoe himself. Sometimes the emphasis is on survival and success; sometimes it is on salvation. There seems no reason to doubt, as some writers have, that this clash was a genuine one. Defoe was a good Christian and he wanted to be saved. But he was also a man of the world who wanted success, not only for himself, but for his country and for the characters he created in his novels. Unfortunately success was not always compatible with a moral code which was likely to lead to salvation,[77] and the Devil's angels were able successfully to tempt Defoe from time to time, both as a man and as a creator of fictional men and women.

[3]

THE WIDER WORLD

THE reader of Defoe is constantly amazed at the breadth and depth of his knowledge. How could the old man have remembered so much? One is reminded of the magic system of mnemonics reputed to have been used by the Renaissance magi with which it was possible to rise above time and keep the whole universe of nature and of man in one's mind.[1] Defoe himself used the same image in an article in *Applebee's Journal* when he described a man, clearly himself, who 'had the history of almost all the nations of the world in his head' and the geography of the world 'at his fingers' ends'.[2] His own works bear out his boast. He clearly had some sort of three-dimensional matrix in his head whose axes were time, space and ideas. From this matrix he could draw at random, immediately relating the effects in Virginia of something happening in the empire of the Grand Mogul, while at the same time retaining a very strong temporal, that is chronological, sense of why the thing had happened in the first place. He may have been a bad historian, and pedants love to catch him out in his facts, but he always explained things in an historical way, whether he was talking about the reformation, the Devil or the gin business. Some idea of his range can be seen by a consideration of two of his works, one basically historical, the other basically geographical. In the *General History of Discoveries and Improvements*[3] he made a bold effort to write the economic history of the world from the building of the Tower of Babel to the invention of the flint-lock musket. Although by no means a great historical work, the book is remarkable in the range of information it conveys to the reader. Even more astonishing is the superb *Atlas Maritimus and Commercialis; or a General View of the World*,[4] a vast and very lovely book in which 340 enormous double-columned pages are given up to a geographical and commercial description of the coasts of the world. Much of this, if not all of it, was written by Defoe[5] and very fine it is, combining useful description with typically Defovian musing on how everything might be improved.

In his younger days Defoe himself had travelled fairly widely and he remarks in the introduction that he had 'indeed seen several of the countries, coasts, cities, and sea-ports' which he described in the Atlas.[6] But it is doubtful if he had travelled beyond western Europe. For the rest he relied on information from others. Much of this he probably received verbally. There were few places like London for meeting travellers and, like most good journalists, Defoe was an excellent listener. Maybe Defoe was thinking of himself when he described Colonel Jack's informal education.

> I was always upon the inquiry, asking questions of things done in publick as well as in private, particularly, I lov'd to talk with seamen and soldiers about the war, and about the great sea-fights, or battles on shore, that any of them had been in . . .

Since Colonel Jack never forgot anything he was told, he became by this means 'a kind of an historian, and tho' I had read no books, and never had books to read, yet I cou'd give a tollerable account of what had been done, and of what was then a doing in the world'.[7]

Defoe himself suffered from no such deprivation and he was able to supplement such oral information by reading in the vast literature of history and travel. His favourite book was perhaps Sir Walter Raleigh's *History of the World*, but it is obvious from the research done for both his historical novels and his histories that he had read very widely in most contemporary history.[8] He was equally at home with travel books, one of the favourite literary or sub-literary genres of his day. The best of these are the accounts of the two English circumnavigators, William Dampier and Woodes Rogers, and the superb descriptions of Turkey, Persia and India by the great French traveller Jean-Baptiste Tavernier, but these books are only the best known of an enormous number of works recounting voyages and feats of exploration. Descriptions of real travels were supplemented by the vogue for imaginary travel books, a medium particularly popular in France. Such books were distinguished by their geographical realism and were often used to make ironical comparisons of an ideal society in such places as the semi-mythical Southern or Austral Land with the decadent, priest-ridden society at home.[9] One wonders if Defoe, always a keen upholder of women's rights,

had read Gabriel Foigny's story of an Australia in which all the
inhabitants were hermaphrodites who looked down on Europeans,
'as upon a sort of beast, whose entire time is taken up with matters
of sex' and who condemned the tyranny of man over woman, on the
grounds that women played the most important part in creation and
no one could be quite certain who was the father of a child.[10] Did
he get any tips from François Misson's story of colonists on a desert
island in the Indian Ocean, written twelve years before *Robinson
Crusoe*?[11] How much Defoe had read we shall never know. What is
clear is that the information he had absorbed in the course of his
lifetime enabled him to roam the world in his mind in a way that
no other writer of travel fiction was able to emulate. Reading did
not only supplement experience. If the reader was an intelligent
man he could learn more from books than lesser men learned from a
life of action. He makes the point in an unpublished work designed
to encourage self-education in gentlemen.

> If he has not travell'd in his youth, has not made the grand tour
> of Italy and France, he may make the tour of the world in books,
> he may make himself master of the geography of the universe in
> the maps, attlasses, and measurements of our mathematicians. He
> may travell by land with the historians, by sea with the navi-
> gators. He may go round the globe with Dampier and Rogers,
> and kno' a thousand times more in doing it than all those
> illiterate sailors.[12]

If this comment refers to Dampier and Rogers themselves it is rather
unfair. They were good observers and wrote interesting books.[13]
But they were not interesting enough for Defoe. Sailing round the
world was now so easy that 'every ordinary sailor is able to do it',
while the writers of round-the-world voyages bored their readers
with a mass of information on sailing instructions, winds, bearings
and depths, but provided little variety of entertainment.[14] This is
fair comment and the truth is that fictional voyages were generally
more fun to read than real ones.

While Defoe's rogues and adventurers are roaming the seas they
are supplying his readers with a non-stop flow of information about
the world they live in. If we concentrate, we can learn an immense
variety of things, from the direction of flow of the rivers of Siberia
to the best way to salt penguins in the South Atlantic, from the
relative prices of gold and brass in West Africa to the length of the

summer night in Nova Zembla. Nothing is more characteristic of
Defoe and nothing more vital in the build-up of his realism than his
detail, whether it is the coordinates of a fictional South Sea Island
or the bill of lading of a ship seized by one of his pirates. Much of the
information supplied is quite accurate. Colonel Jack gives an account
of clandestine trade in the West Indies which squares quite well with
the well-researched efforts of historians.[15] Defoe as a Londoner
with many contacts in the mercantile and seafaring community
would know about such things. The trouble is, how do we know
how much he really knew and how much he simply made up? The
answer is that we either have to read something else to check up or
just relax, roam the world with Defoe and enjoy ourselves.

When Defoe looked at the world he saw it as something designed
by God to provide an intellectual obstacle race for man. The globe
on which men lived had been originally an intellectual blank. Man
had been left by the Creator to discover its secrets.[16] This popular
view of the relation between rational man and God's works had
best been put forward by the naturalist John Ray in 1691:

> Since we find materials so fit to serve all the necessities and con-
> veniences, and to exercise and employ the wit and industry of an
> intelligent and active being . . . and since the omniscient creator
> could not but know all the uses, to which they might and would
> be employed by man . . . it is little less than a demonstration, that
> they were created intentionally, I do not say only, for these uses.[17]

Defoe often marvelled at the ingenuity of God in this respect. How
wonderful, for example, that Providence had adapted nature to trade
by making things float. How much more difficult life would have
been if 'a ship that swims in one sea, would immediately sink to the
bottom in another'. What sort of a world would it be if 'the horse
would not be rid; nor the ox draw, nor the cow be milk'd'?[18]

But perhaps the most remarkable of all God's achievements was
the way in which he had scattered the good things all over the world
so as to maximize the difficulty of discovering them. This not only
made man work hard to find them but gave great rewards to the
finders. It also of course encouraged and maximized navigation since
such things were 'at the remotest distance from each other' and from
the markets in which they would at last be brought together and
consumed.[19] Defoe's contemporaries loved to reflect on this amazing
providence. In 1711 Addison in the *Spectator* remarked on the fact

that 'the simple dress of a woman of quality is often the product of a hundred climates':

> The muff and the fan come together from the different ends of the earth. The scarf is sent from the torrid zone, and the tippet from beneath the Pole. The brocade petticoat rises out of the mines of Peru and the diamond necklace out of the bowels of Indostan.[20]

Defoe is honest enough to point out that God could have arranged that all the produce of the world be found in every part, 'so that no man need to go a mile from home for any thing he wanted':

> As this immediate plenty of all things to all mankind would at once take away all room or pretence for coveting and craving from one another; remove all poverty and misery, tyranny, oppression, and inequallity of poor and rich, and level mankind to one state of quiet, perfect enjoyment, I will not say, but it might be in a better state than we now enjoy.

This utopia, however, would have meant no hard work and no trade, a state of affairs as unattractive to the Almighty as it was to Defoe. God had therefore compromised. The common necessities of life – water, food, fuel and building materials – were found everywhere. But, 'materials for cloathing, varieties for feeding, and many of the numberless *addenda* to the pleasures and conveniences of life' were 'inaccessible . . . but by labour, industry, and correspondence'.[21] Man being what he was had sought out the inaccessible. The whales commanded by Providence to make their rendezvous in the icy waters of the northern ocean had been discovered and now every year 400 or 500 ships sailed to the seas between Greenland and Spitzbergen.[22] In the *Atlas Maritimus* Defoe describes the terrifying business of hunting these whales through gaps in the ice in open boats, 'of all the adventures in trade that are practis'd in the world, the most nice, difficult, and dangerous'. If ever a man earned his living by the sweat of his brow, surely these men had? And yet Defoe can find a fault. For what do the whale-hunters do at the end of the season? They return to Spitzbergen and spend their time hunting and eating the deer which roam so plentifully there. 'This diversion, and the pleasure of their repast, tempts them often to suspend some of that valuable time there, which ought to be wholly employ'd in the business of the voyage.'[23] It was a hard world.

The mention of Spitzbergen reminds us how much of that original blank left to man at the Creation had now been filled in. Here was something in which the moderns had quite clearly outstripped the ancients.[24] Defoe, confident in his modernity, could afford to have a bit of fun at the description by the ancients of Thule (the Orkneys) as the 'last brink of the spacious globe'.[25] Expressions like this which had been handed down to the modern age as the height of wisdom have been found by practice:

> all to be empty, and foolish, nay even ridiculous; for our ships steer not only to their Thule, but beyond it into the frozen seas of Greenland, and Nova Zembla, where we see real wonders, which they knew nothing of, and see also that their wonders, which they made to be so terrible, have nothing in them.[26]

Defoe was rarely as uncharitable to the past as this. He often used a favourite contemporary image by which the moderns were seen to be standing on the shoulders of giants to make their discoveries: 'We stand upon the shoulders of three thousand years application, and have all the benefit of their discoveries, and experiments handed down, gratis.'[27] Nor did he think that change had all been in a straight line towards progress. He liked to remind his readers of the glories of the past in regions regarded in his day as undeveloped and miserable – Greece, the Middle East and North Africa – 'the most delicious countries, formerly flowing with milk and honey', but now turned 'into a desolate howling wilderness'.[28] Much of the desolation could of course be attributed to the Devil's favourite, Muhammad,[29] and his heirs the tyrannous Turks.[30] But as an historian Defoe was aware that the rot had set in earlier. For ancient history had known both progress and decay.

Biblical economic history becomes really interesting for the commercially oriented Defoe with the founding of Tyre, 'the beginner of trade, the mother of merchants; where commerce had its first birth and where all the trade of the world center'd in a few years after, and continued to do so many ages'.[31] But, although a great admirer of Tyre, Defoe reserved his greatest admiration for Carthage, the Queen of the South, whose destruction by the Romans he saw as an unmitigated disaster for mankind. Not only had the English lost an inestimable market for their cloth but the 'gay and delicate' Carthaginians had been replaced as inhabitants of northwest Africa by miserable Moors and beastlike Berbers whose exis-

tence depended on a continual plunder of western European trade.
Defoe's solution to the perennial problem of the Barbary corsairs
was a time-honoured one. He proposed that all the nations of Europe
should join together to conquer Morocco and the Barbary regencies,
driving the corsairs inland to maintain themselves by peaceable
labour.[32]

Defoe was quite prepared to give honour to the ancients where it
was due. He greatly admired the navigational exploits of the Phoenicians, describing their voyage to Ophir (Sumatra) with an imaginative consideration of the difficulties overcome. Here indeed he shows
how a strict interpretation of the Bible need not clash with that first
need of the historian, a sense of chronology, when he comments that
the Phoenicians probably had difficulty in finding provisions since
the coasts they visited might well have been uninhabited 'so soon
after the confusions of Babel'.[33] On the other side of the world,
Defoe credits the Phoenician seamen with the original peopling of
America, thus incidentally saving himself from the heresy adopted
by many of putting God Almighty to the bother of a second creation
for that part of the world.[34] Defoe's view on the peopling of America,
which was a fairly common one, was celebrated in the burlesque
poetry of Ebenezer Cook:[35]

> I hence inferr'd Phoenicians old,
> Discover'd first with Vessels bold
> These western shoars, and planted here,
> Returning once or twice a year,
> With Naval Stoars and Lasses kind,
> To comfort those were left behind;
> Till by the Winds and Tempest – toar,
> From their intended Golden Shoar;
> They suffer'd Ship-wreck, or were drown'd,
> And lost the World so newly found.

Nobody else was to rival the achievements of Tyre and Carthage in
the ancient world. The Romans got a bad press in the *General History
of Discoveries and Improvements*. Not only did they destroy Carthage
but they also failed to encourage commerce and navigation themselves, except for the corn supply to Rome. But they paid the price.
Failure to encourage trade led to their impoverishment and this led
in turn to the success of the Barbarians when they invaded the
Empire.[36]

When all due honour had been paid to the ancients Defoe could turn with satisfaction to his own world. He was continually amazed and delighted at the enormous progress that man had made in his discovery of it in the past three centuries. The ignorance of the twelfth to fourteenth centuries was 'so very near the heels of our times'.[37] Some idea of the achievement can be had from a glance at the sea charts in the *Atlas Maritimus*.[38] The coastlines of Europe, Africa, South America and most of Asia are now known. In the far south, the northern, western and half the southern coasts of New Holland (Australia) have been drawn in, as have parts of Van Diemens Land (Tasmania) and New Zealand. Quite a few of the islands in the western Pacific are there too. No one is quite sure what happens to the north-west of Japan, though the south coast of Korea is drawn, and the coastline of northern Russia only goes as far east as the mouths of the Ob and the Yenisei. North-west America is equally vague. California is still an island, divided from the mainland by the Red Sea, and there is no coastline drawn between the west side of Hudson's Bay and California. To know even as much of the world as this was a remarkable achievement and was a tribute to the persistence, greed and navigational ability of European sailors. But it was not in fact a recent achievement. Defoe's lifetime coincides with a lull in the tempo of exploration.[39] The dates of the latest discoveries give the game away. Most of them are Australasian discoveries made by Dutchmen in the early 1640s, though Dampier's Straits between New Guinea and New Britain (1700) is a sign that the freelance buccaneering explorer still existed. But neither Dampier nor the Dutchmen thought much of what they had seen in Australasia and it was left to Captain Cook a generation after Defoe's death to fill in the gaps.[40] Defoe was aware of these gaps and of the much larger ones that existed in man's knowledge of the interior of continents: 'Neither Africa nor America are yet fully discover'd: there are yet infinite treasures of trade and plantation, to be search'd after, innumerable nations not convers'd with.'[41] Since no one else would explore, Defoe had to do so himself. Most of the geographical discoveries made in Defoe's lifetime were made by his own fictional characters. Some of these discoveries were so realistic that they were accepted as true long after Defoe's death.

The most remarkable achievement of Defoe's adventurers was that of Captain Singleton, who traversed Africa from Mozambique to the Niger more than a century before the birth of Stanley.[42] There was in fact an embarrassing lack of knowledge about the interior of Africa in Defoe's time. Jonathan Swift poked fun at the expense of the map-makers who were loth to leave such a large area empty:

> . . . geographers, in Afric maps
> With savage pictures fill their gaps,
> And o'er unhabitable downs
> Place elephants for want of towns.[43]

But in 1770 the French cartographer D'Anville cut out all these decorative details and demonstrated to his fellow-countrymen how little they really did know.[44] The truth was that people thought that the interior of Africa was so unpleasant that they had no wish to explore it.[45] Defoe would not accept this. In the *Atlas Maritimus* he launches into a panegyric on the dark continent, stressing its central position for world trade, its superb if unimproved rivers, 'the fruitfulness of the soil, the clemency of the seasons, the salubrity of the air, and the suitableness of all these to improvement, were it cultivated by an industrious people'. Even in the very hottest parts, Africa's potential was demonstrated by the density of people 'who do abound in plenty, have cattle, corn, cooling fruits, shade, rivers . . . and live (to them) very agreeably and healthy'.[46] All that was lacking for improvement was trade and even in this respect he was able to report in a stop press item that 'they tell us' that there was a vast commerce between a great negro town four hundred miles north of the Guinea Coast and the Mediterranean. The main trade was northern salt for southern gold and Defoe describes the unusual method by which the trade was carried on:

> They leave the salt in a pot or jar, and retire; then the people take the salt, and put into the pot as much gold as they think it's worth; and if the Moors approve of it, they take it away.[47]

It is rather surprising that the well-read Defoe should have felt it necessary to describe this method of trading in reported speech, for descriptions of it are as old as the hills. A similar story is told by Herodotus of Defoe's beloved Carthaginians whilst the Arab geographers relate the exchange of gold for salt exactly as Defoe reports it.[48]

Even if there was trade in the north there was none in the centre

and it is part of Captain Singleton's mission to demonstrate to
Defoe's readers the possibilities and gains to be had from Africa.
His epic journey has all the trimmings that we might expect. Porters
are acquired by a simple observation of the laws of war by which
prisoners (in Africa at any rate) became the slaves of their con-
querors. Their fidelity is assured by Singleton's astute realization
that one of them is a prince. By getting the surgeon to attend his
wounds he gains the loyalty of all. Carriage is sometimes by water,
sometimes on the backs of tame buffaloes. Food is acquired by hunting or by trading trinkets made by one of the seamen, 'the artist',
with the simple-minded natives, who amazingly have no realization
of the 'real' value of such baubles. Mountains, lakes and howling
wildernesses bar their way. Lions, tigers and elephants abound. But
they really have very little real trouble, just press boringly on where
no man has passed before them till they discover a naked white man
who shows them the way to go home, making sure they pick up
enough ivory and gold on the way to make them all rich.

   More interesting than Captain Singleton as a document of fictional
exploration and perhaps Defoe's best travel book is *A New Voyage
Round the World*.[49] Here, in an amusing way, Defoe puts over many
of his ideas for increasing trade and colonial expansion. The unnamed narrator insists on going round the world the wrong way,
that is in an easterly direction, and tries to demonstrate that more
money can be made that way. The normal route of the circumnavigator, designed for easy navigation and maximum gain, was to
sail from England round Cape Horn to the Chilean coast and then
either to rob or trade clandestinely with the Spanish colonists before
sailing for the East Indies with his hold full of bullion. The return to
England would then be made with a cargo of spices and Chinese
goods. Defoe's narrator sails *via* the Cape of Good Hope to the
Philippines where the governor of Manila winks at his very profitable clandestine trade in European goods. He then sails for Peru
with a cargo of silks, jewels, spices and Japanese gold, all of which is
sold at good prices to the Spanish colonists and he returns home to
England with his ship full of silver.

   The crew are frightened to sail east from the Philippines because
of the dangers of starvation when lying becalmed in the area of
notorious variable winds in the central Pacific. The Spaniards on
their return voyage to Acapulco normally sailed north, until they
found a wind which would take them across to California.[50] But

Defoe's narrator, probably acting on a tip from Dampier's account of his voyages, decided to go south.[51] He argued that north of the line there would be no islands, but south 'we were sure to meet with islands innumerable'.[52] In this he was perfectly correct. A course, east-south-east, from the island of Guam which is the way they eventually sail, would have gone through or near the as yet undiscovered Marshall, Gilbert and Phoenix islands *via* Tahiti and Easter Island to the coast of Chile. And just to make sure that he does not run foul of that worst peril of a long voyage, scurvy, he takes on board plenty of lime, lemon and orange juice mixed with water which he found 'a great relief to our men'.[53] All of which is pretty good going, nearly half a century before Captain Cook's first voyage to the southern Pacific in the *Endeavour* and quarter of a century before the Scottish physician, James Lind, published his famous work on scurvy.[54] Naturally enough, the cruise across the southern Pacific is entirely successful. Many islands are discovered, full of plentiful provisions, gold and pearls. In one of them the natives look seriously at the sky when they make a promise, which bodes well for their eventual conversion. Once converted, there is a good chance that they will cover their nakedness with English cloth.

At long last the intrepid mariners sight the mountains of Chile and drop anchor at the island of Juan Fernandez, eight months out from Manila.[55] Now we come to the main purpose of the book, which was to stress once again one of Defoe's recurring fantasies, the idea of an English colony in Patagonia connected with a trading post in Chile by routes across the Andes.[56] Talking of the southern Argentine he writes in *A Plan of the English Commerce*:[57]

Suppose I should propose a place in the world, where, if the English could plant at this time any numbers of their people, even the poorest and meanest, supposing them only to be industrious, and willing to live . . . where 100,000 people may immediately plant and build, find food, and subsist plentifully; the soil fruitful, the climate comfortable, the air healthy, unmolested by savages and cannibals, as in North America; unravaged by lions and tygers, elephants and monsters, as in Africa; fill'd with cattle useful and eatable, tame and tractable, abounding with fish, fowl, flesh, wanting nothing but to be inhabited by Christians, and ally'd to the rest of the Christian world by commerce and navigation.

It is the real possibility of making this fantasy come true that Defoe
puts over in fiction in the second volume of *A New Voyage round the
World*.

The narrator learns as he trades along the west coast how the
Indians hate the Spaniards and would join in any venture against
them.[58] He learns too that the passes across the Andes are suitable
for mules and that there are villages where they could get provisions.
Later he goes ashore with a Spaniard and stays at his home in
Valdivia. The reader is dazzled with the luxury and good taste of
the Spaniard's home, a way of life which it is understood would be
easily sustainable by Englishmen living under South American conditions. The Spaniard is then persuaded to guide him to the watershed of the Andes so that he can look down on the country beyond.
All of this is superbly done – the landscape, the great precipices and
volcanoes, the abundant game, the hospitality and pleasant manners of the Indians and above all the gold lying around so that it is
hardly worth the trouble of picking it up. Finally they look down
towards the east and see a vast, well-watered and fertile plain
beneath the mountains. The narrator decides to send a party of
fifty men to make the crossing while he goes round by sea to settle
and fortify a port.

Very little was known of this part of South America in Defoe's
day. The routes north-east from the River Plate across Tucuman to
Peru were well known and were much used by smugglers who were
in the habit of using this back-door to the silver mines of Potosi.[59]
There was also a route from Buenos Aires to Chile *via* Mendoza
which Woodes Rogers described as open in the summer.[60] But south
of Buenos Aires was a *costa deserta*. There may have been tracks
across the southern passes but nobody really knew. The achievement
of General San Martín in leading an army across the Andes in 1817
to aid the Chilean insurgents in the war of independence was considered so remarkable that it was compared with that of Hannibal
in crossing the Alps.[61] But Defoe, who elsewhere compared the
mountains of Wales to the Alps and could make a crossing of the
Pennines into something sounding like an expedition to the Hima-
layas, has no compunction in dispatching his fictional characters
across the unknown Andes. Embroidering Admiral Narborough's
description of Port Desire in Patagonia – 'I never saw a country in
the world so like England'[62] – and making a very favourable interpretation of Woodes Rogers' summary of Spanish accounts of Chile,[63]

Defoe decided that the crossing would be easy enough and the anonymous narrator of *A New Voyage round the World* proved him right. He himself sailed to Port St Julian in Patagonia, whose hinterland he described as 'a noble champion country, the plains all smooth, and cover'd with grass like Salisbury Plain'.[64] He forgot to mention that it was in the cold and treeless harbour of St Julian, short of fresh water and inhabited only by a handful of the most primitive people in the world, that Magellan's crew had mutinied on the first circumnavigation of the globe.[65] When Defoe's fifty sailors nearly mutinied on their way across the Andes from Valdivia it was not because they were fed up or hungry, but simply because they did not see why they should press on when there was so much gold lying around to be picked up. It all sounds such an easy formula for the good life that one expects to be knocked down by the rush of Defoe's readers taking passage to Patagonia to stake their claim to prosperity and ease.

We must not leave the subject of exploration without mentioning Robinson Crusoe who, if he discovered nothing new other than his island, did at least travel the farthest of Defoe's heroes. Old age hardly improved him and it was a tedious man who decided to go once more on his travels in his sixties.[66] The reader can feel nothing but sympathy for the crew who, fed up with his moralizing, marooned him in Bengal.[67] But nothing can daunt Crusoe. Off he goes, is mistaken for a pirate in the South China Sea, crosses China with a sneer and then makes his way down the long, long road across central Asia, fighting off Tartars and burning their wooden gods on the way. Finally he reaches the comparatively civilized Gulag Archipelago of Peter the Great. Here, in Siberia, he has a happy winter, swapping philosophy with an exiled Russian prince, before at long last he goes home.

Defoe's heroes, as we can see, quarter the globe between them. The biggest gap is the heartland of North America. There is no Captain Singleton to anticipate the achievement of Lewis and Clark. Many of the novels have sections set in the English colonies: an epic journey from the mouth of the Mississippi over the mountains to South Carolina appears in *Colonel Jack*; various characters toy with the idea of searching for the North-east Passage; but no one goes to have a look at what was known over a century later as the Great American Desert. However, few parts of the rest of the known and unknown world are left out. Within this pattern of constant movement a few exotic places appear again and again in the works of Defoe. The goat-ridden island of Juan Fernandez off the coast of Chile, where the real Alexander Selkirk was marooned,[68] is a constant rendezvous of his pirates, as is Port St Julian in Patagonia – a favourite place for provisioning with salted penguins. And it is here that Captain Avery sets up a board with the inscription 'Gone to Madagascar'[69] which makes the whole world of Defoe sound like a nursery game played on a vast map stretched out on the floor on a winter evening, which of course is what it was. What fun for the dull stay-at-homes, who are following that recipe for contentment which Defoe called the middle station of life, to read of the exotic and to put a little more Newcastle coal on their fires, as they are marooned or endure a hurricane at sea or capture a 46-gun Portuguese man-of-war off the coast of Brazil.

For one thing that is striking about the voyages is just how dangerous they are. Indeed the seas can never have been so destructive as they were in the days of Defoe. Longer voyages increased the danger of death by shipwreck, starvation or disease as leaky, poorly provisioned, unhealthy ships made their way with inaccurate charts through hazardous seas.[70] Crews were often difficult to recruit and inexperienced landsmen were pressed to fill the gaps. Defoe often trumpeted the horrors of the press-gang, painting a pathetic picture of families left starving when the husband and father, by whose labour they lived, was dragged 'from the loom, or from the trowel, to the fleet'. It was all so unfair. 'Why should a brute, a meer tarr, a drunken sailor, judge by the force of his cudgel, who is, or is not fit for the publick service at sea?'[71] It was also inefficient. Professor Boxer recalls how the Portuguese, past masters of the shipwreck, had rustic crews who knew so little of the ways of the sea that the captain tied a bundle of onions on one side of the ship and a bundle of garlic on the other, so that they would be able to distinguish port and starboard.[72] A further danger was that there was no accurate method of determining longitude before Harrison produced the first reliable chronometer four years after Defoe's death.[73] Ship's captains had to rely on dead reckoning to know when to change course. Many captains were superb navigators, like Defoe's own narrator of *A New Voyage round the World*, who hit the poorly charted Juan Fernandez first time after an eight months' voyage through uncharted waters.[74] But even such skill as this could be negated if several days running before a storm, with the masts bare and the galley fires out, had

made casting the log impossible. Western Australia became the
graveyard of many a Dutch ship which failed to turn north for the
Straits of Sunda after the long run east from the African coast, just
as Natal was for Portuguese ships travelling in the opposite direction.[75] But the danger from shipwreck was easily outweighed by the
danger from man, as the editor of one book of voyages reminds us
by including Waller's lines on his title page:[76]

> Bold were the Men who on the Ocean first
> Spread their new Sails, when Shipwreck was the worst.
> More Danger now from Man alone we find
> Than from the Rocks, the Billows, or the Wind.

Waller was almost certainly correct. Never can there have been so
many ships at sea whose sole function was to seize or destroy other
ships. From 1689 to 1713 there was almost continuous warfare
between the leading maritime states of western Europe, and each
nation fitted out privateers to prey on the shipping of its enemies.
Bromley estimates that the French alone took over seven thousand
prizes in the twelve years of the War of Spanish Succession.[77] Privateering was a legitimate activity of seamen, but it was supplemented
by the greatest concentration of piracy in the history of the world.
In the Mediterranean the quasi-legal activity known as the *corso*
continued to flourish and no account of a voyage is complete without
either capture or flight from the corsairs of Barbary and Morocco or
from those of Malta who carried on an equally virulent warfare
against the shipping of Muslims and Greeks.[78] 'Not a sailor goes to
sea in a merchant ship', wrote Defoe, 'but he feels some secret
tremor, that it may one time or other be his lot to be taken by the
Turks.'[79] The author of a book about the Chevalier d'Arvieux, one
of the most readable travellers of the age, pinpoints the nuisance
value of the corsairs when he tells us that travellers' tempers grew
short at 'the almost daily whistle which gave the order to clear the
ship for action, when the passengers had to muster in the waist or
on the deck with their muskets and bandoliers'.[80] In the West Indies
the buccaneers still throve although, from the 1680s, the beginnings
of a settled colonial administration and the enormous expansion of
East Indian trade encouraged some of the bolder of their number to
seek new fortunes in the waters of the Indian Ocean.[81] Here they
were in good company. The formidable Maratha corsairs patrolled
the coast of Malabar,[82] while further to the east flourished the

endemic piracy of the South China Sea which was to survive intact until the days of Conrad.

The great expansion of piracy in the seventeenth century was a backhanded tribute to the great expansion of legitimate commerce in the same period. Never had there been such a chance for so many poor men to get rich so quickly. From the pirates' point of view, their task was made easy by the regularity and seasonality of most of the world's shipping lines and also by the fact that, before the discovery of an accurate method of determining longitude, ships were in the habit of getting on to the latitude of their port of destination and then sailing due east or west till they reached it.[83] Later, such facts were to make protection easier for navies but, in this period, they meant that pirates simply had to sit across the correct lines of latitude at the right time of year and wait for their prey.

Defoe was fascinated by the subject of piracy and he wrote the biographies of many famous pirates as well as introducing them into most of his novels.[84] The biographies of pirates make the profession look temptingly easy for the newcomer to enter, as well as succeed in. Time after time the fledgeling pirate seizes a fishing boat or a small coaster in an English port, then progressively captures bigger ships until he finds himself the proud possessor of a fast, well-armed, well-manned ship of, say, fifty guns. From then on, most merchant ships would be helpless against him and he was theoretically in a position to amass a fortune. And yet, reading Defoe, the life of the pirate does not seem to have been a particularly happy one, though better than starving.

What, then, were the problems for the pirate? The most obvious one was that piracy was illegal and considered so by virtually all civilized countries. Once a man had declared his trade by seizing a few ships, he knew that the normal facilities of the world he had left were no longer at his disposal. If captured at sea or ashore he was almost certain to be hanged and a high proportion of pirates do indeed seem to have ended their lives at the end of a rope, if death in battle, shipwreck or malnutrition had not taken them first. Not that pirates necessarily feared the risk of the gallows. That early upholder of women's rights, the pirate captain Mary Reed, thought hanging no great hardship, for 'were it not for that, every cowardly fellow would turn pyrate, and so infest the seas that men of courage must starve . . . The ocean would be crowded with rogues, like the land, and no merchant would venture out; so that the trade, in a little time, would not be worth following.'[85]

The implications of illegality were immense for the pirate. If he did capture a ship what was he to do with the booty? To sail into a trading port and sell a captured ship's cargo was to invite the gallows. For this reason, Defoe's pirates rarely seize the cargoes of the ships they capture, contenting themselves with ready money or very portable wealth, such as jewellery, and the provisions and equipment necessary for them to continue their voyage. Rich cargoes of sugar, cloth, silks and spices proceed to their destinations with no profit for the pirate. These facts determined pirate policy. No pirate with any sense, for instance, would seize an English East India Company ship on the way home when its hold was full of goods. But it was a very different matter on the outward voyage when the ship was loaded with the silver to pay for them. Not only the cargo but also the crew and passengers of a captured ship were not likely to be of much value to the pirate. The organization of ransom, before the days of wireless, required a settled base and much time to negotiate, and the materialistic pirates of Defoe's day were certainly not likely to take the risks accepted by the modern skyjacker with his political motives. Even to sell their captives as slaves was virtually impossible, since most of the great slave markets of the world were ruled by people as hostile to piracy as anybody else. So, apart from forcing useful members of the crew, such as surgeons or carpenters, to join them and making up their numbers by the recruitment of volunteers, pirates got little from their human captives, a frustration which may well have had much to do with their legendary cruelty.[86]

There were, however, loopholes in the disposal of booty which some pirates were able to take advantage of. The policy of European nations to create trading monopolies in their colonies and of the chartered European trading companies to create monopolies in various parts of the world offered great temptations, both to the colonists and to the junior officers of the trading companies who were left to rot in unhealthy climates while their stay-at-home bosses enjoyed monopoly profits. Hence we can find the governor of South Carolina making a deal with the notorious Captain Teach, *alias* Blackbeard,[87] whilst the Spanish colonists were often prepared to engage in a clandestine trade and few questions asked. On the other side of the world, the scope was even greater. The servants of the English and Dutch East India Companies could only hope to get

rich really quickly by trading on their own account and the temptation to buy pirated goods was more than many of them could resist,
as Captain Singleton and his prudent adviser, the Quaker William,
found to their advantage.[88] And then, of course, there were all the
merchants of Asia, individualists to a man and subject to no
monopolists in London or Amsterdam. A cargo of spices seized in
the Dutch East Indies could be sold well enough in Formosa if you
could get there, even if you did only get 'thieves' pennyworths',[89]
whilst the main problem in the Persian Gulf was that the pirate
himself would be murdered and robbed, rather than finding a
market. But only a really enterprising pirate would enter such
dangerous waters. No such opportunities arose for the small fry in
the West Indies.

Disposal of cargo was by no means the end of the pirate's
problems. A pirate could rarely make use of the facilities of a port to
careen, repair or provision his ship. This was the reason that uninhabited islands like Tortuga and the lesser Bahamas were so
attractive. But, although with good craftsmen a ship could normally
be kept in good trim or even completely rebuilt in these secret, or
not so secret, lairs, they rarely had adequate facilities for the proper
provisioning of a ship. This meant that pirates generally had a very
restricted and often unhealthy diet. They relied for grain and
alcohol on what they could capture; otherwise they seem to have
existed mainly on salted or sun-dried meat (the *boucan* which gave
the buccaneers their name). Both Captains Avery and Singleton fed
their crews for months on virtually nothing but the salted penguins
which they had acquired in Patagonia.

Despite such problems, pirates did of course take prizes, normally
fairly easily, and often the booty in silver coin, jewellery and other
high-value, low-bulk goods could be very considerable. But how
were they to distribute it? One has only to pose the question to see
how difficult it would be to solve amongst such a casually assembled
group as the crew of a pirate ship. A similar problem was how to
keep the crew together once some success had been achieved. A
solution to both problems is suggested by the policy adopted by
Captain Avery:[90]

Here [Juan Fernandez] we shar'd our booty, which was great
indeed to a profusion; and as keeping such a treasure in every
man's particular private possession would have occasion'd gam-

ing, quarrelling, and perhaps thieving and pilfering, I order'd that so many small chests should be made as there were men in the ship, and every man's treasure was nail'd up in these chests and the chests all stow'd in the hold, with every man's name upon his chest, not to be touch'd but by general order; and to prevent gaming I prevail'd with them to make a law or agreement and every one to set their hands to it; by which they agreed that if any man play'd for any more money than he had in his keeping, the winner should not be paid whatever the loser run in debt, but the chest containing every man's dividend should be all his own, to be deliver'd whole to him; and the offender, whenever he left the ship, if he would pay any gaming debts afterward that was another case . . . By this means also we secured the ship's crew keeping together; for if any man left the ship now, he was sure to leave about 6000 pieces of eight behind him.

In this ship one notes a rule of benevolent despotism. Often pirates, considering themselves an assemblage of free men, practised, or at least tried to practise, complete democracy, as for instance in the ship of Captain Roberts where all decisions were to be made according to the vote of the majority.[91] But mistrust and the general nature of the business normally brought such good-intentioned ideas to nothing.

The final problem for the pirate and perhaps the hardest to solve was how to get home with his booty after a successful career. If poverty, greed or ambition drove men 'upon the account', as they euphemistically called piracy, they naturally wanted some day to enjoy the benefits of their enterprise. But getting home could be very difficult. The normal way was for a pirate to go ashore and travel to a seaport and there mingle with ordinary people till he could get a ship home. The dangers were only too obvious. He might well be recognized by a former victim or even more likely by a former colleague who might well turn king's evidence to save his own skin. With so much money on him, the homeward-bound pirate might well be robbed or draw attention to himself by spending it. Once suspected and cross-examined, pirates could be guaranteed to give themselves away by faltering in their stories, by being kept apart and contradicting each other, or by being told and believing that a colleague had betrayed them.[92] So the advice normally given was to take only a small booty home, poor recompense for a life of danger and salted penguins. Many pirates were never prepared to run the risk and, in Madagascar especially, colonies of retired pirates were established, intermarrying with the local population and even founding dynasties and minute states, some with that same demo- cratic bias we have seen in the distribution of booty.[93] Pirates indeed seem to have spent quite a lot of their time drawing up articles of association.

It was sometimes possible for a pirate to get home with at least some of his wealth intact by acquiring a pardon. In 1718, a general pardon was offered to English pirates who surrendered to Captain Woodes Rogers, ex-privateer and circumnavigator, now made governor of the Bahamas, one of the main pirate strongholds.[94] The future safety of shipping was felt to be worth the pardon and several pirates accepted it. When Woodes Rogers arrived in the Bahamas he 'passed between two lines of reformed pirates who fired their muskets in his honour'. But reform was too dull. Soon, many of the pirates were slipping off back to sea and Woodes Rogers was to die in Nassau in 1732 with his task of cleaning up the Bahamas not fully accomplished. Pirates elsewhere managed to buy pardons. In the early seventeenth century some twenty ex-pirates had managed to purchase their pardon from the Grand-Duke of Tuscany with a colossal bribe. Others settled, for a price, in more remote places such as Malabar or South America. But Englishmen of course wanted to return to England (and ideally to buy an estate). In the *Review* of 1707 Defoe reported the offer of an enormous sum by the English pirates of Madagascar in return for a free pardon.[95] Defoe argued that the government should accept. Although ideally the pirates should be rooted out, they were in fact too strong and it would cost too much. By pardoning them England would remove the evil and danger in the Indian Ocean and at the same time receive much needed money for the war effort. The story was probably apocry- phal, but it illustrates the problem well.[96] In fact few pirates managed to get home wealthy; the most successful being those who turned gamekeeper, such as Captain Morgan.

Life might be difficult for the pirate, but this did not deter men from going on the account. A seaman's life was likely to be short and nasty, in any case, and low wages were not an encouragement to a man to be honest. Not much pressure was necessary to induce a sailor to desert from a captured ship, and piracy throve. Merchant ships sailed through dangerous waters and little was done to protect them. Despite the efforts of Woodes Rogers, control of piracy was very limited in Defoe's day, even in peacetime when ships of the Royal Navy could be released for this activity. Several expeditions were fitted out against the pirates of Madagascar but achieved very little. Their historian ascribes their eventual decline to tropical disease and old age rather than to any effort by the British government. And, of course, the most famous pirate-catcher of the Indian Ocean, Captain Kidd, turned pirate himself.[97] However, in the twenty years after Defoe's death, things were to change for the better. The American historian, Gary Walton, has shown that there was an enormous reduction in the number of guns carried by merchantmen as a result of the improved control of piracy in the first half of the eighteenth century. But nearly all this improvement was to come after 1730.[98]

When we look at Defoe's books against this background of maritime violence we can see that he did not use all that much poetic licence in his description of voyages. People were not shipwrecked or captured quite so often in reality but these were both fairly common hazards of the sea. It is hardly surprising that living in such a milieu made sailors hard men. 'Les Enfans Perdus', Defoe called them, 'the Forlorn Hope of the World':

> They are fellows that bid defiance to terror, and maintain a constant war with the elements; who by the magick of their art, trade in the very confines of death, and are always posted within shot, as I may say, of the grave: 'Tis true, their familiarity with danger makes them despise it, for which, I hope, no body will say they are the wiser; and custom has so harden'd them, that we find them the worst of men, tho' always in view of their last moment.[99]

Hard men they were and they lived a hard life. Not a life that many men would seek. Defoe thought that only a desperate man would seek his livelihood on or over the oceans. Desperation could of course lead to success. But for Robinson Crusoe, with his excellent prospects at home, to go to sea was simply foolhardy and he deserved everything he got.

However, violence and danger seemed to suit the European mentality. Although by no means possessed of a monopoly of nastiness, Europeans were already asserting that violent domination of the globe which was to reach its peak in the century and a half after 1750. European superiority is taken for granted by Defoe. China, the only possible rival, is ridiculed in the *Farther Adventures of Robinson*

Crusoe.[100] But Asia was inhabited by rather too many well-armed men for Europeans to be able to throw their weight about in a way befitting their supposed cultural superiority. Elsewhere they could do more or less as they liked. Barbarous and ignorant savages could be induced to trade valuable goods for trinkets. They could be enslaved as useful labour as in *Captain Singleton*. And all this because of the power of the gun, coupled of course with the courage of the European. It is worth noting that both Crusoe and Singleton take very good care to keep their powder safe and dry. For it is only the gun that enables them to survive, whether it is used to shoot goats to fill their stomachs or to keep at bay the savages who tend to be shot down in scores if they get a little out of hand.

Defoe's attitude to the savage reflects the ambivalence of many of his views. On the great chain of being, that hierarchy that stretched from the angels through man to the beasts, the savage clearly had more of the beast and less of the angel than the white man. Defoe regularly uses the adjective 'brutal' to describe the negro, though he never went so far as some who doubted whether the negro was a man at all.[101] There was a hierarchy even amongst the barbarous peoples of the earth, in which the negro was considered by Defoe and his contemporaries to be lower than most other savages. The latter were far more likely to acquire a certain pagan nobility, as for instance in the character of Friday. God had given such savages 'the same powers, the same reason, the same affections, the same sentiments of kindness and obligation, the same passions and resentments of wrongs, the same sense of gratitude, sincerity, fidelity, and all the capacities of doing good and receiving good, that He has given to us'.[102] Why then had it pleased God to keep them as savages, ignorant of His name and His works? There could only be one answer. 'As God was necessarily, and by the nature of His being, infinitely holy and just, so it could not be, but that if these creatures were all sentenc'd to absence from Himself, it was on account of sinning against that light which, as the scripture says, was a law to themselves'.[103] But such sins lay in the past and one could excuse much of their current behaviour, since they were ignorant of the proper way to behave. Even the cannibals are regarded with consideration since they do not know that eating people is wrong, though it is significant that Crusoe's attitude hardens when he discovers that their next victim is a white man.[104] For even the most worthless European must be protected against the hostility of the most admirable savage. Then it is time to close ranks and praise that providence which 'directed our shot so sure that we kill'd fourteen of them'.[105]

In the later eighteenth century the negro was to acquire a nobility, far transcending that of Friday, in the works of the anti-slavery writers. But in the days of Defoe such an attitude was virtually unknown. It comes as something of a surprise to read in Charles Gildon's attack on *Robinson Crusoe* a criticism of Crusoe's activities as a slaver. Gildon even suggests that this was Crusoe's real sin and the one for which he should have been punished.[106] Very few men in the 1720s would have dreamed of taking such an enlightened position. Attitudes towards slavery had hardened in Defoe's lifetime. In 1673 Richard Baxter, in his *Christian Directory*, had no doubt of the essential evil of the enslavement of Africans:

> To go as pirats and catch up poor negro's or people of another land, that never forfeited life or liberty, and to make them slaves, and sell them, is one of the worst kinds of thievery in the world; and such persons are to be taken for the common enemies of mankind; and they that buy them and use them as beasts, for their meer commodity, and betray or destroy or neglect their souls, are fitter to be called incarnate devils than Christians, though they be no Christians who they so abuse.[107]

But, by 1697, Pollexfen could note that when divines were asked whether it was lawful to buy and sell mankind they replied that it was quite all right as long as the slaves were well-treated.[108] By now the words negro and slave were virtually interchangeable. The negro, as we have seen, was regularly described as 'brutal', meaning close to the brutes rather than violent, though even the negro stood high above the Hottentot, 'the worst and most savage of all savages . . . whose understanding is a thousand times below the meanest class of all the rest of God's rational creatures'.[109] The fact of the negro's slavery had served to degrade him in the eyes of the white man so that he became little more than an object of trade, like gold and ivory, 'the product of the country'.[110] Even those other negroes who drove the slaves down to the coasts from the deserts and forests of the interior were little better, despised for their failure to appreciate the 'real' value of the goods they traded in.[111] Defoe often quoted an evocative line from his early poem, *Reformation of Manners*,[112] attacking those who 'barter baubles for the souls of men'. Originally this

was clearly meant as a condemnation of slavery, but when Defoe
quotes it out of context in other works it is equally clearly meant
to be a condemnation of the lack of business acumen of the African
slave trader. Of course, intrinsic value is a tricky concept. In the
Atlas Maritimus Defoe bemoans African stupidity:[113]

> Unhappy nation! who, ignorant of the intrinsick value or virtue
> of things, cast away the richest production of nature as of small
> value to them, and put the same rate upon bits of glass, pieces of
> iron, an old knife, or a pair of scissors, as we do upon jewels,
> ivory and gold.

But listen to Robinson Crusoe:[114]

> I had, as I hinted before, a parcel of money, as well gold as silver,
> about thirty six pounds sterling. Alas! there the nasty sorry useless
> stuff lay: I had no manner of business for it; and I often thought
> with my self that I would have given a handful of it for a gross of
> tobacco-pipes, or for a hand-mill to grind my corn; nay, I would
> have given it all for sixpennyworth of turnip and carrot seed out
> of England, or for a handful of pease and beans, and a bottle of
> ink.

Fine thoughts, but Robinson Crusoe found plenty of business for his
money once he got off the island. Indeed, although Defoe obviously
enjoyed putting over the paradox of money being useless on a desert
island, he never lets his readers forget that Robinson Crusoe kept the
nasty, sorry, useless stuff safe. Africans were not even interested in it.
It was the fact that they seemed content with their miserable money-
less lives that so infuriated Defoe.

On rare occasions Defoe was prepared to show the compassion
towards Africans that he was accustomed to show towards the poor
and miserable of his own country. The Africans were 'a vile accursed
race',[115] but what was the nature of the crime that had led to the
curse of God and had condemned them for ever to such a miserable
existence? The text quoted by divines to justify the enslavement of
Africans was notably ambiguous, even to someone who accepted the
Bible as literally as Defoe.[116] It was clearly extremely rude of Ham
to mock his drunken father, Noah. But it seemed a little hard that
the punishment of servitude should be imposed on Ham's son,
Canaan. Still worse that the inhabitants of the whole continent of
Africa, supposedly descended from Canaan, should be condemned

to perpetual misery and servitude to the seed of Shem and Japheth. But God knew best, and the economist in Defoe could only reflect that the curse was handy, in view of the labour shortage in the American colonies.

This, of course, was the point. In Defoe's view of the world slavery was essential. Economic progress in England depended, as we shall see, on the development of the American colonies.[117] And the colonies could not be developed without a supply of cheap, well-disciplined labour. European labour was cheap, but not particularly well-disciplined, and in any case few Europeans would have subjected themselves voluntarily to work in a sugar plantation. As Defoe points out:[118]

> The work of the islands, which is the planting of canes, and making sugar, whether in the field or in the sugar-works, is of that nature, the labour so severe, the climate so hot, the food so course, that no Europeans were ever yet found that could go thro' it – At least to the profit of the planter – they must have people us'd to the extremities of the weather, entirely subjected to the government and correction of the cruellest masters; that they may be whip'd forward like horses, that can live on what is next to the offall of food, like beasts, and never knew better; that have the strength of the ox, and knew no more of liberty; and that suffer every thing the horse suffers, but being flead when they are dead, which would be done too, if they could get 6d for the hide.

Who else could meet these requirements but an African slave? White convicts and prisoners of war might be sent to the islands, but most of these served only short terms and worked as domestic servants or craftsmen, not as labourers in the plantations. Only a black man enslaved for life could fulfil the needs of a sugar planter. And, since the output of sugar was growing and slaves did not live very long under West Indian conditions, a continuous stream of new slaves had to come out of Africa in order to sweeten life in Europe.

Once the idea of mass black slavery had been absorbed by Europeans, the slave could be seen as a solution to labour problems far less severe than those of the sugar plantations. By the end of the seventeenth century slaves were rapidly replacing white indentured labour in the tobacco plantations of Maryland and Virginia, while slaves as domestic servants could be found all over America and Europe. Indeed the slave could be seen as the answer to any labour shortage and this attitude is reflected in the works of Defoe. Whether the problem was to find men to improve the English roads or to increase the output of timber from the forests of New England the answer was always likely to be the same – send a ship to Africa and buy a few more slaves.[119]

Within this pattern of acceptance of the necessity of slavery, Defoe, as one might expect, occasionally gives rein to his humanitarian instincts. The passage from his poem, *Reformation of Manners*, referred to above, is in fact one of the earliest statements of antislavery sentiments in the English literature of the time.[120] But it is an isolated outburst. Elsewhere Defoe never attacks the institution, but confines his criticism to attacks on the harsh treatment of slaves. The motive for this, it is sad to say, was chiefly economic. This attitude is made clear in a *Review* of 1712.[121]

> He that keeps them [slaves] in subjection, whips and corrects them in order to make them grind and labour, does right, for out of their labour he gains his wealth: But he that in his passion and cruelty, maims, lames, and kills them, is a fool, for they are his estate, his stock, his wealth, and his prosperity.

In *Colonel Jack* there is a long and often mawkish passage advocating the better treatment of slaves, but the motivation is the same. More work will be done by 'the negroes, who shall be engaged by mercy and lenity, than by those, who are driven, and dragg'd by the whips, and the chains of a merciless tormentor'.[122]

That same America which guaranteed the negro slave a life of hell, if he should survive the middle passage,[123] could be a veritable heaven for the white man.[124] Here the dispossessed, the criminal or the unfortunate could start again, reborn in a comfortable anonymity.[125] Here the reprieved Moll Flanders was able to do so well on the capital accumulated in her career of crime that she was able to keep her idle highwayman husband in the state which he, as an impoverished Irish gentleman, deserved to be kept, hunting and shooting in the Carolina backwoods with silver chasing on his gun. Here Colonel Jack, child of the gutter and pickpocket, is able by hard work and good sense to become the gentleman he should have been from birth. This theme of redemption and a new life in the plantations is one that recurs again and again in Defoe. A few years as a transported convict or an indentured servant and then, having worked out his time, the formerly desperate man has the chance to become a planter himself. Nor was the convict forced to work too hard: 'Their labour is not harder, or their usage worse, than many hired servants in England on yearly wages; and 'tis evident, even before their eyes, the negro servants, even in the same plantations, and under the same masters, are in worse circumstances (infinitely worse) than they.'[126] Many a successful planter had arisen, like Moll Flanders, from the condemned hole in Newgate or had been branded on the hand. But America, home of the new-born, was not a place where people asked questions about the past.

Even in America itself there was a chance to escape. For beyond the settled tidewater lay the woods and the possibility of rebirth again. Already the concept of the frontier as both a safety valve and a convenient dustbin beyond the bounds of order existed. As early as the 1630s deviant groups had been expelled from Massachusetts to form new heterodox communities to the west.[127] By the time of Defoe such individualist communities, hostile to tidewater conformity, stretched all the way to the backwoods of the Carolinas. It was here that Defoe's once desperate men and women were likely to find some sort of security to live out their days, if not the wealth which he so confidently predicted for them.

What was good for the individual was good for England. The more people who lived in the mainland colonies,[128] the bigger the market for English goods and the stronger the defence against the French and their Indian allies who, deployed in a great arc from the Mississippi to the St Lawrence, threatened the security of the English possessions.[129] There could never be too many and they could never be too strong. Defoe countered his critics who feared that American strength might lead to American independence in a passage which is often gleefully quoted by transatlantic historians:[130]

I affirm and desire no better quarter than to be oblig'd to prove,
1. That in the nature and quality of trade, it is morally impossible, that any of our colonies on the continent of America, but especially New-England, should ever desire to be independent of England.

The Americans depended too heavily on the English market and relied too much on the continuation of English privileges ever to want to break away.[131] Meanwhile they continued to expand their numbers, both by immigration and natural increase, driving the Indians farther and farther away from the coast.

We have seen Defoe's heroes exploiting or planning to exploit
Africa, America and the South Seas, dragooning whole continents
into satisfying and providing for European greed and ambition. But
in the fourth quarter of the world, the mainland of Asia, there was
no question as yet of European dictatorship. Here lay five great
empires whose wealth and vast resources in manpower had been
able to check the remorseless expansion of Europe. Here the European was a suppliant, clinging to a few trading posts, for the most
part remote from the centres of power, and ready to indulge in a
very un-European humility to attain the trading privileges which
he needed to thrive at all.

But how much longer could these empires afford to remain aloof?
The empire of the Grand Mogul was already in disarray and only
the ferocity and the martial skills of the Maratha warriors kept India
from becoming the anarchic vacuum which Europeans were to fill a
generation after Defoe's death. For the moment Defoe could deplore
the drain of silver which went to pay for the flood of silk and cotton
textiles produced by poor but skilful Indian weavers.[132] It would be a
century before the steam mills of Lancashire would force the Indian
weaver to sell his loom as firewood to stave off starvation, but European military technology was to find a way of exploiting India far
sooner than that. Once Europeans committed to a war in India the
armaments with which they slaughtered each other at home India
would be doomed.[133]

Nearer home the Ottoman Empire, while not yet the 'sick man of
Europe', already bore the marks of incipient disease. Her last great
effort to impose her will on Europe had failed outside the gates of
Vienna in 1683. As Kara Mustafa's defeated army fled back across
the Great Hungarian Plain, the last great tide of Islamic expansion
had been turned. In the works of Defoe, Turkish tyranny is often
criticized as the cause of the impoverishment of the eastern and
southern Mediterranean, but no longer feared as a challenge to the
expansion of triumphant Christendom.

In the very far east Japan, now united under the rule of the
Tokugawa Shoguns, had dallied in the early seventeenth century
with the idea of conquering a far eastern empire,[134] an idea which
was to be put into practice three centuries later. But, by Defoe's
time, Japan had withdrawn from the world. The Jesuit and Fran-
ciscan priests who had achieved so much in the sixteenth and early
seventeenth centuries had been paid the compliment of either

martyrdom or expulsion. Their extremely successful mission of conversion had appeared to threaten the very security of the island
empire, as more and more Japanese had sworn to accept a second
allegiance to the far-off Pope of Rome. Who knew what such an
allegiance meant? Who could be sure that the Christians were not a
fifth column for the better known and much feared King of Spain?
The Japanese decided to cut themselves off from the seditious ideas
of the outside world. One ship a year from Holland bore all that
Japan would know in future of the febrile world of Europe.

There remained two empires, the greatest of them all. In the east
was China, much admired in the Europe of Defoe, no threat but an
intellectual challenge. Defoe himself did not like the idea of a second
centre of civilization, though he was forced to accept the fact that
many of the things which Europe was proudest of inventing had
been invented in China first. Gunpowder, the compass and the
printing press, the fundamentals of European culture and success,
had all been anticipated by the Chinese.[135] It was really rather
humiliating. Nor could Defoe ignore the amazing skills of the Chinese workman, as more and more porcelain and Chinese silks were
imported into Europe. There was no doubt that the Chinese were
'not only the most ingenious, but without exception the most industrious people in the world'.[136] But Defoe accepted such facts with an
ill grace. Hidden behind the fictional character of Robinson Crusoe
he was able to give way to his spite:[137]

> The greatness of their wealth, their trade, the power of their
> government, and strength of their armies, is surprising to us,
> because, as I have said, considering them as a barbarous nation
> of pagans, little better than savages, we did not expect such things
> among them; and this indeed is the advantage with which all
> their greatness and power is represented to us; otherwise it is in
> it self nothing at all.

Crusoe ridicules their buildings, their trade, their farming, their
government, even their porcelain and their much vaunted learning.
On his way out of China he has one last fling, when he passes what
his guide had extolled as the wonder of the world, but what he
dismisses as 'this mighty nothing call'd a wall'.[138]

China's sin in Defoe's view was that she refused to accept that
Europeans had anything to teach her. Quite different was the last
great empire of the east, the Russia of Peter the Great. Here was

that marvel, a humble prince, a 'prince arriv'd to the perfection of knowledge, to know that he knew nothing', and prepared to go to Europe in person to find out the secrets of that knowledge which seemed to make the nations of the west so powerful.[139] He then returned to be 'the general teacher of his own people'. His methods might be cruel, but his achievements were remarkable. During his reign Russia took for the first time a vital part in that game of power played out in the chancellories and on the battlefields of Europe. Russia was still backward and barbarous in western eyes; Peter the Great could still be styled a Siberian bear,[140] but the first moves had been made in that process of westernization which was later to astonish the world. Peter Alexowitz, Czar of Muscovy, was the first ruler of an oriental state to see the light and understand the humiliating truth of the future. The methods of Europe must be adopted, for Europe was about to inherit the world.

[4]

THE INHERITORS

WHEN we move out of that realm of mingled fantasy, fiction and fact which made up three-quarters of Defoe's world and turn our attention to the fourth quarter we enter a continent where hard political and geographical fact takes over from make-believe. Defoe's characters roam Europe just as they roam the rest of the world. But their adventures are firmly rooted in the landscape and events of a factual world which Defoe and his readers knew only too well.

For most of Defoe's lifetime the central feature in the European landscape was the ascendancy of France. Louis xiv's seizure of the reins of power coincided with the birth of Defoe. Within ten years he had created in France the most successful example of absolute power that Europe had seen since the time of the Roman Empire and there seemed little to stop him acquiring a European empire of the same size and magnificence. So mighty and so admirable did French power and culture appear that there were few willing to oppose its inexorable expansion and many who welcomed the day when they too could enjoy the benefits of being the subjects of so magnificent a prince. Defoe, himself, paid tribute to the greatness of the Roi Soleil in a panegyric written in 1712 when it was rumoured that Louis xiv had died:

His genius has been fitted for the part he was to act, as *Flagellum Dei*, the Scourge of God upon the world, even above most of the men that ever wore a crown; a head capable of the deepest councils; a temper fiery, haughty, magnificent, and to his own subjects dreadful; qualified to reduce the nobility to an abject submission, and the commons to the most profound slavery . . . every enterprise has been digested in his own head, and fewer mistakes committed by him, speaking as to his own grandeur, than the wisest prince in the world ever committed.[1]

Defoe's admiration is genuine. He never underestimated the power of France nor the achievements of her great king. For quarter of a century his life and that of his countrymen was dominated by the long and ultimately successful struggle of the two maritime powers, England and Holland, and their continental allies to contain the French colossus. But the struggle was seen to be more than just a reaction in self-defence against the danger of the ascendancy of a single power. From the insular point of view of the Englishman, who was inclined to forget or despise his allies, this was in essence a duel between England and France, the two richest countries in Europe and the homes of two mutually antagonistic views of society and of the world. The victory of what the islanders were pleased to call English liberty over French slavery was a victory which was to have more than a local significance in the history of the world.

The fact that London and Paris should be the focal points of European politics and that the centre of gravity of European power should now lie somewhere in the English Channel was an astonishing change to someone as well versed in history as Defoe. In the course of the seventeenth century Europe had been stood on its head. For more than a thousand years the political, commercial and cultural centre of gravity had been in the Mediterranean. Romans and Carthaginians may have had their day, but they had been replaced by peoples equally powerful and wealthy. In 1600 European civilization was still dominated by the south. If you were looking for culture and wealth you looked to Italy, the Italy of the renaissance, of merchant princes, great industries and great achievements. If you were looking for power you looked to Spain, ruler of the first empire on which the sun never set, stretching from the Philippines to South America, from whence came the constant stream of bullion which paid, albeit with some delay, the finest infantry in the world. These men, pride of Spain and envy of her enemies, were drawn from a bewildering number of European regions, nearly all of them directly under Spanish rule. It was they who held the empire together, marching from province to province to quell revolts or resist the incursions of the envious rivals of Spain. It was they who upheld the ambition of the kings of Spain to be the champions of Catholic christendom, whether they were fighting infidels in Tunis or heretics in Flanders. But, in the end, it was to be the very size of her empire and the cost of maintaining it that led to Spain's downfall. The jealousy of other nations and the particularist ambitions of her own provinces involved Spain in almost continuous warfare for a whole century from 1560 to 1660. Finally she was exhausted, drained of money and men, and no longer predominant in Europe. In 1640, Portugal, herself the ruler of a rapidly dwindling empire, successfully threw off Spanish rule after sixty years. In 1643, the famous Spanish infantry was defeated by the French at the battle of Rocroi; only one battle but a sign of the times. In 1648, the Dutch republic, after an epic eighty-year struggle, was at last recognized to be free of Spanish rule. In 1659, after a quarter of a century of intermittent warfare, Spain made peace with France and tacitly accepted that the Bourbons had replaced the Hapsburgs as the arbiters of Europe. The long reign of the Mediterranean was drawing to a close.

Political decline was coupled with economic weakness. Italy, in particular, had once been the dominant commercial and industrial centre of the European economy, drawing raw materials from the north and shipping out manufactured goods and the luxuries of the orient in exchange. Now the tables had been turned. The English and Dutch, challenged increasingly by the French, drew raw materials from the Mediterranean, shipping cloth and hardware back into the region. Venice, once the middleman between Asia and Europe, now received nearly all her pepper and spices from the holds of the dominant northern merchantmen. Individual Italians were still rich; investment in banking and the silk industry still paid handsome dividends, but the region as a whole was characterized by poverty and a colonial dependence on the rising economic powers of northern Europe.

When Defoe looks at southern Europe it is with a look of contempt, somewhat mitigated by a realization of the past glories of the region. Southerners were scorned on many counts. As Catholics they were, of course, superstitious bigots. This in itself was not too serious a matter, for Defoe, as we have already seen, was relatively tolerant towards Catholics in his works. Nevertheless, it was only wise to check carefully into the religious beliefs of an English suitor who had spent too much time in Italy, 'the very bowels of superstition and the very kingdom of popery'.[2] He might well have caught the infection. But Defoe, unlike some modern historians, never made popery as such a

cause of poverty. After all the south had always been Papist and
had once been rich.

No, it was idleness, not popery, that made the south poor. Italian
idleness was a product of former Italian wealth which had led to the
whole region being given up to an orgy of luxury and debauchery.
Italy was the very symbol of vice. When the Cavalier visits the
country he reflects the views of Defoe and of many of his contemporaries:

> As for what is modern, I saw nothing but lewdness, private
> murthers, stabbing men at the corner of a street, or in the dark,
> hiring of bravoes, and the like; all the diversions here ended in
> whoring, gaming and sodomy . . .
>
> I observed the people degenerated from the ancient glorious
> inhabitants, who were generous, brave, and the most valiant of
> all nations, to a vicious baseness of soul, barbarous, treacherous,
> jealous and revengeful, lewd and cowardly, intolerably proud and
> haughty, bigotted to blind, incoherent devotion, and the grossest
> of idolatry.[3]

The only one of Defoe's characters who has a good word for Italy is
significantly Roxana, great lover of luxury as long as someone else
is paying for it. When she falls 'in love with Italy', Defoe is cursing
the country with her praise.[4] Italy was a place to which an Englishman might go on the Grand Tour to marvel at the wonders of her
past; he might well buy a few paintings and some fine furniture but
he would be unlikely to have much good to say about her present
state, 'so much has sloth, bigottry, and debauchery effeminated the
gallantest and most magnaminous nation in the world'.[5] The glee
with which Englishmen described the moral downfall of Italy was
in part an expression of the cultural inferiority complex that northerners continued to suffer in respect to the cradle of their civilization.
Dudley North had been very pleased to discover that Italians were
adopting English fashions in the late seventeenth century: 'This is
only to show the false relations of many who travel these parts; and
that we have no reason to undervalue ourselves at home as much as
many do.'[6] The Italians were able to take advantage of the Englishman's cultural backwardness. As milord returned from his Grand
Tour he might well be accompanied by a host of Italian musicians
and painters, off to exploit the *nouveaux riches* of northern Europe.
For if Londoners despised the modern Italian, they loved the opera.[7]

Where the Italians were idle because they were too busy debauching themselves, the Spanish were idle because they were too proud to work. The paradox of a country which owned the silver mines of South America and yet was poor had fascinated generations of Europeans. As fast as the silver was brought into Spain it flowed out to pay for the manufactured goods of northern Europe which the proud Spaniards disdained to make. Or so the story went. Even the beggars were gentlemen who refused to soil their hands. The Spaniards had none of the instincts that made other nations rich. When they had money they spent it in a flurry of generosity. When it had gone they starved:

> Lavish of Money, to be counted Brave,
> And Proudly starve, because they scorn to save.
> Never was Nation in the World before
> So very Rich, and yet so very Poor.[8]

The narrator in *A New Voyage round the World* meets a Spaniard who perhaps pinpoints the difference between north and south in the view of Defoe: 'We have so much pride that we have no avarice, and we do not covet enough to make us work.'[9] This apparently attractive philosophy was unlikely to appeal to Defoe.

Spain was England's best market in Europe, so presumably some Spaniards had some money. The country was in fact the contemporary economist's ideal, exporting foodstuffs, raw materials, semi-manufactured goods, such as pig iron, and masses and masses of lovely pieces of eight in return for the homely manufactured goods of England, woollen cloth and knitted stockings. Spain too, although she had lost her political predominance in Europe, had retained nearly all of her vast overseas empire. This alone made her worth wooing. Much of European politics in Defoe's time was to revolve round the future of this empire, who should rule it and who should have the inestimable benefit of supplying it with slaves and European goods.

The decline of Portugal, Spain's Iberian neighbour, was in many ways even more catastrophic. It was the Portuguese who had pioneered that expansion of trade and empire which was Europe's pride. For a hundred years they had been able to dominate the Indian Ocean, unchallenged in eastern waters by any other European power. But now what had happened to their skill and enterprise? 'From being the richest and most famous country for trade, . . .

they have fallen to be the poorest in trade, the most degenerate in their navigating skill.'[10] Captain Singleton learned two things from the Portuguese, 'to be an errant thief and a bad sailor; and I think I may say they are the best masters for teaching both these of any nation in the world'.[11] Could these be the heirs of Vasco da Gama? They too luxuriated in the characteristic idleness of southern climes, and like Spain produced nothing by their own labour and industry, buying everything from other countries.[12] As such, Portugal, like Spain, was a fine market for northerners, a market that was greedily exploited by England in successive commercial treaties from the time of Cromwell. Portugal, too, paid for the goods in the same way, exporting wines, raw materials, Brazilian sugar and, from the end of the seventeenth century, more and more Brazilian gold from the mines and alluvial workings of Minas Gerais. Here, in the 1690s, was seen the first great gold rush of modern times as adventurers from all over South America and from Europe swarmed into the region.[13] Brazil, with its sugar and its gold, kept Portugal going just as Spain's American empire made her still a power to reckon with in European politics.

As the lights of the south began to dim, new cold aggressive lights began to shine from the north. Three Protestant powers burst on to the scene, ready to challenge and overtake the former southern predominance in power, wealth and culture. One of them, Sweden, was to have only a brief period of glory, fated to forego her dreams of Baltic hegemony in the face of the jealousy of her neighbours and the sudden eruption of Russian might. Holland, too, whose rise in the seventeenth century was the period's economic miracle, was to give up her pretensions to military glory in 1713, after successfully holding off for a century and a half the onslaughts of Spain, England and France. Her economy, too, was challenged but not overtaken by her great rivals. Only England was to survive and triumph in the eighteenth century, reviving the glorious days of the middle ages when kings of England had been arbiters and champions of Europe. But England then had been a poor country, dependent like Spain on the courage and technical competence of her ill-paid infantry for her European empire. England in the early eighteenth century was the wealthiest country in Europe, ruler of an empire that rivalled that of Spain, rich enough to hire troops to fight for her from her poorer neighbours and, astonishingly enough, the master of the Mediterranean. Here, where Italian, Turk and Spaniard had challenged each other for hegemony in the sixteenth century, England, with one foot in Gibraltar and the other in Minorca, ruled the waves. No surer sign of the decline of the Mediterranean could be found than the sight of the ships of the Royal Navy patrolling the seas between Italy and Spain.[14]

How had England achieved this remarkable rise to power and wealth? The question fascinated Defoe and the answers appear over and over again in his works. Power and wealth were mutually reinforcing by Defoe's day as they have been ever since. The days of Edward III when a poor country could win an empire had gone. Now wealth was the basis of power, money was the sinews of war and "'tis not the longest sword, but the longest purse that conquers'.[15] Power in turn, particularly naval power, could create wealth by seizing and holding an empire in which Englishmen could trade and get rich, without having to suffer the intolerable hardship of having to compete on equal terms with clever, skinflint Dutchmen. If wealth led to power then the real question to be answered was how had England got rich.

To Defoe the answer lay in the fact that England had really always been potentially rich. The only problem was that past generations had been too stupid to exploit the wealth which lay ready to hand. For God, when he scattered the world with the good things, had been particularly kind to England. In 1711 Defoe devoted two numbers of the *Review* to an impassioned attack on the *Spectator* which had claimed that the native produce of England was of no worth at all and that England was 'a barren uncomfortable spot of earth' before trade had introduced the species and plants which now throve in the island.[16] Defoe would have none of this and accused the *Spectator* of 'disowning the creation-blessings Heaven has bestowed' on England.[17] Chief amongst the blessings of creation was the marvellous English wool, which was in turn the result of a providential attraction that sheep found for the grass that grew on English soil. 'Foreign sheep brought hither improve the fleece, and our sheep carry'd abroad lose their wool.'[18] Defoe had no wish to exaggerate England's natural wealth. He was none of those who said that 'the Creator was in the wrong to place paradise in Asia, or on the banks of Euphrates; that it had been better on the banks of Thames'.[19] Other countries had many good things but no country had the most important. A monopoly of the best wool in the world was God's gift to England.

How astonishing then that the medieval Englishman could be so foolish as to ship the stuff abroad instead of making it into cloth. The people of Flanders grew rich and kept their women and children busy spinning and weaving English wool, while the English sat around in a state of utter idleness and distress:

> Like people buried alive in sloth and idleness they sat still, ploughed and sowed as much corn as served just to feed them, sheer'd their sheep every year, and, as it may be said, threw away their wool; went to the wars, were knocked on the head for the honour of Old England, and the glory of their great kings; and this was the round of life, even from the nobleman to the meanest vassal, peasant or labourer in the nation.
>
> As to the poor women and children, they sat at home, fared hard, lived poor and idle: the women drudg'd at the husbandry, and the children sat still, blow'd their fingers, pick'd straws; and both might be said not to live, but to starve out a wretched time, then die, and go, *where* – who knows![20]

Such expressions of disgust and amazement at England's medieval folly abound in the works of Defoe.[21] But one day a sensible king came to the throne of England. Usually it is Henry VII, but sometimes Edward IV is given some of the credit.[22] Shocked at the poverty of his realm, the king rapidly put his finger on the cause. Foreign workmen were brought over to teach the English how to make cloth. The export of wool was forbidden. Almost overnight England emerged from her lethargy. Those women and children who once sat idly at their cottage doors were now busy indoors spinning away:

> The poor began to work, not for cottages and liveries, but for money, and to live, as we say, at their own hands: the women and children learnt to spin and get money for it, a thing entirely new to them, and what they had never seen before. The men left the hedge and the ditch, and were set at work by the manufacturers to be wool-combers, weavers, fullers, clothworkers, carriers, and innumerable happy labours they perform'd, which they knew nothing of before.[23]

More and more cloth was made, suitable for the peoples of the whole world, 'adapted to all countries, climates, persons and qualities; not too thin for the frozen Laplanders, Swedes, and Russians, or too thick for the scorch'd Americans and inhabitants of Peru and Brazil;

not too light for the Germans, or too heavy for the Italians . . . not too gay for the men, not too grave for the ladies'.[24]

A new phase of expansion was to come in the reign of that great Protestant heroine, Queen Elizabeth.[25] She encouraged the immigration of Dutch, Flemish and French Protestants who taught the English to make the new lighter cloths called the New Draperies.[26] Even more people ceased to be idle, crowds of poor people flocked to the new centres of manufacture 'to reap the benefit of constant employ'[27] and thus was solved the problem of poverty in Elizabethan England.[28] So high a level of production needed new outlets. Previously English cloth had travelled no further than the short sea journey to the Low Countries from whence foreigners redistributed it by land to other parts of Europe. Not only did this limit the market; it also limited the profits to be made by the English merchant and shipowner. England's glorious queen soon solved this problem. 'She open'd the sluices of trade to them, and trade open'd the sluices of money.'[29] Following her lead Englishmen took the distribution of cloth into their own hands, seeking out new markets and new trade routes in Russia, the Baltic and the Mediterranean,[30] thus building up that naval power which was to make possible the development of English plantations overseas in the next century.[31] England may have been a century later in the colonial business than the Spaniards and Portuguese but she very quickly caught up, just in time indeed to prevent the French from acquiring much territory when they in turn sought to expand their empire some fifty years later.[32] Ships full of English cloth now sailed all over the world and came home to England laden with luxuries and silver. England became rich and the world was clothed in English cloth. And all this because of the wool on the back of the humble English sheep, 'an exclusive grant from heaven to Great Britain'.[33]

This expansion of wealth which, according to Defoe, was to continue on a somewhat less heroic scale in the seventeenth century,[34] could not be equated with national power until the political and religious structure of the country had been reformed. The wealth of individuals must be harnessed to a political system whose integrity they themselves believed in and whose policies they were prepared to support with their money. Only then could England become great and the arbiter of Europe.

Defoe, as might be expected, had a Whig view of English history. He believed in the rule of law, in religious toleration and in a constitution subtly balanced between the executive power of the king and the legislative power of the men of property represented in parliament. And he believed that all these principles had been realized in the constitutional settlement which followed the Revolution of 1688. Everything in English history which preceded this great triumph of English common sense was judged in terms of whether it had advanced or retarded the appearance of these 'Revolution principles'. There was much that had had to be done. The anarchic power of nobles and barons had to be crushed. The supremacy of the Pope had to be denied and religion reformed in England. But such reformation must not lead to a new supremacy and a new intolerant orthodoxy which denied freedom of worship to those whose conscience led them to dissent. The autocratic power of the king must be broken and made subject to a parliament which represented the collective views of property.[35] But there must still be a king and a powerful executive to control the tendency towards anarchy and faction of those same property-owners[36] and to keep the mob, that other 'popular' expression of opinion, firmly in its place.[37] Nor was the supremacy of parliament itself an absolute guarantee against tyranny. There was always the danger of a party abrogating unto itself political power, either to feather the nests of its own supporters or, far worse, to undo all that had been done and bring back papism and the arbitrary rule of an absolute monarch. Defoe, like his master Harley and his hero William III, was a man of the middle who hated to see any party dominate English politics.

Like so much in Defoe's views of English history the first move towards a satisfactory solution had been made by the Tudors. Henry VII had bridled the independence of the nobility but in so doing had greatly increased his own power and that of the court.[38] Henry VIII, 'an arbitrary and tyrannical prince', was to go further.

> His haughty spirit perfectly aw'd his nobility, his luxuriant court effeminated them . . . the constant magnificence of a splendid court, brought his nobility and gentry to such an expensive way of living, that soon reduc'd their estates. As poverty came upon them, the dependance upon the king for pensions, places, and preferment, was entirely secur'd.[39]

It was, of course, also in the reign of Henry VIII that 'the reform'd religion . . . advanc't exceedingly, till . . . it crept into, first his cabinet, and then his bed'.[40] 'Nor is it any reproach at all to the Protestant Religion; that, as the Papists say, its first step is deduc'd from King Henry's cod-piece, meaning that the lust of that pretence set the wheels at work.'[41] This was simply a remarkable manifestation of providence that 'the very worst and wickedest of men's designs shall concur to bring to pass the best and greatest of [God's] glorious works'.[42]

The trouble was that when Henry pulled down the supremacy of the Pope he immediately set up his own. The Church remained popish and this of course led to division.[43] Such divisions were to grow wider with the arrival of the Stuarts in the seventeenth century, especially when religious dissent was coupled with hostility to the manifestations of arbitrary government. It was James 1 who brought in the new doctrine 'that kings were immediately clothed with their power from above . . . and consequently must be obeyed as God's ordinance, and without any controul'.[44] But it was Charles 1 who brought matters to a head. Fear of papacy and hatred of arbitrary government led to civil war and the victory of Parliament.[45] But now things had swung too far the other way. Parliament itself had been conquered by a party who were to murder the king and replace him by a government more arbitrary and unrepresentative than anything that had been achieved by the Stuarts. The Cavalier, a moderate royalist, expresses his motivation for his choice of sides in words of which Defoe, despite his father's puritan background, clearly approved:

> Our desires were to suppress the exorbitant power of a party, to establish our king in his just and legal rights; but not with a design to destroy the constitution of government, and the being of parliament.[46]

It was, then, with relief that England welcomed back her king in 1660 after the black days of the 1650s 'when law and justice was under the feet of power'.[47] But Charles 11 was to be a sad disappointment, tainted with that plague of kings, the lust of arbitrary rule. And indeed the English, who greatly loved their merry monarch, were only saved by his idleness. Providence allowed one vice to conquer another. Charles was 'given up entirely to his ease, and drowned in all the pleasures of a life devoted to sloth and luxury. His long lascivious reign was spent wholly in drunkenness, lewdness, and all manner of debaucheries.'[48]

It remained only for James II to do what his debauched brother was too idle to do. Defoe, who was prepared to pity James as a man and admire him as an efficient administrator, was charitable enough to excuse James's failings by blaming them on the party which urged him on. It was the High Tories who led him 'to the brink of the pit' and then when they realized the strength of the opposition to their policies, 'were the first that cry'd fire, and rais'd the whole country upon him'.[49] The desertion of James by his erstwhile supporters made William III's descent on England very much easier, but it was hardly to be admired.

William's success had two admirable consequences for men of Defoe's way of thinking. The settlement of the constitution on 'Revolution principles' removed the immediate threat of an absolutist form of government and thus brought an end to the struggle for power between king and parliament which had dominated English history for so long. But equally important in Defoe's eyes was the revolution in foreign policy which followed the accession of William of Orange to the throne of England. No longer would England engage in shameful, greedy wars designed to destroy her natural Protestant allies, the Dutch. Now, with a Dutchman as king, the wealth and power of England could be harnessed to the honourable task of halting the arrogant expansion of the France of Louis XIV.

Defoe knew that this was no time for complacency. There were many men in England who opposed the French war, once they realized how expensive it was going to be. And there were many who refused to accept that the type of government that evolved after the Revolution of 1688 was perfect. The government on Revolution principles was constantly in danger and Defoe was to spend the next twenty-five years defending both government and war against the men of party on both sides. On one side stood the danger of domination by the Whigs, of the revival of the one-party government of the 1650s. On the other side stood a far greater danger. There were those High Tories who had deserted James in 1688 and who were now plotting to restore first him and, after his death in 1701, his son. In Defoe's eyes they were crypto-Catholics, Francophiles and absolutists to a man. Their triumph, which seemed so close in the last days of the reign of Queen Anne, would undo everything. Once let England be ruled by a Catholic prince and what would happen to the Protestant religion, the rule of law and the liberty of Englishmen? They would all disappear and England would become a feeble satellite of France, as she had so nearly been in the time of Charles II. England was saved from this fate. The failure of the Jacobite Rebellion of 1715 was to destroy not only the Jacobites but the whole Tory party. Defoe could hardly be sorry, though the one-party government which was to survive virtually unchallenged for the rest of his life did not come up to his ideal.

Although Defoe admired and praised the wealth and power of England and was a life-long supporter of the political settlement of the Revolution, he found the English themselves far less admirable and indeed hardly worthy of their good fortune. They had many faults. Prosperity led almost inexorably to vice in all sections of the population, to luxury in the rich and to drunkenness and insubordination in the poor. Liberty was almost invariably misunderstood: 'We are a nation of liberty, that is true! Liberty of speech, liberty of the press, and liberty to be as wicked as we think fit (a few restraints upon killing and robbing excepted).'[50] As for toleration in religion, many people took this as an invitation to be of no religion at all.[51] But perhaps the worst sin of the English was ingratitude and, in particular, ingratitude to those who had made them as rich and powerful as they were. How little credit was given to those immigrants who, from the days of Henry VII, had taught the English how to make use of the bounty left to them by God. How quickly had the English turned their backs on their deliverer, William III; how soon they forgot the dangers from which he had delivered them.[52]

What was good and what was bad about England could be interpreted in the light of the political structure and national psychology of the alternative society across the Channel. The character of the two peoples was quite different. France was the 'dancing nation, fickle and untrue'.[53] The French were 'more volatile, more passionate, and more sprightly' than other nations.[54] This gave them a genius for the unsuspected, the subtle and the superficial, for 'whipt cream, froath and surface'. They could sing and play better than the English; their workmanship was more nimble and often more artful; they were the master of the stratagem and the surprise in war.[55] The English were already the countrymen of John Bull.[56] They were solid and substantial, slow to anger but, when roused, the bravest men in the world. When it came to downright blows, to 'mere desperate fighting, stand clear there!'[57] Even in Defoe's day the English had a reputation of being at their best when their backs

The World of Defoe

were to the wall. In distress they did not give way to despair but showed a greater presence of mind than any people in the world, a trait abundantly illustrated in Defoe's novels. The Spaniard who admired Crusoe's inventiveness and energy when cast away on his island remarked that a Spaniard or a Portuguese in a similar situation would have despaired, lain down and died.[58] Paradoxically, the English also had a reputation for melancholia and suicide which was often attributed to the climate.[59] The English seemed to gain self-confidence the further they travelled from home, a fact, if it is one, which may explain their successful quest for empire.

Sturdy independence and disrespect for authority were the marks of the Englishman. The French, for all their originality and butterfly airs, were a nation of servants. They seemed 'to have no taste of liberty, but to have made bondage their choice; God and their great monarch seem to go halfs in their adoration'.[60] Too often the English had a low opinion of both God and the crown. The French were indeed more religious as a nation or, at least, their habit of accepting authority led them to obey their priests. Such piety, even in the service of superstition and bigotry, could have dangers for the godless English. In 1706, Louis xiv ordered a day of humiliation following the disastrous defeat at the battle of Ramillies. Defoe warned his readers not to mock the Frenchmen who flocked to church to pray forgiveness for their past sins and ask for better fortune in the future. For who can understand the ways of God?

> Blame not the French therefore for looking up to Heaven for help; rather Gentlemen, have a care they don't out-pray you . . . How strange a conjuncture is it . . . that almost ever since their day of general humiliation, God has sent contrary winds to retard and keep back the English navy from invading them.[61]

'If you do not out-pray the French, as well as out-fight them, you will never beat them.'[62]

Modern writers accept the effectiveness of the counter-reformation priesthood in France, but normally cite as an example of this the chasteness of the French compared with the English. Demographers have discovered that the illegitimacy rate in England was much higher than in France.[63] Could it be therefore that England and not France was the land of 'ungovern'd passion'?[64] The Swiss traveller de Muralt did not think so. In his opinion the English preferred wine and gaming to women, 'in which they are the more blameable,

because the women are much better than the wine in England'.[65]
So maybe the English were just careless.

Certainly they were reputed to be lazy, a luxury which perhaps
they could afford to indulge better than most continental peoples
since, when they did work, they worked harder, produced more,
earned more and spent their higher wages on cheaper goods.[66] 'As
they work hard, so they live well, eat and drink well, cloath warm
and lodge soft.'[67] Very few Frenchmen could afford to live in
this style. Maybe they danced and sang so much because few
other pleasures were available to them. For the French were very
poor. The badge of their poverty, their wooden shoes, was already
an English jest, even if the French said that they were 'as happy in
their wooden shoes, as our people are with their luxury and
drunkenness'.[68]

Why were the French who lived in such a fair and fertile land so
poor? Modern writers blame French poverty on the structure of
agriculture. The French were poor because four out of five of them
were peasants, working minute pieces of land with virtually no
capital, little imagination and little incentive to improve in a harsh,
grasping world where up to half of the little they produced was
seized to support the glamorous society of the rich and the luxury
of the court.[69]

Defoe says little about peasants in his works but he does single out
one characteristic of the French which has always been somewhat
of a problem. This was their passion for bread. 'The French usually
eat more than double, if not triple the bread in their ordinary way
of diet, that the English do eat.'[70] The English, on the other hand,
'eat much flesh and little bread', a fact which one traveller assured
his readers gave the Englishwoman her notoriously bad teeth.[71]

The problem about the French love of bread, both in Defoe's day
and in modern times, was that they were not particularly efficient
at producing the grain from which it was made. This was mainly,
once again, because of the small scale and technical backwardness
of their agriculture. But it was also, according to Defoe, because of
the French climate which although 'for vineyards, rich fruits, health
and pleasure, it excels most countries in the world, yet is not the
best for corn, being subject both to hasty storms of hail and rain in
summer, and strong draughts also, much more than we are'.[72]
Whatever the reason the yields of grain grown in France were much
lower than those of England.[73] This sad and fundamental fact of

French history meant that very little else was grown in France and that a bad harvest could lead to the most appalling disasters. Such subsistence crises, as French historians call them, appeared with monotonous regularity leaving a trail of famine, disease and death behind them.[74] England never suffered in this way. As Defoe put it, 'we know not in England what belongs to famine'.[75] One good reason was that agriculture was better organized this side of the Channel. But there was another. If England was short of grain to make bread for the poor there were no less than two great reserves which could be drawn on, the barley which was malted to make the vast quantities of beer which washed down the Englishman's food and the oats which fed his enormous population of horses. Referring to the terrible famine of the winter of 1708-9 which saw hundreds of thousands of Frenchmen die of starvation and the diseases which starvation brought in its wake, Defoe wrote:[76]

> The barley which in England is consum'd in strong liquors; the beans, peas, and oates, which our horses have eaten, how would it have made that whole nation swim in plenty? – And had they not been our enemies, it had been infinitely our profit to have spar'd it, and let our horses, and those worse beasts, our drunkards, feed on something else.

The poor French peasant could not afford horses on his farm and, for some obscure reason, if he drank at all he drank wine, not beer, and so he suffered and died.

The French need to concentrate on grain production to the exclusion of nearly everything else meant that there were very few sheep and thus not much wool in France.[77] And, of course, what wool there was could not stand comparison with English wool, sheared as it was off the backs of sheep which had had the privilege of nibbling grass grown on the heaven-sent English soil. This meant that the French found it difficult to break out of their poverty by developing the industry that kept so many of the English poor busy and happy. In the *Mercator* the cloth that France did produce was described as dogs' hair and cabbage-net.[78] In the next number Defoe was to remark that the 'people of Colchester would roar with laughter if they could see a piece of French bays'.[79] But *Mercator* was written specifically to denigrate French industry, so as to allay the fears of its readers that the commercial treaty with France, proposed by the Tories, would lead to a devastating competition from the skilful and low-paid French. Defoe, in his heart, was by no means so assured of the hopelessness of the French cloth industry. And he could do nothing but admire many of the other industries of France. Ever since his childhood English pamphleteers had become uneasily aware that it was the French and not the Dutch that England would have to fear as competitiors in the future. The 'enterprizing genius' of Louis xiv, coupled with 'the indefatigable vigilance of Monsieur Colbert' had created, with the aid of the nimble French, a whole range of industries.[80] These had first captured the French market behind high tariff barriers and were later to threaten the export industries on which so much of English wealth and employment depended. The truth was that the French were really rather good at making things, as Defoe was to point out in 1713 in a pamphlet written anonymously as an attack on the views of his own paper, *Mercator*:[81]

> The French are an industrious people; they work cheap, and work well; their fancy in contriving fashions, figures and fancies in their work, is very bright and quick, and these things recommend their goods to us; the vanity and levity of their nation prompts them to apply to all the novelties and niceties of dress; they gratify the beaus and the ladies, and this leads us insensibly into the error, and makes our people infinitely fond of their trade.

Such views appear throughout his writing career.[82] The French were the most improving people in the world and, in a world where it was thought that one country's trade and wealth could only expand at the expense of the rest, it had to be accepted 'that by how much the trade, and consequently the wealth of France, is encreas'd for about 150 years past, by so much the trade and wealth of England, Holland, Spain, Flanders, and the rest of the trading part of Europe is decreas'd'.[83]

Nor was it just a matter of silks and toys. The woollens that the French produced were not really just dogs' hair at all. They were very good, as a result of French art, French money and the abysmal treachery of the English who would insist on smuggling their wool, the lifeblood of English prosperity, across the Channel.[84] By the 1720s French competition, especially in the Mediterranean, was to be a very serious matter indeed.[85] Nor was this the end of it. For the French had developed their shipping, too, and had built up plantations in the West Indies which were able to produce sugar far cheaper

than the English islands. It was fortunate for England that the
French had waited so long to build up their naval strength. If they
had done so in the early seventeenth century 'they would have had
most of the colonies in the world'.[86]

It can be seen that France was not really a poor nation, despite
the poverty and frivolity of its inhabitants. One reason was its sheer
size. Defoe thought that it was 'the largest kingdom and the most
populous of any country in the known world, except China'.[87] It
was certainly far and away the most populous nation in western
Europe, with a population estimated at over nineteen millions by
the great military engineer, Vauban, in 1707.[88] This figure is generally accepted as fairly reasonable, if slightly on the low side, by
modern historians. England and Wales at the same time may have
had a population of some five and a half millions. The resources of
France were equally impressive, even if Defoe did think that the
climate was not too suitable for corn. But what made France a really
dangerous rival was the fact that all these Frenchmen and their
resources could be harnessed to a common end in a way that no
other state could ever hope to achieve. The comparative success of
Louis xiv's drive to absolutism meant that France could be subjected to one man's will. By selling jobs in the administration, the
French kings had effectively appealed to the Frenchman's desire for
status and his love of authority over other Frenchmen. They had at
the same time created a bureaucracy loyal only to themselves. Louis
was to perfect this system, using this same bureaucracy and the
enormous army and police force which depended on it to dragoon
backsliders into submission. By the early eighteenth century, as
Defoe pointed out in the first volume of the *Review*, most of the
French gentry were entirely dependent on the king for jobs, and
jobs were found for them in the army, the law, the revenue depart-
ments, the navy and the church.[89] Nor was there much reluctance
to accept them. Apart from the financial benefits that an often
impoverished gentry relished, Louis' success and his genius for
propaganda had created a general atmosphere of *gloire* that nearly
everyone wanted to share in. This made the French gentleman a
very different sort of person from his English counterpart. The first
reaction of an Englishman in trouble was to try and recoup his
fortunes by some ingenious scheme or project in which he hoped to
persuade the innocent to invest their money. 'The first thing a
French man flies to in his distress, is the army; and he seldom comes

back from thence to get an estate by painful industry, but either has his brains knock'd out, or makes his fortune there.'[90] It was a fundamental and very important distinction between the two countries that an Englishman should look to business and a Frenchman to the crown to get them out of financial difficulties. One way led to the Industrial Revolution; the other to that different sort of revolution which was to convulse France in 1789.

Defoe, who had a somewhat ambivalent view of the benefits of English liberty, as we have seen, could not help but appreciate the authoritarian benefits of French society.[91] In his pamphlet, *And what if the Pretender should come?*, published in 1713, he ironically points out the benefits that would accrue to England if the Jacobites were to be successful in bringing in the pretender, James III, at the death of Queen Anne, and thus introducing a French style of government. Although the irony is transparent, like all good irony it has that measure of truth which compels attention and even belief. Indeed he gets a little carried away by the advantages of absolutism and the disadvantages of liberty. No longer would England have to put up with the disgusting ritual of elections to Parliament. No longer would there be any danger of mob rule. A large standing army would cure us 'from our bad habit of destroying ourselves'. Since Defoe had spent much of the past nine years attacking just such abuses of England's liberal constitution, this is not just an elaborate joke. The appalling corruption of elections, in particular, was a bugbear that he attacked over and over again in the *Review*.[92] In the 1710 election he lambasts the voters for selling their 'liberty for the belch of the brewhouse', and notes that those who buy their votes with beer in the country will sell them for cash in the House.[93] And just think of the benefits to the country gentlemen if there were no elections and no parliament. No longer would they be 'unnecessarily exposed to long and hazardous journeys, in the depth of winter, from the remotest corners of the island to come to London, just to give away the countrey's money and go home again'. No longer would they have to suffer the anguish of deciding whether they could afford the money for the journey or 'whether they can trust their wives behind them, or no'.[94]

Again, in 1721, Defoe was to reflect on the effective way in which French authority was able to cope with the bubonic plague which had struck Marseilles the previous year. The whole area was sealed off by troops who had orders to shoot on sight anyone who tried to

escape and thus risked spreading the infection to the rest of the
country. Such a policy would be impossible in England. 'These
happy, unhappy obstructions, call'd privileges and liberties, stand
in the way.'[95]

But it was in time of warfare that the advantages of an absolutist
government were most obvious. It was this that made the French so
difficult to defeat. This was a theme that Defoe hammered into his
readers' heads in number after number of the *Review*. What does
King Louis do if he wants another hundred thousand men? An
order is given to the intendants; the men are levied and then driven
off to where they have to go, 'like a drove of sheep'.[96] Compare this
with England where soldiers can be found only with kind words
and bribes, with 'coats, shoes, stockings etc. and two guineas in
ready money, for every rake that will run away from his wife and
children'.[97] But such volunteers were few. The English had to resort
to an annual round-up of vagabonds, debtors and felons to make up
their numbers, a mere trickle compared with the French levy and
an exercise which made a nonsense of the old view that war was an
employment of honour. Was it not something of a scandal to have
'men taken from the gallows, and immediately from villains and
housebreakers made gentlemen soldiers'?[98]

The French could not only find men, but the efficiency of their
bureaucracy was able to equip them and bring them into the field
in time for each new campaign. Winter after winter Defoe castigates
the optimists who predict that France has at last been brought to
her knees, that there will be no French army in the field for the next
season of war. But absolutism can always find one, larger and better
equipped than the one which Marlborough was supposed to have
destroyed the previous summer:

> Behold, the unprepar'd French are always ready before us; their
> cavalry that had no horses are all mounted, and in the field their
> officers that had no equipages have pass'd in review; their cap-
> tains that had no levy money have fill'd up their companies . . .
> It is not any surprise . . . to find the French, who are the most
> vigilant and diligent people in the world, master by their applica-
> tion insuperable difficulties, and be before us in time, beyond us
> in number, and the like.[99]

Even if absolutism had been unable to fill the ranks of the French
army, poverty would have been as effective a recruiting officer.

The classic occasion was the terrible winter of 1708–9 when it seemed as if the combination of military defeat, economic disaster and famine had at last finished the resistance of France. Many thought that Marlborough would be able to march in triumph to Paris in the spring. Not at all. The lure of bread brought recruits flocking to the ranks and Marlborough's advance was checked at Malplaquet in his most bloody battle.[100] But even in a good year a poor country like France would have little difficulty in finding men desperate enough to volunteer for the army.

Some writers felt that this was a good reason to make the English poor poorer. But not Defoe. That other Defoe who hates absolutism and loves liberty, who praises the wealth of freedom-loving England, can see nothing but matter for self-satisfaction in the fact that the Englishman's wages are too good to find the soldier's life attractive.[101] 'The difficulties to get Englishmen to list is because they live in plenty and ease, and he that can earn 20s. per week at an easie steady employment, must be drunk or mad when he lists for a soldier, to be knock'd o' th' head for 3s. 6d. per week.'[102] The English, like the Dutch, should hire poorer nations to fight for them.[103] This policy was, of course, to be followed by England for the next century. It was not necessary to go far to find poor men. England could draw on the inexhaustible reservoir of poverty in Scotland and Ireland to fill her armies.

The life of the soldier, like that of the sea, was the last resort of the desperate, though a restless, unsettled man like Robinson Crusoe's eldest brother might join up in a spirit of adventure. Needless to say he soon gets himself killed in the Low Countries.[104] In Colonel Jack's opinion, 'no body went into the field but those that cou'd not live at home'.[105] None the less, although the realist in Defoe could see the horror of war, there remained in his breast some admiration for such a noble occupation. For the most part such admiration is, however, for the armies of the past. No contemporary army gets the praise reserved for the Swedes and Scots who fought for Gustavus Adolphus, a modest, clean-living bunch of young men who form a striking contrast to their opponents, Tilly's 'great army of old lads that are used to boxing; fellows with iron faces'.[106] These men were real soldiers who joined the army to fight, not like the mercenary of Defoe's day whose main interest was to avoid trouble and keep the war and his pay going as long as possible. What a shock such men got as a result of the aggressive policies of the Duke of Marlborough.

Those who served for pay and plunder found that they would have to fight as well now.[107] This was as it should be. War was about fighting and fighting was an honourable profession. Service in the army was in fact sufficient, in Defoe's eyes, to make a man a gentleman, 'tho' he was but a private centinel'.[108]

Perhaps this was just as well because there were few gentlemen of birth in the English army.[109] They had long forgotten the chivalrous origins of their status, relying for the most part on Dutchmen, Scots and Germans to officer the armies that protected their liberties.[110] Such was modern chivalry. Of the seventeen members of the higher nobility alive when Henry v set sail for France in 1415, only three did not fight in person during his short reign – two were boys and the third was blind. What was to happen when his great successor, William III, set sail to challenge the might of France?

> Great Britain's Monarch did in Arms appear,
> And scarce an English Nobleman was there.[111]

The reason was obvious. English gentlemen were already too rich. They had no need to go to Flanders to seek their fortunes or their reputation in the cannon's mouth. Better to stay at home and look after their estates or better still use their patronage to get a nice job selling sub-standard supplies to the army commissariat. War was too dangerous for the already rich.

War was indeed very dangerous, despite Defoe's strictures on the reluctance of armies to fight. Each great war brings its death-dealing innovation. Each great war seems to employ more men and kill a higher proportion of them. The wars of the Grand Alliance were no exception. The 1690s saw the general introduction of the flintlock musket in place of the old matchlock, the fuse of which had had the disconcerting habit of going out in rain or a high wind. The new musket was effective up to about a hundred yards and the rate of fire was almost doubled. The percentage of gun-shot wounds, nearly always fatal in the hands of contemporary military doctors, grew. The war saw another innovation which brought cleaner wounds but perhaps little consolation to the wounded. This was the socket bayonet. Earlier, the close order weapon was the pike, often sixteen foot long, or the plug bayonet jammed into the muzzle of the musket. This action took time and reduced fire-power, as General Mackay discovered when Bonnie Dundee's Highlanders poured down on him in the pass of Killiecrankie: 'The Highlanders are of such quick motion that if a battalion keep up his fire until they be near to make sure of [hitting] them, they are upon it before our men can come to the second defence, which is the bayonet in the musle of the musket.'[112] The new socket bayonet, which left the muzzle clear, was to change all that. Defoe was able to assure his readers during the Highland rebellion of 1715 that the English had learned a lot about war since the horrors of Killicrankie. In discussing the relative effectiveness of the thrusting bayonet and the slashing claymore, he concluded that the bayonet was three times as fast and more fatal as it penetrated deeper.[113] The effect of these two innovations was to make war even bloodier and greatly to increase the rate of casualties in action. At Steenkirk, which was considered a very savage battle in 1692, just over ten per cent of the combatants were killed or wounded. At Blenheim, twelve years later, the new weapons and Marlborough's tactics had more than doubled the rate. Malplaquet was to be even worse.[114]

Not that it should be thought that warfare was a matter of battles. Most commanders avoided them at all costs. War was chiefly a question of sieges. In the past two centuries a new system of fortification, based on the bastion, had been developed and had now been brought to perfection by the great French military engineer, Vauban. The dense system of fortified towns along France's eastern borders kept her frontiers as safe from invasion, 'as we are in England by the wooden walls of our navy, and the circumvallation of the sea'.[115] Of course even fortified towns could be taken. Vauban had perfected the technique of siege as well as fortification. ''Tis visible by experience, not one town in ten is besieg'd, but 'tis taken. The art of war is so improv'd, and our generals are so wary, that an army seldom attempts a siege, but when they are almost sure to go on with it.'[116] The main interest was how long it would take. Wagers on the length of sieges kept people interested in the wars in a gambling age, and also stimulated the more enterprising gamblers to establish far-flung intelligence services so that they would be able to adjust their bets to their advance information of the result.[117]

One town captured at enormous expense of money and men was just that. There were always hundreds more to capture. This was one reason why the wars were so long. The other main reason was, as we have seen, the reluctance of the generals to fight, preferring to engage in what was known as manoeuvre. Defoe compared such inactivity with the constant battles of the English civil war:[118]

Now 'tis frequent to have armies of fifty thousand men of a side stand at bay within view of one another, and spend a whole campaign in dodging, or as 'tis genteely call'd, observing one another, and then march off into winter-quarters . . . I grant that this way of making war spends generally more money and less blood than former wars did; but then it spins wars out to a greater length; and I almost question whether if this had been the way of fighting of old, our civil war had not lasted till this day.

It was the genius of Marlborough that he was actually able to bring his enemies to battle. That he could defeat them as well was, of course, an added bonus.

What were the wars about? Why should England, which had kept clear of continental military commitments for so long, be prepared to fight against France for twenty years? Defoe was quite clear. 'Exorbitant power is the wild beast we hunt, wherever he is, we must unkennel and dislodge him; he is now in France, and we have almost hunted him down; if he shifts into Germany, France will help us to hunt him out there.'[119] Defoe was one of the first writers to use the concept of the European balance of power.[120] 'A just ballance of power is the life of peace', he wrote in *The Two Great Questions Consider'd* of 1700. 'Every king in the world would be the universal monarch if he might, and nothing restrains but the power of neighbours; and if one neighbour is not strong enough . . . he gets another neighbour to join with him.'[121] England had particular reasons to fight France, whose protection of the rival Jacobite court threatened the Revolutionary settlement. Such a threat kept England in the war, but there was also a universal duty to curb unbridled power.

There was another reason why England must fight. For England had been guilty in the past of helping France to become the mighty power she was. English neutrality for most of the seventeenth century had been a condition of France's rise to ascendancy. Naturally the subtle French had fomented those divisions in England which had been one of the major causes of neutrality. They were still at it. French money encouraged the Jacobites in England and Scotland. But Major Alexander Ramkins, after a lifetime of fighting in the Jacobite interest, was convinced of French duplicity. Their only object was to divide the English:

My shallow brain told me, expedition was the business of war;
whereas I found afterwards it was the interest of France to spin on
the Irish war, and to order things so, that King William should
always have an army employ'd there; for they look'd upon it as a
chimerical notion that the war could be carry'd on into England.[122]

The English were not always neutral. Their guilt lay deeper than
that. In 1628 they had helped destroy the Huguenot state within a
state by lending the French government ships which joined in the
attack on La Rochelle.[123] Worse was to come. England had become
almost a French province in the reign of Charles II. He it was who
'exchang'd liberty for whores, and English strength for French
money'.[124] It was in Charles' reign, also, that England had engaged
in that anti-Dutch policy which had so strengthened French influence in the Low Countries.[125] Now, with a Dutch king, England
could fight to undo the evil of the past. And when King William
was dead England must fight to maintain the alliance that he had
created and prevent at all costs a French prince sitting on the throne
of Spain. The thought of already mighty France controlling the
enormous Spanish empire, with its silver and its trade, with a joint
coastline that stretched almost without interruption from Messina
in Sicily to Sluys in Flanders was too much to contemplate. England
must fight and the Spanish empire, in default of Spanish heirs, must
be partitioned.[126]

Fighting with allies had its problems. They were constantly letting
each other down and even if they were doing their duty rumours of
treachery often led to strife. The Portuguese got a fairly consistently
bad press, Defoe's conclusion being that they were more use as
trading partners than as partners in war.[127] As might be expected,
Defoe remained loyal to the Dutch. Many Englishmen found it
difficult to think of them as allies, having fought their last three wars
against them. But Defoe saw that competition in trade did not necessarily mean that one had to be enemies in war. 'We will fight hand to
hand, and back to back, against France, against tyranny, against
popery; but we fight hand to hand, and face to face in our trade, in
all parts of the world, where our trading interests clash; nor is it any
breach of our alliance in other things.'[128] Even at the end of the war,
when the Dutch came under more general criticism for not contri-
buting their share to the common effort, he continued to defend
them, characteristically attributing much of the criticism to the

Jacobites. The Dutch were England's barrier against the French on
the continent.[129]

The Austrians were a different matter. Defoe became increasingly
critical of them. The main problem was that they would not concentrate their attention on the main issue. The war could have been
won years earlier if the Austrians had not spent so much time and
effort in trying to subdue their rebels in Hungary. This was a tricky
question since the rebels were Protestants. Many in England supported them. Defoe was able to point up the false logic of such
sympathizers who were at the same time applauding Marlborough
who by winning the battle of Blenheim had just saved the empire
from the French and Bavarians.[130] Still the Austrians were unreasonable. They should make peace with their subjects and get on with
the job of fighting King Louis.[131] It was beginning to be a little tire-
some for the English, fighting all over Europe to support popish
princes in Austria and Spain.[132]

Nor was the Hungarian revolt the only side-show taking attention,
men and effort from the main struggle against France. Defoe constantly had to remind his readers not to encourage Sweden in her
war against Poland, simply because the Swedes were Protestants
and the Poles Catholics. The days of wars of religion were over:
'He that will help French power against us, is an enemy to England,
and the publick interest of Europe, by what name or title soever his
religion . . . is distinguish'd.'[133] Charles XII of Sweden may have
been the victim of an unprovoked attack, and deserved sympathy in
that respect. But success went to his head and his victories disturbed
the balance of power. It was a good thing that he was at last defeated
and the ambitions of Sweden curbed for ever. God forsook him and
threw him from the top of all his glory 'to teach him and all princes,
that tho' they are permitted to do themselves right against the
oppressions of others . . . he will set bounds to the extravagancies of
it'.[134]

Naturally enough the crafty French had been supporting both
the Hungarians and the Swedes. Protestant Hungarian or Catholic
Irishman, what difference did it make, all were grist to the mill of
French ambition. All the same the English must be careful not to be
blinded by concentration on the French. One had to be careful to
see just where exorbitant power was if one was to hunt it. After the
battle of Ramillies in 1706 it seemed that France was ready for the
plucking. Enthusiasts discussed the revival of the empire of Edward

111 with an English Gascony to ship English claret to pour down English throats. Defoe argued against the partition on economic grounds. Cheap wines from Gascony would turn the balance of trade against us.[135] He also argued on political grounds. The object of the war was to curb France not conquer her. A strong France was necessary to retain the balance of power.[136]

France recovered in the following year and there was no longer any question of partition. But when the emperor died in 1711 a new danger arose, the danger of the revival of the Hapsburg empire of Charles v. Austrian control of the Spanish empire was just as dangerous as French. Was exorbitant power moving into Germany? If it was it would be necessary to hunt it there.[137] The new danger reconciled Defoe to the Tory abandonment of the old Whig policy of 'No peace without Spain', that is no peace till Spain had been forced to reject the French candidate for the throne. Some critics have accused Defoe of turning his coat when the Tories came to power in 1710 and Harley continued to employ him as a writer. This is a little unfair. The death of the emperor made a real difference to the European balance of power. Exorbitant power really was moving into Germany.

What sort of war was England to fight? For a very long time England's attitude to continental war had been to keep well out of it, to concentrate on a powerful navy to keep her enemies away from her shores and to use this navy to create as much havoc as possible in the Atlantic and West Indies. This was of course particularly attractive in a war against Spain, as had been seen in the days of Elizabeth. Such a policy was especially favoured by the Tories, the party which drew much of its strength from the poorer country gentlemen who were asked to pay up to a fifth of their net income in a land tax to support the war and thus wanted war to be cheap, short and ideally self-supporting. Defoe had enough of the Elizabethan in him to find such blue water policies attractive. He repeatedly advocated a concerted attack on the Spanish plate fleet.[138] France and Spain could not fight without the money to pay their armies. 'If you get but the Spanish plate fleet you recover Spain in two years ... the money is the victory, and without you do nothing.'[139] He was also keen on using the opportunity of a war against Spain to seize territory in South America, particularly in the vast, unsettled lands in the south of the continent.[140] In 1729, when full-scale war with Spain was once again in the wind, Defoe returns to

his theme, pointing out the advantages of such a war to enable
England to strengthen her position in the West Indies and gain a
firm footing in South America.[141]

Such policies were attractive and Defoe was very disappointed at
the reluctance of the government to invest heavily in a buccaneering
war. But a limited maritime war by itself was not enough. France
could never be brought to her knees by naval war alone. At heart
Defoe was a consistent supporter of the Williamite and Whig view
of the war that France must be defeated in Europe on the battlefields of Flanders. It was no good leaving such fighting to England's
continental allies. If Holland was defeated, then the combined
Franco-Dutch navies and 400,000 men would be ready to fall upon
England.[142] This was the contemporary version of the domino theory.
'It's a known maxim that the preservation of Flanders is more for the
interest of England, than of Spain. If Flanders be an accession to
France, Holland must soon follow, and England next. They are like
nine-pins, the throwing down one carries the rest.'[143] A century of
victory at sea was to give England enormous confidence in the power
of her navy by the time of the Napoleonic Wars. Men in Defoe's
time were not so sure. They still remembered the shock of the
French naval victory off Beachy Head in 1690 when France ruled
the Channel and a Jacobite army was loose in Ireland.

Fighting in Flanders meant fighting in the most sophisticated
military arena in the world. It was no good going over there with a
handful of poorly trained yokels, as had been England's habit in
most of her miserable continental expeditions in the century before
the Wars of the Grand Alliance. England must have a standing
army in peacetime, trained in the latest skills of the art of war,
veterans who could rapidly instruct recruits in the event of war.
There would have to be safeguards to prevent the resurrection of
the dangers of a Cromwell or a James II. But there must be a standing
army. England was too vulnerable to attack from the sea.[144]

Fighting in Flanders was also very expensive. This was why the
Tory gentlemen did not like it. But, in an expensive war, prosperous
England had all the advantages. For ''tis not the longest sword, but
the longest purse that conquers'. France was already poor and could
be made poorer. The stream of silver from South America could be
diverted to England by attacks on the plate fleet. Even more effective in Defoe's view was to trade with France in wartime.[145] French
demand for English goods would drain France of silver to pay for

them. No country could long survive if they could not find enough coin to pay their troops, as Spain had long since discovered. An army where the paymaster is bankrupt and the unpaid troops are mutinying is rarely effective in the field.

There was no danger of English bankruptcy. For the English had at last discovered how to finance a war. English public finance for most of the seventeenth century had been a sorry tale of generally reluctant loans made to dishonest or insolvent monarchs.[146] But in the 1690s the English had learned to imitate the Dutch and Italians and raise money on the credit of the nation as represented in Parliament, rather than on the fickle personal credit of the monarch. The national debt had been born. Slowly the techniques of public borrowing were perfected and the public, once convinced that the investment was really safe, flocked to lend money at attractive rates of interest to finance the war. The innovation spelt disaster to the enemies of England. The amount of money raised surprised everyone, especially the French king, who would never have begun the war if he had 'believed England capable of supporting the war at such a prodigy of expence'.[147] England could now harness her wealth to make her powerful. Much of the credit for this must go to the Lord Treasurer, Godolphin: 'Your Treasurer has been your general of generals; without his exquisite management of the cash, the Duke of Marlborough must have been beaten, and your expeditions been baulk'd, your armies have been backward, and your preparations late; he has recover'd your funds, and restor'd your credit, and fill'd you with money.'[148]

This English money was to check the ambitions of France. In 1713 the wars came at last to an end and peace was made at Utrecht. For the rest of Defoe's life the two countries were to remain at peace, recovering their strength for the next stage in their duel for world ascendancy.

PART III
ENGLAND

THE ECONOMICS OF STABILITY[1]

DANIEL DEFOE had probably seen more of the English economy of
his day than any other writer on economic problems before or since.
He travelled through the whole island several times, and everywhere
he went he not only looked at what could be seen but talked with the
sort of people who would know what was going on. The result of his
journeys can be seen in his superb *Tour*, which describes the working
England of his day in a mixture of pride at its riches and exasperation
at its follies.[2] But the *Tour* and Defoe's other descriptive works on
economic matters do not appear to have much conscious theoretical
background, other than a rather breathless optimism, and it is as an
economic journalist rather than as an economic theorist that Defoe
is normally assessed by historians.[3] This is mainly because few historians have ever read Defoe's excursions into economic theory. He
never wrote a *Discourse of Trade*, the contemporary equivalent to a
modern economics textbook. Instead, his economic theory is scattered through the volumes of the *Review*, a forum not easily accessible
to those who write the history of economic thought.

Taken together this body of writing forms an essential background
to Defoe's better-known descriptive works. Defoe was not a great
economist, nor was he original in any one of his economic ideas.
But the somewhat strange selection which he drew from his contemporaries and predecessors would appear to be unique, reflecting
once again the dualism which we have already noted in his thought.
Defoe's economics combine the archaic with the modern, the pessimistic with the optimistic, in a fascinating, if theoretically dubious
way. Part of the explanation of this arises from the fact that the main
body of economic thought in the early eighteenth century sprang
from four earlier periods of creative economic thinking – the 1550s,
1620s, 1640s and 1690s. These were all periods when the English

economy was in considerable trouble and the economics which
emerged, while not yet the dismal science it was to be in the future,
was often heavily tinged with an atmosphere of gloom.[4] Immersion
in such a literature meant that Defoe's natural optimism was habitually tempered by caution and even alarm when he looked towards
the future. Pride in England's achievements was coupled with doubt
whether such achievements could be maintained into a problematical and trouble-strewn future.

Most modern writers miss this conservative, anachronistic element
in Defoe's writing. They seize on his *Tour* as a superb description of
England on the eve of the Industrial Revolution, which of course it
is, but then select from it material which seems to predict the unique
changes which were about to change the economy of England and
ultimately of the world. The truth is, as we shall see, that Defoe had
no premonition of the Industrial Revolution and that if he had he
would almost certainly have disliked what he foresaw. He thought
that England was the wealthiest country in the world because of the
way things already were in the most advanced parts of the country
and he opposed anything which seemed to threaten this *status quo*,
including many contemporary changes which later writers have seen
as harbingers of or necessary conditions for industrialization.

Industrialization and the changes that it has brought about in
the economic horizons of all men in society has led modern historians
to look at pre-industrial society with a somewhat condescending eye.
The first thing the textbook reader learns about England in the
early eighteenth century is how poor everyone was. To Defoe, however, the most striking thing about England was how rich everyone
was. One sign of English prosperity was the high wages paid to
English workmen, higher than the wages of foreigners and higher
than was necessary simply to survive.[5] Most of Defoe's educated
contemporaries condemned this fact and thought that it had a serious
effect on England's competitive position in her export markets.
Defoe did not accept this argument, as we shall see.[6] He also did not
put quite the same emphasis on exports as most writers, who seemed
to think that export expansion was almost the only object of an
economy. He certainly thought that a high level of exports was
necessary to absorb surplus English production and thus maintain a
high level of employment. But he thought that home demand was
even more important. On his travels round England the thing which
most impressed him was the bustling prosperity of the inland trade.

How could so many people buy so much? The answer seemed obvious. It was the high wages which were paid to the English workman which were both the cause and the effect of English prosperity, and hence it was clear that Englishmen must continue to be paid high wages. If wages were cut the English would never be able to consume all those goods which kept the home market so busy and this would lead to cuts in production and a reduction in employment.[7] As it was, the surplus above the needs of subsistence was available to improve the living standards of the poor, enabling them to buy more food or manufactured goods. Not all men took advantage of this possibility, of course, since many were idle and there was little or no compulsion to do more than was necessary for a bare subsistence. But others were not satisfied with this and worked more for more money, and it was this fact which kept the whole economy going at its relatively high level. By their increased demand for food they enabled the farmer to make sufficient profit to pay a high rent, whilst at the same time paying his own labourers and servants relatively high wages. And by their increased demand for manufactured goods the English workmen provided the demand which caused the employment which paid themselves and their comrades in other industries and other parts of the country the high wages in the first place.[8] High wages led to high demand which led to high employment which led to high wages.[9] Nor was it only the worker who benefited. The clothier who put out the wool to be spun or the yarn to be woven could charge high prices for his finished article because, whether his potential customer was a workman, a farmer or a landlord, all would have the money to buy it. The carter who carried the cloth, the horsebreeder who sold him his pack-horses, the inn-keeper who stabled them and lodged him for the night – everyone could join in the game. Indeed this chain of distribution was one of the most important elements in Defoe's economics. The more hands a commodity passed through on its way from raw material to final consumer, the more employment each article gave rise to and the more wages or profits could be earned on the way:[10]

Every head and hand ought to be employ'd to preserve, support, enlarge, and encrease [circulation], as the main thing on which the health of trade depends; and in the decay, shortning or contracting of which, our trade must necessarily languish, droop, and die.[11]

Ideally everyone in the country – man, woman and child – would be employed, earn high wages and thus keep everyone else employed. England was by no means in such a happy situation and this was one of the main defects in the system which Defoe was keen to eradicate.

Before we come to consider Defoe's suggestions for solving the very serious problem of unemployment in the economy, it would be as well to try and understand how the satisfactory state of affairs by which Englishmen were paid high wages had come about. Defoe has two ways of explaining high wages, depending on whether he is explaining wage variations within England itself or whether he is explaining why English wages are higher than those of foreigners. Although the two explanations are logically connected, neither is very satisfactory. It was clear to all observers that wages in the south of England were higher than in the north. Defoe explains this by arguing that the wage level was a function of the density of population.[12] The greater the number of people in a given area the less self-sufficient they were and the greater the demand that they made on each other's labours. Employers competed for workmen to produce goods to satisfy this demand and so raised the level of wages.[13] Such an argument would not work for England as a whole since it was clear that other areas, particularly the Low Countries,[14] had an even greater density of population and did not have such high wages. This forced Defoe to fall back on a similar but even more circular argument. Englishmen were paid higher wages because there were more job opportunities available to them than people to do them at the starvation wages paid to foreigners.[15] In other countries there were more poor than jobs and so workmen competed with each other until the level of wages had been bid down to the minimum required for subsistence or lower. Why were there more jobs in England? The answer lies in the phenomenon that is being explained. The high wages paid to Englishmen created the demand which swelled the number of jobs to so great a number that employers were forced to pay high wages to fill them. The circle is complete.

Such an explanation presents an obvious problem, since it assumes that everybody who wanted to work in England could find a job, an assumption which was obviously untrue. Full employment, which is hard enough to define realistically today, was even more difficult to define in Defoe's time. It would have been impossible to state at any moment either the size of the labour force relative to the population or what proportion of it was in work. The most that anyone could say was that trade, and hence employment, was brisk or slack. Everybody above the age of five or so was thought able to work and so might theoretically compete with existing labour to bring the rate of wages down to subsistence level. But this was unlikely to happen, despite the contemporary dislike of the sight of an idle child. In any case the labour market did not form a homogeneous and competitive whole in which there was absolute occupational and geographical mobility. Instead it was composed of a series of heterogeneous and for the most part non-competing categories, distinguished by location, sex, age, skill, education and a host of other different features. These facts were obvious to Defoe and it is clear that all that he meant to argue was that for some of these categories of labour the conditions that he described existed. Boiled down to its essentials his argument is that in certain parts of England and in certain jobs at certain times of year the demand for labour was greater than the supply, a fact which meant that employers were in a weak bargaining position and had to pay a wage higher than subsistence. The net result of thousands of such bargains was that the average level of wages in England was higher than that in other countries. This did not mean that everyone was well off all the time. Defoe did not deny that there were many people in England as poor as the average Frenchman or even Irishman, or that there was often seasonal and cyclical unemployment which threw thousands out of work, or that there were many women and children all over the country who would have liked to work in order to increase the family income but could find no jobs to do.

Those historians who accept Defoe's basic proposition, that English workers were paid wages higher than the minimum necessary for subsistence and that these wages were higher than those of nearly all foreigners, use a somewhat more satisfactory explanation of these facts.[16] First they argue that subsistence had become cheaper in England because landlords and farmers had been introducing improvements into English agriculture, at least since the late sixteenth century.[17] These improvements, which included the partial eradication of the fallow and the sowing of new nitrogen-fixing grasses, had much increased the average fertility of the soil and had expanded the supply of foodstuffs on the English market. The supply had also been increased by the extension of cultivation into previously unutilized parts of the country, such as forests, heaths, and fens. However, this expanded output of food had had no effect in reducing the cost of subsistence before the middle of the seventeenth century because the population had been expanding even faster. From the 1640s two things had happened to change the situation. The rate of innovation in agriculture had accelerated, as the new ideas became more widely disseminated, and population had ceased to grow so fast, and may well indeed have fallen. The same number or less people were now in the market for an increased supply of food and this led to a fall in food prices, particularly in a period of unusually good harvests in the 1670s and 1680s. Less money from the same wages could now buy the same amount of bread, and income was available to buy more and better food or to buy manufactured goods. This in turn meant an increase in demand for labour in both agriculture and industry. But now population was no longer rising and so there were not enough people to do the new work at the old wages and so wages rose, once again especially in the 1670s.[18] Although food prices were to rise again, particularly in the 1690s, they did not rise sufficiently to undo the situation and so English workers in the 1710s and 1720s were in the happy position of earning more money to buy goods at cheaper prices than they had in the decade of Defoe's birth.

Defoe never looked at falling food prices in this way. Indeed, when he looked back at the two key decades of the 1670s and 1680s he, like most of his literate contemporaries, saw them not as a boon but as a curse, the curse of plenty.[19] Cheap food might increase the workman's standard of living, though this is not a point that Defoe ever stressed. What it certainly would do was to reduce the standard of living of what seemed to most people a far more important sector of the population – the farmers and landlords. Farmers might well find that when they took their crop to the market the price they received was not sufficient to cover the costs of growing and carrying it, leaving them with no profit and their landlord with no rent.[20] When the income of the wealthiest in the land was reduced this of course affected everyone else. There would be less demand for goods and services, less jobs, lower wages and so the cycle would go on until the workman's lower wages removed the benefit he received from lower food prices in the first place.[21]

Defoe's constant interest therefore was not to lower food prices but to raise them. During the whole of his lifetime England produced on average far more corn than her population would eat or drink.

Satisfactory as this situation was, it posed a very serious problem when seen against the background of Defoe's analysis of the English economy. A run of good harvests, such as those of the 1680s, could spoil his whole system. 'Cheapness of corn is the greatest publick mischief that can befall us', he wrote in 1709.[22] Circulation and employment depended on everything being high – high wages, high food prices, high rents and a high income for the farmer. The problem was made worse for Defoe by the fact that on his journeys round England he was only too aware that there was plenty of scope for further agricultural improvement. Defoe disliked unemployed resources, be they people or land, and so he was always keen on ways of disposing of the surplus, so as to keep the price up, or better still to change the use of the land so as to reduce the heavy dependence on corn cultivation.

One of the most satisfactory ways of disposing of surplus corn was to export it and Defoe was a keen advocate of the system of bounties which had been developed to encourage corn export since the 1670s.[23] But exports only stemmed the tide of plenty and so it was necessary to find other ways of disposing of corn. One way, which was of course implicit in his economic system, was simply for workmen to buy more bread with their high wages. There was however a limit to the amount of bread people could or would eat. On the other hand there appeared to be no limit to the amount they would drink. And so the moralistic Defoe, who in other writings was to describe drink as the father of all vices, became the champion of the drink trade when he was wearing his economic hat. It is with pride that he describes the enormous size of the trade and with much satisfaction that he states that Englishmen drink more per head than any other people in the world.[24] This was just another instance of the enormous value of high wages in maintaining employment, circulation and the landlord's rents. His most succinctly argued pamphlet on the subject was a well-documented puff for the English distilling industry. The distillers were busily engaged in fighting the Dutch for the home gin market, now in the 1720s expanding towards that enormous size which was to inspire Hogarth and give the whole period the nickname of the Gin Age, in which a man could get drunk for a penny and dead-drunk for twopence.[25] Gin was a perfect product for absorbing English grain. It not only had the usual Defovian effects in raising employment and rents but, presumably because of its foul quality, took off the very worst grain that could not be sold in any other market, thus not only swelling the farmer's income but enabling him to till previously unusable ground.

Such expedients for disposing of corn stopped matters getting any worse, at least in Defoe's lifetime, but they did not have the effect of raising the long-term price of grain, nor of raising rents.[26] This was the ultimate motive of all Defoe's cries for high agricultural prices, as we have seen, and it is not surprising that he was interested in other ways of raising rents, apart from the expansion of corn consumption. One answer seemed to lie in not growing grain at all. Defoe claimed that the rents for pasture or feeding land were five times the rents for arable land and those paid for good quality horticultural land could be up to four times those for pasture.[27] The implication was obvious. If landlords wanted to increase their incomes they should cease to allow their land to be used for growing grain and switch it to grazing or market-gardening. There were problems of course. The Englishman would still want his bread and his beer, to say nothing of his gin. But would it not be possible to do as the Dutch did?[28] They imported much of their grain from an area of plentiful land and low wages in the Baltic and paid for it with their earnings from trade and manufacture. Meanwhile their own land was intensely cultivated and raised dairy products, vegetables, industrial raw materials and similar goods whose profits enabled the farmers to pay very high rents for the limited land available.[29] Defoe imagined a similar situation in an England which 'was so full of people that all the low lands of the nation were but enough to make their gardens' and stall feed their horses and cows, while the sheep grazed on the hills.[30] He would no doubt have been much surprised had he known that, two centuries after he wrote this piece, English agriculture was to be very similar to his imagined ideal.

The beginnings of this move towards the growing of high-value crops could be seen even in Defoe's day, as falling or stable grain prices and rising wages encouraged farmers to seek new ways to maintain their incomes.[31] More and more farmers began to experiment with fruit and vegetable growing, with hops or with industrial crops, such as dyes and oil-seeds. More land was devoted to the pasturing of animals whose main purpose now increasingly became the supply of meat and dairy products for the market rather than manure to increase the supply of grain. Such specialists were often each other's best customers, as concentration on the production of one thing made them deficient in others. This general expansion of the market also helped the ailing corn-grower, who found new buyers for his grain in areas which now specialized in livestock husbandry or market-gardening. Slowly the old pattern in which each agricultural region had been nearly self-sufficient was breaking down.

The same type of specialization occurred with the expansion of industry. As more people had income to buy manufactured goods so the entire living of other people came from the wages they received for making them. The process was slow. Most industrial workers in the early seventeenth century were the wives and children of small farmers or, if they were men, combined manufacture with the cultivation of a small farm. But, by Defoe's time, provincial England had a large population of workers completely divorced from the land, living in towns like Exeter or Norwich or in the overgrown villages of the West Riding that Defoe described so vividly in the *Tour*.[32] The parish of Halifax, for instance, was 'if not the largest, certainly the most populous in England', a monster for a country parish.[33] Everyone here was busily engaged in the manufacture and the buying and selling of woollen cloth. The same 'noble scene of industry and application' could be seen all along the road from Halifax to Leeds. 'The country appears busy, diligent, and even in a hurry of work', the villages were large, 'full of houses, and those houses thronged with people, for the whole country is infinitely populous'.[34] Such people relied almost entirely on their industry for food, an alarming thought for government and ratepayer in times of industrial depression, but clear incentive to the farmer to expand his output for the market. The farmers had accepted the challenge. Corn for the cloth-workers of the West Riding 'comes up in great quantities out of Lincoln, Nottingham, and the East Riding, their black cattle and horses from the North Riding, their sheep and mutton from the adjacent counties every way, their butter from the East and North Riding, their cheese out of Cheshire and Warwickshire'.[35]

Provincial towns were growing rapidly in the absence of any real economic constraint on their size.[36] Old fears of urban hunger had disappeared as farmers eagerly sought new markets for their surplus produce. Some of this urban growth reflected the increasing specialization and sophistication in certain processes in industry, particularly in the weaving of cloth which provided the major employment in the examples above. Other towns, such as Bristol and Liverpool, grew as a result of expansion of trade with the Americas and the slackening of the monopoly which London had previously sought to maintain in England's international commerce. But some towns, probably the majority, grew simply because people of means wanted to live in them and enjoy the amenities of what was a much more sophisticated and companionable way of life than had been available to them in the countryside.[37] Defoe has much to say about the delights of such places in the *Tour*. Bury St Edmunds, for instance, was 'thronged with gentry, people of the best fashion, and the most polite conversation', whose expenditure was sufficient to keep not only the town but the whole of the surrounding countryside in a flourishing state.[38] Once a few gentlemen or professional people decided to make their permanent home in a town, other people soon joined them, either to provide for their needs, as domestic servants, craftsmen or shopkeepers, or because where gentlemen led lesser men were sure to follow. Towns seemed to have a natural tendency to grow. Each new immigrant required another immigrant to provide some service for him, whether it was to sell him snuff and brandy or to sweep the street before his house.

Defoe naturally welcomed this development of communities of consumers, though he sometimes attacked some of the forms that such consumption took. The assembly rooms which were being erected everywhere in the late seventeenth century and which seemed to the provincial town dweller the height of urban sophistication were more often in Defoe's eyes temples of vice and lewdness.[39] But towns themselves were the best guarantee of prosperity for the farmer and the continued existence of the consumer society.

Such towns, despite their growth, were minute by modern standards. Very few had a population greater than ten thousand. Most were much smaller. Places with as few as three hundred people living in them might be graced with the name of town. But, added together, the urban population of provincial England was substantial and provided an extremely valuable market for the specializing farmer and industrialist. All the same, it took a man as well-travelled as Defoe to see the real importance of this drift to the towns. Far more impressive to most people, and indeed to Defoe himself, was the astonishing growth of London, the marvel of the age and the model on which the 'little Londons' of the provinces based themselves. Here was a market so big that it absorbed foodstuffs and

manufactures from every corner of the island.[40] By the time that
Defoe was writing London had a population of over half a million,
ten times the size of Bristol, the largest city in the provinces, and
one hundred times the size of the typical medium-sized provincial
town. And London was still growing. At any one time at least one
out of ten of all Englishmen were living in this gross metropolis and,
since it was a very unhealthy place where far more people died than
were born every year,[41] a much greater proportion had to live there
at some time in their life in order to maintain, let alone increase its
population.[42] The rural areas were stripped of people attracted by
the lure of jobs, easy pickings and possible riches in the city. A continuous stream of optimistic farm boys and girls left the villages to
seek their fortunes in London. According to Defoe, in a pessimistic
moralizing mood, most of them ended up as thieves and strumpets.
But whatever they did, they had to eat and most of them could
afford to eat far better in the city than ever they had at home,
whether it was in the pastry-shops whose proliferation so offended
Defoe,[43] or in that boiling cook's in Rosemary-Lane where Colonel
Jack first began to live like a gentleman, off 'three-penny-worth of
boil'd beef, two-penny-worth of pudding, a penny brick (as they
call it, or loaf) and a whole pint of strong beer'.[44]

Supplying the metropolis was the country's biggest business.
Hardly a page of the *Tour* passes by without a mention of some
product of the particular locality which is destined to make the long
journey to London:

> This whole kingdom, as well the people, as the land, and even
> the sea, in every part of it, are employ'd to furnish something,
> and I may add, the best of every thing, to supply the city of
> London with provisions; I mean by provisions, corn, flesh, fish,
> butter, cheese, salt, fewel, timber etc. and cloths also; with every
> thing necessary for building, and furniture for their own use, or
> for trades.[45]

What an enormous co-operative effort was needed to supply the
great city with its fish alone. The seas off the south and east coasts
were thronged with innumerable small boats following the mackerel,
the herring or the cod as the seasons demanded. Most were salted
or smoked, but Londoners liked to have some of their fish fresh or
as nearly fresh as possible. In the summer the Thames boatmen
sailed down to Folkestone to buy the mackerel and then raced back

to market with them, 'with such a cloud of canvas, and up so high
that one would wonder their small boats cou'd bear it and should
not overset'.[46] But even such haste as this could not ensure the
arrival of fresh fish. The best and largest fish from the Essex coast
were sent away on horseback,[47] as were the salmon of Cumberland,
'notwithstanding the distance'. Changing horses frequently, the
carriers rode 'night and day without intermission . . . so that the fish
come very sweet and good to London, where the extraordinary price
they yield, being often sold at two shillings and sixpence to four shillings per pound, pay very well for the carriage'.[48] More prosaic, but
more essential, were places such as Farnham, 'the greatest corn-
market in England, London excepted',[49] or Croydon, another great
corn-market, 'but chiefly for oats and oatmeal, all for London still'.[50]
From such market-towns a continuous stream of river boats, pack-
horses and wagons took the country's produce to the markets of
London, to Billingsgate, Covent Garden, Leaden Hall, Fishstreet
Hill and to the two great London corn markets of Bear Key and
Queen Hith, 'monsters for magnitude, and not to be matched in the
world'.[51]

The sheer size and growth of London was the main reason for the
expansion of both agriculture and industry in provincial England.
But London was even more important as a promoter of employment
in distribution. As we have seen, Defoe felt that the more hands a
product passed through from raw material to final consumer, and
hence the more employment it created on its progress, the better
for the economy. In this respect the fact that London was the only
big city in England was a vital factor in explaining England's
prosperity.[52] So was the fact that 'the manufactures of England are
happily settled in different corners of the Kingdom'.[53] How convenient that God had decreed that coal should come all the way
from Newcastle or metal goods from Sheffield or the Black Country.
That division of England into a highland, pastoral, industrial north
and west and a lowland, arable south and east, which was to be
even more striking in the nineteenth century, guaranteed that the
demand of the great city in the south-east corner of the island would
create almost the maximum employment possible in such a small
country. The more remote any centre of production was from
London, the larger the number of pack-horses and carriers needed to
carry the year's output and the larger the number of inns fully
employed in catering for their needs at the end of each day's slow

travel.[54] The very congestion and physical size of the city was an advantage.[55] How many coachmen, porters and carters were necessary to carry people and goods from the outskirts of the city or the waterfront to the centre? An enormous number, but one that was made even bigger by the fact that each one of them could move only slowly in the crowded streets. From the edge of London, where gardeners grew vegetables for the city or girls cut hay to feed the city's vast population of horses, to the centre was, as Defoe gladly pointed out, far farther than in smaller cities. This led him to emphasize England's advantage in having only one big city. One reason for the poverty of Spain was the fact that the country had several small cities but no one great metropolis.

So far in our discussion, Defoe's economics have an element of unreality. Give the workman high wages which he will spend on food and manufactures to provide the demand to stimulate the employment to pay the high wages. Make sure that the final market is a long way from the centre of production and more people paid high wages will handle the product on the way. It all sounds a bit too easy; or does it? Defoe's formulae for a high level of employment and prosperity have a striking resemblance to the formulae suggested for countries with a high level of unemployment in the 1930s. It is better for people to work than not to work, so give them a job even if it is only digging a hole and filling it up again. Pay them wages which they will spend on things produced by other people and sooner or later everyone will be employed and the world will be a happier place. This was more or less what Defoe was saying, though it was the merchant or tradesman who was the key figure in his system, not the government.[56] The merchant employed the weaver and the spinner, bought food from the farmer, commissioned the carter and sold the goods in the final market. As long as he did all this in the most roundabout way possible and as long as each man in the chain got more for his work than it cost him in food and rent to do, then surely the system would work and England would remain the most prosperous country in the world with a population at once fully employed and well off?

Some people had doubts. Might not high food prices cancel out the benefits of high wages for the workman? Might not high wages cancel out the benefits of high food prices for the farmer? And surely the high wages of English workmen made the prices of English goods uncompetitive in foreign markets? This is in fact what most

of Defoe's contemporaries thought and the general clamour was to
fly in the face of the labour market and demand a legislative reduction in wages.[57] If English wages were to fall, then the price of
English manufactures would also fall. 'Cheapness causes consumption', so England would sell more of her goods abroad. This would
increase employment in England, swell the profits of clothiers and
exporters and reduce the poor rates. On the other hand, high wages
would lead to high prices which would reduce the level of exports
and employment and thus lead to increasing misery and high poor
rates. This pessimistic view regarded the potential market of the
English poor, except as consumers of cheap food and drink and as
occupiers of cheap houses, as very limited and not worth encouraging. Indeed, if you did pay the poor high wages, what happened?
They grew insolent, refused to work for so many days or hours, since
they could get what they wanted in less time, and if they did work
they spent their increased income on drink. High wages simply
meant less output, more drunkenness and led ultimately through a
reduction in exports to widespread unemployment.

Defoe, of course, disagreed with the general trend of such an
analysis. To lower wages would mean the necessity of lowering food
prices and hence rents, 'for the poor cannot earn little and spend
much, the end of that is starving and misery'.[58] Nevertheless, he
reluctantly accepted part of the analysis. He had no wish for wages
to rise continuously. He simply wanted them to remain at the
comparatively high level that they had reached in the early eighteenth century. Then, in his opinion, his analysis would be correct,
though he was the first to accept that many workers simply took
advantage of the new situation and did less work.[59] When wages
appeared to rise considerably above this level in the early 1720s he
was outspoken in his criticism of the way workmen and servants had
reacted.[60] Instead of improving themselves and their standard of
living, instead of putting money aside for a rainy day, they had
squandered their advantage in an orgy of drink, idleness and insolence. Such behaviour often led to their moral as well as economic
ruin, a process which Defoe illustrated by a discussion of the effects
of the lure of high wages on farm servants.[61] The high wages offered
to spinners and weavers attracted the girls from the dairy and the
men from the plough, leaving the farms without labour. But the
opportunity that should have been taken to save up for the future,
even to launch themselves on the road to social mobility, was not

taken. Once the new workers had got a little money they stopped work and spent what they had made on drink and revelry prior to returning to the village to debauch those who had remained. Nor is that the end of the story. A few months later the village is full of girls with big bellies who, after dropping their burden on the tender care of the parish, depart for London and swell the ever-increasing population of whores and thieves.

But, although Defoe disapproved of excess, he did not advocate a major reduction in wages. Sudden increases in wages as a result of a sudden increase in foreign orders could have the disturbing effects described above, effects that were made worse by the fact that, when foreign trade returned to its normal level, servants who had once been seduced by the easy life refused to return to the farms, even though there was now no longer employment to be had as spinners and weavers. But, as long as the wage level was fairly high[62] and was undisturbed by such once-for-all increases in the demand for labour, he anticipated none of the disastrous results predicted by his opponents. For he simply did not accept the analysis which said that high wages would lead to unemployment. He agreed that the prices of English exports, especially the most important export – woollen cloth – were higher than those of her competitors on the continent. But this was because English cloth was so much better. Quality for quality the English product was cheapest. In the case of high-quality goods, the basic maxim of contemporary economics, 'cheapness causes consumption', was just not true. It was true for 'the consumption of trash, and in the consumption of eatables and drinkables', but not for 'things of substance', such as English cloth. People abroad bought English cloth because it was good and because no one else could make such good cloth so cheaply.[63]

To a certain extent this was true. The best English cloth was indeed so good that, within limits, the high-class end of the European market continued to buy it, regardless of the existence of cheaper products. The same was true of other products such as Florentine silks. But this satisfactory condition only applied to a small part of the total European market and hence only to a small part of the English industry. The market for woollen cloth had undergone great changes in the seventeenth century and Defoe's view was now long out of date. There had been a swing in fashion away from the expensive, heavy felted broadcloth in which England had tradition- ally specialized to cheaper, lighter, more colourful cloth. And for

both types of cloth there had developed very much greater competition from producers on the continent.[64] The English clothiers had
managed to cope with the challenge of the change of fashion very
effectively. The old broadcloth industry had kept up its high standards but had been reduced in size, in view of the declining demand,
and was now largely confined to Wiltshire and neighbouring areas
in the West Country. Meanwhile, the other English cloth-producing
regions had switched to making the newer, lighter cloths known as
the 'New Draperies' and were doing very well at it.[65] This may have
been an admirable response to the challenge of a changing market
but Defoe did not like it, though he was quite prepared, when in an
optimistic mood, to praise the size of the industries in Devon, Norfolk
or the West Riding that produced such cloth.[66] He would have much
preferred England to be what she had been in the sixteenth century,
an exporter of high quality broadcloth (a material heavier than that
used for a modern overcoat). It was here that he thought England
had her advantage, in the accumulated skills of her weavers and
even more in God's bounty of the unique English wool which alone
could be used to make such cloth. As long as England kept this wool
for herself and prevented illegal export by the smugglers who
thronged the English coast, no other country could compete and
England could thrive for ever on the monopoly of the raw material.[67]
Despite much evidence to the contrary, Defoe always insisted that
no foreigners could produce such good cloth and no foreign wool
was good enough to make it. The only real danger came from
Ireland whose wool was as good as that of England and whose
workers had acquired English know-how but worked for very much
lower wages. For this reason he supported the legislation of 1698–99
which forbade the Irish to export woollen cloth and encouraged
them to produce linen instead.[68] He admitted it was hard on the
Irish but any other policy would have led eventually to disaster.
Freedom for the Irish producer would mean heavy unemployment
in England and ultimately mass emigration to Ireland bringing the
English workman down to the level of the low-paid Irish. England
should ideally use all the wool of both England and Ireland to
maintain her traditional high-quality industry.

Defoe thought that England had no such overwhelming advantage
in producing the New Draperies. They were made with coarser wool
which could be grown in Saxony and Spain as well as in England
and, since they were of lower quality, foreigners of less skill could

benefit from their lower wages to produce a material that to the ignorant was as good as the English and much cheaper. To make things even worse he thought that the New Draperies used less wool and employed less hands, thus reducing the potential income of sheep-farmers and raising unemployment, to say nothing of the danger of farmers with wool on their hands being tempted to smuggle it across the channel to France.[69]

In fact modern research as well as most contemporary opinion suggests that Defoe was wrong or deliberately blind in most of his views on the cloth trade.[70] To start with Defoe's last point. Most other writers agreed that the New Draperies employed more people at higher wages than the old broadcloth industry and it was indeed because it absorbed the unemployed that the new industry was welcomed by a normally conservative nation.[71] By the early eighteenth century few writers would have accepted that England had the monopoly of high-grade wool that she had enjoyed in the past. The good wools of Saxony and Spain were as good as those of England. Indeed, English wool had deteriorated in quality. Those very improvements in agriculture which had led to better pasture being available to so many English sheep had made much of the English wool longer and coarser, suitable for the New Draperies but no longer the short, fine wool used for broadcloth. One historian suggests that it was this change in the wool that led to the changes in the industry, clothiers being forced to make the best possible use of the wool that was available.[72] Again there seems little doubt that both the Dutch and the French were able to make as good a cloth as the English by the early eighteenth century and, indeed, Defoe himself was increasingly forced to admit the excellence of some of the French products which were rapidly driving English cloth from a number of their old markets.[73] All over Europe new manufacturing areas were springing up, producing excellent substitutes for English cloth. Defoe may have regretted this. He may have wished that foreigners would continue to buy large quantities of the old English broadcloth.[74] As it was, they preferred the new types of cloth and, if England wanted to sell in the European market, she simply had to produce the lighter fabrics and compete with Frenchmen, Dutchmen and Germans doing the same thing.

If we ignore or heavily discount Defoe's idea that England had some sort of monopoly position in producing cloth and concentrate on his other point, that quality for quality English cloth was cheapest despite the Englishman's higher wages, we may well be on stronger ground. In fact, without ever really getting to the point, he was talking about what was probably the most important difference between England and other countries in his day. This was the likelihood that the productivity of the English workman was higher than that of his foreign competitor. If this was true then much of what Defoe discussed could be explained in a more direct way. Higher productivity would explain why higher wages could be paid, why Englishmen were better-off, why the whole of Defoe's circular society in which high wages bought goods at high prices did not just fizzle out as one cancelled the other.

When Defoe suggests that Englishmen could produce more in a given time than foreigners he concentrates his attention on the workman himself rather than on the organization of which he is a part. The English workman was a more effective producer partly because he was more skilful. But it went rather farther than that. The Englishman, though perhaps lazy, found his task more congenial and worked harder and faster than the foreigner when he did work. The reason for this greater application seems to have been because he was happier and stronger as a result of being better fed.[75] And of course he was better fed because he was paid higher wages.[76] In view of studies on the economic effects of undernourishment it would be interesting to test this hypothesis.[77] If Englishmen really did work harder because they ate more and had a more varied diet it would help to explain why they were able to compete so effectively with their low-paid rivals.

Defoe was prepared to admit that there were exceptions to his observation that quality for quality English products were always the cheapest. If the wage differential was too great not even English strength and skill could overcome it. No English workman could hope to compete on level terms with the workmen of Asia. And yet they were increasingly forced to try to do so as the markets of Europe were flooded with more and more Indian and Chinese silks and cotton textiles. Defoe estimated that wages in Asia were only twopence a day, about one-ninth of a contemporary English labourer's wages.[78] Englishmen certainly could not work nine times as hard as Indians. Indian goods therefore sold well in Europe because they were attractive, skilfully made and very cheap, even after the East India Company had taken its large profits. But at what a cost. Defoe invites his readers to imagine how terribly the Indian poor must live and, even worse, how terribly the English poor would live if they were forced to work for the same wages in an attempt to increase sales. The answer in a nationalistic age was quite simple. The English workman must be protected. In the end he was, despite the well-argued and well-financed defence of the East India Company.[79] After a long debate in which Defoe played his part, retained imports of most Asian textiles were prohibited, thus incidentally giving a boost to the struggling and technically backward English cotton textile industry which expanded to try and satisfy demand.

In the end this new industry was to be able to overcome the wage differential between England and India by a revolution in its organization and technology. And it is in terms of the organization of industry and its technology rather than the nutrition of the workers that productivity is normally discussed. In Defoe's day, the benefits of the division of labour were already well appreciated,[80] and the period saw a considerable quickening in the pace of technical change in English industry. This was particularly marked in mining and metallurgy but could be found in practically all parts of the economy.[81] Labour-saving devices, such as the knitting-frame and the ribbon mill, were being introduced into the textile industry, and the cloth industry as a whole had undergone considerable rationalization in its organization and methods of distribution in the course of the seventeenth century.[82] Such changes would almost certainly have increased the average productivity of the workers in the industry far more than could the difference between their diet and that of foreigners.

Defoe's attitude to such change was ambiguous, to say the least. One maxim which he often repeated was that the English were not inventors but were great improvers of other people's inventions.[83] This was certainly true of earlier periods, for example the late sixteenth century, when a very wide range of continental technology was introduced and adapted to English skills and needs. It was then, for instance, that the New Draperies themselves were introduced from the Low Countries.[84] It was the time when such diverse industries as glass, paper and copper-smelting were first established in England, nearly always with the aid of foreign workmen and often foreign capital as well.[85] But in Defoe's own lifetime it was far less true that the English were simply borrowers of other people's technology. New industries, such as diamond-cutting, were still introduced from the continent, but most of the technological changes in the mining and metallurgical industries were of English origin and gave a foretaste of that remarkable period of English invention and innovation associated with the Industrial Revolution. Late seventeenth-century England was in fact seething with new ideas. This was, after all, the time of Newton, Boyle and Locke, when English science and philosophy were respected, admired and imitated all over Europe. Scientists, both individually and in the forum of the Royal Society, took much interest in the problems of industry and some of their ideas were developed by practical men.[86] Even more, the spirit of the Royal Society, with its emphasis on observation and experiment and above all its insistence on the possibility of change, had had its effect. It was now felt that problems could be solved and a host of greater and lesser men rose to the challenge with projects which they were eager to foist on a not normally very critical public.[87] Some such projects were bizarre, others were simply fraudulent, but many were quite genuinely useful and were to give England a considerable technological lead over other countries.

Defoe ignores much of this change. In the *Tour* there are many surprising gaps in what appears at first glance to be a superb description of the economy of England. Industrial areas in which cloth manufacture was not very important, such as the West Midlands,[7] are virtually left out.[88] Birmingham, the most rapidly developing industrial town in the country, is hardly mentioned[89] and the reader has to be content with one short paragraph to describe the vast Northumberland coal-mining industry.[90] Nowhere is there much emphasis on new technology. The result is a very distorted picture in which the cloth industry and the distribution of goods to and from London get a considerably greater prominence than they should.[91] They were the two most important aspects of domestic trade and industry, certainly, but not as important as Defoe makes them out to be and relatively not as important in 1724 as they had been a hundred or even fifty years before.

There are several reasons for this distortion in Defoe's economic reporting. The first is the obvious fact that he knew the south and the east of the country best. He wrote his descriptions of these parts first and clearly got bored with the project as he went on. Once he gets past the West Riding he covers the rest of the north of England at indecent speed. Also, as G. D. H. Cole pointed out some time ago,[92] Defoe was far more interested in distribution than in the means of production and it is this aspect of the economy that gets most emphasis. Industry in any case was not so visible in the early eighteenth century as it is now. Conducted for the most part in small workshops or the worker's own home it did not have the same visual impact as a modern factory or refinery, whereas distribution was bound to be observed by the man on horseback all the time. In the inn at night it would be the merchant or carter with whom Defoe shared his meal, not that immobile and socially insignificant person, the industrial worker.

Defoe also saw what he wanted to see, and hence his emphasis on the cloth industry to the exclusion of practically all other sectors of industry. Such an emphasis is clearly implicit in Defoe's historical approach to economics. In the past the cloth industry had been virtually the only important industry in England. It was also implicit in his conviction of England's monopoly advantages in this industry and his belief that it was the cloth industry alone which would be able to maintain the very satisfactory economic position which England had achieved in the world.

Such distortions apart, Defoe had other reasons to play down the degree of technological change. As we shall see later in this chapter, the apparently optimistic, forward-looking Defoe feared the very changes which were to make the English economy more powerful in the future.[93] The reason for these fears is only too familiar to Englishmen today. Defoe feared change because he believed it would lead to redundancy and unemployment. He was convinced, probably rightly, that he lived in a world where the level of trade was stable. He glimpsed vaguely that England was able to compete effectively in such a world because the English workman or woman had higher productivity than their European counterparts, but he feared a situation where that productivity became even higher. The extra flow of goods, even though they might be cheaper, would not sell or not all of them would. So, just as in his discussion of high wages, he preferred the *status quo*.

As we have seen, contemporary writers saw foreign trade as a means of providing a market for the products of English manufacture and thus as a means of maintaining the level of employment in England. But foreign trade was also the means by which the merchant could earn foreign exchange to finance England's imports. Or, to look at the matter the other way round, England's imports enabled foreign countries to earn the foreign exchange necessary to finance their purchases of England's exports. Indeed some writers, including Defoe on occasion, saw this as the only function of imports. Writing in the *Mercator* he remarked that the silk trade 'is useful and advantageous as it is a return for and encourages the exportation of the woollen manufacture, and no otherwise'.[94] This was rather a limited viewpoint and the economist could normally see many benefits in imports, apart from their role in enabling other countries to buy England's cloth. Wool and oil from Spain, silk from Italy, even elephants' teeth from Africa provided raw materials for industries which employed the poor.[95] Even if the goods were re-exported without alteration they were bound to pass through many hands and thus add to employment. And bringing the goods to England employed ships and seamen, thus not only providing jobs but also maintaining the supply of ships and sailors to protect England in time of war.[96] None the less, in the last analysis, Defoe did not welcome imports and he was proud to point out that one of England's great advantages was that she, of all countries, had the least need for imported goods because of her own abundant resources.[97]

For imports, although they obviously had their uses, had many disadvantages. They had a debauching effect on both rich and poor. This was of course their main attraction to most people who revelled in the enormous increase of goods available to them as a result of the expansion of trade in the seventeenth century. They were now able to buy the products of almost the whole world in the shops which had sprung up in nearly every town. But, neither the moralist nor the economist in Defoe could really approve of this flow of luxuries which had so expanded the Englishman's range of choice. He agreed with Sir William Petty that most imports were 'superfluities tending to luxury and sin',[98] though he had to admit that some such 'superfluities' had now become necessities, if only because they provided employment for the poor.

The normal objection to imports was that they had to be paid for. An historian has described the seventeenth and early eighteenth centuries as a period of import-led growth where the new appetites of Englishmen for the products of the world provided the impetus for foreign trade and the main economic problem was to maintain the exports to pay for them, a problem solved for the most part by selling such luxuries at high prices to the European mainland.[99] Defoe would probably have accepted such an analysis but, without the benefit of hindsight, he could never be complacent about

England's ability to pay for her greed. It was alarm about this which led Defoe and practically all his contemporaries to spend so much time worrying about the balance of trade. The main point was that foreign trade provided the specie and bullion which, when minted, provided the cash in which high wages were paid.[100] England had no gold or silver mines worth the name so that the only precious metals available to mint were those already in the country, in the form of coin, bullion or plate, or those that could be brought in through foreign trade. Because coins got lost or worn and because home trade and population were slowly expanding, it was therefore necessary for England to have a balance in her favour in foreign trade, a balance paid ultimately in coin and bullion which could maintain the stock of money.[101] In the absence of such a balance England's cash would ultimately dwindle away to nothing. There were no printing-presses turning out banknotes of small denomination, as there are now.

Defoe accepted this analysis, though he rarely discussed it in much detail. This was simply because the need for a favourable balance of trade was accepted by most economic writers of his day and it was therefore not really necessary to discuss it.[102] What was discussed were the finer points of the doctrine; such as whether it was necessary to have a favourable balance with each individual country or simply with the world as a whole. Most writers, including Defoe, realized the impracticability of a surplus with everyone. Nevertheless, when discussing trade, Defoe, like most of his contemporaries, tended to praise those trades where it was thought England had a surplus and condemn those where she had a deficit. Nearly all writers thought the best trade was with the Mediterranean, particularly with Spain, a trade where England not only received a surplus of silver drawn from Spain's South American empire but also exported manufactured goods in return for raw materials which employed the poor. This was the ideal towards which the ingenuity of economists and government alike was turned.

By the time that Defoe started writing on economic matters, England had already adopted a very complex system of controlling trade. The aim was to maximize the benefits that England and her empire received from foreign trade, whilst at the same time attempting to ensure that the balance of trade remained favourable to England. Most of this system of control was enshrined in what were called the Navigation Laws.[103] Very simply, these laws stated that, with a few exceptions, all trade between England and her American and West Indian colonies had to be carried in British ships and that the trade between the colonies and Europe had to go *via* England. Further regulations governed the trade between England and other areas. An elaborate system of check and counter-check was developed to ensure that the Navigation Laws were obeyed, in which colonial governors, customs officials and the navy all had a part to play. The navy, in particular, stood to gain by enforcing the law, since half of all goods carried illegally were considered as prize goods to be shared between the officers of the ship which seized them.[104] As a result, although there was of course some smuggling, the risks of financial loss were too great for wholesale evasion of the law and trade was largely forced into this somewhat unnatural pattern.[105]

The Navigation Laws were much admired by Defoe. They had led to a great expansion in the size of the British merchant fleet and, since the routes taken were of necessity somewhat circuitous, each ship was more fully employed than would have been the case if trade between America and Europe had been direct. The fact that American goods had to be landed in England before shipment to European ports meant that employment was created, not only in the double handling involved, but also in the refining and alteration of the goods themselves. And the fact that English merchants handled the re-export of these goods to Europe meant that their profits swelled the export earnings of England, thus helping to maintain a favourable balance of trade.

In the 1690s further improvements were made in the system.[106] The government's wartime demands for increased taxation led to a considerable increase in the level of the customs tariff. But duties were not raised all round. Those on exports remained low, or were even removed, whilst duties on imports were raised, sometimes to prohibitive levels. At the same time trade with France was prohibited altogether. The result was obviously to make the whole system much more protective and exclusive. New industries grew up to take advantage of this protectionist legislation, whilst those former French imports which could not be made in England had either to be smuggled or sought from elsewhere. It was in this period that port began to replace claret as the drink of the wealthy and cheap Dutch gin to replace cheap French brandy as the solace of the poor.

By the early eighteenth century the aim of the legislators to create

an imperial system of trade, in which the English merchant, manufacturer and workman had a privileged position, had been largely
achieved. England produced textiles, hardware, coal and grain
which were sold on the continent and in the colonies. The southern
mainland colonies produced tobacco, the bulk of which after being
processed or at least handled in England, was sold by English merchants in the markets of Europe. The West Indian colonies had a
similar but much more valuable trade in sugar. New England and
the Central Atlantic colonies produced foodstuffs and caught fish
which were sold to the southern colonies, who concentrated so
heavily on tobacco and sugar that they were unable to feed themselves. Meanwhile the monopolist joint-stock East India Company
sent to England the products of India, Persia and the Indian Ocean
to be once again redistributed in Europe.

Much as Defoe admired this remarkable system he was aware of
one potentially weak link. The main hope for expansion of English
commerce lay in the development of the complex system of inter-
locking triangular trades in the Atlantic. But the whole of the
Atlantic trade depended ultimately on West Africa. As Defoe
succinctly put it in a *Review* of 1713:[107]

> The case is as plain as cause and consequence: Mark the climax.
> No African trade, no negroes; no negroes no sugars, gingers,
> indicoes etc; no sugars etc no islands; no islands no continent;
> no continent no trade . . .

Not only was the African trade the key to the whole system but it
was in itself potentially the most profitable trade of all.[108] English
merchants exported baubles of little or no intrinsic value and
received in return ivory, gold and, above all, slaves. No other trade
returned so much for so little. The slaves were shipped by the middle
passage to the West Indies and increasingly the tobacco colonies,
where they not only created the demand for food which provided
the northern mainland colonies with an outlet for their surplus, but
also of course provided the labour to produce the sugar and tobacco
sent to England. The whole of American trade therefore depended
on an adequate supply of slaves. Defoe thought that such a supply
could only be maintained if the existing Royal African Company
had a monopoly of the business. Only a powerful company could
maintain the forts and men necessary to control what was often a
potentially explosive situation in Africa. Only a company could be

required by its charter to maintain a steady flow of slaves at a reasonable price to the American colonies. Slaves died fast, particularly in the sugar islands, and a check to the supply would soon bring the whole imperial edifice tumbling down.[109]

Unfortunately the company on which Defoe pinned his hopes had had a very chequered financial and commercial history.[110] Chartered in 1672, it had originally paid reasonable dividends to its often distinguished shareholders. As late as 1688 it was in good shape. One of the wisest things the often foolish James II did was to sell out his share after his ignominious flight from England. For in the 1690s the Company began to run into trouble. Over-expansion of the supply of both sugar and tobacco had brought their prices tumbling down throughout the second half of the seventeenth century with the result that planters were often unable to pay for the slaves supplied. The bad debts incurred forced the Company to borrow more money at high rates and threatened it with bankruptcy. The threat came closer with an all-out attack on the Company's ships by French privateers operating from French west coast ports and the West Indies. All this might have been bearable if the Company had been able to maintain its monopoly. But monopoly itself, especially those established by Stuart charter, was under fire in the 1690s. As a result the government tended to turn a blind eye to the rapid increase of interlopers who had far lower overheads and were able to make profits out of the same business which was ruining the official monopolists. In 1698 a short-term solution to what was becoming an absurd situation was evolved. The interlopers were now to be styled Separate Traders and to pay an export duty of ten per cent to the official company to help pay for the maintenance of its forts in Africa. But this was to be only a passing phase. From 1708 onwards the Company was once again under fire.

For years Defoe tried to defend the Company's monopoly position. Using all the polemic at his disposal he attacked the Separate Traders who by competing with the Company had educated the Africans in the arts of commerce, thus driving the price of English goods down and the price of slaves up. He proved beyond all doubt that the slave supply could only be maintained by an exclusive company bound to ship a minimum of so many slaves across the Atlantic each year. Separate Traders would only keep the forts in good repair and ship slaves when it was profitable for them to do so. A run of bad years would stop the supply of slaves, with the inevitable disastrous consequences. But Defoe for all his fire (possibly paid for by the Company) was fighting a losing battle. The Company was doomed, and in 1712 the trade was thrown wide open. In the years that followed it would have been hard to sustain the argument that in the absence of monopoly the supply would be inadequate, as the merchants of Liverpool and Bristol rose to the challenge and made their fortunes in what under the new conditions was clearly a very profitable business.

Whoever ran the African trade, whether Company or Separate Traders, Defoe had to admit that it was an admirable business from the point of view of the balance of trade, whether the visible signs were the increased minting of guineas made from West African gold or the re-export of the sugar and tobacco produced by African slaves. Other trades were far less satisfactory, and Defoe, like most contemporary economists, worried about such areas of the world which took English silver and not English manufactured goods in return for their products.

One of the worst regions was the Baltic.[111] It was impossible to sell sufficient fish and cloth in the Baltic to pay for the huge imports of forest goods, iron and naval stores that England bought from the area. Nor was there much compensation in re-exports since England herself used most of these imports. The matter was made worse by the fact that all these materials were of the utmost strategic importance and their supply could easily be cut off by an enemy gaining control of the narrow waters of the Sound through which virtually all Baltic goods had to travel.

Defoe reluctantly had to admit that, although England's exports to the Baltic had increased in his lifetime, the chances of covering the deficit were not very good. For England's major competitor in Baltic trade, the Dutch republic, had enormous advantages. As the major centre of both the fish and grain trades, as the biggest buyer of timber and naval stores and as an equally well-endowed supplier of colonial and exotic goods, Holland had little problem in maintaining her strong position in Baltic trade.[112] And even if Holland had had a deficit in this particular trade it would have made little difference. For contemporaries thought that a country like Holland, which seemed to rely almost entirely for her wealth on buying and selling, did not have to worry very much about the balance of trade. Since Holland sold again at a profit what she bought and consumed little of the goods she traded in, she was like a shopkeeper who, so long as he made a profit, had no need to bother about the supply of money.[113]

Such an analysis was a travesty of the real Dutch situation. The Dutch had probably the highest level of consumption in Europe.[114] But there were not very many Dutchmen. England seemed to pose a very different problem to Defoe and his contemporaries. If England could not sell more in the Baltic then she must buy less. Where else in the world could iron, forest goods and naval stores be bought? The answer was obvious. In England's own colonies on the mainland of North America. The only problems were that they were rather short of people and a very long way away.

As might be expected, Defoe was able to suggest ways to solve such problems. In 1704 he dismissed the fact that shortage of people in the colonies made labour dear by remarking that if hands were scarce we could always send more from Africa.[115] In general Defoe was an advocate of increasing the population of the northern colonies, both as a means of extending the market for English goods and as a bulwark against the danger of French encroachment from the Mississippi and the St Lawrence. But he normally advocated emigration as the means and not slavery, an institution which was not very well suited to either lumbering or the production of iron. The problem of distance could be solved either by accepting New England goods duty-free or alternatively by paying a bounty on them.[116] A third idea which he put forward in 1728 was to subsidize the commanders of the ships carrying naval stores from New England by a ten per cent duty on all English goods sent to the colonies. The torrent of complaint which might have been expected was dismissed. 'The colonies will never complain of such a duty, because 'tis in a manner paid to themselves, and is but taking the money out of one pocket, and putting it into the other.'[117]

Defoe's suggestions to remove England's dangerous dependence on the Baltic for naval stores were fairly commonplace in his time. It was an obvious problem and his remedies were the obvious remedies of the day. Some such solutions were tried.[118] But in fact none of the apparently tempting offers did much to overcome the enormous competitive advantage held by Norway and the Baltic in carrying such bulky goods. And in any case many contemporaries preferred the disadvantage of reliance on the Baltic to the danger of making the colonies too strong. As they were, they performed a valuable function in England's trading system. But if they expanded

they would withdraw labour from what already seemed an England
with too little labour and too high wages. Worse still, they might use
their strength to declare their independence or to ally themselves
with another colonial power. After all, most of the colonies were born
of political or religious dissension.

As we shall see, Defoe in his more pessimistic moods was worried
himself about the level of population in England. He was also aware
that further expansion of the sugar and tobacco colonies in the
present glutted state of the market would pose more problems than
it solved. None the less his usual view was that more and bigger
colonies were a good idea, not only, as in this example, to provide
much-needed strategic goods, but also to consume the products of
England. Defoe considered the possibility of American independence
to be totally unrealistic.[119] Because of the colonies' position in the
English trading system and because of their privileged markets under
the Navigation Laws they could not afford to be independent.
England had only to prohibit the import of mainland food to the
West Indies and replace the supply by provisions from Ireland for
the whole New England economy to collapse. And no other metro-
politan country could replace England, since no other country had
sufficient population in the West Indies to absorb the North American surplus of food.[120] The dangers dismissed, Defoe concluded that
the only way to protect the colonies in the long run was to make
them strong enough to defend themselves. The colonies did get
strong enough to defend themselves, but they were never able to
replace the Baltic and Norway as suppliers of England's vital naval
stores.

The two other areas where England traditionally had a deficit on
her balance of trade posed rather different problems. The first was
the east, which since time immemorial had absorbed European silver
and for the most part neglected European goods. One reason was
that the Indians in particular put a much higher value on silver than
did the Europeans. In some years a good profit could be made
simply by shipping silver out and gold back since the ratio between
the two metals was different in the two areas.[121] The other reason
was that the oriental simply did not want very much of what the
European could produce. Most goods they could themselves produce
better and more cheaply, drawing as they did on a huge supply of
very cheap skilled labour. The result was that Europe had an enormous balance of trade deficit with the east. This fact had worried

those Englishmen who were not enjoying the reputedly high profits
of the East India Company ever since the trade began in 1601.
Whenever for any reason the English economy was in trouble, such
as in the 1620s and the 1690s, the debate came to a head. By the
time that Defoe started writing, the argument had become somewhat stereotyped. Advocates of the Company admitted that they
shipped very considerable quantities of silver to the east. But
this silver came not from England, but from the continent – in
particular from the great bullion markets of Amsterdam and Genoa.
The reason that the Company was able to acquire silver in this way
was because the goods they bought at low prices in India, they re-
exported at very high prices to Europe. Such a business not only
enabled them to acquire the bullion required to keep the trade
going at all but also brought back to England much more bullion
as profit. So the oriental trades, far from being a drain on England's
specie, actually increased it as few other trades could do.

Except in a very polemic mood Defoe accepted this analysis,
which was almost certainly true.[122] His main objection to the East
India Company was to the nature of their imports rather than to
the necessity of carrying them on their business by shipping silver.[123]
In the first half of the seventeenth century both the English and
Dutch East India Companies had made most of their returns in what
had been the staples of oriental trade since the middle ages – pepper,
spices, jewels, dyes and saltpetre. But falling prices of most of these
goods and changes in European fashion led them to alter completely
their pattern of imports by the end of the century. By the 1690s silk
and cotton textiles dominated the trade from Asia to England.[124]
Such imports of course upset the Defovian system whether their
final point of sale was in England itself or in Europe, since they
competed directly with English cottons and silks and acted as substitutes for woollens. But although prohibition in England could and
did have satisfactory results, prohibition of their re-export abroad
was a different matter.[125] For the European market had already
become debauched by these oriental fripperies and if the English
did not supply them, then the Dutch would.

Indeed, Defoe considered prohibition of the sale of any commodity to a foreign market to be poor economic thinking, with the
single exception of raw materials of which England had a monopoly.[126] The only important example of this was his consistent
approval of the prohibition of the export of English wool. No other

exports should be prohibited since whatever England did not export or re-export some other country would. For this reason Defoe's attitude to France, the third area where England was traditionally supposed to have a deficit on her balance of trade, was rather different from that of many of his contemporaries. Most writers thought that England had a serious deficit on trade with France, buying a far greater value of French wines, brandies, luxuries and other goods than the French bought of English cloth and metals.[127] Partly as a result of this, but also because of the wars, trade between the two countries was prohibited on several occasions from 1678 onwards.

Defoe thought that prohibition had been necessary in the 1690s.[128] French tariffs had been progressively raised against English goods whilst French wines, brandies and industrial goods continued to pour into England. The result in his opinion was not only that England helped to maintain the level of employment in France but that a great flow of silver went across the Channel to help the French pay for the war.

But Defoe thought it absurd to continue the prohibition in the early eighteenth century simply because England was once again at war with France. The short period of peace from 1697 to 1702 had demonstrated that matters had changed considerably and that in fact it was now England, not France, who gained by the trade. The English gentleman had been prevented from drinking French wines for several years, unless he paid inflated prices to the smuggler, and so had developed a taste for the now much improved wines of Portugal. So long as a differential duty was kept in Portugal's favour the change of taste would become permanent, even if the prohibition was removed. Some very expensive French wine would be imported but the bulk would come from Portugal, whose empire took off a far greater value in cloth than she received for her wines and paid the balance in that most desirable of commodities, Brazilian gold. Other even more satisfactory changes had occurred in the course of the wars. Huguenot refugees had introduced new branches of several industries from France, including hat-making, fine glass, white paper and silk-making, all of which had flourished in the absence of French competition. These industries were not yet capable of survival if the trade between the two countries was completely opened. But, so long as there were sufficiently high import duties, they would be able to develop until they no longer needed any

protection at all. With so many former French imports now supplied
at home or from areas with which England had favourable trading
relationships, Defoe was quite certain that the selling power of
English cloth would ensure a favourable balance of trade with
France if the prohibition was removed but high duties on imports
were retained. With his usual confidence in the English cloth industry, he ignored the threat of competition both in France itself and
in third markets from the rapidly improving French industry.[129]

In 1704 Defoe summed up his views on the subject of trade in
wartime in a classic statement of his particular brand of what was
later called mercantilism:

> If it be to our gain, it must be to their loss; and if we are, as by
> the declaration of war, by all means to annoy them both by sea
> and land, let us trade with them. We shall beggar them by it,
> and all men will allow that's as quick a way of beating them, as
> to fight them.[130]

Prohibition under conditions where England stood to gain from the
trade was absurd. If the French could not buy English cloth, corn
or metals direct they would buy them from other suppliers or would
buy English goods re-exported by the Dutch or the Italians. The
Dutch, in Defoe's view, only supported the war because they were
able to keep an open trade with the enemy.[131]

What good did it do the English merchant if the Dutch made
enormous profits by re-selling English goods? What good did it do
the English shipmaster and the sailors he employed if Dutch ships
carried English goods to the Texel only to send them straight on to
France? Surely the English soldier lying dead in the Flanders mud
would have been happier had the bullet that killed him provided
employment for the miners of Derbyshire rather than of some foreign
land, or the man that fired it had his belly full of corn from Sussex
rather than the Baltic? And what was the net result for England?
The exceptional prices paid by the French to the Dutch or Italian
go-between tended to reduce the total world market for English
goods and hence to put a strain on the balance of trade. France with
a population of twenty million was by far the biggest market in
western Europe and the English were not getting the benefit of it.

Political requirements forced Defoe to go much further in promoting an open trade with France towards the end of the war. In
order to seal the peace, the Tory ministry which employed him

was determined to conclude a commercial treaty with France which would incorporate a far more liberal view of trade than that which Defoe advocated. In essence, the treaty would have returned to the situation existing in 1664 when duties in both countries were relatively low, long before the new industries had been established in England and before the rapid growth of the French woollen industry. The Defoe of five years earlier would never have approved such lenient terms. But now in 1713 it was Defoe who had to defend the treaty in the last numbers of the *Review* and in a new paper, *Mercator*.[132] Given his habitual method of economic reasoning he was in a somewhat uncomfortable position. For now he had to prove that even before the wars England had gained from her trade with France, despite having often stated the opposite in earlier numbers of the *Review*.[133] The result was some quite incredible statistical juggling.[134] He also had to exaggerate the strength of the new industries to suggest that they would not collapse under free or relatively free French competition. He had to belittle the French cloth industry even more than was his wont. He had to argue that even if the sale of Portuguese wines in England declined they would still buy as much of our cloth. And so on. Defoe tried hard, but it is clear that his heart was not in it; in fact he was also writing anonymously and persuasively for the other side.[135] And in the end he failed. A large Tory minority, convinced by the arguments of Defoe's opponents in the *Guardian* and the *British Merchant*, joined the Whigs and threw out the treaty.[136]

In general, as we have seen, Defoe's view of trade policy, like that of virtually all of his contemporaries, was to try to expand exports and encourage the development of import-substitute industries. In the course of his lifetime England had very considerable success in reducing the imports of goods which could equally well be made at home. Whether it was the trash sent out to West Africa to be exchanged for slaves and gold or the gin which was degenerating the poor at home, what had formerly been bought in the Low Countries was now being made in England. English industry was becoming increasingly diversified. But expanding exports, despite Defoe's optimistic assumptions about the English cloth industry, was a very different matter.

The European economy of his day was in a period of stagnation which we can now see with hindsight lay between two remarkable periods of expansion. But from 1620 to 1730 or 1740 a great gloom

hung over much of European commerce. The main stimulus to
economic development before modern times has been an increase
in population, preferably in conjunction with an increase in the
productivity of the land. This period of over a century sees very little
population growth anywhere in Europe, even in England. The
population of some countries, including France, actually fell. Nor
was there much improvement in agriculture, except in England
and the Low Countries. The result was a stabilization of national
incomes, usually at very low levels *per capita*. In such conditions the
demand for goods in international trade was unlikely to grow
rapidly, especially when so much of the available purchasing power
was siphoned off in taxes to pay for the wars which occupied much
of Europe between 1680 and 1720.

The reactions of most countries to such an unpromising world
were similar to the policies adopted by England and supported by
Defoe. If world trade was only growing slowly they would fight to
keep what they already had and if possible increase their share at
the expense of other countries. The situation was similar to that of
the 1930s. Most countries strove to increase their exports and restrict
their imports, building up often with state assistance import-substitute industries at home. The French were perhaps the most
successful. Colbert and those who followed him introduced a wide-
ranging programme of legislation in a determined attempt to expand
French industry, trade and shipping. Navigation laws were passed
which were similar to those of England, if not even tougher. New
industries were developed, often by foreign immigrants who were
begged, bribed or blackmailed to move their homes to France. The
results were impressive. In the Mediterranean the French built up a
large merchant fleet which successfully challenged the English and
Dutch. In the Atlantic it was the more fertile French sugar islands,
especially St Dominique, which were now beginning to dominate
the market. And at home an increasing share of the market previously supplied by English, Dutch and Italian industries was now
being supplied by the French themselves. Other countries pursued
similar policies. The Virginian planter discovered that much of the
European tobacco market had disappeared by the early eighteenth
century as government after government created tobacco monopolies
fed by home-grown tobacco.[137] Similar developments were taking
place in the cloth industry as states like Prussia fostered high-cost
textile industries behind equally high tariff barriers. Even those

countries which had little success in developing their own industries were able to protect the trade and industry they already had. The great Spanish empire remained closed to direct trade from the thrusting economies of northern Europe. All trade to Spanish America was supposed to go *via* Spain in Spanish ships and most of it did, despite the existence of various loopholes such as the English and Dutch entrepôts in Jamaica and Curaçao.[138]

Defoe was aware of all this. He might try and run down the French achievement, but when he was really honest with himself he was prepared to admit their successes. He might stress the quality and selling power of English cloth but he was too close to government sources not to know that English cloth exports did not grow at all during most of the period when he was writing.[139] In particular he saw that expansion of exports to Europe was very difficult to achieve. It was therefore on the extra-European world that he based his hopes. There is hardly a place in the settled or unsettled world that he does not advocate as a market for English woollens in one or other of his works. If only the Czar of Muscovy would order that all his subjects should wear English stockings or we could establish a trade to China for English broadcloth and stockings.[140] And what about Ethiopia? It is the only country in the world known to Europeans with whom Europe has no trade. And yet we know they wear clothes and have gold, copper and emeralds. Perfect for the English balance of trade.[141] If the Ethiopians wore clothes many other people did not, and Defoe often bemoans the failure of the English to civilize the natives. He was particularly impressed with the achievement of the Portuguese in this respect. The Indians of Brazil had been instructed by the Jesuits in the art of covering themselves and now there was a large and growing market for English cloth.[142] One fantasy which often recurs is for civilization to operate a pincer-movement in West Africa. In the north the Barbary robbers should be pushed back from the coast into the mountains and replaced by civilized people with the same cultured tastes and effective demand as the former inhabitants of the region, the much-admired Carthaginians. In the south a civilizing movement should start on the Gulf of Guinea. In the end civilization in the form of European clothes would sweep from the mangrove swamps of the West Coast across the savannah, the desert and the High Atlas to the Mediterranean. Millions of Africans, now ashamed of their nakedness, would regularly demand suits of bays and English stockings.[143]

Defoe's hopes for English trade in Asia and Africa border on the fantastic. But he is at his most serious and persuasive when he is urging the development of the South American market. Throughout the War of Spanish Succession he urged the government to take the war into the West Indies, to seize the treasure fleets on which both the French and Bourbon Spanish governments depended and to take advantage of the clauses in the Treaty of Grand Alliance which stated that the English and Dutch could seize territory on the South American mainland.[144] His alarm at England's failure to use her naval superiority grew as the French began to build up their commercial power on the west coast and in the West Indies.[145] Once entrenched they would be very difficult to remove. The problem of course was that there were two rival kings of Spain. To seize territory from the enemy was thus at the same time to seize territory from friends. In any case Defoe felt that to conquer lands already settled by the Spaniards would never be acceptable in Spain whoever ruled.[146] As a good nationalist himself he had little hope of the Spanish people accepting anything more than a token inroad by the English into the direct trade with South America. But in fact it would not be necessary to clash with Spain. In the south of the continent there were vast unsettled lands which in Defoe's imagination were ideal as a site for an English colony. Here were well-watered plains where Englishmen could settle and thrive, growing their own food, provisioning ships, trading into Spanish territory along the Plate, Parana and Paraguay rivers and providing a vast new market for English cloth which they could pay for with the silver and gold which literally lay on the ground in the mountains of the interior. It was the promise of such a settlement which led Defoe to support the South-Sea Company which was chartered in 1711.[147] We have seen earlier how little Defoe actually knew about the geography of Patagonia and Aracania, let alone of Ethiopia.[148] It is some measure of his desperate view of the future possibilities of expansion that he should continue to advocate for more than twenty years such fundamentally unrealistic schemes. And indeed as he grew older, although he continued to press his fantasies on his public, he was becoming less and less optimistic about the chances of extending English export markets.[149] By 1729 in *An Humble Proposal* he accepted that growth had reached a standstill, as a result of foreign competition and foreign prohibitions, and would soon decline if nothing was done. When he asked himself the question whether trade was growing or decreasing he answered, 'we are rather in a state of ballance between both, a middle between the extreams; I hope we are not much declin'd, and, I fear, we are not much advanc'd.'[150] Pride or rhetoric sometimes led him to deny this stable situation, but it is clear from the whole trend of his economics in the 1720s that he feared decline despite the fact that English cloth was sold everywhere, 'all the world wears it, all the world desires it, and all the world almost envies us the glory and advantage of it'.[151]

Unable to expand abroad, Defoe turned his attention to the home market. Here he was able to give full rein to his rage and frustration. For what did he find? Instead of spending their money on the product that the whole world coveted, the vicious, unthinking English were buying silks, cottons and linens instead of woollens, thus threatening employment in England's major industry and thus of course threatening to bring down the whole shaky structure of the Defovian economy.[152] How blind could people be?

> We see our trade sick and languishing, and our poor starving before our eyes; and know that we our selves are the only cause of it, are yet so obstinately and unalterably averse to our own manufacture, and fond of novelties and trifles, that we will not wear our own goods, but will at any hazard make use of things foreign to us, the labour and advantage of strangers, pagans, negroes, or any kind of people rather than our own.[153]

In fact, as Defoe knew very well, and was indeed to praise in its place, fewer of these goods were produced by pagans and negroes and more by the British as time went on. But he would never accept that other textiles could be substitutes for woollens and create a permanent change in the structure of employment in England. Cottons and linens could never be more than a backwater which was able to absorb some of England's underemployed resources:

> As if an upstart, and in it self trifling manufacture, however increas'd by the corruption of our people's humour and fancy, could be an equivalent to the grand manufacture of wool in England, which is the fund of our whole commerce, and has been the spring and fountain of our wealth and prosperity for above three hundred years.[154]

In reality, of course, it was just these new textile industries, these trifles, which were to enable Britain to break out of that long period of stability which roughly coincides with Defoe's lifetime. But Defoe with his mind in the past could not really welcome such changes.[155]

The stagnation in exports and apparent decline in home consumption was made worse in Defoe's eyes by the fact that there was such enormous potential to expand the production of woollen cloth in England. It was remarkable that so much cloth could be produced in so few counties and that even the cloth-producing counties were not wholly devoted to cloth. Even in the very centre of the cloth-producing regions there were innumerable other employments, particularly for men. 'In a word, except the weaving part, and the managing part, the main stress of the manufacture depends upon, and is perform'd by the women and children, and that of those few counties only.'[156] In these few counties life was satisfactory with little misery or distress.[157] The children were happy. The father earned their food and the mother earned their clothes. And as they grew up they did not have to run away to become 'footmen and soldiers, thieves and beggars . . . but have a trade at their hands and everyone can get their bread'.[158] The point was, of course, that even in comparatively high-wage England the father's income alone was not sufficient to keep the whole family at a reasonable standard of living. The irregularity of work in the seasonal rhythm of agriculture and the overall low productivity meant that in a region where there was little industry there was likely to be poverty. Defoe describes such 'unemployed' counties. 'The countries look desolate, the people sad and dejected, poor and disconsolate, heavy and indolent; not for want of will to labour, but for want of something to labour profitably at.' Here what seemed to romantics to be a rural idyll was in fact an economic disaster. The women and children were idle, 'These sitting at their doors and those playing in the streets.'[159] Modern research tends to bear out Defoe's sad observations. In those areas where industry and agriculture could be combined by the same family there was least rural poverty. It was in the great arable farming belts which supported neither mining nor textile industries that the poor rates were high.

Such waste appalled Defoe, for both humanitarian and economic reasons. How much bigger the cloth industry could be, he mused, if 'all the looser inhabitants, such as are fit to work . . . were set in upon it'.[160] But if more cloth was produced who would buy it? Some might be bought by the women and children set on work but between them they could never buy all the extra production. In a pessimistic stable world there would be cloth unsold, stocks would rise, clothiers would cease to distribute yarn and wool and the country would return to the *status quo*. In fact the situation was likely to be worse. The low wages of the new workers would take away the employment of an established worker somewhere else in the country. 'Can the poor of one town be employed in the business another town did, and not that town, or some other, do the less.'[161]

It was just such a depressing trend of thought that led Defoe to attack with much vigour Sir Humphrey Mackworth's Workhouse Bill of 1704.[162] The object of workhouses was to relieve the rates by employing the poor. Wool or yarn would be handed out to inmates who, in return for their keep, would work the materials up to be sold in the market. Defoe thought this would be completely counter-productive. First, all those spinning in the Bishopsgate or Bristol workhouse would deprive others spinning elsewhere.[163] There was no point in increasing supply without increasing the market. Secondly, by dispersing manufacture into workhouses all over the country one of the major pillars of Defovian economics would be pulled down. For now, with a workhouse in each parish turning out cloth for the local market, there would be no need for anything like the same number of people to distribute the wool, yarn and cloth all over the country. Since Defoe thought that there were more people employed in distribution than in manufacture the result would necessarily be economic disaster.

The only legitimate use of a workhouse was to produce something that was not produced before, preferably something that was previously imported from abroad. The Reading workhouse could therefore be praised for setting the poor to make sailcloth, previously imported from France or Holland.[164] Similar praise was given to workhouses in which children were taught to spin cotton, a skill thought by some to be impossible for Englishmen to learn.[165] The same approach is taken in respect of the 'unemployed' counties. It would have been ideal if all the idle wives and children of the poor could have been set to making woollen cloth. But in the present state of stability this would have been absurd. They, too, like the workhouses must make something previously not made. Defoe is delighted by the enormous expansion of the bone-lace industry in Buckingham and Bedfordshire, previously largely unemployed counties. Now the 'most idle, useless and burthensome part of our people', the younger women and girls, have work which saves their parents having to pay for their maintenance.[166] The fact that an increase in lacemaking in England meant a decrease in lacemaking in Flanders was an added bonus, a turn of the balance of trade in England's favour.[167]

Although Defoe felt some sympathy for the people of the un-employed counties, as was seen above, he was not always quite so sure that their poverty was not their own fault. After all they had legs. In some regions of the country there was work to be done and not enough poor to do it. This was of course one of the basic tenets of his economics and the explanation of English high wages. Could it therefore be idleness which kept the poor poor in the non-industrial counties? Internal migration was not quite as simple as this in the early eighteenth century. It took quite a brave individual to divorce himself completely from his parish of birth for the un-known. For only in his birthplace did he have a settlement and hence only here could he receive poor relief should he run into hard times. Defoe tends to ignore this problem. It may not have been so serious in reality as it appears in the statutes.[168] There was certainly a very high level of internal mobility in England and had been for a long time.[169] Many did migrate permanently to London or to the rising industrial districts. The real problem was that the unit of labour in Defoe's time was the family. The man might have work in farming in a region where there was very little industrial work for his wife and children. Elsewhere there might be work for his family but not for him. In such conditions it seemed best to stay on the farm and hope for the best. As a farm labourer he might well have advantages which would not be available to a worker in an industrial region or in a town:

> The poor cottager and labourer can glean his corn, brew his beer, raise his poultry, keep a cow upon the common, and a hog in his yard, can dig and trench in a little enclosure for his vegetables, gather and cut his fewel on the heaths and in the woods.[170]

Such bounty could well be more valuable than a second wage.

In any case Defoe was not quite sure that it was any gain to England for a man to move from one job to another, even if he was moving to a job with better wages. Indeed, without any concept of comparative productivity it would be difficult to show any advant-age. Once again we run into the problems of a stable economy. For 'that hand is wanted where it was employ'd before, and the gain is only transpos'd; rais'd here and sunk before'.[171] The situation was obviously very different from that in which the unemployed family of a worker got employment in a new industry.

None the less there were many unused resources in England and it was desirable that people should work on them to raise total output and increase England's wealth. Theoretically, it should have been possible to redistribute the people that already lived in England in order to maximize employment and output. Defoe was only too aware that the present distribution was unsatisfactory:

> I will not say but our poor may be ill-sorted in England, too many in one work, too few in another; too many in our manufactures and too few in our husbandry; too many in our corporations and too few in the country; too many on shore, and too few on our ships.[172]

But, as we have seen, the movement of people was likely to lead to more problems than it solved and it seemed necessary to accept a fairly high level of both underemployment and unemployment amongst those people who already lived in England. More people seemed to be the answer. New people who were not already tied down by habit, family and the Settlement Laws to their existing location could work on the unused resources. In the long run more people could have been produced by a natural increase of the population, as was in fact to occur after 1750. But in his time Defoe thought that the population of England was falling, as the result of the wars and emigration to the plantations. The best short-term solution was therefore to encourage migration to England from the continent, particularly from the Palatinate, which had been laid waste by the French.

Defoe's desire to increase England's population was common to nearly all the writers of his day. Population was fairly stable and many writers were dimly aware of this, despite the enormous growth of London. In an age of low productivity and only limited techno-logical change an increase in population was the most obvious way to increase output.[173] In an age of warfare more people meant more cannon-fodder. And in an age of high wages more people would mean more competition for jobs, bringing wage levels down, improv-ing England's competitive position and incidentally helping to swell recruits for England's army since only a poor man would be fool enough to volunteer to be hit on the head for sixpence a day.[174]

Despite such arguments, Englishmen, then as now, were hostile to immigration, and for very much the same reasons. Immigrants were foreigners and hence inferior. They were different, dirty, probably Papist, poor and beggarly and hence would swell the poor rates. They would compete with Englishmen for jobs and in a stable economy would thus further increase the poor rates by throwing Englishmen out of work.

Defoe's views on immigration were completely different. He thoroughly approved of immigrants, who were, he thought, the means by which practically all industry in England had first been introduced.[175] Descended from immigrants himself, Defoe often ridiculed English pretensions to purity of race, most scathingly in what was perhaps his most readable poem, *The True-born Englishman*. On the other hand, as a believer in the importance of high wages to maintain the economy at its existing level, he was unable to accept the arguments of those who supported immigration because it would reduce the general level of wages. The easiest way to resolve this paradox would have been to argue that an increase in population expands the possibilities of specialization and thus increases the division of labour. This in turn would raise the general level of productivity and hence, because more people led to a more than proportional increase in output, there would not necessarily be any fall in wages.[176] This in effect is what Petty and other writers were arguing when they advocated an increase in population. Defoe, as we have seen, never argued like this and in any case would have been worried about the disposal of the increased output.

Defoe's solution, although quite neat, is not very realistic. He argued that high wages were found in the more densely populated parts of England because more people create a more than proportional number of jobs.[177] The answer therefore was to settle immigrants in the empty parts of England where wages were lower; the increased density would raise, not lower, the wages of such areas.[178] 'Want of numbers has always made a want of work for the people.'[179] A million new people settled in a fairly empty area would not only create jobs for each other but also for the people already living there. There was no need for the immigrants to compete for scarce resources with the existing population. Much of England was still undeveloped. Immigrants could be settled in forests, wastes or unenclosed commons in colonies of up to a hundred families, no larger because otherwise it would be difficult for the newcomers to become assimilated and to learn English. Each colony would have a due ratio of farmers to artisans and professional people; Defoe suggests twenty farmers to support those families in other occupations. Since the colony would be largely self-supporting the immigrants would not compete with existing trades; and indeed since they would be unable to satisfy all their requirements from within the group their demand for those goods which they themselves did not produce would increase employment outside the colony, while their demand for wool would swell the income of the grazier. The initial capital required to clear the land and build houses would be lent to them by the government, as would the cash necessary to compensate landlords and commoners for the loss of the use of the waste land.[180] Once the colony was well established the immigrant farmers would repay the loan by paying rent to the government, so that in the end the whole project would cost nothing, unused resources would be exploited and England's population and wealth correspondingly increased. Defoe never discusses where the colonists would acquire the cash to pay their rent or to buy goods from outside, but one assumes that the system is completed by specialization on the part of some colonists in producing goods previously imported to England from abroad.

Hardly surprisingly, Defoe's ingenious ideas fell on deaf ears. Indeed it is difficult to imagine an eighteenth-century government or an eighteenth-century landlord accepting such ideas, even if a hundred immigrant families with the correct mix of skills had come forward or land suitable for their support could be discovered in the uncultivated parts of England. Defoe's schemes for immigration belong to the same world of fantasy as his schemes for the settlement of Patagonia or the clothing of West Africans. The only one of his major suggestions for expanding output and employment which had any great likelihood of success was the introduction of import-substitute industries to absorb some of the rural unemployment.

This was to be the real area of growth as cotton, linen and metal industries expanded in the half century after Defoe's death. But, although Defoe was prepared to give praise where it was due, his obsession with woollen cloth led him, as we have seen, to underestimate the possible contribution of such industries. They were useful in absorbing some of the rural unemployment but he would have thought it somewhat fantastic to suggest that they could lift England out of her current position of stability.

Faced with this stable world in which expansion seemed to be so difficult, Defoe could at least be pleased at the fact that it was England which seemed to do best in such a world. To ensure the continuation of England's prosperity it was necessary to maintain the existing economic system in all its complexity. All change which threatened that system was immediately suspect and was nearly always condemned by Defoe.

We have already seen how Defoe thought that a change in the location of industry simply provided work in one place at the expense of another. The expansion of the stocking-knitting industry in London could only be achieved by the decline of the same industry in Norwich.[181] In the *Review* of 1705 he challenged his readers to prove him wrong.[182] 'Will any man tell me of a manufacture started up, but I shall tell him of another fallen down; of a manufacture begun in one town, but what sunk in another?'

Indeed, in the stocking-knitting example quoted above, the result was more serious than just a transfer of employment from one town to another. For the London industry used the knitting-frame which, according to Defoe, could produce in a day what would otherwise keep a poor woman busy for eight or ten days.[183] In stable market conditions this, or indeed any new labour-saving equipment, could only lead to redundancy and unemployment. 'All methods to bring our trade to be manag'd by fewer hands than it was before, are in themselves pernicious to England in general, as it lessens the employment of the poor, unhinges their hands from the labour, and tends to bring our hands to be superior to our employ, which as yet it is not.'[184]

Innovation in selling methods and in distribution were likely to have even worse effects because of the importance of employment in distribution.[185] And it was in this field that most labour-saving improvements were made in his lifetime. In *The Complete English Tradesman*, for instance, Defoe attacks the now common practice of selling corn by sample.[186] His chief complaint is that if farmers come to market with only a small bag of samples and then, having made their sale, deliver in bulk to the nearest river or straight to the miller, a large population of horses, carters and porters who previously carried the corn in bulk to the market and then took it out again would be unemployed. That pattern of circulation which by its very complexity created employment was being short-cut.

Exactly the same effects on employment were caused by changes in the routes or methods of circulation. Ideally everything should be brought to London and then sent out again, if employment was to be maximized. 'If Norwich trades with Exeter, if Exeter trades with Leeds, if Leeds trades with Canterbury directly, and not by London, a model too much practis'd',[187] then the goods would pass through fewer hands and hence deprive many men of their jobs.

> The circulation of trade is ruin'd, and things go in strait lines that formerly took large circles . . . there are fewer hands engaged in every commodity than there used to be between the maker and the consumer . . . so that tho' six times the quantity of the manufactures were made and consumed, yet not one sixth part of the people shall be employ'd in the doing it. This is depopulation in trade, in the grossest sense, and leaves a vast chasm to be fill'd up.[188]

Particularly guilty in this respect was the pedlar or hawker who, 'thinking to put all the gain of five or six stages of the trade into his own pocket . . . contrives or at least pretends to carry the goods a shorter way to the last consumer; so bringing things to an immediate period, making himself the carrier, factor, wholesale-dealer, chapman and retailer all in one hand'.[189]

Similar observations could be made of some of the improvements in inland waterways which were taking place in his lifetime.[190] Defoe, both as traveller and economist, was a man of the roads. He was a keen advocate of their improvement, since if a road was a sea of mud there could be no circulation at all. The farmer's produce stuck at the farm gate in such a county as Sussex where the roads were impassable, employed nobody and earned no money for the farmer. A good road increased circulation and kept a vast population employed carrying things along it. But a river was different. A barge drawn by a single horse could carry many times as much as a wagon drawn by four or more horses. Each new navigation scheme therefore deprived hundreds of horses, carters and innkeepers of a living, to say nothing of the threat to the rents of the farmers who had previously fed them all.[191] The fact that the reduction in costs brought about by such innovations might make the goods cheaper at market might well not be sufficient compensation for the reduction in the level of employment.[192]

It can be seen that Defoe was seriously alarmed at the thought that England's prosperity might be undermined by individuals

introducing innovations which might swell their private profits at
the public expense. But even to maintain the existing prosperity had
some very unsatisfactory consequences. As we have seen, the whole
structure depended ultimately on the maintenance of a high level
of consumption. The main benefit of high wages was to enable the
poor to buy goods produced by the farmer and manufacturer. Sale
of produce by the farmer enabled both himself and his landlord to
maintain high incomes which when spent would employ the poor.
It was the increase of the level of consumption in Defoe's lifetime
which had raised England to that peak of prosperity which he
praised and tried to explain. But to the moralist practically any
increase in consumption meant an increase in vice. If more beer,
gin or wine was drunk this led to more drunkenness. The motives
for fancy clothes, more carriages, more fine houses and furniture
were pride and vanity. To eat more food than was sufficient for
subsistence was gluttony. And yet, unless more was eaten and more
was drunk, unless more people imitated the rich by buying finer
clothes and furnishing their houses in an extravagant style, there
was no hope for economic progress. Even to maintain the *status quo*
meant it was necessary to maintain the already high level of vice.
Moral reform would be an economic disaster. No wonder, wrote
Defoe in 1713, that the preachers have ceased to preach against
pride and vanity, since the whole of England's commerce now
depended on a 'confederacy with Sathan'.[193]

Defoe was not of course the first or the only writer to note the link
between vice or luxury and employment. The speculative builder,
Nicholas Barbon, writing in 1690, pointed out that 'prodigality is a
vice that is prejudicial to the man, but not to trade'.[194] Bernard de
Mandeville was to write a whole book on the subject.[195] But the
paradox was particularly disturbing to Defoe, a moralist as well as
an economist, and was to lead to some startling contradictions in his
writings. He could write a whole pamphlet in support of English
gin-distilling, praising the new industry for employing the poor and
using up English grain.[196] In other works he is as virulent an observer
of the evils of gin as any other critic.[197] In *The Complete English
Tradesman* he boasts of the number of tradesmen in the liquor business on one page; on the next he is describing public-house keepers
as brokers to the Devil. Three pages later he is boasting again that
Englishmen drink more per head than any other people in the
world.[198]

Some writers have suggested that the moralist in Defoe is simply a conventional pose.[199] This seems an unnecessary resolution of his contradictions, It is common enough for a man to dislike the means and praise the end. Economic historians do it all the time. It might be unfortunate that Englishmen were not so abstemious as the Turks; but, if they had been, they would also have been as poor as the Turks, and England would not have been the powerful and rich country that she was.[200] For Defoe consistently argued that it was luxury which led to trade and employment, not the other way round.[201]

Defoe was perhaps happiest when he was attacking those vices or sins that had no economic benefits. Then he felt that he could really let himself go, without feeling any twinge of conscience about the effect of his moralizing on the employment prospects of the poor, in the unlikely event of anyone taking any notice of him. The most useless of all sins was profanity, which gave no benefit to either the individual or the community. Most sins had some motivation or cause, but swearing was useless, a nonsensical and ridiculous vice.[202] Equally useless from an economic point of view, at least in the days before leisure was fully commercialized, was the very common sin of failing to observe the Lord's Day. In *The Family Instructor*, Defoe makes clear in what order he placed the various possible abuses of the Sabbath:

> I must own, I think people had better open their shops as soon as sermon is done, and fall to their business every Sabbath evening, for sure it would be less sin to spend the day in lawful employments, than in sports and recreations. Worship and diversion is putting the two extreams next to one another; and it seems a contempt of the day to set one piece of it apart for the best things, and the other for the meanest, for recreation is the meanest lawful thing that can be done.[203]

We may think it harmless to take a walk in the fields after spending the whole morning in church, but that just shows how degenerate we have become. Walking in the fields might do no economic harm, but it was certainly a sin if you did it on Sunday. The only vice which is condemned as actually doing economic harm is gaming. It wasted time, it drew people away from legitimate economic activities and it had a very serious effect on the country's liquidity. In a world which was already short of cash, the revolving funds in the gaming clubs and the wager offices could be seen in the same light as the miser's hoard.[204]

Most other vices had economic benefits. Recognizing this, Defoe normally attacked the consumer and not the purveyor of vice. The consumer called the tune and the purveyor had a living to make. This is seen most clearly in his attack on the playhouses, which received the same sort of criticism for their exploitation of sex and violence and their general condonation of low moral standards as do television and the cinema today. The playhouses were 'nurseries of crime, colleges or rather universities of the Devil', and should be closed.[205] But the players themselves were not condemned for acting in lewd plays. Defoe was enough of a realist to know that if they had put on virtuous plays, no one would have come to see them and they would have gone bankrupt.[206] They had a right to live and, if the playhouses were closed as a result of the pressures of the godly, the players had a right to compensation for loss of income. Defoe suggested that a charity should be set up to pay off the players; the equivalent of twenty years' income would purchase an oath from them that they would never play again in the queen's dominions and thus ensure an improvement in the morals of the nation.[207]

Defoe's clear view of the links between vice, consumption and economic growth, coupled with his historical approach to economic problems, led him to write at length on the history of the increase of vice. In the old days it had not been necessary for vice to increase for England to become more prosperous. In the sixteenth century, for instance, economic growth depended on the expansion of exports of English cloth and merchants, graziers and cloth-workers alike could make England rich and powerful and grow richer themselves without doing any moral harm to anyone. In fact the morals of the nation were actually improving, since the reformation in religion had led to a reformation of manners, the Protestant religion having in itself 'a natural tendency to virtue'.[208] But with the death of Elizabeth the rot began to set in. 'In King James the First's time, the Court affecting something more of gallantry and gaiety, luxury got footing; and twenty years peace, together with no extraordinary examples from the Court, gave too great encouragement to licentiousness'.[209] Things were not much better under his son, though the common people had not yet caught the infection. They were still plain, fair-dealing, sober and humble.[210] But not for long. It was in the reign of Charles II that vice really got a grip on the nation, when 'lewdness and all manner of debauchery arriv'd to its meridian'.[211] The shocking example of the court had been followed only too eagerly by a nation which seemed happy to discard the stringent moralistic government of the 1650s. Luxury, ostentation and insubordination flourished. But it was drink which became the national vice.[212] As time went on the nation became more and more a nation of drunkards. A great boost was given by three general elections in quick succession during the Exclusion Crisis, which so accustomed the English workman to swilling vast quantities of free beer that he was never again able to break the habit.[213] More and more beer was drunk, as the 1680s continued, to reach a peak in 1689 when the annual consumption assessed for excise was over fifty gallons per head of men, women and children.[214]

England's new king and queen were not happy at the moral state of the country; not that much else could be expected after it had been ruled for twenty-eight years by Papists and debauchees. Queen Mary 'rais'd the value of virtue and sobriety by her royal example'.[215] It was soon followed. The revolution in politics was paralleled by a revolution in morals. Societies for the Reformation of Morals were set up all over the country, pledged to root out and prosecute drunkards, fornicators, swearers and profaners of the Sabbath.[216] Their organization and enthusiasm was quite remarkable. Blank warrants for particular offences were circulated, as were directives for the instruction of informers in the finer points of their trade. Little books were published for free distribution to the poor, earnestly dissuading their readers from the commission of various sins.[217] The Societies claimed for themselves very considerable success in the suppression of vice. They certainly drew up impressive lists 'of the names of a vast number of lewd and disorderly persons' who had been brought to punishment.[218] Maybe they were successful. Beer consumption fell heavily in the 1690s. Even more to the point, the economy was in a severe state of depression. Already the English were finding that they could not afford to be virtuous. Or, at least, that was one way of looking at it. Historians might suggest that they could not afford to drink so much beer because of the high price of bread, the disruption of trade in the war and the abysmal state of the currency. Whatever the reason, the check to the triumphant march of vice was short-lived. In the eighteenth century the Societies failed to control the licentious English and the economy flourished once again. It is true that beer consumption never returned

to its peak of 1689, but that was only because the English had found
something stronger to drink. All classes had found ways of getting
drunk quicker. The rich were drinking arrack instead of French
brandy, or port instead of claret. The common drinkers of ale or
beer were moving over to stout.[219] But the most astonishing change
was the vast increase in spirit drinking. The English had been introduced to a cheap but satisfactory form of Dutch courage, called
geneva, by their allies in King William's War.[220] Back home the
new drink soon became popular. The average consumption of spirits
in the 1680s had been about half a million gallons a year. By 1710
the figure was over two million gallons and was to rise virtually
continuously for the next thirty years to reach a peak of over eight
million gallons in the 1740s.[221] And this with very little increase in
the population.

One would have thought that the consumption of drink on this
scale might obliterate the possibility of pursuing any other vice. Far
from it; while gin conquered the poor, luxury, ostentation and greed
in a bewildering range of forms conquered the middle classes and
the rich. By the 1720s England had long since passed the levels of
vice achieved in the degenerate reigns of Charles II and his brother.
Catering to sin had become big business:

> If a due calculation were made of all the several trades besides
> labouring, manufacturing and handicraft business, which are
> supported in this nation merely by the sins of the people, as I
> may call them, I mean the sumptuary trades, the ribbons, the
> perfumes, the silks, the cambricks, the muslins, and all the number-
> less gayeties of dress; as also by the gluttony, the drunkenness, and
> other exorbitances of life, it might remain a question, whether the
> necessary or unnecessary were the greatest blessing to trade; and
> whether reforming our vices wou'd not ruin the nation.[222]

This was a worrying question. Towards the end of his life, Defoe's
reflections on the necessity to maintain the level of vice in order to
maintain the level of employment had led him to a very pessimistic
view of England's future. For vice, luxury, call it what you will, had
reached such high levels by the 1720s that he felt certain that
nobody, not even such a wicked country as England, could keep it
up.[223] The possibilities of a moral backlash, of a new and successful
reformation of manners driving rich and poor alike into the paths
of the righteous, alarmed the economist as much as it delighted the

moralist. The truth was that, with exports stable or falling, England could not afford to reform. But the dying Defoe did not need to worry. England was hooked. That pursuit of vice which we now call materialism was here to stay. It would soon lead to the complete disappearance of the world that Defoe knew and loved.

A MOBILE SOCIETY

ENGLAND could be a disturbing place for a foreigner in the days of
Defoe. Many of the social signposts with which the visitor was
familiar at home had vanished or had become so mutilated that
they provided little assistance to the stranger in his passage through
English society. What was a man to do in a country where lords
played bowls with tradesmen and peasants rode on horseback,
where many women of the lower orders did not work and those who
did were so well dressed that they were hard to distinguish from
their mistresses.[1] Nothing was clearly defined, not even the most
important social frontier of all, the borderline between those who
were gentlemen and those who were not. The status of gentleman
had no real definition in law[2] and was open at the bottom to anyone
who looked and behaved like a gentleman and indeed to many who
did not or could not do even that.

The real problem was that a new sort of gentleman had appeared
on the English scene.[3] In the past the word gentleman had been
loosely defined as a man who did no manual work and had the
means to live like a gentleman. What this meant in the majority
of cases was that he lived off the rents which he received from an
estate. There were in fact few other safe forms of investment and the
nouveau riche, when he had made his pile, almost inevitably bought
an estate in his turn. In Defoe's time two things happened to
change this pattern. The commercial boom of the 1670s and 1680s
had greatly expanded the number of rich men seeking the status
of gentleman, while the developments in banking and in company
and government finance had almost simultaneously made available
a far wider range of safe rentier incomes and had incidentally
enabled more people to get rich. A man who prospered in London
was likely to want to remain in London and enjoy the amenities of

the metropolis. The thought of having to buy an estate in the middle of nowhere in order to finance his leisured life was not very attractive. Now he did not have to. He might buy a park and a fine house in Middlesex or Surrey. But his income came from pieces of paper, not land. It was his holdings in Bank of England or East India Company stock, his investments in government debt, his loans on mortgage to needy landowners which provided the safe and easily managed income which enabled him to live the life of a gentleman without any of the bother and doubtful returns of managing an estate in the countryside. He was in fact what the French called a *bourgeois*, a wealthy urban rentier. But, since the English did not use this word, it was very difficult for the foreigner to distinguish between a *bourgeois* and a real member of the landed gentry who happened to live or be staying in London. Both were called gentlemen and the ambiguity enabled lesser men who were neither to call themselves gentlemen too.

The English did not need to have two words to distinguish their two types of gentleman because they alone of European peoples did not wish to emphasize the contrast between a gentry based on land and one based on money. Both were firmly rooted in the absolute, unfettered control of property and this was what mattered. Movement between the two was constant. No one was surprised if the son of a landed gentleman used capital derived from the land as the basis of a city fortune or if the son of an urban gentleman withdrew money from the funds to buy himself a landed estate. Nobody would be surprised if he became a knight or even an earl in the process. Nobody, that is, but a foreigner. They found the concept of the English gentleman rather difficult to understand and writers tried hard to explain it to them. As the Swiss author of one guidebook to England's social chaos put it 'the title of gentleman is commonly given in England to all that distinguish themselves from the common sort of people by a good garb, genteel air, or good education, wealth or learning'.[4] This might seem confusing to a foreigner, used to clearer demarcations of status. But an Englishman knew exactly where he stood and half the fun of social intercourse lay in adjusting his behaviour to his company.[5] Another Swiss, the artist Jean Rouquet, who knew the English well after thirty years in London, described them in words which seem to have a striking familiarity. 'Every Englishman', he wrote, 'constantly holds a pair of scales wherein he exactly weighs the birth, the rank and especially the fortune of those he is in company with, in order to regulate his behaviour and discourses accordingly.'[6]

The scales that the English held had become more and more finely calibrated. Two centuries of social change and economic development had played havoc with the structure of the past in which a man's relationship to the land he owned or worked was sufficient guide to his standing in the world. A graduated society, in which everyone from nobleman to cotter knew his place, had now been permeated by several kinds of disturbance.[7] Most important was the growth of towns. By the early eighteenth century it is probable that at least one in every five Englishmen was a townsman[8] and so not subject to the much clearer hierarchy of the countryside. An urban hierarchy existed, but based as it usually was on money, rather than birth or land, it was bound to be more fluid and difficult to determine. Nor was it easy to determine the relationship between the urban and rural hierarchies. Who should have precedence, the country squire or the alderman, the yeoman farmer or the shop-keeper? It was often very hard to say.

The rapid growth of the professions had simply made things even more difficult.[9] Many professional men were gentlemen by birth or education. But they might also be gentlemen by the nature of their profession. Army officers, for instance, even the very meanest, were considered gentlemen,[10] though it was difficult to treat as such the hungry half-pay men who roamed the streets after the end of the French wars. And then each profession had its own hierarchy, some with a clear and intelligible chain of subordination like the army or the established church, others less easy to determine. Why, for example, should a barrister figure above an attorney? And did he figure if he was, like most barristers, a failure?[11]

The social distinctions in trade were just as problematical. A long tradition had established that a merchant trading overseas ranked above a wholesaler, a wholesaler above a retailer and a retailer with a shop above a pedlar. But, by the late seventeenth century, such distinctions were breaking down. Many shopkeepers were far richer than overseas merchants and, just to confuse the issue, many overseas merchants kept shops. And once wealth became the criterion, it was obvious that a rich shopkeeper or merchant could be richer and live far better than the bulk of the landed gentry. In any case, the rich tradesman had only to retire from business and invest his capital in the funds, to become that new phenomenon, the urban gentleman.

In the world of handicrafts the same confusion reigned. Here we get the familiar modern distinction of employer and employed, of master and man. But such distinctions do not really take us very far since few masters employed more than one or two men and many men became masters. More important to many contemporaries was the distinction between different trades. The range of specialized trades seems fantastic. The single gold and silver lace-man, an aristocrat among tradesmen, provided work for a vast range of lesser tradesmen, including wire-drawers, silver-thread spinners, orrice-weavers, bone-lace makers, silver and gold button-makers, spangle-, bugle-, button-ring, fringe-, frog- and tassle-makers and embroiderers, to name but a few, each a separate trade with a separate workshop and specialized skills and its own rung on the ladder which ran from less genteel to more genteel occupations.[12] The gentility of a trade did not of course guarantee the financial success of those who worked at it and authors warned parents not to let their fondness for their children push them into genteel trades for which they had no aptitude or which were so overcrowded with social-climbing optimists that there was no money to be made out of them.[13] Everybody was trying to push themselves or their children upwards in society, to get their foot on that vital first step of the ladder and to work themselves 'out of the dross of mankind'.[14]

The dross itself had become larger and much more mobile. The decline of peasant cultivation and the increase of population in the sixteenth and seventeenth centuries had created something approaching a genuine proletariat, dependent for their livelihood on paid work either within someone else's house or workshop as a servant or in the shifting, uneasy world of the casual labour market. Such people probably made up half, or even two-thirds, of the total working population, an astonishing contrast to France where the great majority of the people were still peasants and more or less fixed on the piece of land where they were born.[15] By contrast the English workman had considerable freedom of movement. It is true that such independence normally meant simply the freedom to be poor in the countryside, but it also meant that even the poorest had some choice, at least the choice to work or not to work at any particular moment, to stay in the country or to go to London

and the growing industrial areas to try their fortunes in a new world
where the details of their background were not known.

When Defoe looks at the mobile and diffuse society of England
he looks at it from his own particular viewpoint, that of a widely
travelled but essentially London-based member of the middle classes.
He was not very interested in the people who lived in the countryside, or even those in the provincial towns. He was not terribly
interested in either the very rich or the very poor, though they
enter into his analysis. What he was fascinated in and wrote about
at enormous length was the shifting fortunes of the commercial
classes of London. It is these people who are the dynamic element
in his analysis of the way that society worked. It is possible to
summarize his model of society very simply. There were three main
groups each with their own particular role to play and each of
course producing their own particular problems. At the bottom
there were those who worked with their hands and who then
either sold the product of their own labour or were paid wages.
Defoe tends to lose sight of what seems to modern writers the
important distinction between the self-employed craftsman and the
wage-earner. He realized that there was a hierarchy of labour in
which a smith or a weaver might earn in a year several times as
much as a casual labourer, but from the point of view of his analysis
the role of all these people was the same. Their duty was to work
hard and to spend what they received for their labour in order to
help provide employment for their fellows. Spending was also the
main function of those at the top of society. These were the people
who did no work but lived luxuriously off rentier incomes. Their
duty was to spend these incomes in a way which provided the
greatest possible employment for those at the bottom. In the
middle were the tradesmen, shopkeepers and merchants who
employed the poor and provided and sold the goods on which both
rich and poor spent their incomes. It was this middle group which
kept society going.

Defoe was not a great one for political arithmetic but he did make
one attempt to guess the numbers in these various strata of society.
This was in a paper on recruiting which he published in *The Review*
of January 1709.[16] His main object was to demonstrate the ease
with which England should be able to supply the required number
of men and the high proportion of 'the most useless and unprofitable'
from which they could be drawn.[17] He began by assuming, 'I need

bring no authorities to justifie my suggestion', that the total population was ten million.[18] He guessed that one-fifth of these, or two
million, would be fighting men. He then divided the two million
men into four groups, the gentry and professional men; the tradesmen, farmers and employers; the sailors and all those employed in
navigation or shipbuilding, who were exempt; and finally 'the
meer labouring people who depend upon their hands, such as
weavers, butchers, carpenters, shoe-makers etc. including apprentices, servants of all sorts, with vagabonds, loiterers and unaccountable people'. It was from this last group that all the recruits would
be drawn. The fighting men were divided between the four groups
in the following proportions:

1. Gentry and professionals   8 per cent
2. Merchants, shopkeepers, employers of others
   in trade and manufacture, farmers, publicans
   etc.   40 per cent
3. Sailors etc.   4 per cent
4. Mere labouring people who depend on their
   hands.   48 per cent

The most striking feature of Defoe's estimate is the enormous size
of the second group, what we can call the commercial middle
classes. It is doubtful if Gregory King, had he divided the nation
on the same basis as Defoe, would have put more than a quarter
of Englishmen in this group and, as we have seen, he would have
put far more than 48 per cent into the group of 'meer labouring
people'.[19] Since modern research suggests that we should always
believe King rather than Defoe in anything which involves the
use of figures, we must assume that Defoe was wrong and that he
had grossly inflated the strength of this group. The reason for this
distortion is fairly obvious. Defoe's London bias had led him to
project for the whole country the predominant position that the
commercial middle classes held in the life of the metropolis. It is
quite likely that he believed his own figures. Nearly twenty years
later he estimated the total population engaged in trade and
distribution, together with apprentices, servants and journeymen, as
two million, an enormous figure and equally unrealistic.[20]

A few months after the estimate discussed above Defoe divided
up the people of England on a different basis, this time without
attempting to quantify those in the various groups.[21] The division

was based on consumption, a sensible enough criterion for a man who saw consumption as the main driving force in the economy. The population was divided into seven groups:

1. The great, who live profusely
2. The rich, who live very plentifully
3. The middle sort, who live well
4. The working trades, who labour hard but feel no want
5. The country people, farmers etc. who fare indifferently
6. The poor, that fare hard
7. The miserable, that really pinch and suffer want

Within these seven groups we can see the tripartite division in society that has already been mentioned. The first two groups are those who spend but do not work. Here they are divided into two to distinguish the bulk of the urban and landed gentry from the handful of great magnates with princely incomes of £5,000 a year, and sometimes much more, who effectively ruled the country. The last four groups are those who work with their hands.[22] As can be seen, their potential as consumers varied considerably, the most important contribution coming from the working trades, by which Defoe meant craftsmen such as carpenters, smiths and weavers. He compared their consumption with that of a gentleman:

> If the gentleman eats more pies and puddings, this man eats more bread; if the rich drinks more wine, this drinks more ale or strong-beer, for it is the support of his vigour and strength. If the rich man eats more veal and lamb, fowl and fish, this man eats more bread and bacon, and add to it, has a better stomach, a happiness almost as great as to have food to eat. As to the milk, if the rich man eats more butter, more cream, more white meats, or as the song calls them, fools, flawns and custards, our workman eats more hard cheese and salt-butter than all the other put together.[23]

In order to demonstrate with slightly more precision the difference between feeling no want and really pinching we can translate Defoe's vague description of how these four groups fared into the more concrete estimates of family incomes made by Gregory King.[24] King's equivalents for Defoe's fourth and fifth groups, the artisans and farmers, had estimated family incomes of £40 and £44 a year respectively, only slightly less than such sterling members of the middle sort as the shopkeepers. But descent into the world of faring hard was rapid. King's labourers, roughly equivalent to Defoe's poor, received only £15, whilst his paupers and cottagers were surely miserable since they are only credited with an annual income of £6½.[25]

This great range of incomes was one of the most striking facts of life in the world of Defoe, but we can learn little about it from him. All these incomes tended to be subsumed into the single observation that the English received high wages, an observation which suited his purpose as an economist but was not very useful from the point of view of analysing social structure. But Defoe never really tried to do this. He wrote voluminously on the sections of society which he knew best or whose problems interested him but he never really tried to analyse society as a whole, except in the very sketchy way outlined above. We can tell from his writings that there was a great industrial labour force in the countryside but it is difficult to learn much about them, except that they were better off when they were working than when they were not. We can find out still less about the even larger group of people engaged in agriculture. Even in the London world which provides the scene for most of Defoe's writings the treatment is very selective. He is happy to boast about the number of industrial workers in London, the silk-weavers and the stocking-knitters, the glass-workers, bottle-makers and brewers, and above all the vast numbers of workers in the service industries who provided for the needs of the port in the East End and the gentry in the West End and whose whole gamut of subordinate trades helped to house, clothe and feed the half million inhabitants of the greatest city in Europe.[26] But the reader of Defoe will find that he discovers far more of the problems and life-style of a pick-pocket or a whore than of any one of these legitimate occupations. This may seem regrettable since one must assume that if he had written more about such people he would have had something interesting to say, judging by the fascinating sketches he gives of the lives of Derbyshire lead-miners or Leeds cloth-workers in the *Tour*.[27] All the same, it is the fact that Defoe wrote about what he wanted to that makes him enjoyable to read. Those who write about him can only follow where he leads. For the rest of this chapter, then, we will discuss the four sections of society about which he had most to say, the middle sort, servants and labourers, the poor, and the gentlemen of leisure. Not even these groups are treated comprehensively. In particular, Defoe's generalizations nearly always apply only to London and not to the country as a whole.

We will start with the only group who really met with total approval, the middle sort of people, 'who in short live the best and consume the most of any in the nation, and perhaps in the world, and who are the most numerous also among us, and with whom the general wealth of this nation is found'.[28] The actual composition of the middle sort varies somewhat in Defoe's writings. At its widest it stretched from the lower echelons of both the landed and urban gentry to the smallest shopkeeper, taking in most of the farmers and professional people as well. The essential characteristics of the middle sort in this broad definition were the fact that they did not work with their hands, were not 'meer labouring people', and that it was a nice condition of life to be in. Their good fortune in this respect was often contrasted with those above them as well as below. They were 'not expos'd to the miseries and hardships, the labour and sufferings of the mechanick part of mankind, and not embarass'd with the pride, luxury, ambition, and envy of the upper part of mankind . . . but in easy circumstances sliding thro' the world'.[29]

This was the audience to whom Defoe spent most of his life preaching. These were the people whom he told how to vote and save their souls, who to marry, how to make money and how much of it to spend. This was the great new middle-class reading public who read and welcomed Defoe, though some of them were still too busy trying to establish themselves to have much time for books. But those who already had were prepared to pay good money to read and improve themselves.[30] Now they could sit back in comfort and take a vicarious delight in the adventurous life of a man like Robinson Crusoe who had been so foolish as to give up the advantages of the middle station. As they slid gently through their world they could only marvel at the desperate straits of those so unfortunate as not to belong to it. Or, in more serious mood, they could absorb themselves in the rather gloomy upper middle-class comfort which formed the social background to Defoe's works of moral instruction. There some of them might feel at home and others might wish that they did, though there is too much oak panelling, long faces and family prayers for modern (and probably for much contemporary) taste.

In fact the characters in these pious books belong to the very top of the middle sort. Some are lesser country gentlemen or else members of the new urban gentry. Many of them are successful merchants and clothiers, well on the way to becoming rentiers in their turn, inhabitants of that watershed between the gentry and the successful commercial classes across which Defoe so often stressed movement in both directions. Many of them were indeed so elevated that they did not really perform the functions of the middle sort, which were to keep everything going, to run the shops and foreign trade, to organize the vast distribution network of the inland trade, to employ the poor and in general to operate as the entrepreneurial group in society. This would necessarily exclude most gentlemen, whose main function was to spend rather than work, to 'live on estates without the mechanism of employment'.[31] Even the farmers, much the largest group within the income limits of the middle sort, are normally excluded from discussion. Defoe recognized that they performed essential middle sort functions, such as trading and employing the poor, but he could never raise much enthusiasm for their rustic way of life. Defoe's world was a world of towns and of the roads that connected them. On the road he would meet fully paid-up and essential members of the middle sort, such as innkeepers, maltsters and country shopkeepers. But the only really admirable activity for someone who actually lived amongst the trees and fields of the countryside was to do nothing and spend a lot of money, in other words to be a country gentleman.

Even in the towns many middle-income people tended to be excluded from the ranks of the middle sort proper. Such were the professional men whom Defoe regarded, as did many of his contemporaries, as leeches on society. Lawyers were notorious for their grasping, time-wasting practices, whilst the medical profession were often even more maligned. It was an old joke to regard the doctor as the enemy of the commonwealth, since the normal result of his ministrations was to reduce the size of the population.[32] Worst of all was a new group who were hard to fit into anyone's scheme of society. These were the intermediaries in the new financial world, the dealers in money and in stocks and shares. The bits of paper which they dealt in were an admirable innovation which, as we have seen, provided a new secure income for the urban rentier. But there were no kind words about the stock-jobbers and very few about the bankers. Defoe was to attack these drones on numerous occasions but he was unable to think of any way of doing without them.[33] As a great believer in the virtues of money's 'little sister', credit, and as a convinced supporter of England's excellent new system of public finance, he was forced to accept that such men were a necessary evil.

We are left with the commercial middle classes proper, those actually engaged in trade, the 'most noble, most instructive and improving way of life'.[34] Not everyone agreed with Defoe. The old hostility to the distributor still existed and many people thought the shopkeeper or the corn factor as much of a drone in society as Defoe considered the doctor or the stock-jobber. In 1662 Sir William Petty described distributors as 'onely a kinde of gamesters, that play with one another for the labours of the poor'.[35] But attitudes were changing fast. For a long time writers had been trumpeting the glory of the merchant, the 'steward of the Kingdom's stock', as Thomas Mun called him.[36] By the Restoration many were prepared to believe Mun. The merchant had become an eminently respectable person whose daughter could provide a much-needed injection of capital into a decaying noble house and whose counting-house was no longer too sordid to offer an education and a living for the younger sons of the gentry.[37]

Defoe has remarkably little to say about the overseas merchant. His main role as writer was to glorify the lower strata of the middle sort. As one of the first writers to point out the enormous importance of the inland trade, he necessarily takes as his heroes the shopkeepers and wholesalers rather than the merchants trading overseas. In Defoe's scheme of things the shopkeeper, previously a figure of fun or a money-grabbing parasite depending on one's point of view, becomes an essential element in the commonwealth. No doubt shopkeepers had for a long time had a sneaking suspicion that they were doing good by doing well, but it was nice to have someone tell them so as often and at such great length as did Defoe.

Retail shopkeeping was an occupation which had grown very rapidly in the seventeenth century, a product of urban growth, new wealth and the enormous expansion of the range of goods available to the consumer.[38] By the end of the century there were shops in every country town and even in small villages,[39] while the number of shops in London was one of the city's main attractions to the visitor. Indeed some people thought that there were far too many shops and that shopkeepers were competing with each other out of existence.[40] A fairly genteel occupation in which success could launch a man's family into virtually unlimited social mobility was bound to attract recruits, especially as it seemed at first sight to be such an easy job. 'An easie life, and hence many are induced to run into it', as one writer put it in 1684.[41] According to Pepys, shopkeeping absorbed most of the disbanded parliamentary army at the Restoration;[42] it was certainly a very common occupation for a Dissenter. The very easiness of entry meant that it was easy to fail. The early years could be a frightening experience as small retailers tried to raise themselves up, 'by their bootstraps on borrowed money'.[43] Many ended up in a debtor's prison or returned to the dross from which they had temporarily lifted themselves, only to find that without the knowledge of a craft they must sink to the very bottom of the pile.[44]

Much of Defoe's most famous book on shopkeepers, *The Complete English Tradesman*, consists of advice to the novice on how to avoid this disaster without doing too much damage to his immortal soul.[45] For the most part he takes as old-fashioned a view of retailing as he does of most other sections of the economy. Once again nearly all innovation is attacked, whether it was the fashion for bow-windows and fancy shop-fittings or the frivolous taste of the consumer which led to the best sites in town being occupied by pastry-cooks or toy-men instead of drapers selling good old-fashioned English cloth.[46] But his severest criticism is of price-competition.[47] He accepted that it was the normal impulse of a shopkeeper to increase his business at the expense of others, but such things should not be overdone. To compete in quality and service was all right, but to compete in price was likely to undermine the stability of the commonwealth. Price-cutting by the big businessman would lead to the destruction of the small shopkeeper who could not compete.[48] Similar attitudes to business were to survive a long time. In nineteenth-century France the price-cutter and excessive competitor was known as 'le mangeur des hommes', a description which perfectly accords with Defoe's views. The ideal business was small and was an offshoot of the household in which it was carried on. Housekeeping and shop-keeping were simply different aspects of the same business, the business of living. Such an attitude to business led to a safe but unprogressive way of trading, a dislike of partnership and a hankering after a slow and steady rate of accumulation with very high unit profits and a very slow turnover.[49] Many years of high profits

carefully gathered together, of thrift and a tight hold on the housekeeping pursestrings could lead to sufficient accumulation to enable
the shopkeeper to retire and purchase an income from the funds.
Yes, comfortable and easy as it was, the middle station of life was
for many only a means to an end, a means to achieve the most
satisfactory way of life of all, to be a gentleman of leisure and do
nothing at all.

Defoe has nothing but admiration for the middle sort of people
as a group, although there were individuals within the group who
received sharp criticism. He praised their function in society and he
admired their ambition to improve themselves and, if possible, raise
themselves out of the ranks of the middle sort of people altogether.
He was rarely as enthusiastic about the other sectors of society. In
this he was often inconsistent. We have seen how alarmed he was
that the high level of consumption which he advocated as the best
means of achieving full employment and economic growth should
almost inevitably lead to the increase of vice. He was equally
worried by the effects of social ambition. This was admirable in the
middle sort and should, theoretically, have been equally admirable
in those below them. On one occasion Defoe went so far as to hope
that one day all Englishmen might be masters: 'I wish for my
country's good that it might please God that all our people were
masters and able to keep servants, tho' they were obliged to buy
their servants, as other nations do, and as we do in His Majesty's
American dominions.'[50] But this of course was only rhetoric. As the
quotation implies, Defoe could not envisage a society without
servants. And servants with ambition or with a taste for independence were sure to be bad servants. Indeed once servants forgot
their place the whole order of society was threatened: 'The poor will
be rulers over the rich and the servants be governours of their
masters . . . in a word, order is inverted, subordination ceases, and
the world seems to stand with the bottom upwards.'[51] This should
remind us that Defoe, author of *Legion's Memorial*, the 'hard-headed
tribune of the people', was not a democrat but a Whig. No society
could survive once the poor got above themselves, for 'subordination
is the soul of law'.[52]

Service in the world of Defoe took various forms.[53] He distinguishes three main groups, each of whom posed rather different
problems, though they were all deemed guilty of the most appalling
insubordination. The smallest group were the apprentices,[54] an

élite among servants whose numbers included the sons of gentle-men.[55] Much more numerous were the 'indoor-servants', a group which included not only what we today think of as domestic servants but also servants in husbandry and industrial servants who lived in their masters' homes. Altogether this group may have comprised half a million people or ten per cent of the entire population, a percentage which was concentrated in the younger age-groups[56] and formed, together with the apprentices, a potentially explosive adolescent force that state and family alike tried uneasily to control. Finally, the word 'servant' could be applied to the whole of the labouring poor, the out-servants, a status that not all of them were prepared to accept.

Defoe's discussion of these three groups is very uneven. For a man whose economics rested so largely on the payment of high wages he really had very little to say about the wage-earner himself, except to generalize that he did not work as hard as he should or as hard as he had done in some probably mythical past. This simply reflects the fact that Defoe looked at the world from the viewpoint of a Londoner of the commercial classes and not from that of a clothier or a coalmine owner. The shopkeeper's main contact with those below him in the social scale was not in their capacity as workmen, but as customers. In this role they were, of course, admirable. 'Those we call poor people, journey-men, working and painstaking people', Defoe reminded his readers, 'are the people that carry off the gross of your consumption; 'tis for these your markets are kept open late on Saturday nights; because they usually receive their week's wages late.'[57] The shopkeeper might suspect that such people did not work very hard and did not really earn the wages that they spent, but he did not have first-hand evidence to support these suspicions. What he did know was that the subordinates with whom he dealt directly, his own domestic servants and his apprentices, had many undesirable qualities. Defoe agreed, and it was these two groups of the subordinate population whom he discussed in most detail.

Apprenticeship was defined by the author of a guidebook for young apprentices as 'that genteel servitude which by a few years' service faithfully and diligently performed towards their masters, lays a certain foundation for attaining riches and honour in this world, and by God's grace everlasting happiness in the life to come'.[58] The servitude was in fact genteel for only a minority of apprentices, but it was about this minority which Defoe wrote. He has nothing to say about what must have been the typical apprentice, a young man learning a craft such as carpentry or weaving in preparation for a life-time of hard work with little prospect of either riches or honour. What he does discuss, as we might expect, were the young men who were being apprenticed to the commercial trades, to shopkeepers, wholesalers and merchants. Such apprentices posed many problems. What was perhaps the most important problem was not discussed by Defoe, whose glorification of the shopkeeper seems to have blinded him to reality in this respect. This was the fact that a long apprenticeship was not really of much practical use in these trades. As a later writer pointed out, what was actually taught to the apprentice shopkeeper could be learned in a few weeks and parents would have done better to have used their money to provide capital for their sons rather than to buy them seven years of servitude.[59] The only real value he could see in such apprenticeships was that they were a good way of keeping a boy out of trouble during his adolescence, a motivation which is clearly reflected in the second, religious objective in the quotation above. Despite the obvious truth of such observations, apprenticeships in retailing continued, partly because it was the good old traditional way of doing things and partly because it was the normal way of acquiring the freedom of the City of London and hence the right to run a business there. But even this was becoming less important as London itself grew in size. Now it was possible to run a very successful business in such areas as Westminster or the West End, which were beyond the old limits of the City and where a businessman did not need to be a freeman of London to set up shop.

Under such conditions it is not surprising that the London apprentices tended to be bored and frustrated and to cause trouble quite out of proportion to their numbers. The ability of the individual apprentice to make a nuisance of himself had been much increased in Defoe's time. The main reason in his view was the enormous growth in the size of premium that parents had to pay to the master when their children's indentures were drawn up.[60] Defoe explained this by the growing wealth of parents and their conviction of the wealth to be made by their sons once they had served their time. This was probably partly true though, as we have seen, a successful career in business did not necessarily require an apprenticeship at all. Another reason for the growth of premiums seems to have been a complete change in the service conditions of apprentices. In Elizabethan times the apprentice had been unpaid and the only money which he was likely to have would be tips from his parents. But, by the late seventeenth century, most apprentices were paid wages by their masters, normally more the longer they had served and the more use they were.[61] Premiums could be seen as a compensation to masters for having to pay wages.

Whatever the reason, the combination of high premiums and regular wages made the apprentice extremely difficult to control. As a character in *The Family Instructor* remarked of his apprentice, 'now we get a hundred pound, or two or three hundred a piece with them; they are too high for reproof and correction'.[62] They fancied themselves to be way above the other servants and refused to be treated like them. 'They did not give such sums of money to be confin'd like prisoners, or to be used like footboys.' If their masters did not like their behaviour they would go, but before they did they would like part of the premium back.[63] Since the master had almost certainly invested the premium in his business this could be an embarrassing threat. The fact that they were paid wages only increased the scope for their insubordination, as it provided the means for them to buy fancy clothes, frequent taverns and, horror of horrors, seek female company.

The results of such flamboyant behaviour to a man of Defoe's views were disastrous, offending both his moral and his economic code. In the past parents had seen apprenticeship as a period of moral as well as business instruction, and to some it was the moral instruction which was the most important. They felt that it was easier and more effective for a stranger to instil the correct pious attitude to life than the perhaps too fond and indulgent parent. Some writers even went so far as to emphasize godliness over business competence as the vital quality to be sought in the selection of a master for their son. *The Apprentices Companion* of 1681,[64] for instance, has virtually nothing to say about the work that the apprentice shall do and consists mainly of biblical quotations and cautionary tales of what happens to those who profane the Lord's Day, swear or drink. When the author discusses the selection of a master he says that 'there is more real profit to be obtained by following the spiritual directions of religious masters than by the most subtle and cunning artifices they can learn from the wittiest and over-reaching person in the way of their trade and employment'.[65] But such views must have been extremely old-fashioned even in 1681. They may well only reflect that pious wishful thinking so characteristic of the didactic literature of the time. Contemporary opinion is perhaps better illustrated by the strictly businesslike attitude of the master in Defoe's *Family Instructor* who could not care less what his apprentices' morals were like as long as they did their work.[66]

The problem was, however, that even in this respect the modern apprentice was a failure. The unpaid menial apprentice of the past had cleaned his master's shoes and waited at table. But no young man whose father had paid £100 or more for his premium was going to behave like that. Now the master had to employ porters and footmen to wait on the apprentices and poor women to clean the apprentices' shoes.[67] Yet another good reason for raising the level of premiums.

Domestic servants were just as irresponsible and, since there were many more of them and they formed the background against which all life in the middle station (and sometimes below it) was lived, they posed a far more universal problem to Defoe's readers. Nowadays we may find it difficult to appreciate the problems of living in a house where servants were nearly always present or at least just round the corner. Master and mistress spent their lives on a stage and, if they should be so foolish as to forget their lines or their manners, the fact would be the common gossip of the neighbourhood taverns in no time.[68] Defoe seems so terrified at the scope that servants had for character assassination that one suspects that he must have something to hide. What that something was may well have been a fear that his own gentility did not match up to the standards that his servants had seen in other people's houses. His frequent observations that maidservants' clothes were so fine that it was difficult for the visitor to determine who was the maid and who the mistress may just be hyperbole, but they may well be a sign of insecurity. Robert Dodsley, a very puffed-up footman who replied to some of Defoe's attacks on servants in the postscript to his poem, *Servitude*, has some heavy irony at the expense of a gentleman who was unable to recognize a lady when he saw one. 'Indeed, with a gentleman of Squire Moreton's elegant taste we find a cook or a house-maid, if she appear in any thing of a tolerable dress, is easily mistaken for a fine lady.'[69]

Defoe thought that one of the main reasons for the bad behaviour of servants was that they had more money to spend.[70] 'I never knew a servant, or a workman in England one farthing the better for the encrease of his wages', he wrote in 1724, 'it is so natural for him to think he deserves it, or that else you would not do it; that instead of mending him, it always makes him worse.'[71] This may seem a rather inconsistent point of view for a high-wage advocate like Defoe to take. He goes even further in his second major work on servants, *Every-Body's Business is No-Body's Business*, where he proposes a fairly considerable cut in wages.[72] But, as we saw in the last chapter,[73] Defoe did not wish to see wages rise continuously. He also tended to treat domestic servants as a special case. A rise in wages for anyone was more than likely to lead to vice and insubordination, but this could be accepted as a necessary evil since the resulting consumption helped to sustain the level of employment and prosperity in the country as a whole. But vice and insubordination in a domestic servant were less easy to condone since they actually occurred in one's own house. It was also possible to argue that a cut in a servant's wages would not lead to a fall in consumption. High wages for servants merely meant that their employers had less to spend on other things; in other words it was simply a matter of the distribution of spending power within the family. Defoe, as an employer of servants, naturally felt that the master and not the servant should decide what the household spent.

There seems little doubt that Defoe was right in saying that domestic servants were becoming better paid, though he may have exaggerated a little in his details.[74] It is probable that his explanation is also fairly accurate. The growth in numbers of the middle sort and their increasing ostentation naturally led to a greatly increased demand for servants. To be served is, after all, a continuous and satisfying reminder that one is a master. But while demand grew there is no indication that supply grew at the same rate. Population growth appears to have been very small, especially in the south of England. Defoe thought that numbers were actually falling as a result of emigration and the wars.[75] This disequilibrium between demand and supply led inexorably to a rise in servants' wages, which could not be halted even by the continuing exodus of young people from the countryside.

Wages were by no means the only income of servants. The extortion of tips from visitors had been brought to a fine art, doubling servants' wages according to one writer.[76] It became a contemporary joke to say that you could no longer afford to dine with the wealthy

because of the long line of stretched-out hands that you would have
to pass on the way to the door. Refusal to pay could mean an
unpleasant experience if you dined out again, word having gone
through the servants' grapevine of the visitor's meanness or poverty.
Long tradition had established that servants could also increase
their income by demanding a percentage from the tradesmen with
whom they chose to place their masters' business.[77] Those who did
not have access to shops could cheat their master in different ways.
Your huntsman, for instance, could take tips from poachers and
when you yourself went out to hunt he could lead you away from
the game so as not to spoil his own business.[78] The scope for petty
pilfering and general dishonesty must have been considerable,
though, after reading a few contemporary works on servants, it is
refreshing to appreciate the obvious truth of Robert Dodsley's
indignant statement that not all servants were rogues.[79]

None the less, if contemporary comment has any value at all,
servants seem to have made good use of their improved bargaining
power. A young girl coming up to London as a maid at 50 shillings
or 3 pounds a year had 'scarce been a week, nay, a day in her
service, but a committee of servant wenches are appointed to
examine her, who advise her to raise her wages, or give warning;
to encourage her to which, the herb-woman or chandler-woman,
or some other old intelligencer, provides her a place of 4 or 5 pounds
a year . . . and so gives warning from place to place, 'till she has got
her wages up to the tip-top'.[80] And if the girl servants got more
money then the male servants also had to have a rise. It would
never do for a footman to be paid less than the chambermaids.
There was no guarantee that the girl just up from the country
was as green as she looked in any case. The very worst girls, whose
behaviour was so bad that they could not get a job at all, were in
the habit of going down into the country, to 'return perhaps with
the next wagoner; and being made free of the wagon (which
is the phrase amongst those sort of gentry for the last favour) the
honest fellow gives them a character, knows abundance of aunts
and cousins, all extremely honest etc.'[81]

The conditions of service by which a servant could 'give warning
from place to place' are an illustration of a change that had come
about in the relationship between master and servant. Servants
were no longer forced by the difficulty of finding a job to enter
into long-term contracts with a master.[82] In fact, according to

Defoe, an employer had to give a servant a month's notice but the servant could leave when he wished if he did not like the job.[83] Dodsley echoes this at the end of his poem of advice to masters and servants on how to improve their relationship:[84]

> If we dislike, and think it too severe
> We're free to leave, and seek a place elsewhere.

As a result the turnover of servants seems to have been extremely rapid, the impetus coming from both sides. The famous Scots footman, John Macdonald, who wrote his memoirs later in the century, served twenty-eight masters in thirty years.[85] This does not seem to have been all that unusual. One result was that London had a considerable population of servants 'out of place', either because they had been sacked or because they had left in an effort to improve themselves. Contemporaries felt that unemployed servants almost inevitably sank into the underworld, selling information about their former masters' possessions and way of life, engaging in theft themselves or, if they were girls, going on the streets.

Defoe deplored not only the spending patterns of servants, the drink and fancy clothes which made them bad servants and an embarrassment to unsubtle visitors, but also their improvidence. Why did they not use their advantages to put something aside for a rainy day or even to place themselves on the first rung of the ladder which led to social improvement? But they never thought like this. If a maid-servant thought about improving herself at all she took the quicker but potentially disastrous method of seducing an apprentice or, better still, the master's son. And servants never saved money. Once out of work they therefore found themselves under the necessity of resorting to petty crime or the brothel to save them from starvation until they found a place again. And, since they had not served a proper apprenticeship to crime, more often than not they were ineffective criminals who ended up on the gallows, while the girls made neither good whores nor good servants.[86]

Were servants really as awful as Defoe and other writers made them out to be? It is impossible to say. The appalling behaviour of servants has always seemed to be the main topic of conversation among masters, but on the other hand few periods can have been so favourable to servants as the early eighteenth century. Perhaps one should leave the last word on this subject to the historian

Dorothy Marshall, who found the insubordination of servants proved, 'a degree of drunken insolence which would not be tolerated today', a verdict which may well tell us as much about the 1920s as it does about the 1720s.[87]

It would be doing Defoe an injustice to suggest that he placed the whole blame for their bad behaviour on the servants themselves. Implicit in any paternalistic view of society is the assumption that society will degenerate if the father does not set a good example to the son and the master to the servant. Much of Defoe's criticism, therefore, is levelled at the incompetent, overkind or vicious master or mistress. It was not servant girls who did all the seduction.[88] In all his works on the family Defoe emphasizes the role that both master and mistress have to play in ensuring that there is good government and moral behaviour within the family. It is their duty to instruct and improve their servants, to see that the Lord's Day is properly observed, that family prayers are attended by servants and that the door to the cellar is kept firmly locked. The fact that proper family government had broken down was one good reason for the improper behaviour of servants. The other problem was that English masters were too easy and kind. 'Easy masters make sawcy servants', as he reminds us in *The Great Law of Subordination Consider'd*.[89]

One aspect of English kind-heartedness which he particularly deplored was the giving of good references to bad servants, a practice which, apart from being a lie, might well let a thief or a moral degenerate into the house of another member of the middle station.[90] One character in *Religious Courtship* is made to point out that if every servant's references told the whole truth no one would get a job, but Defoe is adamant.[91] The truth must be told. Employers who failed to provide an accurate reference should themselves be punished. Such a reform would play an important part in a paternalistic solution to the servant problem which Defoe advocated. Turnover could be reduced by registering all contracts between master and servant before a Justice of the Peace. Then, if the servant left without due cause, he or she could be summoned before the justices and punished. No such contract was to be made unless the servant could produce a genuine, and good, reference. Like most of Defoe's reforms, however, this was destined to be just so much paper. Neither the justices nor the servants would have welcomed it and employers would have soon grown to dislike it once they realized that its effect would be further to reduce supply and thus of course to raise the wages of servants even more.

It is difficult for the commentator on Defoe to see exactly how servants could have behaved in a way that would have satisfied his programme for the social and economic improvement of society and the individual. If they had had their wages cut this must have had some effect on consumption and employment, though not as much as one might think. Farmers would not have been hit very much since the servants would still have eaten at their masters' expense. And even the textile industry would not have suffered, since nearly all the fancy clothes that servants wore were either purchased for them by their masters in an effort to bolster their own vanity or else were their mistress' cast-offs. The result of servants wearing the drab liveries that Defoe recommended would therefore have been an expansion in the supply in second-hand silks and cottons to the old-clothes men of Rag Fair and Rosemary-Lane. The major sufferers from a cut in servants' wages, apart from the servants themselves, would have been the drink trade. This could have had serious results, since the drink trade, in all its ramifications, was one of the major employers of the poor. The drink trade would also have suffered if servants had had the same money and saved it as Defoe recommended. Worse still, if servants had used their savings to improve themselves and move into the lower echelons of the middle station it would have led to vastly increased competition for small shopkeepers, bakers, cook-shops and other trades which servants would have had the skills to take up. But competition in the trading world was also something that Defoe opposed, as we have seen. It was a rather tricky problem. If servants really had been sober, god-fearing and well-behaved; if they had worn linsey-woolsey and saved their pennies, then society might have been satisfactorily paternal but there would have been a higher rate of unemployment, a higher rate of bankruptcy and higher poor rates.

Defoe was on the whole more charitable to the rest of the working classes than he was to domestic servants. The working trades and the labouring poor, though they had their faults, were after all the same marvellous people who by producing such high-quality goods and working so hard were able to outshine the French and other foreigners. They were also outside the house, not inside being saucy all the time like domestic servants. Nevertheless, much of Defoe's discussion of labourers is similar to his criticism of domestic servants. They spent their money unwisely and viciously; they were improvident and lazy; they aped their betters and in general found it easy to forget the place that a good Lord had provided for them.[92] Few demonstrated the servility which an hierarchical society expected of them.[93] Fewer still were content with their lot. How many had read their Baxter and realized how fortunate they were not to have the temptation of riches to deter them on the road to salvation?[94] Only one character in the works of Defoe earns full marks as an honest, god-fearing workman. This is the poor labourer in *Religious Courtship* who manages to convert his godless landlord.[95] But this very example shows the other side of Defoe. For the landlord gives him a farm, fully-stocked and at a very easy rent, as a grateful reward for his conversion.[96] Could honest William have had the possibility of that in his mind when he began his pious task?

This is perhaps too cynical. All the same, one thing that rings out loud in Defoe's writings on the labouring poor is that they had a good eye for the main chance. We have seen how well domestic servants exploited their scarcity value. Labourers, too, might well find themselves in a strong position in the early eighteenth century, in good times at least. This is not to deny that they were poor and lived a hard life by twentieth-century standards. But, within the limitations of a pre-industrial society and labour market,[97] they were able to look after themselves fairly well. By doing so they of course infuriated their masters and the moralists and commentators on their society. Such people tended to look backwards to an ideal society where the poor had been really poor and were obliged to spend their whole time working hard for the greater glory of the gentry and the men of the middle station, touching their forelocks as they did so. But the utopia of the poor was rather different.

The commonest complaint about the labourer's actual work, rather than his behaviour, was that he was lazy. What this actually meant was that he did not do as much work in a given time as his employer would have liked him to. A man's time, once contracted for, was felt to belong to his employer. To be idle was therefore tantamount to robbery.[98] 'He that defrauds me of any part of the time that he makes me pay for', wrote Defoe in *The Great Law of Subordination*, 'is as much a thief as if he broke open my cabinet and took away so much money, as those hours (so wasted) came to.'[99] This attitude is illustrated by a story about a delightfully idle gardener who, instead of working, spent most of the day watching some young lads playing cricket over the wall. His employer accused him of theft and gave him the sack, at which the gardener asked him for a reference. The employer gave him one. 'He is a person capable of discharging the place of a gardener, but was dismiss'd by me for neglecting his business, robbing me of my time, and for his saucy tongue.'[100]

Impudence, insubordination and a general disinclination to do any work at all was the common mark of the worker in the eyes of those of the middle station. Even old men had forgotten the good ways of the past. In another delightful cameo, Defoe tells of a wheelwright mending a cart. 'While he was busy at his work, comes by a countryman that knew him, and at some distance salutes him with the usual compliment: "Goodmorrow Father Wright, God speed your labour". The old fellow looks up at him, for he did not see him at first, and with a kind of pleasant surlyness, answered: "I don't care whether he does or no, 'tis day-work".'[101]

Not only did labourers idle on the job but they would not work at all if they did not want to. The day-worker would stop work when he felt that he had earned sufficient to maintain his family and then spend the rest of the week in the alehouse.[102] The piece-worker was no better. The man or woman to whom the clothier handed out wool or yarn to work up in their own home took their own time over the job. If they were hard up they would work quickly. If they were in easier circumstances or the price of corn was low they might take weeks or months to do a simple job. There was very little the clothier could do about it. Unless the worker was an apprentice 'or a hir'd covenant-servant, bargain'd with for the year', his employer could not summon him before the bench for not working. He could only 'sue him for his bargain, and would recover damages against him at law'. But such a suit would take a long time, cost a lot of money and the result was always uncertain. Even if the clothier won the case, the workman was almost certain to be a poor man by the time that damages were settled, 'so that you sue a beggar and catch an English proverb'.[103]

The fact that nobody would work longer than they felt was necessary was of course made worse by the rise in wages and the fall in the price of bread. What was necessary could now be earned in far less time. Fortunately for employers, however, necessity itself had changed in character, as new products were introduced

on to the market and as the spirit of emulation kept the worker busy
in his drive to keep up not only with his neighbour but with those
above him. Such emulation might make a mockery of order and
degree, but it was the only thing which kept men working at all.
Defoe knew this, even if he regretted it. It was, after all, the basis of
his economics. Other writers were also beginning dimly to see that
it was true.[104] Some writers even recommended the creation of
wants in order to stop workmen being idle. Bishop Berkeley of
Cloyne found it difficult to think of a way to get the Irish to work.
They could live too well in total idleness. He posed the question,
'whether the creating of wants be not the likeliest way to produce
industry in a people? And whether if our [i.e. Irish] peasants were
accustomed to eat beef and wear shoes they would not be more
industrious?'[105] Exactly the same creation of wants has been a
concern of modern writers trying to induce a spirit of acquisitiveness
in the Third World.[106] There is nothing more annoying to the
promoter of change than a man who is happy without it.

Wants were not always satisfied so easily in the world of Defoe.
The happy picture of the well-fed, well-dressed labourer who worked
when he liked merges imperceptibly into that equally common
stereotype of the early eighteenth century, the men and women who
could not work when they wanted to, 'the poor that fare hard'
and 'the miserable that really pinch and suffer want'.[107]

The main problem facing all writers on poverty in the days of
Defoe, and for a long time before and after him, was to sort out the
deserving from the undeserving poor. Everyone accepted that the
community at large, and especially the wealthy, had some responsibilities to the poor. All agreed that the poor orphan or the widow
with a young family, suddenly left destitute by the death of the
breadwinner, were entitled to a dole to save them from starvation.
But, even in these cases, relief was no absolute right. In particular
it was felt that such people, however young they were, should do
all they could to maintain themselves and so relieve the community.
Most writers felt that the sick and the aged, too, had a claim on
society, though many thought that the world would have been a
much better place if the aged at least had saved up in the time of
their youth and strength to provide for such a predictable disability
as old age. The most passionate debate, however, was about the
people known as the able-bodied poor, those men, women and
children who, although apparently able to work, expected society

to support them in idleness instead of doing so. Most, but by no means all, writers thought that such people had deliberately chosen to be idle and that they should be forced to work if they refused to find a job for themselves.

Defoe, himself, had proved, at least to his own satisfaction, that there was no such thing as involuntary unemployment for the able-bodied. He argued that there could be no want of work in England because English wages were higher than was necessary for the workman's subsistence. If there had really been people looking for jobs, then the level of wages would have fallen to the bare minimum necessary for survival, to level of the wages paid to the French or even to the Irish.[108] "'Tis undeniable, that where a labour-ing man can by his single hand earn more money than will maintain himself, in that nation, let it be where it will, there is no want of work.'[109] When a hypothetical opponent points to the number of beggars, Defoe simply dismisses him. Begging was just another profession and obviously a profitable one, since otherwise beggars would be competing with existing workers for jobs. 'The reason why so many pretend to want work is that they can live so well with the pretence of wanting work, they would be mad to leave it and work in earnest.'[110]

Defoe gets a bad press from the Webbs in their history of the poor law for his complaisant discussion of the problems of the able-bodied poor, and he is dismissed as holding attitudes common to the wealthy of his day.[111] This is a little unfair on Defoe. In 1704 and 1705, when he developed the arguments discussed above, he was engaged in a specific polemical task, the destruction of Sir Humphrey Mackworth's Workhouse Bill.[112] In this he was totally successful. But in other works Defoe is by no means so harsh, though he does not abandon his central proposition.

In fact few early eighteenth-century writers had such a clear idea of the causes of poverty as Defoe and, in many of his works, he is remarkably tolerant towards the poor and shows a keen under-standing of their problems. This is hardly surprising. Defoe was almost the only writer on poverty who had mixed with the poor himself. His experiences as a debtor and his sojourn in Newgate in 1703 had taught him things that he never forgot. One thing was a lifetime concern for what he called the poverty of disaster, that poverty which came as such a shock to the middle sort of people who 'by misfortune or mismanagement, or both, fall from flourishing fortunes into debt, bankruptcy, jails, distress, and all sorts of misery'.[113] But he also learned more about the poverty of inheritance and the people who had to suffer it, 'the people born to labour, that work for bread, and depend upon either labour or charity for subsistence'.[114] He might agree with other writers that many people were poor because, like the bad servants and labourers discussed above, they were idle and drunken. Such people deserved no pity. But Defoe did not leave it at that. He saw that there were other reasons for poverty and those who were poor because of them received his sympathy.

The most obvious cause of poverty for the able-bodied in the days of Defoe was the fact that there was never enough work for every-body all the time. The farmers needed to employ vast numbers of extra workers at the peak times of the farming year. Many of the harvesters and haymakers were migrants who had jobs elsewhere for the rest of the year, but this was by no means true of all of them. The same seasonality operated in many other occupations. Water mills did not work in the summer when there was no water; building workers could not work in the winter when it was too wet. A brick-layer, for example, could expect to be out of work for five, if not six, months of the year.[115] In London a vast number of workers only had work to do during the season when gentlemen and lawyers with their families and servants came to town to do the year's business and enjoy themselves, spending freely as they did so. A tailor or a milliner could well be idle for a third of the year and there was little likelihood of them finding alternative work to tide them over till the gentlemen and their ladies returned.[116] It was unlikely, for instance, that a man could be a tailor in winter and a bricklayer in the summer. Of course nine months' work would have been a luxury for many. A great army of stevedores and porters was necessary to unload and distribute the goods brought in by England's fleet of merchantmen which made London's river such a memorable sight. But there was not a regular flow of imports and many, if not most, of these workmen were idle on any particular day.

Seasonal unemployment was fairly predictable and a clever work-man might be able to dovetail several jobs to keep himself reasonably well employed. Even the stevedore who had no work because the wind prevented shipping sailing up the river could console himself with the thought that an English wind was not likely to blow the same way for very long. But much unemployment was caused by the vagaries of governments or the rich and could not be predicted by the poor. The fortunes of war or a change of fashion could suddenly put thousands of people out of work throughout the country. With no wages they could no longer afford to maintain their standard of consumption, thus throwing a far larger number of people who had previously depended on supplying their wants into the ranks of the poor.

The vulnerability of labour in such an economy is well illustrated in the *Journal of the Plague Year*. Here Defoe points out that it was among the poor that mortality was highest. This was because they were forced by their poverty to spend much of their time out in the streets mingling with other poor people, many of whom were infected. They could afford neither to escape the city, as many of the rich had done, nor to lay up a stock of provisions and shut themselves up in their houses till the virulence of the plague had passed. Poverty dictated their behaviour. They had to go out to the shops and markets every day to buy food in small quantities. But they also had to go out to look for work. For the plague had led to a massive fall in regular employment. The virtual closure of the port had meant that not only had all the seamen, dockers and porters been dismissed but also that a vast range of skilled workmen from rope-makers to anchor-smiths had been laid off. The flight of the court to Oxford and of many of the well-to-do to their country homes led to the unemployment of all those who catered for the fashions of the wealthy and of that great army of servants normally employed in the city. Finally, the heavy mortality had brought all of the building work in the city to a halt.[117] Since the main alternative employments were digging plague pits and carting the dead it is not surprising that many poor people died. Only the merciful coincidence of a good harvest in the plague year had prevented mortality from being even higher.

Plague was of course an exceptional occurrence, but intermittent unemployment was a normal phenomenon in Defoe's world. Moreover, even in good times, the available work was not spread evenly across the country.[118] This normally high level of unemployment could be greatly increased if some structural change occurred in the usual pattern of employment. Defoe draws our attention to the plight of the English silkworkers, forced to turn to lesser occupations by Indian competition.[119] The long-term solution for a problem

like this and similar problems was government legislation, in the
case of silk a ban on retained imports. But what about the already
underemployed coalheavers, porters and fish-sellers who must
have found it even more difficult to make a living when a flood of
unemployed silkworkers began to compete with them for the available work?

The truth is that, although Defoe had more understanding of the
causes of poverty than most of his contemporaries, he never really
considers the endemic problem of underemployment in any depth.
At the back of his mind he always has his basic proposition that
overall there must be sufficient work for everybody or else the level
of wages would have fallen. As a result, he is immediately suspicious
when he sees a coalheaver or a porter out of work or when he is
asked to provide a dole for their support through the poor rate.
How could such a man, clearly fit and able to work, find himself
unemployed? There must be something wrong with him and the
most likely thing to be wrong is that he is idle and realizes that
people in the middle station are a soft touch for alms, if not a
regular pension.

So perhaps the Webbs were not all that wrong in their assessment
of Defoe's analysis of poverty. It certainly requires little ingenuity
by the student of Defoe to find references linking idleness with
unemployment, and hence poverty. That thoughtful observer of
human nature, Robinson Crusoe, was able to note that in the
community that had grown up on his island the iron law of idleness
was in operation. The five English mutineers whom he had marooned had reacted in different ways to the challenge of their new
environment and had been rewarded according to their merits.
'The diligent liv'd well and comfortably, and the slothful liv'd
hard and beggarly; and so I believe, generally speaking, it is all
over the world.'[120] Defoe, when he wrote this, may well have had
in his mind a passage from the *Review* of 1707 where he had argued
that in any given population there would be some diligent and some
slothful and that, as a result, there would always be rich and poor.
'Equality of division cannot possibly last. There will be rich and
poor; the diligent will improve, and the slothful decay; the sluggard
will be cloth'd in rags, and the good-wife will be array'd in purple;
the waster will starve, and the good-husband will be rich.'[121]

The diligent man had a genius for improving himself and for
recovering from disaster. He would never be poor for long. If he

was out of work through no fault of his own, and Defoe was suffi-ciently realistic to admit that this could happen, he would look after himself, not come running to the rate-payer for support.[122] He would look for work and support himself and his family in the meantime with the money which he had saved in anticipation of just such a period of difficulty.[123] This conviction that self-help could overcome all problems is the basis of the only fully-worked-out cure for poverty that Defoe wrote. This is in the early *Essay upon Projects* and it is perhaps significant that he does not repeat it in his later works. The scheme is for a Pension-Office to which all labouring people should pay a compulsory shilling a quarter and draw free medical treatment or, if necessary, a pension for life 'if they become lame, aged, bedrid, or by real infirmity of body (the pox excepted) are unable to work'.[124] This was the basis on which friendly societies were to develop in the nineteenth century. But, although mutual insurance might make good sense for a craftsman with his relatively high wages and regularity of employment, it was totally unrealistic for the mass of the underemployed poor. Defoe's scheme does not even mention unemployment; not that a contribu-tion of four shillings a year would have done much to alleviate it in any case. Nevertheless the Pension-Office was confidently announced as a method of banishing beggary and poverty forever out of the kingdom. Who could ever feel sorry for the poor man who had failed to pay his contribution? 'Who, indeed, wou'd ever pity that man in his distress, who at the expence of two pots of beer a month, might have prevented it, and wou'd not spare it?'[125]

The 1690s was a time of soaring poor rates, caused by high food prices and high unemployment. As usual a crisis produced its crop of panaceas and the decade was a great time for utopian schemes for curing poverty. The most popular were those which advocated a new world where the poor had been swept away out of sight and at the same time were made to pay for themselves. Old ideas that there was something admirable, even saintly, in poverty had long disappeared. Poverty had become just rather untidy and very expensive.

The idea that the able-bodied poor should pay for their keep had been incorporated in the famous Elizabethan Poor Law. The poor were to maintain themselves by working in their own homes on a stock of material provided by the parish. Such schemes norm-ally foundered because the overseers were unable to sell the resulting

goods. By the second half of the seventeenth century most parishes
had probably discontinued the practice. They found it cheaper and
much easier to support the able-bodied poor by handing out a dole
to those who could convince the overseers that they needed it. There
was inevitably much criticism of such a policy. The sight of fit men
doing no work and spending public money on drink was calculated
to make the contemporary rate-payer gnash his teeth in uncontroll-
able fury and to stimulate intellectuals to an orgy of pamphlet-
writing, in which schemes from the fantastic to the apparently
realistic were presented for the attention of a gullible public and a
parliament of rate-payers.[126]

Nearly all the solutions that poured forth had two aspects in
common. The poor must be made to pay for themselves and they
must be herded together in an institution. An optimistic belief
in the power of institutions to cure or at least obliterate all distress
and all vice can be seen in most schemes of reform in the period
1650–1750. A shining example had been set by the French. In
1656 a decree founded the Hôpital Général in Paris. In the following
year, the Paris militia, 'the archers of the Hôpital', began their
task of hunting down beggars and herding them into the different
buildings of the new institution. Within a few years five or six
thousand men, women and children had been shut up. The great
confinement had begun.[127] The English were not slow to see the
beautiful simplicity of such a scheme though, lacking the effective
central government of the Bourbons, they were unable to operate
on such a grand scale. London tried hard but it was to remain an
untidy city, in bureaucratic terms, compared with Paris. The
English multiplied the existing public institutions, such as hospitals,
gaols and houses of correction, and expanded their functions to
absorb more of the human litter which formed such a blot on an
otherwise industrious and prospering society. New institutions, such
as the private mad-house, were developed to fill in some of the
gaps.[128] Different men might have different solutions to the same
social problem but all solutions were likely to incorporate some sort
of institution. Mandeville, for instance, thought that prostitutes
should be herded into municipal brothels; other writers thought
they should be in reformatories or even public laundries; but
everyone, including Defoe, thought they should be swept off the
streets where they openly plied their trade and made London a
scandal, the lewdest city on earth.[129] Defoe in his old age was indeed

obssessed with order. In *Every-body's Business is No-body's Business*
he attacked the 'ten thousand wicked, idle, pilfering vagrants'
called the Black Guard 'who black your Honour's shoes', corrupt
servants, pilfer and act as fences for indoor-servants' thefts. He
proposed that they should be rounded up and set to work. If they
proved refractory they should be sent to the mines where hard
work was required or set to clear the Thames of obstructions under
guard of soldiers.[130] Whatever would have happened to Colonel
Jack?

The institution which was expected to tidy up poverty was the
workhouse. Many schemes were propounded but they were for the
most part repetitions of each other. Parishes or groups of parishes
would set up a workhouse and provide a stock of materials and an
efficient overseer who would see not only that work was done, but
also ensure that the inmates followed a strict regime calculated to
make them think twice about ever being poor again.[131] The workhouse as such was an old idea. Indeed many of the Elizabethan
houses of correction were little more than workhouses. But the
modern workhouse movement is conventionally considered to have
begun in 1696 when Bristol obtained a local Act of Parliament
which, amongst other things, authorized the establishment of a
workhouse to be financed and managed by a union of the city's
parishes. Other towns followed Bristol's example and in 1723 a
general enabling act was passed which led to a boom in workhouse
creation in the mid-1720s.

Defoe, as we have seen, objected to workhouses on principle, on
the grounds that giving the poor work in a workhouse deprived
another poor man of similar work somewhere else in the country.[132]
His pamphlet on this subject, *Giving Alms no Charity*, effectively
killed Sir Humphrey Mackworth's attempt to introduce a major
revision of the Poor Law, by which a public workhouse would have
been set up in every parish.[133] But, significantly, Defoe has nothing
much to say about workhouses in his later years. His well-reasoned
fears of 1704 and 1705 had no basis in reality. The workhouse as a
self-financing institution for employing the poor was a complete
flop. It was much cheaper to relieve a man in his own home. Nor
did the pitiful output of the supervised labour within the workhouse
compete seriously with national production. Much of the work was
geared to supplying the needs of the inmates themselves. When
goods were produced for sale they often did not compete directly

with work outside. Picking oakum was a favourite task, although occasionally one finds a more imaginative use of the captive labour, such as the St Paul's Covent Garden workhouse which specialized in beating carpets for the West End.[134]

The able-bodied poor, for whom the workhouse had been originally designed, were very rarely to be found within its walls. The reason for this is interesting and shows that late seventeenth-century views of poverty, though muddled, were not totally wrong. The workhouse, in fact, was an effective method of distinguishing between the idle and the 'accidental' poor who were genuinely looking for work. Few idle men would willingly accept the workhouse regime. A man genuinely looking for work might, if he was desperate. But once he had established his credentials by accepting the workhouse there was no point in admitting him, since this would prevent him from looking for work. He would therefore be relieved in his own home, which in any case was cheaper, and the workhouse was filled up with long-term cases of poverty. Such people could look after each other and, if they were children, be prepared for the inevitable day when they too would have to go out into a pitiless world and look for work. With a clientèle consisting mainly of children, old people, invalids and deserted mothers it is hardly surprising that productivity was low and that the workhouse was unable to pay for itself, as the author of an anonymous book on workhouses points out:

> The failure of most attempts for improving the poor has been generally owing to the expecting too much profit from their labour: for, alas! What great gains can be hop'd for, from old, infirm people, who are past labour, or young inexperienc'd children, who have everything to learn.[135]

But on the next page he tells us the real object of the workhouse. 'No vagabond poor dare come into, or stay long in a parish, where such a house is erected.'[136] The 'workhouse test' which was to play such an important role in the nineteenth-century Poor Law was written into the general enabling act of 1723. 'In case any poor person shall refuse to be lodg'd, kept and maintain'd in such house or houses, such person shall be put out of the parish books and not entituled to relief.'[137] As a result of the difference between the avowed original intention of the workhouse and the reality, Defoe did not find it necessary to repeat his attacks on the economic effects of the institution when he wrote his savage criticism of local government, *Parochial Tyranny*, in 1727. All he was worried about was the fact that the workhouse, as a general dustbin for the unfortunate, made no attempt to separate the good from the bad. What would happen if some honest man of the middle station should suffer the poverty of disaster? 'We all, alas, are subject to misfortune! and if an honest gentleman or trader should leave a wife or children unprovided for, what a shocking thing is it to think they must be mix'd with vagrants, beggars, thieves, and night-walkers.'[138] The answer was to have a strict partition of the workhouse between those shabby genteel ex-members of the middle station who might be so unfortunate as to seek its protection and the 'vagabond wretches' who were its normal inmates.

Alongside the promoters of workhouses were some much more utopian schemes with which Defoe probably had more sympathy. They were virtually identical in spirit with Defoe's plans for absorbing the poor immigrants from the Palatinate, which were discussed in the last chapter.[139] One such proposal was put forward by the Quaker John Bellers in 1696.[140] His idea was to set up a college of industry where two hundred people of all trades would provide the necessities of life for three hundred, leaving the output of the rest as a profit for those who put up the estimated capital investment of £18,000. The poor in this college would 'be a community something like the example of primitive Christianity, that lived in common'. Such schemes had an attractive and plausible simplicity. It was obvious that it was unnecessary for the whole population to work in order for the basic needs of everyone to be satisfied.[141] Therefore, if everyone did work there must be a surplus which could be used either, as in this example, to produce profit for the investor or for any one of a host of attractive utopian objectives. If there had been a prize for the most fantastic scheme of the early eighteenth century it would surely have gone to the delightfully crazy idea of Lawrence Braddon, who proposed to set up one general corporation for relieving, reforming and employing all the poor of Great Britain.[142] A million and a half poor people would be settled in collegiate cities all over the country and half a million of this population would be producing goods surplus to the subsistence requirements of the whole. The sale of their output would undercut and eventually destroy the economies of both France and Holland, leaving Britain with an enormous surplus on her balance of trade.

The earnings would be used, amongst other things, to pay off the national debt within twenty years. How happy a country it would have been if only George 1 had listened to Braddon. There would have been no more poor, no more poor rates, virtually no taxation and all this without doing any harm to any existing interest. Unfortunately, no such scheme was ever attempted but, before we write off Braddon and his friends as harmless lunatics, it is worth remembering that the settlement of North America, especially of Massachusetts, was based on very similar reasoning. The trouble was that there were few empty areas the size of Massachusetts in Great Britain.

Overall, the new ideas, whether realistic or fantastic, had little effect on poverty, except perhaps to brand as hopelessly idle any man too proud to accept the workhouse test. More poor people were shut away in institutions but, for the most part, poor relief in the eighteenth century, as it had been in the seventeenth, was a matter of handing out doles to the poor in their own homes. Defoe was quite happy about this. Despite his somewhat confused views about the able-bodied poor, a confusion which he shared with most of his contemporaries, he knew that they would always exist and that there would always be even more widows and orphans, aged and sick. Some would be idle and these should be sorted out and punished before being relieved. But most would be genuine and deserved to be supported, 'for no man ought to starve'.[143] Indeed, so certain was Defoe that poverty was ever-present that he was prepared to have a shot at estimating how many poor there would be in any one parish. In a London parish of four hundred houses, for instance, he thought that forty poor would be 'a competent number'.[144] Defoe also knew that the existing Poor Law had many anomalies and that many people fell through its net. Many people, especially in London, had no settlement where they lived and worked and so were not entitled to poor relief if they fell on hard times. But even if they had a settlement there was no guarantee that they would receive adequate relief. The eighteenth-century ratepayer was not particularly altruistic and, if Defoe is to be believed, much of what he did pay in poor rates stuck to the hands of the parish officers and never got near the poor.[145] Charity, therefore, must fill the gap.

'Charity', as the cynical Mandeville reminds us, 'is that virtue by which part of that sincere love we have for our selves is transferr'd pure and unmix'd to others.'[146] Self-love was certainly part of the motive but, for Defoe at least, self-help was just as important. The good uncle in *Roxana* makes the point. 'He that gives to the poor, lends to the Lord ... I only talk of putting out a little money to interest, our Maker is a good borrower, never fear making a bad debt there.'[147] But the good Lord himself would not approve of indiscriminate charity. It was the duty of the charitable to sort the deserving from the idle, to do the workhouse test in his head. The problems in doing this are illustrated by an article that Defoe wrote in *Applebee's Journal*.[148] It had been a wet summer and Defoe made a plea for the migrant haymakers who were suffering because they could get no work. There had been a generous response to their plight, but the word had quickly gone round the underworld and 'all your common beggars, mumpers, and street runners' had armed themselves with fork and rake and joined the army of haymakers in the hope of sharing in the hand-out.[149] How were the charitable to distinguish a genuinely unemployed haymaker from an habitually idle beggar? Defoe's answer must have appealed to many. Wait for a sunny or windy dry day, for then haymakers would be making hay and only beggars would be begging!

When we come to examine the other large group of idle able-bodied men and women in the world of Defoe, the ladies and gentlemen of leisure, we find as many anomalies as in the discussion of the poor. The very fact that they were leisured was anomalous. How could one preach work to the poor and teach the middle station that every minute of their time was precious, when the most alluring objective of such a close attention to the main task was to attain the blissful state of gentility, and hence be idle?

This paradox is always at the back of Defoe's discussion of gentlemen. One part of him admired the ease of upwards social mobility in England and welcomed that climax of the career of a successful man in the middle station which enabled him to convert his capital into a rentier income and buy himself a life of genteel leisure. It was after all his own ambition. But the other part of Defoe spent much of his writing career lambasting the life-style of existing gentlemen. The confusion is made worse by the fact that he only rarely distinguishes between the two types of gentlemen which we discussed at the beginning of this chapter. Some of his attack is certainly aimed directly at what he saw to be the typical country gentleman, but much of it is simply abuse of all gentlemen of leisure.

There was also another problem. Implicit in the concept of the gentleman was an almost mystic belief that gentlemen were somehow different from the rest of mankind. Such a belief posed difficulties for the *nouveau riche*, who was soon made to realize that the combination of wealth and idleness did not automatically create a gentleman. The rich man might try to behave like a gentleman, but even if he moved into a new circle which did not know his real origins he was likely to be unmasked. There was in fact a certain quality by which the discerning could distinguish the English gentleman however well he might be disguised. What was it about the Englishman whom Captain Singleton met in his journey across Africa which led him to remark that 'he appeared to be a gentleman', although 'he was stark naked, and had been so, as he told us, upwards of two years'?[150] It can hardly have been his appearance, despite his very fine skin. Presumably it was the very fact that he could retain his dignity even in such unfortunate circumstances. And where had he acquired such dignity? Gentlemen of old families liked to think that it was something to do with birth and breeding, something in fact that no new man could possibly acquire.

Defoe, the advocate of such new men, refused to accept these mystical properties of the English gentleman. He preferred to emphasize the often sordid origins of both the gentlemen and the nobility of England. Scratch a pedigree and what did you find? 'French cooks, Scotch pedlars, and Italian whores'[151] were the progenitors of much of the existing nobility, while the best that one could say of most 'ancient' families was that their 'ancestors have at least for some time been rais'd above the class of mechanicks'.[152] Gentlemen were really made, not born. Even those who had acquired the status of gentleman at birth needed a proper education in order to attain that virtue which was so essential if they were to behave like a gentleman as well as be one. If all gentlemen required to be educated, this meant that there was theoretically ample scope for the new man to satisfy his ambition. He might even be a better gentleman than the gentleman born.[153]

In fact he almost certainly would be. It was possible to make a gentleman, but those who were already gentlemen behaved in the most appalling and ungentlemanlike way. It seemed almost as though a man ceased to behave like a gentleman the moment he became one. It looked as though the net result of that social ambition which pushed successful members of the middle station into the leisured classes would be the moral degeneration of their sons. This was hardly a very satisfactory situation and moralists leaped into action to try and do something about it. The writers of the day poured out non-stop criticism of the morals of their social betters and at the same time produced a flood of conduct-books from which fond parents might learn how to bring up their sons to be ideal English gentlemen.[154] When such literature was written by Locke or Addison, or even Defoe, it was excellent, though it probably did more to improve the morals of the middle classes than of the gentlemen it was supposedly aimed at. But most of it, as one might imagine, was impossibly dreary and one suspects that the gentry, if they sought advice on the ways of the world, would have preferred to receive just one letter from Lord Chesterfield.

The main reason for the bad behaviour of gentlemen was also the main attraction in being one. They had no work to do. This itself in a work and time-conscious society was something to be condemned. When Robinson Crusoe became a gentleman of leisure, in the interval of chasing foolishly round the world, he found it a very attractive way of life but was forced to comment on its irrelevance. 'I had . . . nothing to do but to saunter about like an idle person, of whom it may be said, he is perfectly useless in God's creation; and it is not one farthing matter to the rest of his kind whether he be dead or alive.'[155] Defoe knew God better than that and elsewhere, while condemning the idleness of gentlemen, he is able to improve somewhat on Crusoe's limited understanding of economic realities:

I allow, there are a sort of drones in the hive, who live on the said labour and industry of the others – And were intollerable in the nation, but for two things; 1. that they help to consume the produce; and 2. that they pay for it. Otherwise some of our gentry, by their course of life, would almost give occasion for blasphemous thoughts of their maker, as if he had done something in the world to no purpose at all.[156]

Needless to say, gentlemen, particularly country gentlemen, were continuously criticized for what they consumed, even if it was accepted that maintaining a conspicuous level of consumption was their only function in society.

Ideally the country gentleman was supposed to do far more with

his time and income than simply to spend money. He was supposed
to look after his estates, be kind to his tenants and the poor and to set
them a good example of behaviour. He should maintain the old
traditions of hospitality by keeping an open house and, if he were
rich enough, he should play a responsible part in county society, a
role which involved a considerable number of unpaid duties, such
as service on the bench, as a member of parliament or as an officer
in the militia. In other words he should be like Sir Roger de Coverley, though even such an attractive upholder of the traditional Tory
virtues as this was something of a figure of fun to his Whig creators.[157]
Such people probably did exist, though we hear little of them, and
when we do hear of a gentleman behaving himself there is usually
more than a touch of irony, as in Swift's delightful description of
Henry St John at his country estate. 'Mr. Secretary was a perfect
country gentleman at Buckleberry; he smoakt tobacco with one or
two neighbours; he enquired after the wheat in such a field, he
went to visit his hounds; and knew all their names; he and his lady
saw me to my chamber just in the country fashion. His house is in
the midst of near three thousand pounds a year he had by his lady.'[158]
But the normal comment on the country gentlemen was that they
were a failure on nearly all counts.

Indeed the moralizing literature of the early eighteenth century
produced a stereotype of a country gentleman, the antithesis of Sir
Roger de Coverley, and as far removed from reality. The only thing
that such a gentleman might do properly was to look after his
tenants, the source of his income and a rather shaky source at that
in a period of low or falling prices.[159] Even if he looked after his
income as best he could he was not encouraged to mix socially with
his tenants, for 'peasantry is a disease (like the plague) easily
caught by conversation'.[160] It was not a disease that many such
gentlemen seemed likely to catch, since they systematically neglected
those duties which might have led to increased contact with the
humbler elements of the countryside. They neglected the poor and
failed to employ them. They no longer maintained the traditional
hospitality of the big house and in fact shut it up for much of the
year while they were in London, thus failing to support the local
tradesmen and farmers. If the richer of their number took their
duties seriously enough to sit on the bench they were shockingly
corrupt and maintained a double standard of tolerance of the vices
of the rich and vindictive punishment for the same vices when

practised by the poor. They might not even be able to read the laws which they so scandalously administered. For one of the more reprehensible things about the country gentlemen was their ignorance. Education, they said, was for their younger brothers who had their way to make in the world.[161] As for themselves they were proud to be illiterate.[162] The results of such an attitude were appalling. 'This is the reason why a man may venture to say there perhaps never was a H.... of C....s in England till now, where there has not been a hundred men could hardly spell their own names, and some that could not write them.'[163]

And what an example these ignorant men set to those beneath them. If contemporary opinion was correct their lives must have been one long debauch, the sordid routine of drinking, gaming and whoring only occasionally interrupted by chasing round the countryside after a fox or having a romp or a snooze in the kennels with the dogs. The foppish London gentleman was no better. He simply added vanity to the other genteel vices, being the sort of man, 'that seeing but a new-fashion'd shoe will look upon their own and blush, and can no longer believe themselves dress'd'.[164] No wonder that vice had triumphed since lesser mortals were bound to ape their betters. If only their betters would reform. A reformed upper class would lead to a reformed people. Defoe was just one of a long line of writers who begged and bullied the gentlemen of his day in an attempt to make them just a little more virtuous and public-spirited. They were wasting their time. The country gentlemen of England preferred their bottles and their dogs.

In any case sober and well-behaved gentlemen would have had the same deleterious effects in Defoe's view of society as would sober and well-behaved servants. For, as he loved to point out, it was the irresponsibility of the rich which kept the whole social machine going. Thank goodness their vices were not cheap. The fact that they kept on spending was the fact that kept a considerable proportion of the people employed. Gregory King estimated the income of the nobility and gentry, despite their small numbers, to be thirteen per cent of the national income.[165] How could the tradesmen and the poor have survived if they had not spent it? Fortunately for the economy they did. Indeed many of them did even better than this, spending more than they received as income.[166] This, in Defoe's eyes, was one of the main differences between the gentry and the people of the middle station, a difference which he

loved to proclaim in the language of Micawberish accountancy.
Year after year, the middle station saved a little of their income and
so got rich. If only, as Sir Robert Clayton explained to Roxana, 'the
gentlemen of England wou'd but act so, every family of them wou'd
encrease their fortunes to a great degree, just as merchants do by
trade; whereas now, . . . by the humour of living up to the extent
of their fortunes, and rather beyond, the gentlemen, says he, ay,
and the nobility too, are almost all of them, borrowers, and all in
necessitous circumstances.'[167]

It was not only extravagance which put them in this plight. Most
of the income of the country gentry, particularly the lesser gentry,
came from the land and landed incomes were in considerable
trouble in the early eighteenth century. This was particularly true
during the war when efficient assessment of the Land Tax could
mean that some gentlemen were paying twenty per cent of their
net income to support what many of them thought was an unnecessarily long and expensive Whig war. But, even after the war,
the generally low level of agricultural prices made it difficult to
raise or even maintain the level of their rental income.[168] Life
could be difficult for a gentleman caught between a stagnant income
and the temptations of an increasingly luxurious and ostentatious
metropolis. There were, of course, ways of supplementing a landed
income. 'Frequent war, a flourishing court, and the increase of public
business' could all provide jobs for the boys.[169] Trade itself was open
to the sons of gentlemen as well as to the sons of tradesmen, and
many gentlemen's sons were not too proud to serve an apprenticeship to a merchant or a shopkeeper. Even if he could not improve
his income, a sensible gentleman could go back to his estates 'till
time and his real estate will redeem him'.[170] But gentlemen, as we
have seen, were not famous for their good sense, luckily for the
tradesmen who were the most likely group to benefit from their
stupidity.

These very men who had emptied the gentle coffers were able to
replenish them. For who had the mobile wealth to be able to lend
money to the impoverished gentlemen; who had the money to buy
his estate when it came on the market; who had a plump and
genteely educated daughter with a dowry big enough to tempt a
duke in danger? And there was no point in being snobbish about
it as a nobleman explained to a titled lady who scorned her monied
husband.[171]

In former days ... it was indeed beneath a man of quality to
match among the vassals. But then two things are to be observed,
which have happened in England since that time.

1. The Commons have grown rich by industry and commerce.
2. The Nobility are become poor, or at least poorer; be it by
   sloth and luxury, I do not determine ... [Nowadays] we
   often go into the City to get fortunes for our sons; and many
   noble families, sunk by the folly and luxury of their predecessors, are restored, by marrying into the families of
   those that you call mechanicks.

The thrifty members of the middle station took their chance and
the days of Defoe were days of great social mobility as he loves to
tell us.[172] 'The merchant grows rich, lays up vast sums, and being
able to give great portions, his daughter marries my lord duke's
son, and in time becomes a dutchess; and his son marries my
lord's eldest daughter; and thus the tradesman's grandson becomes
a duke, and my lord's grandson goes prentice to a merchant; their
coats of arms are quarter'd *parte per pale*, and posterity knows no
difference.'[173]

Such dramatic changes of fortune did indeed happen in the
world of Defoe, but the usual elevation of a successful member of
the middle station was more modest and did not take him far from
the bustling world where he had made his money. He was interested
neither in the vices nor the virtues of the country gentleman. Not
for him the broad acres of the shires with their poor tenants, poachers
and soaring poor rates. His country house was more likely to be in
Surrey villages such as Peckham or Camberwell, Carshalton or
Tooting, one amongst many. Each house had its fine garden and
was built 'with such a profusion of expence, that they look rather
like seats of the nobility than the country houses of citizens and
merchants'.[174] Here he might have retired completely but more
likely would still keep a finger in several city pies, like the rich
inhabitants of Tottenham, half citizens, half gentlemen, people
'generally belonging to the middle sort of mankind, grown wealthy
by trade, and who still taste of London; some of them live both in
the city, and in the country at the same time'.[175] His business in the
city was bound to bring him into contact with those members of
the nobility and the country gentry whose incomes now so depended

on the rise and fall of stocks and shares, 'that they find themselves
obliged to come up and live constantly here, or at least, most part of
the year'.[176] The rich citizen retired or semi-retired from the daily
grind of business, and the former country gentleman happy to spend
most of his time in the metropolis, merged to produce that new
sophisticate, the urban gentleman of leisure. He, too had his faults.
He was vain and he was covetous; he drank too much and he
whored too much and he spent too much time at the theatre or the
masquerade. His life-style had the flavour of *Vanity Fair* but it
was a long way from the bottle and the dogs of the stereotyped
country squire.

That Vanity Fair which was London society outlasted both
Roxana and Becky Sharp. In the last quarter of the nineteenth
century, in the heyday of the Victorians, we find a world which is
strikingly similar to that of Defoe. Here too we find that gentlemen
are having difficulty in maintaining their incomes; here too we find
a big increase in the real incomes of the middle classes and of the
poor. A similar economic background produced similar social
change. Late-Victorian gentlemen were busy looking for city money
and city marriages, as their forebears were in the days of Queen
Anne and the first two Georges. The shopkeeper is once again the
beneficiary as increased real wages are translated into spending
power. Once again middle-class money buys leisure and a rentier
income as soon as possible. In the later period the English rentier
was to secure a steady income by lending to foreign governments and
railway companies rather than to his own government, but like his
predecessor he used his income to acquire what appeared to be
necessary to the good taste of the time. In the 1880s as in the 1720s,
moralists attacked the *nouveaux riches* for their ostentation, and
writers of conduct-books taught them to be genteel. And, strangely
enough, both the ideals of middle-class gentility and the idea of a
desirable expenditure pattern seem to have changed very little.
There was no great rush to install a bathroom in the 1720s but
otherwise we might be in the same world. In both periods the men
and women who formed the leisured society of London wanted
more servants, a carriage, to be seen riding in the park, good food,
good wine, clothes from Paris and in general wished to give the
impression by the scale of their ostentation that they had even more
money than they had. By the time of Defoe a standard of wealthy
London consumption and behaviour had been established which

was to last virtually unchanged up to the First World War, and even later.[177] All that the Industrial Revolution had managed to achieve in one sector of English society, and a fairly large one at that, was to ensure that in the 1880s even more people had servants and a coach and horses than in the 1720s.

PART IV

THE INDIVIDUAL IN SOCIETY

THE MAKING OF THE INDIVIDUAL

MAN in the world of Defoe, as in ours, was inevitably moulded by the society in which he lived. That providence which determined that he should be born the child of an Englishman, rather than of a French peasant or an African slave, naturally set the scene for the drama of his life. An observer might even think that he could predict the nature and the pattern of a man's life, armed with the single fact of his birth. But he would usually be wrong. Man was not a cog in a machine programmed to behave in a predictable way. He was an individual, driven by self-love and aided by self-help, who could himself, with the all-important assistance of divine providence, determine the conditions of his own existence.

What was the object of that existence? At the very least a man must do all that he could to ensure that it continued. No man should let himself die.[1] But satisfaction with a mere state of survival was not enough. Defoe would never have echoed Richard Baxter's advice to the poor: 'Be willing to dye. Seeing the world giveth you so cold entertainment, be the more content to let it go . . . For what is here to detain your hearts.'[2] A man should never be content to let the world go. Nor should he be content with the state of existence in which he was born. He had a duty to improve himself, for 'Nature dictates to life that it should be progressive and increasing; and improvement is a study of the greatest minds, and the greatest men upon earth.'[3] But in the process of improvement, with all its worldly excitements and distresses, a man should never think that secular improvement was the only end of life. He had a duty to make the most of his innate capabilities, to improve himself in this world, but he also had a duty to prepare himself for the next.

Defoe felt it was possible to get the best of both worlds, to be a happy and successful worldling and still go to heaven, but he offers no false optimism. Those who hope for success in both this world and the next will have to work hard for it. And they could never start too early. Ultimately, success must depend on the efforts of the individual, but the early preparation, the moulding, was a responsibility and a duty that fell on his parents. It was a responsibility that they only too easily forgot.

A modern parent might well feel some disgust if his son resembled the appalling child who appears in the first dialogue of *The Family Instructor*.[4] This precocious creature, a 'thinking and inquiring' child of about five or six years old, cross-questions his father about God and his soul and, when the father has scraped about in his mind for the correct answers, sternly rebukes him for allowing him to be ignorant of such matters at such an advanced age. But, nasty as the child was, one has to accept that he was perfectly justified in taking such an attitude. In an age of enormously high child mortality his parents had already gambled recklessly with his chances of salvation. Many of the child heroes and heroines of the best-selling *Token for Children* were only four or five when they died, having already spent years on their knees in their rooms, where their sobbing and groaning as they wrestled with their sins was faithfully reported by those listening outside.[5] The author asked his child readers some terrifying questions. 'How do you know but that you may be the next child that may die? And where are you then, if you be not God's child?' The answer is spelled out in no uncertain terms. The wicked child will go to the Devil, 'into everlasting burning', to that terrible place called Hell, 'that's worse a thousand times than whipping'.[6]

No wonder, then, that most writers of conduct-books and books on education stressed the need to start the educational process as early as possible when the child was like wax 'ready to be moulded into any form, and receive any impression'.[7] 'While you lay them in your bosomes, and dandle them on your knees, try by little and little to infuse good things, holy truths into them', wrote Benjamin Wadsworth.[8] The need for an early start was given added weight if the writer believed in original sin. If the child was born evil and his heart was 'a mere nest, root, fountain of sin, and wickedness',[9] it was clearly essential to start at once if the child was to have any hope of salvation. Fortunately the child was born ignorant as well as evil, and his parents were thus offered the opportunity to make the correct impressions on the *tabula rasa*.

In fact, contemporary ideas suggested that the parents, particularly the mother, could have done considerable harm to the child long before he was old enough to dandle on her knee. It was felt that, from the moment of conception, the mother's imagination could affect both the appearance and the personality of the child. Her influence was particularly strong in the last weeks of pregnancy when 'the impressive force is made highly conspicuous, marvelously altering the infant'.[10] Judging by contemporary male views of what went on in women's minds such an influence could have serious implications for the moral future of the race. Female failure to think correct thoughts was reinforced by the common custom of mothers of the middle and upper classes to put their babies out to nurse. The motivation was said to be the vanity and idleness of the mother who forbore to feed her own children, 'for fear of their shapes',[11] and because they hated to be tied to the nursery and thus unable to mis-spend their days and nights.[12] The practice was also condemned because of its effects on the child. Defoe, amongst others, held that a baby took in the nurse's temper with her milk, one reason amongst many for the degeneracy of the modern gentleman whose character was irredeemably sullied by the milk that he had sucked at the plump breast of the ploughman's daughter.[13]

Mothers were not only criticized for neglect. A common complaint was that they were too fond of the child, pampering it and shielding it from the harsh blast of reality that was necessary if the child was to be prepared to face the world. In behaving like this the mother was simply reflecting a new attitude to the child, quite often shared by her husband. There is considerable evidence that the eighteenth century saw an improvement, from a modern point of view, in the domestic conditions of at least the children of the higher income groups.[14] They were treated more as children and less as erring sinners to be whipped into a state of grace. It is in this period that can be seen the real beginnings of a culture specifically for children and of the commercial enterprise to provide it. Children began to wear special children's clothes, instead of miniature adult clothes, when they came out of their infant dresses. They began to read books written specifically for children, or rather books which seem to us more suitable for children than the largely undifferentiated religious diet of the seventeenth century.[15] Children were also provided with a far wider range of toys and amusements than they had had in the past. This trend, which has continued to our own day, was partly a result of increased material prosperity. Many more people could now afford to spend money on superfluities and expenditure on children was just another form of ostentatious consumption. The child, like his mother, could reflect the new-won economic status of the successful man of the middle station. But the changes also reflected a new view of childhood as something completely different from adolescence and adulthood. Children were no longer seen as young adults. They were more like pets and were pampered accordingly.

Writers on education were wary of this trend. This is hardly surprising. Whether the particular writer's background was puritanical or not it was hardly in the spirit of the age actually to recommend a pampered way of life for the child. Perhaps the most influential educational writer of the time was John Locke, who argued for a stoical régime on the basis that if the child was used to hardship in his youth, hardship would never hurt him as a man. He recommended 'plenty of open air, exercise and sleep; plain diet, no wine or strong drink, and very little or no physick; not too warm and straight clothing, especially the head and feet kept cold, and the feet often used to cold water, and exposed to wet'.[16] 'Brawniness and insensibility of mind is the best armour we can have, against the common evils and accidents of life.'[17] Locke was against beating a child unless the circumstances were exceptional, preferring a system of reward and punishment in which the child received praise and esteem if he did well and felt disgraced if he did wrong.[18] But most writers held that the rod was an essential part of the child's education. Cotton Mather's famous epigram, 'better whipt, than damn'd',[19] belongs in spirit to the seventeenth century but the biblical equivalent, 'spare the rod and spoil the child', still held sway.[20] 'Correction is of great use and often necessary,' wrote Archbishop Tillotson, 'and parents that forbear it are not only cruel to their children but to themselves.'[21] He also emphasized the double sanction available to parents who could reinforce the immediate effect of punishment in this world by the warning of eternal punishment in the next. 'And because fear and hope are the two passions which do chiefly sway and govern human nature ... children are to be carefully inform'd that there is a life after death ... or a terrible and endless punishment, according as they have done or neglected their duty in this life.'[22] There was no need to be a puritan to frighten a child. For all that, Tillotson's advice is kind and sensible.

Like Locke he stressed the carrot rather than the stick. They should be lured to do their duty, not driven to it. For 'how can it be expected that children should love their duty, when they never hear of it but with a handful of rods shak'd over them?'[23]

Defoe agreed with Tillotson, although as one might expect he was slightly more severe. The subject of punishment is introduced in the first volume of *The Family Instructor*. The wife in one of the dialogues tells her husband that it is nonsense to try and educate a child at the age of three. But the husband points out that a child of that age has already grasped the idea of cause and effect:

> *Hus*. Does he know you have a rod, and that he must not be a naughty boy, and that if he does, he will make you angry, and you may correct him?
> *Wife*. What's all that to the purpose?
> *Hus*. By the same rule he is capable of receiving due impressions of his maker.[24]

Later, Defoe was to go into greater detail about the correct way of punishing a child. His advice was fairly straightforward. The object of punishment was to amend the child's behaviour, not to assuage the father's anger. What was essential was that the father should never lose the love and respect of the child. The children of the savage, passionate father, whom a neighbour discovered quite exhausted from the effort of beating them, very sensibly kept out of his way and so were no longer amenable to his instruction. The children of the good father, who carefully explained to them the nature of their offence and the necessity he was in to punish them for the good of their souls, were mortified by their foolishness and by their unkindness to their father who was now obliged to whip them so much against his will.[25] They naturally resolved to behave better in the future. 'Correction! the most necessary part of family-government, and the best part of education, how difficult a thing is it!'[26]

The object both of correction and the early start in education was, as we have seen, to instil religious ideas into the child. But this could not happen in a vacuum. The whole family background must be correct. Defoe wrote his *Family Instructor* and his didactic works of the 1720s in the tradition of the conduct-books which had a continuous history stretching back a very long way.[27] Such books, though too pious for modern tastes, have much good sense in them and were much appreciated by their readers, who could consult them for an answer to many a knotty domestic problem. Defoe's books follow the morality of the conduct-books though, by his use of dialogue and dramatic situations, he is able to bring the family to life in a way that the older authors were never able to achieve. All the same he follows tradition in setting an ideal standard of family conduct which it is difficult to imagine ever being achieved in reality. The essence of family harmony was the acceptance of the absolute authority of the father. Wives must submit and children and servants obey. The father in turn had his duties, to love his wife, to instruct his children, to look after the interests of his servants and above all to maintain a rigorous standard of behaviour. Nor must he abuse the absolute authority which he exercised in his little commonwealth by behaving like a tyrant.

The secular authority of the father was reinforced by his role in establishing a religious setting for family life. The child who was learning to respect the authority embodied in his father would also be set a constant example of truly religious behaviour by both his parents. A father who drank or a mother who spent her time at balls and masquerades had little hope of instructing their children in a proper way of life. Good behaviour in children, and in servants, required good behaviour by their parents. Religion in the home should also be formalized. Parents should take every opportunity to instruct and catechize their chidren. But it was also necessary that there should be a regular time for family worship. The whole family should ideally meet twice a day for prayers and of course keep the Sabbath together.[28] Some idea of what the perfect household was supposed to be like can be seen from the description made by one of the children in *The Family Instructor* of the pious household of her aunt. Everything there was 'so sober, so pretty, so grave, so exact, and so regular, and yet so chearful, so pleasant, so innocently merry, and withal, so pious, and so religious, that I thought nothing so happy in my life'. The Sabbath at auntie's involved a succession of prayers at home, going to the meeting-house, returning home, reading from a good book, singing psalms and more prayers and 'when that is over, they go to supper, then they spend an hour perhaps or two in the most innocent and the most pleasant dis- course and conversation imaginable, it is always about something religious . . .'[29] And so to bed. In this sort of setting the young child could not fail to grow up a godly, serious child who would honour

God and his parents and be well prepared for that greater common-wealth, the world.

The failure to educate and discipline the child and above all the failure to provide a proper background of family religion for his education could have appalling consequences. The household which provides the setting for the first volume of *The Family Instructor* has completely fallen apart as a result of the parents' neglect of family government and family worship. We have already seen how the religious education of the child of six has been neglected. The elder children are naturally in an even worse state and have developed some very bad habits in the absence of any direction from the parents. Things get worse before they get better. Shocked by their youngest child's ignorance, the parents determine on a programme of reform. Family worship is to be reinstituted and a tight rein kept on all the children. In future their daughters will be more modest in dress and conversation, no longer wear patches, go to plays, play cards or walk in the park or fields on the Lord's Day. Predictably the eldest children object to this sudden, unexpected and apparently unreasonable attack on behaviour which had never been rebuked before.

The oldest daughter refuses to conform. She can see no reason why she should not walk in the park after the Sunday service and, when her mother remonstrates with her, she contemptuously hums the tune of a playhouse song. Furious, her mother strikes her and later goes up to the girl's room and burns all her plays, songs and French novels, replacing them by religious books. Of course all parties are at fault, the girl for disobeying her parents and the parents for letting her run into such amoral behaviour in the first place. Things get to such a state that the girl leaves home to stay with an aunt, but fortunately she is a good woman who keeps a pious house so all is well in the end.

The greatest failure is the eldest son. Inured in vice, he refuses to conform and makes a fool of himself before his friends. He refuses to give up the park or the playhouse, 'the study of the most accomplish'd gentlemen'. He refuses to be confined to the house on the Sabbath, save by his father's threat of never letting him return until he repents. However he has a way out of his predicament. Even if his father is determined to thwart him he can make an independent life for himself because he has a small estate left him by an uncle. He leaves home but perhaps inevitably comes to a grim end. He spends his estate and then, like many another down-at-heel gentleman, drifts into the army, is crippled and dies miserable, but still proud and unrepentant.

At the same time that a child was supposed to be absorbing a moral and religious education within the family he would probably be receiving some sort of schooling. Ideally this would reinforce the moral influence of the home. Indeed the practical and worldly was inextricably bound up with the religious side of education. Learning to read, which would often start at the mother's knee, meant more often than not learning to read the Bible or the catechism. Most theorists thought that a child should learn to read as soon as he could talk. A beginning would be made with the horn-book, a sheet covered with transparent horn to protect it from the child on which was printed the alphabet and the Lord's Prayer. Having mastered his letters, the child would move on to the catechism or to the small condensed Bibles which were specially prepared for children.[30] Later in the eighteenth century attempts were made to provide a rather more imaginative introduction to reading, but in Defoe's lifetime most children would have associated the written word with an almost totally non-secular literature. For many children this was all the education that they would receive, if indeed they received as much as this. Writing was normally regarded as superfluous for the children of the poor, a fact which bedevils any attempt to estimate the level of literacy. A population which can read but not write leaves no record of its literacy. All the same it is likely that a very high proportion of the population could read, if only because of the very considerable religious emphasis on the need for everyone to be able to read the Bible.[31]

Before Defoe's time there had been only two important types of school, the 'petty' or elementary school usually run by an elderly lady or the minister which taught reading and sometimes writing and mathematics, and the 'free' grammar school which provided a grounding in the classical languages and prepared the student for the university. In the century after 1660 the grammar schools, with a few notable exceptions, were to enter a long period of decline, both in numbers taught and in the standard of education.[32] Their insistence on continuing to teach a dull and repetitious curriculum consisting almost entirely of Latin grammar was unlikely to attract new funds in an age which was beginning to demand a more utilitarian type of education. They were also attacked because of what seems to us to have been their most praiseworthy function, the provision of free education for the more intelligent sons of the poor. White Kennett thought that the intentions of their founders that a number of poor children should have learning *gratis* was 'no doubt good and honourable'. But it was mistaken. Such an education was 'too high for the meaner boys, born to the spade and the plough . . . [and] it gave them such an imperfect tast of learning, as when they were called out to labours, and lower trades, did but fill their heads with noise, and help to make them more vain and conceited'.[33] The main problem, however, was the inability of the schools to move with the times. Many closed down, unable any longer to afford the salary necessary to attract a teacher qualified to teach the classics. Others just became very bad, turning out students who were still unable to understand the Latin which had theoretically been drilled into them for seven or eight years.[34]

At the same time as the general standard of education offered was declining, a few of the grammar schools were acquiring the élitist reputation which they have maintained ever since. It was in the late seventeenth and eighteenth centuries that it became more and more the right thing to send your son to the so-called public schools. Nicholas Hans has examined the educational background of a sample of 3,500 top people of the eighteenth century drawn from the Dictionary of National Biography. Over six hundred of them came from just four schools – Eton, Westminster, Winchester and Merchant Taylor's. The attraction of these schools was not their standard of scholarship, but the social cachet they gave and it is perhaps even more significant that nearly a thousand of Hans' élite never went to school at all, but were taught at home by their fathers or by private tutors.[35] Schools were considered by many to be beneath the sons of gentlemen, who it was felt would gain little in return for the irreparable damage caused by 'conversation with ill-bred and vicious boys'.[36]

There was also a decline in the standards of the two universities, a decline which is reflected in the numbers of students which reached their lowest mark in the third quarter of the eighteenth century.[37] Classical studies continued to predominate but the level of scholarship seems to have been much lower than it had been in the early seventeenth century. There was some realization of the need to introduce new subjects, especially science and mathematics, but the contemporary accusation that the main function of Oxford and Cambridge was to teach young gentlemen to drink and gamble had

considerable justification. In 1728 Defoe added his criticism to
what was by then a fairly general condemnation of both the grammar
schools and the universities, when he expressed his 'deep sorrow for
the present decay of learning among us and the manifest corruption
of education; we have been a brave and learned people, and are
insensibly dwindling into an effeminate, superficial race: our
young gentlemen are sent to the universities 'tis true, but not under
restraint or correction as formerly; not to study, but to drink'.[38]

However, all was not depression in the educational world.
Defoe's lifetime sees the beginnings of a number of very important
new ideas in education. Many of these ideas had been discussed by
Puritan thinkers in the intellectual excitement of the Civil War and
Interregnum.[39] When such people were debarred from teaching
in the English universities or were ejected from their livings in the
Anglican backlash which followed the Restoration some of them
were determined to set up institutions of their own which would
incorporate some of the new ideas. Defoe himself was the beneficiary
of this ironic result of Anglican persecution. He had an astonishingly
modern education which was to affect both his way of thinking and
his mode of expression all his life. Following a good grounding in
private schools he was sent at the age of fourteen to Newington
Green Academy, ostensibly to read for the Presbyterian ministry.
This academy which was run by Charles Morton was two or three
decades ahead of its time.[40] In addition to the normal classical
studies, Morton taught maths, science and modern languages,
but perhaps the most remarkable innovation he introduced was to
teach in English, not Latin as was normal in the universities.
English, both written and spoken, was also studied for its own sake.
The fact that it was an innovation to teach in English may seem
surprising, but it was, and it was obviously a very important
one if more modern subjects were going to be taught in higher
education.

Such a wide range of subjects meant that Defoe was never able
to achieve that facility in the classics which was the hallmark of the
contemporary scholar but, on the other hand, his education provided
him with the foundation of that almost universal knowledge of
modern subjects and the modern world of which he was so rightly
proud. Defoe always felt a little touchy about his lack of classical
learning and was often at pains to let the world know just how
widely educated he was. He was particularly upset by the jibe of

Swift who in 1711 had brushed him aside as an 'illiterate scribbler'.[41] Fourteen years later this still rankled. Writing in *Applebee's Journal* Defoe discusses his memories of an 'unnamed' author. 'I remember an author in the world, some years ago, who was generally upbraided with ignorance, and called an "illiterate fellow" by some of the *Beau-Monde* of the last age.' He then went into the author's study and discovered the illiterate fellow's knowledge of languages, geography, history and science. 'This put me upon wondering, even so long ago, what this strange thing called a man of learning was, and what is it that constitutes a scholar? For, said I, here's a man speaks five languages, and reads the sixth, is a master of astronomy, geography, history, and abundance of other useful knowledge, (which I do not mention, that you may not guess at the man, who is too modest to desire it,) and yet, they say, "This man is no scholar".'[42]

Next week, in the same journal, he drew a portrait of what the world called a scholar:[43]

> He knew no more of the world abroad than if he had never seen a map, or read the least description of things. He could give no more account of Africa or America than if they had never been discovered; only, that he knew St Cyprian and St Augustine, but not whereabouts they lived, or whether Africa was divided from America by water, or by land.
>
> He understood not a word of French, Dutch, Spanish, or Italian ... Take him among his books, everything that was ancient, crabbed, and critical, suited; everything modern, smooth, eloquent, and polite, provoked him to wrath ...
>
> In a word, he knows letters, and perhaps could read half the polyglot Bible, but knows nothing of the world, – has neither read men nor things; and this, they say, is a scholar.
>
> Why then that SCHOLAR is a LEARNED FOOL.

Defoe may exaggerate but one can think of no better description of the difference between the ancient and the modern.

Defoe's distinction between the learned fool and himself was a valid one and owed, as we have seen, at least something to the excellent education he had received from Charles Morton at Newington Green Academy. Morton was unique in his time, most Dissenting academies concentrating on classical studies with the particular object of preparing young men for the Nonconformist ministry. But in the early eighteenth century more of the Dissenting academies began to add modern subjects to the standard classical curriculum and to teach in English.[44] Some of these academies set an extremely high standard and their curricula foreshadowed the period of their greatest reputation in the second half of the eighteenth century when many of the academies specialized in giving a good general education to young men who were going into business, and thus incidentally produced an élite of educated Dissenters who would be able to make their mark in the Industrial Revolution.

It would be wrong to think that the Dissenting academies made all the running in modern education, or indeed that all 'academies' were run by Dissenters. In any case it must be remembered that Dissenting academies were more like contemporary universities than schools, most of their students being fifteen or sixteen when they entered, having already had a classical education at grammar school or its equivalent.[45] The truth is that there was a bewildering variety of choice for a parent seeking secondary education for his child in the eighteenth century. The grammar schools might be in decline but their very decline had called forth private classical schools, mainly run by Church of England clergymen, who used more imaginative methods to coach students in the classical languages in preparation for the universities.[46] Alongside these were a host of new schools, often short-lived, which offered a wide range of new types of education or specialized in training children for particular careers, such as the army, navy or for commerce. Most of these schools were distinguished by teaching in English and offering maths, accounting, science and modern languages as well as or instead of classics. Some schools specialized in providing the students with the social graces, teaching them to dance, to hold a cultured conversation or to write in the style of Bacon, Steele or Addison. Their predecessors had only been taught to write in the style of Cicero. Obviously the standard of such schools varied enormously. Many were simply the product of an educated man or woman's economic necessity, one man teaching a few children for a few pence in very cramped conditions. But, at their best, the new schools could be extremely good, such as the fashionable Hackney Academy which flourished from 1685 to 1820 or Little Tower Street Academy which opened in 1720 offering maths, book-keeping, natural philosophy, French, writing, English and a number of other subjects.[47] One way and another it would be fair to say that the aspiring parent of the middle station was being given an increasingly satisfactory choice of schools to which he could send his son, if not his daughter.

All these schools were of course financed by fees and were designed to provide a variety of secondary education for children from the more privileged groups in society. A tradition of providing free education for the children of the poor still existed, but the number of places available in the 'free' grammar schools for the occasional bright lad of parts had dwindled, as rising costs since their foundation in Tudor times had forced more and more schools to charge fees or go out of business. In any case, as we have seen, a growing body of critics felt it wrong to educate the sons of porters and ploughmen above their station. At the elementary level there was also some free education provided by the old parish schools, but most petty schools were obliged to charge fees. The dame who ran the dame school had to live.

Towards the end of the seventeenth century a new movement to provide free education for the poor got under way. The middle-class charity which had in former times so bountifully provided for the building and maintaining of England's splendid grammar schools was now to be diverted to the support of charity schools for the elementary education of the poor.[48] Unlike the existing elementary schools, which were seen as a means of preparing the child for grammar school, the new schools were to be an end in themselves. The poor were to be educated but they were not to be taught too much.

The thinking behind this very successful campaign reflected the philosophy of the new age. The homes of the poor bore little resemblance to the homes portrayed in *The Family Instructor*. There was a notable absence of family worship and family discipline. There might not even be a Bible from which the children could be taught to read. Few good things or holy truths were infused into the children as they were dandled on their mother's knee. We might think that she was too busy. Contemporary critics thought it more likely that she was too idle or too drunk. As a result of this early neglect the poor were lazy, vicious, dangerous and ungrateful. Those who did not behave like uncaged wild beasts had a hateful tendency to ape the manners of the rich and even to seek to lift themselves out of the dross to become rich themselves. This would never do. What the poor should be was humble, hard-working, god-fearing and eager to please the generous members of the middle

station who scattered crumbs before them. How was the wild beast
to be tamed?[49] The answer seemed obvious. Remove the children
from the appalling influence of their parents and educate them just
sufficiently to make them content to exist 'in that station of life
wherein Providence hath placed them'.[50] The charity schools, which
really got off the mark in 1699 with the foundation of the Society
for the Propagation of Christian Knowledge which operated in
its early years as a promotional body, tried their hardest to fulfil
these conditions. The children of the poor were cleaned up, dressed
in neat but modest uniforms and given 'a Christian and useful
education'[51] which taught them to read but little more. Throughout
their education the Christian virtues of humility, obedience, subordination and respect for their betters were drilled into them. A
charity-school child was said to make a very good servant.

From the beginning the charity schools found much support
from the urban middle classes who saw them not only as the most
acceptable medium of the charity which the scriptures demanded
of them but also, if their critics can be believed, as a vehicle for
promoting their own importance.[52] The schools were locally
supported and financed and a charitable shopkeeper could derive
much satisfaction from the file of tidy, obedient children whom he
could feel that he himself had transformed from the socially dis-
ruptive hooligans they had once been. By 1729 the charity schools
of London and Westminster had over five thousand pupils, a fairly
moderate proportion of the total number of poor children in the
metropolis, but quite an achievement, and an indication that the
servant problem might not be quite such a problem in the future.
London was proud of its charity children, who were regularly
marshalled, tidy and clean, two by two, to march through the
streets behind their ministers and teachers and so to proclaim to
the world the charity, benevolence and good sense of its public-
spirited and Christian citizens. Regular charity sermons were
preached by famous divines in which the charitable would be
praised for their work and the assembled children would be told,
as if they did not already know, how lucky they were. 'You therefore,
little children, who are born of meaner parents,' boomed White
Kennett in one of the best argued of such sermons, 'rejoice in this,
that God provides you friends better than your parents, charitable
friends, who clothe your bodies, and new-dress your minds and
souls. . . . You will come to say, Oh what had we been, if left unto

our selves, and to our parents unable to help us! Left to play in the streets, and to linger and pilfer from door to door! What had we been, when come to age, but the lowest servants, and hardest labourers; or perhaps idle wanderers and beggars, or possibly strouling thieves and robbers!'[53]

The development of charity schools was hardly likely to proceed without criticism. Teachers were criticized for their incompetence and organizers for their corruption, often with good reason. Other people pointed out that when children went home to their parents at night all that had been achieved in the day was undone.[54] But most criticism was about the principle of the charity schools rather than the inevitable difficulties of actually providing such free education. A large and vociferous group thundered against the inequity of the schools in removing from the children of the poor the opportunity to provide for themselves and for their parents. This was particularly strong in the countryside, where farmers who demanded an ever-ready pool of children to perform the meaner tasks of the field, such as bird-scaring and stone-picking, were able to prevent the rural schools from ever having much success.[55] Even more fundamental was the criticism led by Bernard de Mandeville, who held that it was dangerous to teach the poor at all, that reading which taught them to be humble could be used for other purposes. Knowledge itself was subversive. 'To make the society happy and people easy under the meanest circumstances, it is requisite that great numbers of them should be ignorant as well as poor. Knowledge both enlarges and multiplies our desires, and the fewer things a man wishes for, the more easily his necessities may be supply'd.'[56]

Defoe was to reply to Mandeville's attack on education for the poor.[57] As might be expected, he thoroughly approved of the charity schools, considering them a much more satisfactory and cheaper approach to the rehabilitation of the poor than the workhouse, which was the only available alternative. But it is significant that Defoe supported the schools for exactly the reason that Mandeville opposed them. He did not see them simply as a means of making the poor content with their lot, as did their promoters, but thought that they could be an important and valuable vehicle of social mobility. 'To repine that our poor should be enabled to make themselves rich, this is such an unnatural piece of policy as I never met with before.'[58]

It may be interesting in this context to look at the education of the heroes and heroines of Defoe's novels. It is noteworthy that Defoe places considerable emphasis on both their formal and informal education as a major part of the explanation of their remarkable performance as individuals in their various activities. He also makes sure that their education realistically reflects their original station in life. The cavalier, the son of a gentleman, goes to Oxford, where he concentrates on reading history and geography, 'as that which pleased my mind best, and supplied me with ideas most suitable to my genius: by one I understood what great actions had been done in the world, and by the other I understood where they had been done'.[59] He then wanted to travel before getting married and settling down. His father asked him in what capacity he would travel: 'You must go abroad either as a private gentleman, as a scholar, or as a soldier.' When the cavalier shows his preference for the military life, his father replies, 'Truly, I see no war abroad at this time worth while for a man to appear in.'[60] The cavalier disagrees and completes his education on the staff of Gustavus Adolphus.

Robinson Crusoe, the third son of provincial members of the middle classes, has a more modest education, but one suitable to the profession which his father had chosen for him and which he foolishly rejected. His father gave him 'a competent share of learning, as far as house-education and a country free-school generally goes, and design'd me for the law'.[61] Roxana, who was also a child of the middle station, being the daughter of wealthy Huguenot refugees, probably went to some of the new types of school described above. All she tells us, however, is that she 'went to English schools, and being young, I learnt the English tongue perfectly well, with all the customs of the English young-women'. We do not know if it was her own personality, her home or her school which made her 'sharp as a hawk in matters of common knowledge; quick and smart in discourse; apt to be satyrical; full of repartee, and a little too forward in conversation; or as we call it in English, bold, tho' perfectly modest in my behaviour'.[62]

Moving down the social scale we come to Moll Flanders, or Betty as she was known as a child. She got a very good education for the daughter of a convicted felon, brought up by gypsies and then dumped on the tender mercies of the parish officers of Colchester. The parish put her out to nurse with a woman who kept a dame school where children were taught to read and work, in other words to become adept at the skills required to be a good servant. But later Moll goes into the home of a gentlewoman, as companion to her daughters, where she learned as much as them from the masters who came to the house to teach them. For, 'though the masters were not appointed to teach me, yet I learned by imitation and inquiry all that they learned by instruction and direction; so that, in short, I learned to dance and speak French as well as any of them, and to sing much better, for I had a better voice than any of them'.[63] Moll Flanders was obviously very lucky to get such a good education, but it is significant that even Captain Singleton, kidnapped at the age of two, brought up by a beggarwoman and then a gypsy till she was hanged, was able to go to a parish-school where the minister told him 'to be a good boy; and that tho' I was but a poor boy, if I minded my book, and served God, I might make a good man'. Although he was moved from parish to parish and went to sea when he was twelve, his education had been sufficient to enable him to write a tolerable hand and understand some Latin.[64] The fact that both Moll Flanders and Singleton could read and write was not all that unrealistic in the world of Defoe, though it would perhaps have been more true to life if they had only been able to read.

The only one of Defoe's heroes who has no formal education at all as a child is Colonel Jack, a fact which leads him in the preface to make a plea for charity schools, the best means of preventing 'the destruction of so many unhappy children, as in this town are every year bred up for the gallows'.[65] But since, as we have seen, the object of the charity school was to inculcate in the children of the poor a prudent, pious acquiescence in the humble but useful station assigned to them by providence, Jack may have been fortunate to escape it.

Jack makes up for his lack of formal education by his eagerness to learn from experience and from those whom he met in his adventures. Eventually he acquires a proper classical education from an educated felon, transported from Bristol to Virginia where he becomes Jack's servant. When describing this process Defoe has a little dig at the pedants who taught in the grammar schools. 'He taught me not only with application, but with admirable judgement in the teaching part, for I have seen it in many histories since that time, that every scholar is not fitted for a school-master, and that the art of teaching is quite different from that of knowing the language taught.'[66] Captain Singleton, too, is fortunate to meet a good tutor in his travels. This time it is a Portuguese gunner, 'an excellent mathematician, a good scholar, and a compleat sailor', one of the few Portuguese to come out of the works of Defoe with any distinction. It was through conversing with this man that Singleton learned 'the grounds of what knowledge I have since had in all the sciences useful for navigation, and particularly in the geographical part of knowledge'. The Portuguese was able to lay 'the foundation of a general knowledge of things in my mind'.[67]

Defoe thought that such education in the school of the world or in the school of affliction was as important, if not more so, than what one learned in formal schooling. He also felt that it was never too late to learn. This was not just a question of the education of the underprivileged. Even a gentleman, despite the fact that his ignorance when he came of age was almost total, could educate himself and fit himself for polite company and a useful role in life. Adult education had become very much easier in Defoe's time because of the wide range of titles now available in English translation. In *The Complete English Gentleman* Defoe discusses how an uneducated gentleman, with the aid of a tutor and a good library, could in four and a half years make himself master of geography, philosophy, history and other subjects, without needing to learn either Latin or Greek.[68]

This was all very well for a gentleman of leisure to whom the main disadvantages of a lack of education appear to have been the fact that he might be cheated by a book salesman or unable to take part in a dinner-table conversation on astronomy.[69] But far more interesting to Defoe was the further education of the children of the middle station. We have seen them as small children, learning to be pious and well-behaved. What sort of schooling should their parents choose for them? Defoe does not spell this out but it is fairly clear what his feelings were. A man in trade needed to know neither Latin nor Greek, but must be hard-headed, sensible, able to make judgments and have a good general knowledge of trade.[70] 'The compleat tradesman is the middle among these extremes [wit and fool]; he knows more than he has an immediate use for, and is capable of learning more than he knows; he loves knowledge enough to make him seek it, and knows he wants it enough to make him love it; he has knowledge enough to make him diligent, and not so much as to make him loose and aspiring'.[71] So, unless the child had a vocation for the professions, there was no point in sending him to a grammar school to have his head crammed with the classics. It would be better to send him to one of the new types of school where he would be able to acquire a facility in his own tongue and in modern foreign languages, a knowledge of maths and book-keeping, and a sound understanding of science, geography and history.

The provision of such an education was not the end of the duty of parents. They must still see 'their children well dispos'd of, well settled in the world'.[72] A good settlement in the world depended on two major decisions by the parents, the choice of a wife[73] and the choice of a career. Parents were also expected to finance their children's future if it was in their power, providing a dowry for their daughters, a premium for their son's apprenticeship and a capital stock on which he could start his business. To be able to do this was one good reason why parents should try to improve their own estates. 'Although this must be done without covetousnesse', wrote Jeremy Taylor, 'without impatient and greedy desires of making them rich, yet it must be done with much care, and great affection, with all reasonable provision, and according to our power, and if we can without sin improve our estates for them, that also is part of the duty we owe to God for them.'[74]

Choosing a career for his children was a very serious responsibility for the parent who was expected, by prayer or inspiration, to assist his child in discerning the call of God, a call which was by no means always very clear.[75] Since the normal age for beginning an apprenticeship was fourteen or less the child was likely to be too young to make a sensible decision by himself. The guidance of a child into the correct vocation or calling and the selection of a suitable master for his apprenticeship was a tricky task where parental ambition or fondness could easily lead to serious mistakes, mistakes moreover which were likely to harm not only the child but the commonwealth. 'If the genius of young people were suited in their professions', wrote Jeremy Collier, 'the world would improve faster, and there would be a greater progress made in arts and sciences. But pride and interest spoils all.'[76]

Once the boy had been apprenticed he of course had to leave home. Now he was on his own with the world ahead of him. But this was no time to stop learning. In many ways the beginning of his apprenticeship was when he really began to learn. 'His apprenticeship is his grammar-school', wrote Defoe of the fledgeling shopkeeper in the *Complete English Tradesman*.[77] It could be a dull schooling. The apprentice was not expected to learn much in the first four years, except submission and how to sweep the floor of the shop. Later he would be given more responsible work in the shop and the counting-house, where he would be able to learn book-keeping and the art of mercantile correspondence, get thoroughly acquainted with the nature and provenance of the types of goods sold and also get to know his master's major customers and suppliers, some of whom would be his own when he finished his term and set up shop for himself.

But a boy who only learned in the shop itself would be getting too limited an education for success in the world. For this it was necessary to get outside, to keep one's eyes and ears open, to talk to men in different trades and find out what sort of behaviour led to success or failure. In this way the young tradesman would get a proper knowledge of business in general, so that he would be able to judge new ideas and projects and if necessary change the nature of his future business if he saw a new opportunity for profit. This education in the university of the world never stopped. A tradesman should be learning till the day he shut up shop.

It is interesting to compare Defoe's advice in *The Complete English Tradesman* with that of Richardson, the next great English novelist, who had himself been an apprentice and is credited with *The Apprentice's Vade Mecum* of 1733.[78] Both writers advise young men to make good use of their leisure time to improve themselves. But where Defoe advises the apprentice to go out into the streets and learn about the world at first hand Richardson's apprentice is expected to get his learning from books. When he himself was an apprentice he claimed to have stolen 'from the hours of rest and relaxation my reading times for improvement of my mind'. And so righteous was he that he would not even use his master's candle, lest he 'make my master a sufferer'. Can we see the result in the rather different behaviour of their two great maid-servant heroines, the eminently literate Pamela who has learned about the world in books and can pick up an allusion to the fate of Lucretia, and the worldly, but rather foolish, Moll who receives no reward for her virtue?

THE ROAD TO IMPROVEMENT

AMBITION was the driving force in the world of Defoe. It was the individual's desire to improve himself which kept everything else going:

> Being discontented with our present condition gets all our thoughts to work to mend it. This sets the wheels of industry and application a-going; all the springs of our faculties are wound up, the whole machine, call'd man, is put in motion, for the great end of transposing the situation of his affairs, and altering the circumstances.[1]

But ambition and discontent were hardly a satisfactory recipe for a well-ordered society. Such characteristics led to that shocking insubordination amongst servants that we have already discussed. What was true of a class was likely to be true of the individual. Man's discontent with his state was 'the essence and beginning of crime',[2] a fact which is illustrated in every one of Defoe's novels. To be ambitious, to succeed and not at the same time be criminal was perhaps the hardest task to be faced by a man or woman in the world of Defoe, but it was a task that had to be faced if that world was not to collapse.

The actual process of improvement was quite simple. The first thing to remember was that the main affair of life was getting money.[3] And, although the spending of money by other people was the way in which the individual bent on improvement got it, he himself must be careful not to spend it all. Part of it should be salted away to be periodically counted and the amount noted for his personal satisfaction. This might be added to his trading capital or might simply be a precautionary nest-egg, the best insurance against hard days in the future. In either case the growth of a man's money, his stock, was a sign of improvement, a sign that he was gradually moving along that path by which a man hauled himself out of the common rut to a position where survival was no longer something to be worried about every day and where he might take a slightly less selfish view of the society he lived in. With diligence and application a man or woman might make his or her way from the very bottom to the very top, but instances of this were of course rare. But anybody who followed the simple rules, who worked hard and saved some of his money, could improve himself.

Throughout this process the individual must keep his eyes wide open to avoid at least the most obvious pitfalls in the road that led ultimately to the improved state. This could be extremely difficult. Each level of society had its own particular mode of behaviour, each calculated to hinder the progress of the individual, while at the same time promoting the progress of the society of whom the individual formed a part. At the top and the bottom, the gentleman and the labourer or servant had each a very similar attitude towards life, an attitude which if pursued energetically enough was almost bound to lead to disaster for the individual. Both liked living and disliked working; both loved spending and hated to save. Most gentlemen could afford to live like this but no labourer or servant could. And so if a labourer wished to improve himself he had to behave in a fashion not typical of a labourer, in other words he had to acquire the virtues of the middle station long before he acquired the income which made the maintenance of such virtues relatively attractive.

Even those of the middle station had their problems. In a fickle commercial world they were forever threatened by the poverty of disaster and, the faster they tried to move, the more likely they were to suffer, as Defoe himself had discovered as a young businessman. Patience might be a middle-station virtue but it was a difficult one to practise for a man who could see the prize of leisure and ease dangling temptingly close to the man who brought off just one lucky coup. But impatience was not the only pitfall for the aspiring man of the middle station. Since the aim was to be a gentleman, there was that ever-present temptation to neglect his business and to practise what seemed to be gentlemanly behaviour long before he had the income or the time to support the behaviour pattern of a man of leisure. How different from the position of the aspiring labourer. If he behaved like a man of the middle station he might

well become one. But for a tradesman to ape the manners of a
gentleman was a sure formula for failure.

The problem was in fact a little deeper than this. Could a man of
the middle station ever become a gentleman? Could he suddenly
throw off the habits of a lifetime? If he had really followed the
gospel of work; if he had stayed at his counter and practised that
servility so necessary for success in the world of the shopkeeper,
he might with luck amass sufficient cash to buy himself a life of
leisure and call himself a gentleman. But what sort of gentleman
would he be? On the other hand if he prepared himself for the idle
life, spent long hours in the coffee-house or with his dogs, practised
the arts of conversation and got to know what gentlemen called
the world, he would be that 'amphibious creature', that 'land-
water thing, called a gentleman-tradesman',[4] a fool who ended
up being neither.

One way and another, it can be seen that the road to improvement, though quite well signposted, was a tricky one to stay on.
Many fell by the wayside but this did not mean that they never got
back on the road again. For one virtue, shared by all real members
of the middle station was that, like Defoe, they never gave up:

> To fall is common to all mankind; to fall and rise is a particular
> that few men arrive to, and no man so easy or so often as the
> tradesman; but to fall into the very dirt of scandal and reproach
> and rise with reputation; to fall with infamy and rise with
> applause; to fall detested and rise caressed and embraced by all
> mankind; this I think is a kind of peculiar to the tradesman; nay,
> to the unhappy unfortunate tradesman, who by this one turn
> of his affairs is lifted out of the mire into a station of life, infinitely
> superior to the best condition he was ever in before.[5]

A tradesman never gave up hope of improving himself till 'he is
nail'd up in his coffin and six foot under ground'.[6]

Life, then, to vary the metaphor, was a game of snakes and
ladders. Not all people started at zero but they could all see the goal
at the top of the board. The mouths of the snakes were often disguised. Many of the ladders had broken rungs. And the dice could
certainly be manipulated, by the individual himself or by other
individuals. Some such individuals, in a world of patronage, could
be benevolent;[7] but most were cheats who could weight the dice
of life as effectively as they could those with which they reduced

the incomes of young gentlemen in the Groom Porter's or other gambling clubs. The dice were also, of course, manipulated by God, sometimes in the player's favour, sometimes against him. Such manipulation was implicit in the rules of the game but it was difficult to predict.

The mention of God reminds us that, if life was a game, it was not one that was played on only one plane. For, at the same time that a man was working his way up and down the snakes and ladders of the game of the world, he was busily or should be busily engaged in a simultaneous game whose prizes were theoretically even more attractive. This was the salvation game. The problems of playing two games at once, in which an apparently logical move in one game can prejudice one's chances of success in the other, will be apparent to all who have struggled to find their way through the permutations and patterns of three-dimensional noughts and crosses. The same problems faced man in the world of Defoe. What seemed to be a good move on the success board might well be a bad one on the salvation board.

Collectively, the works of Defoe offer a guide to the man or woman struggling to do his or her best in the double game of life. One can think of few people better equipped to write such a guide. Who else had had his enormously wide experience, not only of life as it was lived but of the varying fortunes which could fall to the lot of one single man? Who else had been trained both for business and the ministry? Who else had lived in a situation of familiarity with thieves as well as kings? The only problem, perhaps, was that there was no evidence that Defoe himself had reached the top of the board in either game. But that could be an advantage, as he pointed out to an imaginary objector. 'An old sailor that has split upon a sunk rock, and has lost his ship, is not the worst man to make a pilot of for that coast; on the contrary, he is in particular able to guide those that come after him to shun the dangers of that unhappy place.'[8]

Despite his experience, Defoe is not an altogether satisfactory guide, particularly when he is writing his novels rather than his didactic works. For Defoe the novelist kept up his sleeve a gambit which, to modern readers at least, he seems to have used somewhat immorally – the repentance gambit. It has always seemed a little unfair that a man can have a good time being bad and then wipe out his sins by a well-timed repentance or a death-bed conversion, however sincere. And it has to be admitted that some of Defoe's fictional repentances ring with all the sincerity of a very cracked bell.

A tolerant God would not expect perfect behaviour, especially in a man who was striving to achieve success in this world. In *The Complete English Tradesman* Defoe outlines what seems to him at least to be a reasonable compromise. Since perfect honesty was unlikely on this earth, the intention to be honest and to reform and repent if you slipped was the ideal, and it was this that the good tradesman should aim at.[9] This might be acceptable, though it is doubtful if many divines, even in the 1720s, would have put it in quite these words. But what exactly does Defoe mean by the intention to be honest and how long is a slip? In the tradesman's case a slip clearly means what we take it to mean, a minor moral error which God can easily condone if the tradesman is sorry and resolves not to do it again. In the novels the position is often quite different. The slip may last half a lifetime and the intention to be honest not become a real intention until the hero or heroine has hoarded enough loot from a career of sin never to need to be dishonest again. Only then do they reform and repent.

The worst case is surely that of Captain Singleton. At first he seems to have some of the attributes which Defoe normally ascribes to the poor. When he has money he spends it with no thought for the future. This is because he has 'neither friend, relation, nor acquaintance in England'; no Defoe, in fact, to tell him what to do with the fortune he had picked up in Africa. 'I had consequently no person to trust with what I had, or to counsel me to secure or save it; but falling into ill company . . . all that great sum which I got with so much pains and hazard, was gone in little more than two years time.'[10] But, later in the book when Singleton has made a second fortune as a pirate, he is better advised by one of Defoe's most interesting fictional characters, the Quaker William, who directs many of Singleton's battles without, of course, as a Quaker fighting himself. William advises Singleton to give up piracy, while the going is good: 'Well then', says William, 'I would ask, whether, if thou has gotten enough, thou has any thought of leaving off this trade; for most people leave off trading when they are satisfied with getting, and are rich enough; for no body trades for the sake of trading, much less do any men rob for the sake of thieving.'[11] Captain Singleton sees the logic of this. Following William the Quaker's advice he welshes on his piratical colleagues and eventually

manages to get back to England from Basra disguised as a wealthy
Armenian merchant, with all his loot intact. At the same time
Captain Singleton is trying to repent, but is worried that God will
never let him off while he has so much plunder. William reassures
him: 'To quit what we have, and do it here [i.e. Basra] is to throw
it away to those who have no claim to it, and to divest our selves
of it but to do no right with it.'[12] What Captain Singleton must
do is to get the plunder back to England and then providence may
give him an opportunity to do some good with it. God plays the
game; William has a poor sister who is relieved with some of the
loot; Captain Singleton marries her and they all live happily ever
after.

One might wonder what the tradesman working away in his
shop thought about a novel like this, if he had time to read it.
Why on earth did Defoe let Captain Singleton get away with it?
Here was he toiling away, putting a little money aside each year
and slowly working himself towards a comfortable retirement.
What right had such a rogue to end up so much better off than
him, and be saved? Why did his creator not send him to the gallows
he so richly deserved?

It is very difficult to say. The Defoe who wrote the novels seems
to be a very different man from the Defoe one gets to know in the
rest of his works. He sets out to be a moralist but the moral he makes
is often a very doubtful one. He pretends to judge his fictional
characters but the judgment is rarely one with which the world
would agree. It is almost as if he got carried away by the exciting
adventures of the characters he created and felt reluctant to give
them their due. He started off all right. Robinson Crusoe gets
punished regularly by God, though both his crimes and his punish-
ments may seem a little far-fetched, if not absurd, to us. But from
then on, as a moralist, Defoe goes downhill.

The themes of his later novels are all very much the same. The
main character is either born poor or becomes poor and the story
is about the process by which they eventually become secure from
their original poverty and the temptations which the state of poverty
holds. So far so good. This is what much of Defoe's didactic writing
is about as well. But in the process of getting rich they commit sin
after sin, whether it is the comparatively innocent picking pockets
of Colonel Jack or the much more premeditated crimes of Moll
Flanders, Roxana or Captain Singleton. The characters are all

made to suffer, both mentally and physically, as a result of their sins. But this is not very convincing. Nor is their ultimate repentance, except perhaps in the case of Colonel Jack. The only one who is left to suffer for ever is Roxana, whose guilty conscience condemns her to a hell on earth, albeit a very comfortable one, and the possibility of eternal damnation to follow.[13]

Defoe would never have allowed the fictional behaviour of his heroes and heroines to be condoned in real life.[14] He allowed for slips, as we have seen, and expected God to do the same. But the characters in his novels do not slip, they fall. And they do not fall, like that phoenix called a tradesman, because of error or misfortune in the pursuit of their business career. They fall because they have deliberately chosen to fall. It is all very well remarking, as he often does, that necessity knows no law. But the truth is that necessity plays only a small part as a motivation in Defoe's criminals. Necessity may start them off but greed and even love of crime carries them on.

Defoe wrote a stirring piece in the *Review* of September 1711 in which he exposed the hypocrisy of the rich towards the poor and the poverty that made the poor commit crimes:

> I tell you all, gentlemen, in your poverty, the best of you all will rob your neighbour; nay, to go further, . . . you will not only rob your neighbour, but if in distress, you will EAT your neighbour, ay, and say grace to your meat too.

> Men rob for bread, women whore for bread; necessity is the parent of crime; ask the worst high-way man in the nation, ask the lewdest strumpet in the town, if they would not willingly leave off the trade, if they could live handsomely without it – And I dare say, not one but will acknowledge it.[15]

But he contradicts himself as he says it. There is a world of difference between necessity or distress and living handsomely, as any casuist knows. And how handsomely do you have to live before you leave off? When Captain Singleton and William the Quaker arrived safe in Venice with all their treasure, it was 'such a cargo, take our goods, and our money, and our jewels together, as I believe was never brought into the city by two single men, since the state of Venice had a being'.[16] One could live handsomely on a fraction of that. Colonel Jack and Moll Flanders were somewhat more modest but they were certainly not on the bread line. Crime seemed to be not only an alternative to honest work but an alternative that paid.

It seems unlikely that Defoe really wanted his readers to believe this. He was aware, of course, that there were other ways to improve oneself than the normal middle-station way of diligence and application in the performance of one's business. He lists a few in *The Compleat English Gentleman*. 'Law, trade, war, navigation, improvement of stocks, loans on public funds, places of trust, and abundance of other modern advantages and private wayes of getting money . . . have rais'd a great number of familyes to not onely prosperous circumstances . . . but to immense estates, vast and, till of late, unheard of summs of money amass'd in a short time.'[17] Some of these were the sort of activities open to those of the middle station; some of them, such as improvement by war or by places of trust, were more likely to be taken up by a needy or ambitious gentleman. But there were also other ways of improvement not mentioned in this list. A good marriage was certainly one.[18] Crime might well be another, though the crimes which took men to the top in the real world of Defoe were not the crimes of Moll Flanders or even Captain Singleton.[19] They were the crimes which went unpunished, even when discovered, the 'crimes' against society of the speculator and the monopolist, the 'trade pyrates' who made life so much more difficult for the honest struggling man of the middle station.[20] They prospered, leaving smaller men bankrupt in their wake. Meanwhile, what society branded as criminals, the real Molls and Captain Singletons of the world, finished their short lives at the end of a rope or mouldered away their days in Madagascar. Defoe the crime reporter knew this only too well, since much of his copy was the so-called confessions of convicted criminals. But Defoe the creator, despite his love of realism, was reluctant to doom his creations to such a realistic end. The Devil's angels whisper in his ear, Moll and Singleton speedily make their peace with God and move on to a comfortable retirement, if not the honourable one that was part of the prize of success in the conventional middle station.

Before we leave the picaresque world of the novels for the plodding world of the shop and counting-house it is worth noting the fact that, criminal or not, Defoe's fictional characters reflect faithfully the strengths and weaknesses of the middle-station way of life. Above all they have that ambition to improve themselves which was so vital to the proper functioning of the world of Defoe. Moll Flanders's ambition expands with her understanding of the world. When she is only eight, she has 'a thorough aversion to going to service' and wants to be what she calls a gentlewoman, by which she only means that she wants to be independent and get her bread by her own work. Her horizons soon widen. Before she is twelve she realizes the importance of not only earning her keep, but having money in her pocket as well.[21] Colonel Jack has a rather different sort of ambition. The illegitimate son of people of quality, he has been told by his nurse to remember that he is a gentleman. What this means is by no means clear to the young boy who is so innocent of the facts of life that he does not even know that picking pockets is wrong. But once he begins to find out, he sets out to become in fact the gentleman he should have been by birth. Neither are content to remain poor. Both acquire the instincts of the middle station and realize that if you can only safeguard your money, however you come by it, you will not be poor for ever.

Robinson Crusoe offers an interesting variant on the theme. For he was born in the middle station and yet rejects its comfort and the means of improving himself still further that his father offers. For such disobedience and ingratitude he is quite rightly punished. But it is striking that, despite his wanderlust and his misfortunes, Crusoe is able to survive and prosper because he has the diligence, the application and the ability to overcome disaster which are the recipe for success in the world of Defoe. He survives his slavery in Africa and succeeds as a planter in Brazil. He survives his shipwreck and succeeds in solving every problem that he faces as a castaway. And he would clearly have been a very successful lawyer if only he had followed his father's advice. How strange that a man should have so much common sense as Robinson Crusoe and yet not have the sense to stay in York and slide gently through the world.

Robinson Crusoe may be an admirable character who shows good sense in times of trouble, but he illustrates only too well one universal trait, the folly of the young. And, unfortunately, it was the early moves in the game of life that determined its pattern. One act of foolishness led to another and Crusoe's decision to ignore his father and go to sea was just the first folly in what was clearly a foolish life for one on whom fortune was smiling so sweetly. But no one could really call Crusoe a fool. If we want to meet a really foolish young man we have to look in other novels, especially in

Roxana and *Moll Flanders*, who were both foolish enough to marry one. Moll's fool at least gave her a good time and, despite her horror of wasting money, she is prepared to forgive him. But Roxana's fool was a total disaster. In a few lines his business career sums up everything that the man who is seeking success in the world of Defoe should not do:

> He had no genius to business; he had no knowledge of his accounts; he bustled a little about it indeed, at first, and put on a face of business, but he soon grew slack; it was below him to inspect his books, he committed all that to his clerks and book-keepers; and while he found money in cash to pay the maltman, and the excise, and put some in his pocket, he was perfectly easie and indolent, let the main chance go how it would.

Naturally, such an approach to business led to disaster, 'his trade sunk, his stock declin'd', even his tools of trade were seized to pay the excise. Finally he sold what was left of the business and wasted what remained of his fortune in foolish pursuits such as hunting.[22]

If we want to find out what a man should do if he wants to succeed in the humdrum world of reality then we have to look at *The Complete English Tradesman*, the longest and the most interesting of all Defoe's didactic works. The formula for success is a dull one, as one might expect, and it is hardly surprising that the sales-conscious Defoe never wrote a novel about a conventional success story. It is even duller than it perhaps needed to be in reality because of Defoe's distrust of too rapid acquisition of riches. This was partly a reflection of his own experience. 'The plodding fair-driving trades-man that goes on safe and sure, and is always moving; he, I say, is the man that bids fairest to be rich.'[23] But the emphasis on slow and steady is also a reflection of that dislike of big business which we have already discussed.[24] Many plodding, fair-driving tradesmen slowly improving themselves were much better for the economy and society as a whole than one or two men in a hurry who, if they succeeded, did so at the expense of their slower and probably more honest brethren and, if they failed, brought many better men down in their wake.

The word 'tradesman' meant different things in different parts of England, but to Defoe in London it meant a shopkeeper and it is the world of the shopkeeper that is dissected in *The Complete*

English Tradesman. The shop, symbol of the consumption that made the world go round, is taken as the forcing ground of the middle-station virtues. This might seem surprising, since the clothier, the wholesaler or the overseas merchant were all more likely to improve themselves than the shopkeeper. But the shop, with its permanence and the routine of its management, offered a better opportunity to rub in a few home truths applicable to all business. In particular, the virtue of constantly attending to one's own interest could much better be taught to the man who conducted all his affairs under one roof than to the more peripatetic clothier or merchant.

Defoe never lets us forget that there is a double aim in life, that worldly success earned at the expense of salvation is a poor bargain. But, although no one should forget God, it was necessary for the proper fulfilment of both roles that there should be a strict partition of the working day between the hours devoted to God and the hours devoted to Mammon. The achieving man rose at six, broke his fast and heard family prayers in his home. At seven his shop would be unbuttoned and the next five hours would be spent in strict and personal attention to the affairs of the shop, which he should never leave unless the business itself demanded that he go out to meet his suppliers or to soften up a prospective customer. From noon till two was the time to eat. Then he was back in the shop till nine o'clock before returning home for further prayers and so to bed. Every hour thus had its set purpose from which there should be no deviation. Sermons in business time and drinking in sleeping time were both wrong.[25] This routine was broken only one day a week when the shopkeeper forgot business and praised the Lord, dividing his time between prayer at home and prayer in his place of worship through all the rigour of a Dissenter's sabbath.[26]

Constant personal attention to his shop was necessary because only the tradesman himself could be trusted to make a success of his own affairs. The moment he left the shop to be looked after by his apprentices he was asking for trouble. If they were bad they would be robbing him. If they were good they would be ingratiating themselves with his customers, hoping to take them with them when they in turn opened a shop after completing their apprenticeship.[27] Every minute that the shopkeeper was away from his place of work he should be asking himself what was happening to his business while he was out taking the air. This was not just a question of the obvious dangers of wasting time and money and endangering his immortal

soul in the tavern or the playhouse. The innocent, but foolish, tradesman might try to persuade himself that he was simply taking
exercise for the sake of his health. But such exercise was bound to be
a thief of his time. Even worse, the exercise might cost money and
be just the first step in an attempt to acquire at second-hand the
bearing of a gentleman. 'When I see young shop-keepers keep
horses a hunting, learn dog-language, and keep the sportsmens'
brogue upon their tongues, I will not say I read their destiny, for I
am no fortune-teller; but I do say, I am always afraid for them.'[28]
Such a way of life could only lead to disappointment. Success in
trade depended on keeping to the company and ways of a
tradesman.[29]

Simply being in the shop might be a good start but it was hardly
likely to lead to prosperity by itself. When Defoe discusses the actual
management of the shop, he gives full rein to his old-fashioned
prejudices. He is forced to make some concessions to the changes that
have occurred in retailing, but he is reluctant to do so, since he
considered that most of them were unnecessary and only tended to
increase the dangers of failure for the young and inexperienced
shopkeepers whom he was advising. His main dislike was for the
extravagant shop-fitting that was now becoming typical of the
London shop, the bow windows, finely joined display cabinets, the
gilding and the well-lit and well-laid-out shelves which showed the
goods in their best, and sometimes in more than their best light.[30]
Defoe's objection, which was a common one, was based partly on
the cost. A shopkeeper should spend his money on goods, not fittings.
'A gay shop and a mean stock is something like the Frenchman
with his laced ruffles, without a shirt.'[31] For a young shopkeeper to
put two-thirds of his capital into shelves and glass windows was
obviously to put himself into a very vulnerable trading position.
But shop-fitting was also seen to be dishonest, a way of deceiving
the customer into thinking the goods on display were better than
they were. This was an old problem which Baxter had considered
in his *Christian Directory*:[32]

Is it lawful to make a thing seem better than it is? It is lawful to
dress, polish, adorn or set out your commodity to make it seem *as it
is indeed*; but not to make it seem *better* than it is; except in some
very few cases . . . You ought not to deceive your neighbour, but
to do as you would be done by.

To do as you would be done by. This was the watchword of Baxter's commercial ethics. But it was a hard code for the shopkeeper. Defoe, although he accepts the principle, was prepared to bend the rules a little. The tradesman was allowed a certain latitude in honesty. He could, for example, tell unavoidable lies. When he said that a price was the lowest price he could possibly take he was lying, but it was a lie that God himself would overlook in the days of haggling and before the arrival of that marvel of truth and clarity, the fixed price.[33]

A much more serious problem concerned the maintenance of one's own and one's neighbour's credit. All shopkeeping was conducted on credit from suppliers. Defoe thought that the stock of a shop should be two or three times the shopkeeper's own capital.[34] By the 1720s many of the goods sold at retail were also sold on credit. 'How many thousands of families wear out their cloaths before they pay for them, and eat their dinner upon tick with the butcher? Nay, how many thousands who could not buy any cloaths, if they were to pay for them in ready money, yet buy them at a venture upon their credit, and pay for them, as they can?'[35] Defoe, while he welcomed the increase of business, saw retail credit as a great danger, both for the gentleman who slowly eroded his income in interest payments and the tradesman who might find himself with a capital consisting entirely of bad debts.[36] Still retail credit, like shop-fitting, was here to stay and the tradesman who refused to engage in either would be forced to go out of business. 'Every tradesman both gives and takes credit, and the new mode of setting it up over their shop and warehouse doors, in capital letters, NO TRUST BY RETAIL, is a presumption in trade . . . and most of those trades, who were the forwardest to set it up, have been obliged to take it down again, or act contrary to it in their business.'[37]

Such dependence on credit had obvious dangers. Credit, as Defoe had written many years before in the *Review*, was a coy lass who, if disobliged, was most difficult to be friends with again.[38] A tradesman could maintain his credit only by letting the world know he was an honest man, by his industry and by the punctual payment of his bills.[39] But a tradesman's credit, like a virgin's virtue, was particularly susceptible to the evil tongues of men. It only required one idle remark in the coffee-house or at the newly fashionable tea-table for creditors to close in and a lifetime of industry and honesty to be undone. Defoe imagines such a conversation:[40]

First Lady Alas he has no bottom.
Second Lady No bottom! Why you surprise me; we always look'd
upon him as a man of substance . . .

No bottom, no credit; no credit, no business.

Under conditions of such fragile personal credit, the tradesman
himself was faced with some very tricky moral temptations. What
was he to do, for instance, if someone asked him his opinion of
another tradesman, his rival? If he praised him too much he would
improve his rival's credit and thus increase his competition. To
decry him was tempting but unjust, and quite likely to rebound on
him in the future. The best thing to do was to refuse to give opinions
on other tradesmen's characters, though silence in such circumstances was likely to be interpreted as implying a bad character.[41]

It can be seen that the tradesman who wished to succeed without
doing too much harm to his hopes of salvation had to be a very
subtle casuist.[42] He also had to be the perfect hypocrite. He had to
learn to keep his temper, to remain calm and courteous when
people came into his shop, were rude to him and turned over the
whole of his stock with no intention of buying.[43] He had to remember
that in trade the seller is servant to the buyer:

> His shop is a place to be invited into, not to be commanded
> into; and therefore we see the best shopkeepers do not think it
> below them to stand at the door, and with cap in hand, that is,
> with the utmost respect, to ask their customers to come in, to see
> if they can please themselves, and find what they have occasion
> for.[44]

If he did all these things, if he remained a servile hypocrite, if he
kept a well-stocked but not over-stocked shop, if he avoided the
temptation of extending his credit beyond the bounds of caution,
if he maintained a careful check on his expenditure and kept a good
set of books, the shopkeeper might find that he received his reward
in the form of an annual addition to his capital. He might even
manage to do so without offending God. But even then he would
not have done enough to satisfy Defoe. For the tradesman, like all
men in society, had a duty to his neighbour, even if that neighbour
was his closest competitor in business. As a man grew richer he
would be faced with an increasing temptation to compete too much.
He must resist it. A man was not in business to destroy the livelihood
of his neighbours, but to do as he would be done by.

The worst sin was price competition. Nothing better illustrates the new world of Defoe, where the men of the middle station have grown so numerous, than the fact that their welfare as well as that of the poor must be of concern to the state and to the writer on economic matters. For centuries, moralists had attacked the trader for charging too much. William Ames stated the still current orthodoxy in 1639: 'To bee willing to buy cheape, and sell deare, is (as Augustine observes) common, but yet a common sinne, except it is bounded within a certaine measure and limits.'[45] How different was the attitude of Defoe, the champion of the small shopkeeper whose body of economic ideas depended upon the maintenance of high prices. His greatest fear was that the successful shopkeeper would cut prices, not raise them. 'Nothing is more frequent among tradesmen than to supplant and underwork one another in their business, by sinking or abating the value or price of the goods they sell, that is, in a word, to under-sell one another, to carry away the trade.'[46]

> 'Tis fatal to the poorer and little dealers about him; for they stand still, with their fingers in their mouths, as we call it, or walk about at their shop doors, and have nothing to do, while they see all the trade run in the great channel of their neighbouring alderman's shop; who gives large credit at a ready-money price, or sells for ready-money ten *per cent* cheaper than they can.[47]

How well Defoe understood the first principle of retail price maintenance, that your competitor is your friend. The only enemy is the consumer.

A man who could tread the delicate path that Defoe advocated, who could make money without offending God or his neighbour, deserved his success. But it certainly was a hazardous path. There was always the fear of falling. Sometimes, of course, only the tradesman could be blamed for his fall. He had broken the rules, over-extended his credit or spent too much in aping the gentleman before he had the money or the time to do so. But often he was the innocent victim of circumstances beyond his control. A change of fashion or a few royal deaths and a long period of mourning could make his stock unsaleable.[48] The successful operations of his rich price-cutting neighbour could remove his profit-margin, and no amount of paring his consumption and attention to his books could change the fact that he now spent more than he earned. Commonest of all, in

a world of extravagance, scandal and fickle personal credit, would
be the failure of one of his debtors, leading to the bankruptcy of a
whole sector of the business community in a chain reaction.

Defoe felt that the danger of bankruptcy was increasing in the
1720s. Every new trend was calculated to magnify the chances of
the individual trader's fall. Whether it was more credit, and
particularly more retail-credit, greater outlay on shop-fitting or
greater expense on an ostentatious way of life, the innovations of
the day were bound to undermine the stability of the business. And
yet, as we have seen, the shopkeeper could not afford to behave
contrary to the custom of his neighbours. If one tradesman took on
more servants, dressed in the height of fashion and entertained his
friends to exotic meals, then all tradesmen had to follow suit, or run
the risk of the world thinking that they could not afford to.[49] The
maintenance of 'bottom' was a trying task. No wonder that many
tradesmen fell, even while their own forced extravagance made
many others rich.

What should the tradesman do when he felt himself slipping?
Defoe was in no doubt. A man in trouble whose business was basically sound, whose good debts were greater than his liabilities, should
retrench, seek to recover his own debts and treat honestly with his
creditors, 'that they may be easy with him till he can get in his
debts'.[50] But a man in real trouble, whose books tell him that his
business is unsound, should never hang on in the hope of some good
fortune. He should break at once. To do so was both more honest
and more prudent. It was honest because it meant that he was not
robbing his creditors any more than he need. It was prudent
because, by so doing, he would get the name of an honourable man
who, although unfortunate, was able to pay perhaps fifteen shillings
in the pound. Breaking early also gave the bankrupt peace of mind.
It got the unpleasantness over as quickly as possible and avoided the
terrible strain of trying to patch up a rotten business.[51]

When the bankrupt had made his composition with his creditors
and been discharged he should never despair. It was now that he
would be able to prove Defoe right in calling the tradesman a
phoenix who could rise from his own ashes.[52] Now was the time that
the fallen tradesman must really work hard to rise again. And, as
he rose, he would be able to demonstrate to his former creditors that
they were right to treat with him as an honourable man. For now
he would be able to repay them, or their widows, the five shillings

in the pound that they lost by his fall, even though he was not required to do so by law.[53]

The natural corollary of honourable behaviour by the bankrupt was decent treatment from his creditor. Here again it was a question of do as you would be done by. Show charity and compassion for the fallen, for who knows when it may be you. 'Let him that thinketh he standeth, take heed lest he fall.'[54] And indeed, as so often in the world of Defoe, the creditor was likely to do well by behaving well. By an early settlement he was likely to recover more of his debt. And, by a private composition, he could avoid seeing his money disappearing into the insatiable stomach of the law.

Good treatment of their debtors was just one instance of the exemplary behaviour that Defoe expected of those who made it to the top in the world of the shopkeeper. We have already seen how the successful must avoid the temptation to destroy the weak by competition. Avarice tempted the rich man just as necessity tempted the poor. But there was no excuse for avarice. The rich man was 'tempted by that which is in itself a crime: 'tis not criminal to be poor'.[55] There were many other temptations for the rich. The most obvious were covetousness and pride. The rich man always wanted more. Defoe reserved his strongest invective for the man he called the purse-proud tradesman, 'the most troublesome and intollerable of all God's two-legged creatures', the tradesman who failed at the post by never learning to be rich with dignity, never learning to be a gentleman in fact.

> The man I am speaking of is first a poor, empty, bloated-up animal who, rising from nothing, or something very mean, and having been lifted up beyond what he was, continues always lifted beyond what he is: He is so, and will be so, because, though his stock of money may encrease, yet his stock of pride encreases still faster than his wealth.[56]

What then was the proper behaviour for the man who had succeeded in business and made his way to the top in the game of success? The first thing he should do was to take his capital out of his business, buy rents or invest in the funds, and retire. This was for his own good, in that a businessman was never out of danger 'till his bottom is wound up; and if he continues in trade, we may say of him, he is never perfectly safe till he is nail'd up between two elm boards.'[57] Nor should he have one last fling. The last adventure

could be the one to send him to the bottom once again.[58] But the
retirement of the rich was not only for their own good. It was also
good for society. The gap that he would leave in the business world
would increase the possibilities of mobility for those who remained.
Several aspiring young men could take up the business of one rich
man, working their way up the board in their turn till they too
grew rich and retired and made way for the next generation.[59]

The retired tradesman should not simply disappear to a new-
bought estate and lead the life of a country gentleman. That could
be done by his son. There was much that he could still do in the
city. He could be an arbiter in the disputes of other businessmen
who would respect the decisions of such a man who had not only
proved his worth by making money, but had gone off the stage with
his reputation unblemished. 'The old, approv'd, experienced tradesman . . . is the oracle for trade, every one goes to him for advice,
refers to his opinion, and consults with him in difficult and intricate
cases.'[60] He could also be a friend to the poor. He could even
become an adviser in the councils of his country, and who could be
a better one than a man with his experience of the world? Above all,
he could afford to be a nice chap, worldly but honest, generous but
not ostentatious, saving a little of his income from the funds so
that he became a little richer each year. By the time that he died,
honoured and respected by the whole community, who would ever
remember that this nice, kind old gentleman was once a penniless
apprentice? Certainly not his son.

THE INDIVIDUAL AND HIS WIFE

So far in our discussion of the individual in the world of Defoe there has been an almost inescapable tendency for that individual to turn into a male individual, for the non-specific plural 'they' to degenerate into the specific singular 'he'. This may be regrettable, and indeed historians are often accused of denying the existence of half the human race, but it is virtually impossible to write otherwise of the male-dominated and male-oriented society that existed in the days of Defoe. Women were not expected to be individuals; in law they were not supposed to live by themselves or, as the contemporary phrase had it, to live at their own hands. Unless they were widows, they were expected to spend their whole life in legal and physical subjection to a man, whether he be father, master or husband.[1] A woman on her own was an anomaly subject to harsh treatment by the law and the disapprobation of society.

The subjected woman had many duties, but few rights. She was expected to breed and rear children, as many as possible since a high level of population was seen to be the best guarantee of continued prosperity in the commonwealth. She was expected to work, not just to look after her master's or husband's household, but as a vital part of both the national and the family economy. Ideally a woman or girl should never be idle. This was particularly true of the wives, daughters and servants of country folk. When they completed their household duties, if they ever did, they were not supposed to relax in the satisfying glow of a job well done but should immediately address themselves to their spinning wheels or their knitting to earn a few more pennies for the family budget. Such earnings could make the difference between comparative comfort and the state of want, but work also had another function. Tired women were more likely to be virtuous. For women were expected by society to be models of chastity and virtue, unlike their husbands, whose sins were laughed away as excusable trifles.[2]

A male world not only subjected women, but had conveniently developed a set of hypothetical female attributes which justified that subjection. Naturally, the fundamental justification for the subjection of women, as of Africans, was biblical. Eve had sought to be wiser than Adam so that she might govern him, an ambition still entertained by her descendants. Defoe imagines Eve using some very unbiblical language, as she offers Adam the apple. 'Here,' says she, 'you cowardly faint-hearted wretch, take this branch of heavenly fruit, eat and be a stupid fool no longer; eat and be wise; eat and be a God; and know, to your eternal shame, that your wife has been made an enlightn'd Goddess before you.'[3] God's punishment for her ambitious folly was of course to make her even more subject to her husband. Eve has much to answer for, but the daughters of Eve also had many faults. They were vain, deceitful, passionate rather than rational, shamelessly wanton in their sexual appetites, stupid and quite incapable of making an independent decision. One quotation will be enough to illustrate the general feeling of the age. Listen to the Reverend Richard Baxter's warning to a potential husband:[4]

It is no small patience which the natural imbecility of the female sex requireth you to prepare. Except it be very few that are patient and manlike, women are commonly of potent fantasies, and tender passionate impatient spirits, easily cast into anger, or jealousie, or discontent: and of weak understandings, and therefore unable to reform themselves. They are betwixt a man and a child: some few have more of the man, and many have more of the child; but most are but in a middle state.

Women were halfway between men and children. Men were halfway between the beasts and the angels.

In Defoe's lifetime a new type of woman was appearing in increasing numbers on the English scene, especially in London. These were the wives and daughters of the successful men of the middle station who, together with the wives and daughters of the gentry, produced a somewhat alarming phenomenon, a large group of women who did not work and whose husbands and fathers did not make them work, preferring to see them as a means of displaying their own economic success.[5] Roxana's Dutch lover describes the

woman's role in the modern marriage. 'The man had all the care
of things devolv'd upon him; the weight of business lay upon his
shoulders, and as he had the trust, so he had the toil of life upon
him, his was the labour, his the anxiety of living; the woman had
nothing to do, but to eat the fat, and drink the sweet; to sit still,
and look round her; be waited on, and made much of; be serv'd,
and lov'd, and made easie.'[6] A new class of idle women had been
born. And what did idle women do with their time? Naturally,
they tended to vice. The age-old sins of adultery, drink and a
scolding tongue were joined by a new range of vicious pursuits born
of idleness and vanity. The endless round of visits in which idle
woman chatted to idle woman, the newly fashionable tea-table with
its scandal and its gossip, the masquerade and the assembly rooms
with their endless opportunities for anonymous vice, patches, hoop-
petticoats and painted fans, window-shopping and the glorious
game of 'tumbling' goods with no intention of buying, getting up
and going to bed late, gambling at basset and backgammon, all
were condemned by a long line of male moralists who denounced
from the pulpit or ridiculed from the pages of the *Tatler* or *Spectator*
the displeasing spectacle of idle womanhood.[7] Later the new woman
was to change. In reality and in the kingdom of the novel from
Richardson onwards the idle women of the middle classes were to
be tamed, to turn into the demure, asexual prudes that a new race
of Christian gentlemen would place on pedestals safely out of the
reach of sin.[8] But in Defoe's time women were still scarlet, avid for
sex and the good times which their husband's incomes placed within
their reach. And far too few gentlemen were Christian.

Defoe had no more time for such conspicuously idle women as
these than any other writer of the day. In *Religious Courtship* he refers
to the fate of a man married to such a woman, 'a wild, giddy, play-
house-bred wife; full of wit, and void of grace . . . a tempter at his
elbow, instead of a wife to help him on to Heaven. She has led him
hood-wink'd to the gates of Hell and goes chearfully along with
him.'[9] But he is remarkable in his generation for the good opinion
that he had of the fair sex in general. Throughout his life he advocated better treatment for women, both by society and by their
husbands. He was sufficiently authoritarian to think, like everyone
else, that a wife should be subjected to her husband, but he thought
that the nature of their subjection should be that of a junior partner,
not an upper servant.[10] He refused to believe that women were

mentally inferior to men and felt that the main problem was that women did not receive a good enough education to fit them for their main role in life, to be the companions of men.[11] To most Englishmen of his time an educated woman was a joke. There was nothing in London to compare to the salons of the *précieuses* in Paris. But to Defoe a well-bred, educated woman was 'a creature without comparison; her society is the emblem of sublimer enjoyments; her person is angelick, and her conversation heavenly; she is all softness and sweetness, peace, love, wit, and delight. She is every way suitable to the sublimest wish; and the man that has such a one to his portion, has nothing to do but to rejoice in her, and be thankful.' Unfortunately he belies these sentiments when, on the next page, he sinks into a typical piece of Defovian bathos. 'Bless us! What care do we take to breed up a good horse, and to break him well! . . . and why not a woman?'[12]

Defoe reserved his strongest criticism for his own sex, considering them not only vile in their own right but responsible for most of the bad reputation of women as well.[13] An early shot in his campaign for the better treatment of women by their husbands was his poem, *Good Advice to the Ladies*, which was published in 1702. The good advice was not to get married because men were so awful. They kept whores, went out and got drunk, kept their wives short of money and often did all this in an hypocritical way so that the world saw only a smile. Such criticism crops up repeatedly throughout his writing career. Men drank, got the servants pregnant[14] or spent their wives' portions in a flurry of high living before going bankrupt and leaving them destitute.[15] People were so used to husbands beating their wives that the screams did not even bother the neighbours. 'The common answer to one another is only thus; " 'tis nothing neighbour, but such a one beating his wife"; "O dear", says the other, "is that all?", and in they go again, compos'd and easie.'[16] If all else failed, the very worst husbands had their wives committed and locked up in a private mad-house. Naturally, while their wives were inside, the husbands spent their dowry on their mistresses, while the wife was so badly treated that she finally really did go mad. 'Is it not enough to make any one mad to be suddenly clap'd up, stripp'd, whipp'd, ill fed and worse us'd?'[17]

Defoe's criticism of the poor treatment meted out by Englishmen to their wives stands out the more since England was proverbially 'the paradise of women', a piece of chauvinism endorsed by many men, if few women, throughout the seventeenth and early eighteenth centuries.[18] 'For such is the good nature of Englishmen towards their wives', wrote Edward Chamberlayne, 'that if there were a bridge over into England . . . it is thought all the women in Europe would run hither.'[19] The same sentiment was expressed in 1703 in a satirical attack on the current vogue for all things French. 'I hate everything that Old England brings forth', says a lady of fashion, 'except it be the temper of an English husband, and the liberty of an English wife; I love the French bread, French wines, French sauces, and a French cook; in short, I have all about me French or foreign, from my waiting woman to my parrot.'[20]

Those who trumpeted the English woman's good fortune realized that there were some legal disadvantages in being a wife in England. Chamberlayne himself pointed out the extreme legal subjection of the English wife. 'Women . . . so soon as they are married are wholly at the will and disposition of the husband. They can own no goods, not even their clothes.'[21] This was certainly true in common law, by which a wife was treated as a minor.[22] Since all that 'the wife hath is the husband's',[23] it was not even possible to give one's wife a present, as the father in *Religious Courtship* points out. 'Presents to a wife! What do they signify? 'tis but taking his money out of one pocket, and putting it into the other.'[24] A husband had full control not only of his wife's dowry but of all her property, though the courts accepted that a widow had a right to a part, normally a third, of her late husband's property after his death. Indeed virtually the only way a woman could become a full legal individual was to outlive her husband, as many did. As a wife she had no control over the disposition of either her money or her children. She could make no contract since she had no full legal personality. There were occasions when this legal subjection could work for her. If a wife committed a crime in her husband's presence he was liable to be charged with it, since it was assumed that she could not be held responsible for her actions.

Some beginnings were made in improving the financial and legal position of married women in Defoe's lifetime. Much was made of the new institution of pin-money, 'that foundation of wives' rebellion', as Sir Harry Gubbin put it in Steele's *Tender Husband*.[25] Pin-money, which could be a large sum, was often agreed before marriage. The customary anti-feminine bias of the common-law courts was also challenged by the courts of equity, who increasingly

held that a wife could have property settled on her.[26] But, until the
1740s, such a settlement normally required the husband's consent.
So even what improvements that there were rested, as did the
paradise of marriage itself, on the hypothetical good nature of the
English husband. There may have been a few legal loop-holes but,
for the most part, Roxana sums up the position of a wife in an
English marriage very accurately.'The very nature of the marriage
contract was in short, nothing but giving up liberty, estate, authority,
and every-thing, to the man, and the woman was indeed a meer
woman ever after, that is to say, a slave.'[27]

Roxana develops the logic of her attack on marriage in the
splendid satirical comparison between the condition of a wife and
a mistress which she makes when she discovers that she is at last
free to remarry, as a result of the death of her ne'er-do-well first
husband:

> I had no inclination to be a wife again; I had had such bad
> luck with my first husband, I hated the thoughts of it. I found
> that a wife is treated with indifference, a mistress with a strong
> passion; a wife is look'd upon as but an upper-servant, a mistress
> is a sovereign; a wife must give up all she has; have every reserve
> she makes for herself be thought hard of, and be upbraided with
> her very pin-money; whereas a mistress makes the saying true
> that what the man has, is hers, and what she has is her own; the
> wife bears a thousand insults, and is forc'd to sit still and bear it,
> or part and be undone; a mistress insulted helps herself im-
> mediately and takes another.[28]

Few of Defoe's female contemporaries would have gone as far as
Roxana, but there were many critics from both sexes prepared to
join Defoe in doubting, or at least questioning, whether marriage
was really quite the paradise for women suggested by proverb.[29]
Richard Baxter, apparently happily married himself,[30] spelt out in
pitiless detail what marriage was likely to bring to a woman:

> Women especially must expect so much suffering in a married
> life, that if God had not put into them a natural inclination to
> it, and so strong a love to their children, as maketh them patient
> under the most annoying troubles, the world would ere this have
> been at an end, through their refusal of so calamitous a life.
> Their sickness in breeding, the pain in bringing forth, with the

danger of their lives, the tedious trouble night and day which
they have with their children in their nursing and their childhood,
besides their subjection to their husbands . . . All this and much
more would have utterly deterred that sex from marriage, if
nature it self had not enclined them to it.[31]

What made things even worse was that this state of slavery and
degradation was so incredibly easy to enter. The normal procedure
when two people wished to be married was for the banns to be
called publicly three times before the solemnization of the marriage
by a clergyman. But many people did not relish this publicity and
there was provision for marriage by licence without the calling of
the banns.[32] All that was necessary was for one of the parties to make
a sworn statement that there was no legal impediment to the
marriage and that, in the case of a minor, parental consent had been
obtained. A considerable proportion of all marriages in the seventeenth century appear to have been by this more expensive method.[33]
Less regular, but still legal, was the trade in clandestine marriages
which was carried on by the so-called Fleet parsons. According to
Lecky, almost every tavern and brandy shop in the neighbourhood
of the Fleet Prison had a parson in its pay who would willingly
hitch a stupefied heir or a kidnapped heiress to some sprig of the
underworld.[34] In law the forced abduction of an heiress was a felony
without benefit of clergy, as Defoe was to point out in 1727, but
there were more subtle ways for the fortune-hunter to work.[35]
'Buying and selling fortunes, a trade never practised so much as
now', he wrote in 1713. 'The most busy brokers in this employ make
it their business to betray ladies of estates into the hands of beggars
and bankrupts, under the title of wealthy citizens.'[36]

There was no real need to have a parson at all for a marriage
to be legal. A mutual agreement between the parties was a binding
marriage, though it might be difficult to prove at law.[37] Writing
in the *Review* Defoe stated that 'marriage being nothing but a
promise, the ceremony is no addition to the contract, only a thing
exacted by the law to prevent knaves [breaking that promise]'.[38]
In *Robinson Crusoe* the French priest defines the minimum requirements of marriage somewhat more strictly. 'A formal contract on
both sides, made before witnesses, and confirm'd by any token
which they had all agreed to be bound by, though it had been but
breaking a stick between them, engaging the men to own these

women for their wives upon all occasions, and never to abandon them or their children, and the women to the same with their husbands.'[39] Crusoe accepted this, but in fact Defoe's earlier statement that marriage was nothing but a promise seems to have been perfectly correct in English law. Thomas Salmon, in his *Critical Essay concerning Marriage* of 1724, quotes a resolution made in the King's Bench in the early years of Queen Anne 'that a contract in words of present time was a marriage; as where it is said, I marry you; you and I are man and wife etc. and such contracts are not releasable'.[40] No wonder that people went to bed drunk and woke up married, the fate of Colonel Jack who, 'in an unusual height of good humour' brought about by drink, consented to marry his second wife.[41]

Marriage might be unpleasant and for life, but most women still sought it. The chances of a woman achieving anything in the market place, of improving herself, were negligible. This sad fact, together with human nature, habit and fear of the scorn reserved for the old maid ensured that this somewhat unsatisfactory method of guaranteeing the future of the human race was the main issue in most young girls' minds. This being the case, Defoe applied himself to issuing advice to both men and women on whom to marry and how to catch the object of one's choice once it had been made. His first venture in the marriage-guidance business appeared in the agony column, called 'Advice from the Scandalous Club', which he ran in the early volumes of the *Review*.[42] In this light relief from the main political business of the paper, he answered readers' letters on a host of problems including courtship and marriage. Most of the ideas developed in this forum were retained when he wrote his didactic works on marriage and his novels later in his life.

Women were doubly cheated by marriage in the world of Defoe. Not only did they get a poor deal in marriage, but marriage itself was a man's market. This was particularly true in London where there was habitually a surplus of women,[43] many of whom only came to the metropolis to find a husband. But Defoe thought, probably wrongly, that there was also a considerable surplus of women in the countryside.[44] The most obvious explanation of this imbalance between the sexes was the high level of male mortality in the wars and the very considerable preponderance in male emigrants to the Americas.[45] The female surplus may have been aggravated by a lack of enthusiasm on the part of men to marry in a world where the financial benefits of bachelorhood and the easy availability of prostitutes made a single life a very attractive alternative to matrimony.[46] The result, in any case, was to make life even more difficult for women. When the man who was eventually to marry the young Moll Flanders praised her beauty, his sister pointed out that beauty would be of little use to her without money. 'The market is against our sex just now; and if a young woman has beauty, birth, breeding, wit, sense, manners, modesty, and all to an extreme, yet if she has not money she's nobody, she had as good want them all; nothing but money now recommends a woman; the men play the game all into their own hands.'[47] Moll, of course, proved her wrong, but then she was an exceptional woman.

Moll had even sacrificed the only other currency which a woman without money had to offer.[48] She sold her maidenhead for a hundred guineas and the promise of the same every year till marriage. This was a bad bargain, as she later realized: 'If I had known his thoughts, and how hard he supposed I would be to be gained, I might have made my own terms, and if I had not capitulated for an immediate marriage, I might for a maintenance till marriage, and might have had what I would ... but I had wholly abandoned all such thoughts, and was taken up only with the pride of my beauty, and of being beloved by such a gentleman.'[49] Too many girls fell for such snares. This was not the age of the virginal miss of the Victorian novel and most writers assumed that young girls were torn between 'their naturall wishes and the inborn modesty of virgins', like the very physical Antonia in Mandeville's *Virgin Unmask'd*.[50] Jeremy Taylor thought that the answer was to keep girls ignorant of the 'distinction of sexes or their proper instruments, or, if they accidentally be instructed in that, it must be supplied with an inadvertency or neglect of all thoughts and remembrances of such differences.'[51] Defoe, too, realized the potency of maiden sexuality but he was normally scathing in his criticism of those who gave up the bargaining power of their virginity so cheaply. As he put it in the *Review*, 'he that lyes with a woman on a promise of matrimony is a knave if he does not perform his promise, and a fool if he does.'[52] For why should a man trust a girl who has just given him the best proof of her dishonesty? 'He can never believe she will be honest, because, once a whore and always so.'[53] If a woman was so foolish as to 'yield up the last point before wedlock', she should never marry her lover, the only man that could upbraid her with her lack of chastity.[54] There were ways of disguising her former incontinence[55] and there was no obligation for anyone to accuse themselves.[56]

There was no need for a woman to run the risk of such deception. She should play a man carefully, not show herself aggressive and eager for marriage, not show herself fond of the man but cool and indifferent. 'The weak, tho' fair part of the rational world, are desir'd to observe how much they expose themselves, when they become aggressors in love; 'tis the honour of the woman to preserve the negative power in her self, and if ever she loses it, she is sure to go a begging for her own misfortune.'[57] Mandeville ridicules this conventional view of courtship, the one time in her life when a woman was supposed to call the tune. The courting woman 'sits in state, insults over the man, and treats him with as much scorn as if he was not worthy to wipe her shoes; and why does she do all this? For no other reason, but because she designs to make him her master and give him all she has in the world.'[58] In any case a lack of aggression could be taken too far. With the market in the man's favour he could better afford to be indifferent than the woman, as Colonel Jack's first wife discovered before she changed her tactics. First she teased him to arouse his interest, but then kept herself on the reserve so that he could not speak to her alone. 'She soon found she had gone too far with me; and in short that she was extreamly out in her politicks, that she had to do with one that was not listed yet among the whining sort of lovers, and knew not what it was to adore a mistress, in order to abuse her; and that it was not with me, as it was with the usual sort of men in love, that are warm'd by the cold, and rise in their passions, as the ladies fall in their returns.'[59] But a woman who knew how to play the game should be all right, if she stood her ground and fought off the fear that she might never get married at all if she did not accept the first proposal. 'There is no woman, deformity or lost reputation excepted, but if she manages well may be married safely one time or other.'[60]

Such tactical manoeuvres imply a previous choice. Who should a girl marry? A typical answer to this eternal question comes in a discussion on how to choose a husband between the two eldest daughters in *Religious Courtship*:[61]

> *1st. Daughter* O! I'll explain it in a few words; a good estate, and a man you like.

2nd. Daughter Nay; you might have stopt at the first: it's no matter what the man is, if the estate be but good.

Money was of course a vital element in the choice of marriage partner, at least for those of the middle station. When the poor married they just felt in their pockets to see how much money they could bring together to start them in the world.[62] But, amongst the even moderately wealthy, the importance of the commercial element in marriage was probably on the increase in the time of Defoe.[63] But those who benefited were likely to be men rather than women. In the current state of the marriage market a man was able to make an extremely good bargain, offering a much smaller jointure in relation to his wife's dowry than had been the case in the early seventeenth century.[64] Moll Flanders realized that a woman must have money to buy herself a husband and tried to hold herself true to the maxim that 'a woman should never be kept for a mistress that had money to make herself a wife'.[65] But even if women of the middle station, or their fathers, had to buy their husbands it was necessary to make sure that what they bought was a good bargain. Careful investigation was required to ensure that a man who appeared to be well off was not just a cheat who was creating on tick the impression of wealth, in order to rob a girl of her dowry and then send her home a beggar.[66] Even if a man did have money there was no guarantee that he would keep it. It was necessary to discover his debts and obligations, his pattern of expenditure and his ability in business, not just to 'run into matrimony as a horse rushes into the battle'. Moll Flanders argued that even the man she married would have a low opinion of a girl who 'having but one cast for her life, shall cast that life away at once, and make matrimony, like death, be a leap in the dark'.[67] Roxana, rich from the proceeds of her life as a whore, is careful to refuse the offers 'which came generally from gentlemen of good families, and good estates, but who living to the extent of them, were always needy and necessitous, and wanted a sum of money to make themselves easie, as they call it; that is to say, to pay off incumbrances, sisters' portions, and the like'.[68] She had good reason to be careful since she had married as her first husband the most despicable sort of man, not only a spendthrift but a fool. In a *Review* of 1707 Defoe asked his readers what was the worst kind of husband. There were many candidates, such as the drunken, the debauched, the fighting and the extravagant husbands, but all these might 'have something attendant, which in the intervals of their excesses may serve to alleviate and make a little amends to the poor woman, and help her to carry thorough the afflicting part; but a FOOL has something always about him, that makes him intollerable.'[69] A fool would never be a phoenix, would never raise his fortune from the ashes of his disgrace and would leave his wife in poverty and distress all her life.

Money, then, was a vital element in marriage. Love was not forgotten, but it was felt by most commentators to be something that came after marriage, not before. Benjamin Wadsworth argued that love was the chief duty of husband and wife towards each other, but did not think it necessary that they should love each other before they got married. All that was required was that they should marry someone whom they thought that they would be able to love in the future.[70] Defoe, while he accepted this general proposition, was rather more romantic. Love was required even before marriage. Some people held, he said, that let a couple be but married, 'they will toy together till they love afterwards; that property begets affection, and that if all other things hit, they may run the risque of the love with less inconvenience. But I must enter my protest here: I think they that make a toy of the affection, will make a toy of the matrimony.'[71] Young people should not only get to know one another before marriage but 'should be engaged to each other by a solid and durable affection, professing to love, and not only professing but sincerely loving one another above all other persons'.[72] He accepted that the young could make foolish mistakes, that affection was not always grounded on merit, but all the same love was so essential to happiness 'that however absurdly that unaccountable passion may be grounded ... a woman ought to choose a man she loves best'.[73] A man who wrote to the *Review*, saying that he loved a woman but was unwilling to marry her because her fortune was not equal to his, was unequivocally advised to marry her, 'if what you have of your own will but give you bread'.[74]

Few writers had Defoe's confidence in the power of love to create a happy marriage. Baxter, whose gloomy views on marriage have already been quoted, thought that few people could love each other and that even a state of compatibility was virtually impossible. 'There is so great a diversity of temperaments and degrees of understanding that there are scarce any two persons in the world, but there is some unsuitableness between them, ... Some crossness there will be of opinion, or disposition, or interest, or will, by nature, or by custome and education, which will stir up frequent discontent.' The crosses of marriage were not for just a year, he reminds us, 'but during life: they deprive you of all hope of relief while you live together. Death only must be your relief.' And, if you did happen to love your partner, not even death was a relief, since 'one of you must bear grief of their death'.[75] Defoe would have agreed that marriage was a lottery, but not one with quite as many blanks as this.

Love might be more important than money in Defoe's didactic works, if not his novels where Moll and Roxana, though loving, behave in a more businesslike way, but it was still not enough. Or, if it was enough, there were other attributes which it was important that the loved one should have. A wife should be a good housewife as well as a good woman if she was to do her job properly, though the former might be a virtue difficult to determine before the fact.[76] But some men could pick well. The five English mutineers who had settled on Crusoe's island drew lots as to who should have first choice of the five savage ladies they had brought to the island. Everyone laughed when the winner chose 'the homeliest and the oldest of the five ... but the fellow consider'd better than any of them, that it was application and business that they were to expect assistance in, as much as any thing else; and she prov'd the best wife of all the parcel'.[77]

Far more emphasis is placed by Defoe on what he called inequality in marriage. This expression could be interpreted in many ways, but usually meant that religious persons should not marry those that were not, even if they loved them. Only if both partners were religious could there be harmony in the marriage. Ideally husband and wife should not only both be Protestants and truly religious, but should also belong to the same Protestant sect. Otherwise their different views of family worship, one perhaps using the Bible and the other not, would be likely to lead to a family schism. And what sort of marriage would it be if one partner went to church on the Sabbath and the other to the meeting-house?[78] But Defoe did not like to stress this ideal too much, since he was hoping to find as wide a pious audience as possible for his books. In *The Family Instructor*, for instance, there is a couple who are both sober and pious and whose household is described as a paradise of harmony with 'no difference in their conversation', although the wife was a Dissenter and the husband a churchman.[79]

The theme of religious inequality is worked out most fully in *Religious Courtship*. The dying mother's last plea to her three daughters was that they should all marry religious men and the book considers their differing interpretations of this injunction. The message is that it is no good simply accepting a man's claim that he is religious. One must investigate the sincerity of the claim and make absolutely sure that his religion is the right one. The second sister's slackness in this respect leads to disaster. She is sprightly, gay and the best-looking of the three, by no means without religion, but not as careful as her sisters. Her main interest in a suitor is that he should have a good estate and, when a rich Leghorn merchant courts her, she is not too bothered about anything other than his wealth, accepting his unqualified assertion that he is a religious man. Her elder sister is very worried. 'Did ever a young lady, that had any regard to religion and the future happiness of her life, suffer herself to be courted two months by a strange person coming out of Italy, from the very bowels of superstition and the very kingdom of popery ... and never know what religion he was of, or whether he had any religion, or no; except that she had heard by accident that he was not an atheist?'[80] Needless to say the worst happens. When her sisters visit her after her marriage she is living in a magnificent house, furnished with every luxury and with walls lined with pictures. But these pictures, although beautifully painted, have suspiciously religious subjects. Suspicions of idolatry are confirmed when a crucifix is discovered over the bed. The full story comes out after the merchant's death. He had always been kind and loving, but he was a confirmed Papist and had continuously tried to convert her, bribing her with presents and subjecting her to an affectionate, but subtly logical, demonstration of the danger in which her soul was placed.[81]

The youngest daugher is determined to follow her mother's advice. A good-looking, wealthy suitor comes to seek her hand in marriage and her father enthusiastically accepts his suit. But the girl, though clearly smitten, is determined to discover whether he is a real believer before she makes her final decision. For a long time he parries her attempts to discover his religious beliefs, but finally he gives the game away by saying flippantly that the gentlemen of

England choose their wives first and then their religion. The girl is very miserable at this evidence of his religious insincerity and is now determined not to go through with the match, despite her love for the man and her father's fury at her disobedience in not marrying the man whom he had approved.[82]

Defoe and his characters are fully conscious of the danger of hypocrisy involved in such a situation. The girl's suitor was quite honest and sincere about his lack of religion and so he lost his lady; but she admits that if he had been a hypocrite and had simply made a show of religion, the fact that she already felt herself in love with him would have carried the day.

It is also interesting to note how often those who have no religion or the wrong religion are in every other respect such nice people. Defoe was far too much of an artist and a realist to assume that only religious people could be pleasant and lovable. Both the suitors in the stories discussed above would have made ideal husbands from a purely worldly point of view. But marriage was a partnership whose end was death and the hope of salvation, and thus for a religious person to tie herself to a non-believer was a sure recipe for worldly unhappiness and the possibility of eternal damnation. In *The Family Instructor* one wife is described as 'housewifly, frugal, quiet, mannerly, tender and kind', apparently a model list of feminine virtues. But she is not religious.[83] She mocks her husband's performance at family worship and ostentatiously reads a book or sleeps during prayers. In a huff the husband discontinues family worship and this in turn leads to a total breakdown of relationships within the household. There are quarrels between the parents in which the children take sides until finally the wife leaves home.[84]

A difference in matters of religion was not the only type of inequality which Defoe condemned in marriage. Any sort of inequality, in age, estate or temperament, could lead to strife. He was particularly opposed to the marriage of old women to young men, quite a common arrangement in a world where a widow left with a family business might well need a man to help her run it and provide the cash to educate her children and set them forth in the world. That man might be the apprentice who already understood the business and stood to get a good settlement by marrying his master's widow.[85] Defoe may have recognized the business sense in such a marriage but he saw the main motive on the woman's part as one of pure lust. He illustrated this point by the story of a widow whose justification of her need to remarry was that the Devil appeared to her in dreams, beseeching her to let him come to bed with her. She needed a man in her bed because she was frightened.[86]

Defoe in fact doubted whether it was lawful for a woman past childbearing age to marry, since she would be unble to satisfy any longer the proper end of marriage.[87] Such an approach led to yet another variation of the double standard, since it was all right for an old man to marry a young girl. For, although it was a bit of a joke, he could still have children and might need an heir.[88]

It can be seen that the individual was likely to undergo considerable difficulty in selecting the ideal partner. To find someone whom you not only loved, but who was also genuinely pious and belonged to the same sect, who was roughly the same age and whose fortune was not too far removed from yours, was quite a tall order. But the individual choice was in any case considerably circumscribed by the need to obtain parental consent, by law if one was a minor, and for long afterwards by the customary respect which a child should have for his father. An authoritarian society naturally put much emphasis on the fifth commandment, and nearly every writer on moral affairs had his bit to say on just how far a child was obliged to obey his father's commands in the choice of marriage partner, and to what extent the father should determine that choice.

Many moralists assumed, quite rightly, that the father's choice of spouse for his children was likely to be dictated by an ambition to raise his family in the world, rather than by any great interest in the young people's happiness. 'Parents oftentimes measure their affections rather according to the humour they have themselves, (being old), than regard the good liking of the young folks to be matched. And therefore rather seek to bestow their children in wealth, or honour, or strength of friends, than are willing to suffer them to bestow themselves according to their own choice.'[89] Under such conditions writers were practically unanimous that the father should not be able to force his children to marry against their will.[90] The father could use persuasion but not force, although the degree of persuasion was not well defined. It was wrong for a father to tie his daughter to the bedpost and whip her until she consented to marry the hideous but rich and influential man that he had chosen for her,[91] but there were other less painful but more permanent methods of persuasion. The father of the youngest sister in *Religious Courtship* who refused to marry her irreligious lover, discussed above, threatened to turn her out of the house and send her into service,[92] and many a father, both in fiction and reality, disinherited his children for their refusal to obey him.

Defoe's position in this debate reflected the general opinion of his day. A father could refuse his consent to his son's choice, though if the boy was over age he should be prepared to defend his refusal.[93] On the other hand, although a father must be allowed to select the field, his child had the right to refuse any individual within that field, 'to be at liberty to like or dislike, receive or refuse the person and that absolutely'.[94] Defoe's views are summed up in *Religious Courtship*. 'If your daughter desires to marry any person you do not like, I grant that you have power by the law of God to forbid her positively; the scripture is plain, you have power to dissolve even a vow or promise of hers, to marry or not to marry at all. But if your daughter is not willing to marry one you may like, I do not think you have the same right of command.'[95]

One thing which must have militated against parental control was the extremely high age at marriage in both sexes. Historians have discovered with some surprise that the median age at marriage of women in both England and France was twenty-four or twenty-five or more, with the men normally being a year or two older than their brides.[96] Such averages naturally conceal a wide range. The legal age of consent was twelve for girls and fourteen for boys and many children were married at these ages. Betrothal and the formal bedding of the espoused pair might take place at the age of seven. But such marriages as these were nearly always to be found in the dynastic alliances of the landed classes, and even then only rarely. The truth is that the vast majority of all people of both sexes were married after they had reached the age of twenty-one, and thus did not require the legal consent of their parents.

Contemporary advice mirrors the discoveries of the statisticians. Men of the middle station were given the almost universal advice to marry late. The rationale was of course the weak economic position of young men. Marriage was nearly always strictly forbidden in apprenticeship contracts,[97] and a young man out of his time would need all his cash to set himself up in business and he was likely to be twenty-five or even thirty before his trade was

sufficiently flourishing to 'carry two'.[98] Similar restraints operated
in the countryside where the controlling factor was the need to
possess a house and land on which to support a family, a require-
ment which might well have to await the father's death or retirement from farming.

From an economic point of view the age at marriage of girls was
obviously less relevant and indeed the contemporary emphasis on
the need for a large population might have been expected to have
led to the encouragement of girls marrying early. Modern writers
suggest, however, that exactly the opposite reasoning led men to
choose older girls. In a world without efficient mechanical means of
contraception a bride of thirty was the best possible insurance of a
small family and a good life. Few women were likely to have more
than four or five children if they started at this age and a couple
of these might well die in the conditions of high infant mortality
that existed.[99] Children might be able to pay for their keep when
they were five or six in exceptional circumstances, but these were not
the children of the middle station and, in any case, they would
obviously have been cheaper if they had not existed.

Defoe advocated a high age at marriage for girls, but naturally
not for the reasons suggested above. He thought that one of the main
reasons that marriage was so often a disaster for wives was because
they were scared of never marrying and so accepted the first comer.
But the longer they waited, the more experience they would have of
saying no and so the more choice. A lady who signed herself Lady
Marjory in *Applebee's Journal*, but who writes suspiciously like Defoe,
said that after discussion with her friends she had decided that
between twenty-five and forty was the best time to get married.
She was determined 'to run the risk of staying, and being taken off
to my advantage, rather than of being boy-match'd in my youth,
and tied down too early to a fool or a fop'.[100]

Saying no might be a frightening proposition, the marriage
market being so favourable to men, but many girls obviously did.
Some may never have been asked. But the fact of late marriage,
together with the greater survival rate of women, meant that there
existed a vast number of unmarried adult women in England. If
Gregory King's figures are correct, over forty per cent of all adult
women were unmarried, either widows, servants or simply single
women, a fact which was good news for those looking for cheap
labour and which made rather a nonsense of the law, since a

considerable number of them were single women living at their own hands.[101]

Modern research has enabled us to snoop unmercifully on the behaviour patterns of the past. One thing that is striking is the very high proportion of girls who were pregnant when they got married.[102] As we have seen, for Defoe and the middle station generally, the sacrifice of her maidenhood was considered to be a disastrous mistake on the part of a girl. Of course they may just have been talking a lot of pious nonsense. These girls may have been as promiscuous as the girls from poor, rural backgrounds whose behaviour pattern must dominate any such statistical generalization.[103] What seems probable, however, is that the mores of the vast majority of the population who did not belong to the middle station were strikingly different from those of their better-off compatriots. There seems to be too much contemporary evidence of the loose morals of the poor for there to be no truth in any of it. Much of the motivation and argument which occupied the moralists must have seemed totally irrelevant to the poor. They could never expect to inherit a farm or build up a business; most of them never served an apprenticeship. Parental authority, equality of fortune, even decency must have seemed of little consequence. And yet it is of course, their late marriages which make the average high. Economic pressures against an early marriage and a large family were as relevant, if not more so, for the poor as they were for the rich. Negative evidence for this can be seen from the fact that people married younger and had larger families in the industrial areas where there was more, and more regular, work for young people with no land and no expectations.[104] How do the pregnant brides fit into this? Did the poor play Russian roulette with their economic chances, avoiding the sexual frustration of the middle classes, but marrying when they had to? Or did they see premarital sex as a process of natural selection by which they made love to their intended brides but did not marry them unless they proved fertile? Whatever the answer to such delicate questions the English poor seem to have made more enjoyable use of their short lives than their French counterparts, who had an equally high age at marriage and very low levels of both bridal pregnancy and illegitimacy.[105] What they did to quiet their frustration is now a subject of passionate debate among French historians, whose discussion of what their forebears did in the long period between puberty and marriage has led to the creation of two schools, those who believe they masturbated and those who believe they prayed.[106]

Whether the bride was pregnant at marriage or not she was likely to become so soon afterwards and so enter the miserable state of life described by Baxter.[107] Of course some of the horrors of child-rearing could be farmed out by the women of the middle station, who could irritate the moralists by putting the child out to nurse and could rely on the servants rather than themselves being woken by the children in the night. Certainly those who wrote books of advice for such women and their husbands have for the most part little to say about the physical aspects of bringing forth and bringing up children, concentrating as we have seen on their moral and religious education. How then did they see marriage itself?

In his novels Defoe passes over the actual details of marriage with indecent haste. Years of marriage pass in a few lines and the interest is concentrated on the process of choosing a partner or the conditions under which the marriage finally dissolves. The children who are born to Roxana and Moll are treated in an abominable way, farmed out, killed off or forgotten, never brought up but occasionally brought in to provide some sort of dramatic tension. In his moralizing works, however, marriage itself is often the centre of attention and we can find ourselves inside an early eighteenth-century household with all its inevitable stresses and strains. The recipe for peace is fairly predictable. As we have seen, Defoe did not put the same emphasis on female subjection as other writers. Marriage was something in which husband and wife were partners:

> The great duty between the man and his wife, I take to consist in that of love, in the government of affection, and the obedience of a complaisant, kind, obliging temper: the obligation is recip-rocal, 'tis drawing in an equal yoke. Love knows no superior or inferior, no imperious command on one hand, no reluctant subjection on the other; the end of both should be the well-ordering their family, the good-guiding their household and children, educating, instructing and managing them with a mutual endeavour.[108]

Such an ideal of partnership extended to the husband's business. One reason that Defoe opposed the marriage of young tradesmen was that their wives would be forced to do the housework, as they would not be able to afford servants, and so would not have time to learn the business and help in the shop. This was the place for the wife of a shopkeeper. No woman should think herself above businesss and just sit upstairs dispensing tea. Not only could she help her husband if she understood his business, being able to run the shop for instance if he went out, but later, if he died, she could manage the business herself and not get cheated as so many ignorant widows of businessmen were.[109] Defoe does not go into many details of the woman's function in business but, at the very least, she could act as some sort of moral support, like the wife of the tradesman who, when he could no longer bear the impertinence of his customers, used to rush upstairs, beat her and kick his children around like dogs till he had recovered his temper. 'After the fit was over he would go down into his shop again, and be as humble, as courteous, and as calm as any man whatever; so absolute a government of his passions had he in the shop, and so little out of it.'[110]

The household was as much a part of the business as the shop in the world of Defoe.[111] A woman therefore needed to know how trade was going so that she could govern her expenditure accordingly. Everyone knew that marriage was expensive,[112] and becoming more so in the ostentatious days of the 1720s. But it was no good brimming over with pride at the thought of your servants and carriage or at the sight of your well-dressed wife presiding at the chocolate-pot in your expensively fitted parlour and then blaming her for her extravagance when things started to go wrong in the business. If you were not honest with her, how was she to know that her little parties were taking you to the brink of bankruptcy?

Rows about money were just one of those many trifles which could lead in marriage to a fatal breach. 'How simply, how weakly, and indeed how wickedly such people act when they run little family bickerings up by rash and impudent degrees . . . to real quarrels.'[113] Trifles might be simply a matter of temperament, but they were far more likely to occur where Defoe's injunctions on the choice of partners had not been observed. Now was the time to say 'I told you so'. Those who married too young and struggled to run a business and a household on a pittance were bound to be unhappy. What else could be expected? At least such people presumably married for affection or, at any rate, one must hope so since they had so foolishly renounced all the worldly benefits of marriage. A worldly marriage without affection was likely to be even worse,

almost inevitably a seed-bed of strife and hate. But even if you loved
your wife, that inequality in marriage which Defoe so condemned
would soon sow its seed. Think of the horrors faced by a religious
man tempted by money to marry into an irreligious family. One
such unfortunate described to his friend the first six months of his
marriage which he had spent with his wife's family. It was one long
orgy of luxury and drunkenness. Worst of all was the fact that no
grace was said at meals. 'We all sat down to table without a chaplain, and as Sir Richard made no offer to stand up, so no sooner
was the dinner set on, and the ladies plac'd, but my lady had her
knife in a boil'd turkey, and we all fell to work.' His friend was
shocked, indeed amazed. He had never thought that there was any
Protestant in the world that would eat 'with as little regard to him
whose hand fill'd us, as any pack of hounds in the country'.[114]

Such situations were not irreversible. Wives could be converted.
Patience and love could overcome religious indifference. Once
unbelief had been stormed, affection, a shared responsibility for
children and household, and mutual prayer should do the rest. But
there was no denying it was a hard task and those who made a poor
first choice got what they asked for.

It is amusing to compare Defoe's pious, idealistic, hopeful, but
ultimately rather pessimistic view of marriage with the ideas of the
best-known and most cynical commentator on the realities of
marriage among his contemporaries. There is no nonsense about
partnership in the advice given to his daughter by George Savile,
marquis of Halifax:[115]

> You must first lay it down for a foundation in general, that there
> is inequality in the sexes, and that for the better economy of the
> world, the men, who were to be the law-givers, had the larger
> share of reason bestow'd upon them, by which means your sex
> is the better prepar'd for the compliance that is necessary for
> the better performance of those duties which seem to be most
> properly assigned to it.[116]

But subjection does not mean defeat. On the battle-field of marriage
wives have many countervailing strengths. The very worst faults of
a husband can work to her advantage. When he, almost inevitably,
commits adultery she should ignore it. The 'complaint makes a wife
much more rediculous than the injury that provoketh her to it'.
But there was more to forgiveness than fear of the laughter of the

world, for the husband's knowledge of his own injustice 'will naturally make him more yielding in other things. And whether it be to cover or redeem his offence, you may have the good effects of it whilst it lasteth.'[117] Indeed no woman should welcome a husband without faults who can with justice condemn her for her own. In many ways the ideal was a weak incompetent husband whose very weakness 'giveth you the dominion, if you will make the right use of it'.[118] One can imagine what Defoe, with his contempt for fools, would have made of this, perhaps realistic, view of contemporary marriage.

Defoe, with his ideals of love before marriage and partnership within it, may seem fairly 'modern', if overly pious, in his views of the relations between the sexes. But he is 'puritanical' in his attitude to sex itself. The very word puritanical is a popular misconception in this context. Historians have been able to show that the puritan moralists were remarkably tolerant and understanding of the role of sex within marriage. They accepted the biblical view of the ends of marriage as procreation and the avoidance of fornication, and they decried immoderate intercourse as they decried all forms of immoderate behaviour. But they certainly realized that there was more to sex than simply a rather distasteful necessity if the world was not to come to an end.[119]

When Defoe comes to discuss sex he, rather prudishly, tries to avoid any possible charge of obscenity by quoting at length from the work of Jeremy Taylor, an Anglican but, like many other Anglican moralists, a writer in the tradition of the puritan conduct-books of the first half of the seventeenth century. Taylor preaches moderation like all moralists. 'Chastity', he wrote, 'is the cutting off all superfluity of naughtinesse, and a suppression of all irregular desires in the matter of sensual or carnal pleasures.'[120] But, when he comes to define the legitimate objects of sexual intercourse, he defines them quite widely as 'a desire of children, or to avoid fornication, or to lighten and ease the cares and sadnesses of household affairs, or to endear each other'.[121] In other words sex was all right as long as it was not for pleasure alone.

Defoe pays little attention to Taylor's two last, delightfully worded objects of sex, although he quotes them.[122] For him it was mainly a matter either of lust or procreation. Such an attitude leads him to condemn intercourse in many situations where other moralists saw no harm. He repeats the conventional advice that a man should not have intercourse with his wife when she is menstruating.[123] He also said that, once his wife has conceived, the object of marriage was fulfilled and the man should no longer lie with her.[124] 'The woman is with child, that's supposed ... The end of the conjugal act is already answered; wherefore does he come near her? 'Tis only to satisfy the cravings of his vice.'[125] This was not exactly illiberal since, although some writers saw nothing wrong in making love to a pregnant woman,[126] many including Defoe thought that it could cause damage to the unborn child. Defoe specifically rejected one common theory by which it was not only lawful but necessary to continue to have intercourse, since conception was held to be continuous and so, 'there is a supply wanting to compleat the formation of the foetus'.[127]

Where Defoe really was illiberal and indeed thoroughly unkind was in his attitude to the sexual relations of the elderly, which he condemned entirely as motivated only by lust. Since they were no longer able to have children, it could only be 'for the frailer part' or to gratify the beast in them.[128] There is no mention of companionship as a motive for sex among the old or their need 'to endear each other', as Jeremy Taylor put it.[129]

It is hardly surprising that Defoe, with such a view of sex, should come down very heavily against contraception and abortion. Condemnation of such practices was universal. What is interesting, however, is that he assumes that both practices were common and needed to be denounced. Modern demographic historians have been able to demonstrate the probability of the use of birth control on a considerable scale,[130] but there is little evidence of the methods used. It is generally assumed that the normal methods were abstinence or *coitus interruptus*. Defoe mentions both these, condemning *coitus interruptus* as the sin of Onan,[131] and abstinence if it is caused by the wife refusing to accept the husband and thus denying him the possibility of achieving fatherhood.[132] But he also certainly implies the wide-scale use of both spermicides and abortifacients by women, supporting his moral view that the use of both is child-murder by more practical arguments about the danger of quack medicines. A woman who uses such mixtures to prevent pregnancy now may find she is sterile later when she really wants a child.[133] Such preparations have a history nearly as old as man and their manufacture must have been an important part of the business of herbalists and midwives, though some historians rather condescendingly assume that contemporaries had no idea which ones worked and which did not.[134] Defoe also considers supernatural methods of contraception. In his section on the use of spells and witchcraft to prevent conception he has a rather muddled discussion of whether the Devil in fact has the power to prevent a woman having a child, concluding that the crime remains the same whether the Devil can work effectively or not. 'To go to the Devil to prevent God's blessing!'[135] Later he considers the farcical situation of the husband praying to God for children on one side of the bed and the wife praying that she shall not get pregnant on the other.[136]

Abortion, like contraception, has a long history and we must assume that it was common in Defoe's time. One of Moll Flanders' confidantes was an abortionist, as well as a baby-farmer and provider of secret places for girls to have awkward babies. ' 'Tis scarce credible what practice she had, as well abroad as at home, and yet all upon the private account, or, in plain English, the whoring account.' But Moll, who was very much against abortion, warns her readers, 'let none be encouraged in their loose practices from this dexterous lady's management, for she has gone to her place, and I dare say has left nothing behind her that can or will come up to it'.[137] That others besides whores might seek to procure an abortion can be seen from a pathetic letter in the *Review*. A lady, living in poverty with five children, denied her husband the marriage-bed, but persuasion of friends, love and obedience to her husband overcame her. She was now pregnant again and had resolved to get something from the midwife to cause miscarriage. Defoe reinforces his moral veto with some cruel logic: 'If she must kill one of them, 'tis less crime to kill one of them that is born, and has enjoy'd some part of life, than that which has not yet seen the world.'[138]

One interesting aspect of Defoe's writing on both contraception and abortion is his assumption of their motivation. Modern writers all seem to assume that the main motivation was economic, an assumption which is given some support by the apparent correlation between falls in the birth rate and the short-run state of the economy. In such circumstances the husband has as much or more interest in a small family as his wife, since the extra burden will have to be paid for by him. This seems a good reason to assume that *coitus interruptus*, a method of contraception controlled by the husband, was widely used. But Defoe never mentions the economic motives for contraception. The whole responsibility is placed on the woman, who is said to want no children because of the pain and danger of bearing them, the work of bringing them up and the havoc that they are likely to play with her figure. 'She would have the pleasure of lying with a man, but would not have the least interruption from her usual company keeping; the jollitry and mirth of her younger years; that she would not abate her pleasures, she would not be confined at home, or loaded with the cares of being a mother.'[139] It is always assumed that a man who did not want children would not marry. After all, what other reason was there for undergoing the expense and strife of matrimony?

In the world of Defoe, the sexual frustration and the sheer incompatibility between partners, which leads to such a high level of marital disorder in the modern world, must have been even greater. The comparative absence of choice of marriage partner, the lack of room, the lack of privacy, the general acceptance of male infidelity and drunkenness must have led to a very considerable amount of irretrievable breakdown in marriage. Yet the solution of the modern world did not exist. It was virtually impossible to divorce and remarry.

England, alone of Protestant countries, followed the canon law which took marriage to be absolutely indissoluble. Indeed, practice in England after the Reformation was even more unrelenting than it had been in the middle ages, when various loopholes by which a marriage could be judged invalid enabled people to slip through the harsh requirements of the canon law.[140] In Defoe's time it was possible to obtain a separation[141] in the ecclesiastical courts on the grounds of adultery or desertion, but such separation did not permit either party, not even the innocent, to remarry. The only way in which remarriage was possible was by the new and extremely expensive expedient of a private Act of Parliament which annulled the original contract of marriage. 'In this case the thing appears with another face, the persons are to be esteem'd as two that had never been married at all, and are doubtless free, both by the laws of God and man to marry who they please.'[142] Defoe knew the law, but he did not point out how extremely rare such Acts of Parliament were. For all practical purposes there were only two alternatives open to the man or woman who would have liked to remarry: to live in sin or in that more refined form of sin, bigamy. The farcical and extremely unfair nature of the situation is summed up in some

famous and much-quoted remarks made as late as 1845 by Justice
Maule to a man who had committed bigamy after his first wife had
robbed and then deserted him:

> Prisoner, you have committeed a grave offence in taking the law
> into your own hands and marrying again. I will now tell you
> what you should have done. You should have brought an action
> in the civil court, and obtained damages, which the other side
> would probably have been unable to pay, and you would have to
> pay your own cost – perhaps £100 or £150. You should then have
> gone to the ecclesiastical court and obtained a divorce *a mensa
> et thoro*, and then to the House of Lords, where, having provided
> that these preliminaries had been completed, you would have been
> enabled to marry again. The expenses might amount to £500 or
> £600 or perhaps £1,000. You say you are a poor man, and you
> probably do not possess as many pence. But, prisoner, you must
> know that in England there is not one law for the rich and
> another for the poor.[143]

Even a separation was not that easy to obtain. Desertion was often
difficult to prove and was not always accepted as adequate grounds.
And adultery, until very recently the mainstay of the modern
divorce courts, appears to have been extremely difficult to establish.
Defoe tells a story of a husband who caught his wife and her lover
together, both undressed but not actually making love, and was
told by the ecclesiastical courts that this did not constitute sufficient
evidence for a separation on the grounds of adultery.[144] The Swiss
traveller, de Muralt, confirms this. In England, he wrote, husbands
'must be posted behind their wives, and see all with their own eyes,
for no other proof will do'.[145] In the absence of a legal separation,
the husband was still liable for maintenance not only of his wife but
of any bastards which she might have by her lover. A troubled
husband wrote to *Applebee's Journal* describing the situation he found
himself in when his wife was unfaithful. If he turned her out she
could go and take a house next door and make him pay the rent;
if her associates lent her money, they could arrest him for the
debt. He was obliged to own her bastards or at least pay for them.
What could he do?[146] Even if he managed to prove that his wife was
a notorious adulterer, she might be granted 'a large allowance out
of her fortune, nay almost equal to it, for her subsistence'.[147] In
other words, she got some of her own money back to support herself.

'Cuckoldom is the liberty, and a separate maintenance the property, of the freeborn women of England.'[148]

It is not surprising that most people found such laws extremely difficult to understand and there were numerous popular misconceptions about the law of divorce. In particular many thought that desertion constituted immediate grounds for divorce and enabled the innocent party to remarry. After Roxana has been deserted by her first husband, her landlord argues that, since they had both been abandoned by their respective spouses, 'the end of marriage was destroy'd by the treatment we had either of us receiv'd; and it wou'd be very hard that we should be ty'd by the formality of the contract, where the essence of it was destroy'd'. When he had made a contract, 'wherein he engag'd himself to me; to cohabit constantly with me; to provide for me in all respects as a wife', both he and Roxana's maid, Amy, considered the new relationship to be a valid marriage, but Roxana quite rightly knew it to be adultery.[149] Colonel Jack thought that, after he had successfully sued his first wife in the ecclesiastical court for adultery, he was 'a freeman once again'.[150] But he was wrong and his later marriage was bigamous.

There was naturally much opposition to such inflexible divorce laws. Many of the moralists criticized the law and compared it very unfavourably with that of other Protestant countries.[151] The influential Ames held that both desertion and adultery were grounds for divorce and, since they removed the possibility of the true performance of matrimonial duties, the innocent parties were free to remarry.[152] Milton took this liberal view much further, arguing in effect for divorce on the grounds of the irremediable breakdown of the marriage and pleading 'that some unconscionable and tender pity might be had of those who have unwarily, in a thing they never practised before, made themselves the bondmen of a luckless and helpless matrimony'.[153] The views of Milton, Ames and other reformers were well known and widely discussed, but Defoe was adamant in his defence of the indissolubility of marriage. He discusses the views of the famous Mr Milton, 'that disagreeableness of tempers, when it once appeared to be irrecoverable, was sufficient to justify a separation; and to leave either party, or both parties, at liberty to try their fortunes in another venture'.[154] But he laughed them out of court, since it was well known that Milton himself was seeking a divorce when he wrote it. The unwary get no pity from Defoe: 'No, no; if you will rush like the horse into the battle; if you will be mad, and follow rashly, and without consideration, the raging heat of corrupt inclination only, and go hood-winked and blinded, you must take the consequences to your selves; if you will wed without affection, you must be content to live without affection.'[155] Household strife might be a terrestrial hell, but the only road to freedom lay in death.

THE WORK OF DYING

THE man or woman struggling to succeed, or at least to survive, in the world of Defoe was uneasily aware that the business of living, whether it was pleasant or not, must one day come to an end. And there was no need for them to study contemporary vital statistics to know that such a day was likely to come sooner rather than later. No amount of absorption in work, no amount of concentration on leisure could hide the fact that death was ever-present. Even a lady of quality, surrounded by plenty, had to admit to an admirer that the pleasures of life were somewhat tarnished by the thought of death. 'I live very agreeably,' she said, 'and if it was not for this dying it would be all very pretty; but that cursed article takes away all the comfort of my life.'[1]

It was true that the highest rates of mortality occurred before a man really stepped onto the stage of the world. Indeed, so high was the rate of child mortality that it might take two live births to produce one live adult,[2] a fact which led parents to arm themselves with what seems to us a certain callousness in order to cope with repeated grief. The man or woman who survived the testing time of childhood might expect to enjoy a fairly long life,[3] particularly in England where neither famine nor war was a serious danger. Defoe was not all that unusual in reaching the satisfactorily biblical age of seventy before he in turn succumbed. But, for all that, the incidence of mortality among young adults and men in their prime was far higher than it is now and few men were able to forget it. No one could expect with confidence to survive from adolescence to retirement. This fact was naturally disturbing to the individual who never knew if he would live to satisfy his ambitions. But it was likely to pose far greater problems to those who survived.

A man who died in his prime left dependents who had relied on his continued existence to fulfil their role in the world, half-educated children and financially dependent and sexually active wives, who were supported by earnings which in nine cases out of ten required the dead man's own individual application and knowledge.[4] No wonder that Defoe begged the men of the middle station to instruct their wives in the ways of their business.[5] No wonder that he pleaded for a system of mutual insurance to provide pensions for their widows.[6] But, alas, few people took any precautions at all against the only too likely eventuality of the death of the breadwinner.

For some wives, of course, such a death was no disaster. Those who had been so fortunate as to marry a man with an unearned income, a landowner or a fundholder, were entitled to their dower rights, normally one-third of their late husband's income.[7] They might get even more. Such wives were able to survive their husbands' deaths with impunity. Indeed they might look forward to such an event as the only possibility of a much desired financial independence in an unequal world. Peachum was to expound the facts of death to Polly in the *Beggars' Opera*:[8]

> PEACHUM. And had not you the common views of a gentlewoman in your marriage, Polly?
>
> POLLY. I don't know what you mean, Sir.
>
> PEACHUM. Of a jointure, and of being a widow.
>
> POLLY. But I love him, Sir: how then could I have thought of parting with him?
>
> PEACHUM. Parting with him. Why, that is the whole scheme and intention of all marriage articles. The comfortable estate of widowhood is the only hope that keeps up a wife's spirits.

But there were few women lucky enough to marry a successful highwayman, an ideal husband who was not only rich but was unlikely to survive more than a couple of sessions' days at most. Some widows were sufficiently pretty and young or were the heirs to a sufficiently attractive business to find themselves besieged by a host of urgent suitors. Many of these remarried with indecent haste, often within days of the decease of their husband. But most widows could look forward to no such good fortune. There were far too many of them for all to hope to find another man to support them. Gregory King thought there were a quarter of a million widows in 1696, one in six of the adult female population.[9] Most were poor, unattractive and burdened with children and care. They could look forward to nothing but misery, the workhouse or the brothel, or a hard, soul-destroying life spinning or knitting all the hours of daylight in a never-ending attempt to survive. Few women on their own could earn enough to support themselves in comfort, let alone a family of young children. Survival for the poor widow might well seem worse than death.

This could be equally true for a man. It was not necessarily an advantage to live long. Even for the successful, for the English tradesman, retired from the daily cares of the world and basking in the glory of an unsullied reputation, old age could be a sad time, and one that was almost bound to be extremely painful. In Defoe's time, as in ours, the problem of what to do with the old, even if there were less of them, was not always satisfactorily solved. The traditional answer was that old men and women should live out their lives in the company of their children, who could now repay the debt incurred by the provision of their education. But, sadly, children then as now were not always too keen to fulfil such obligations. Too often, old age was not the idyllic rocking in the chimney corner that it should have been. 'The old man, or the old woman can do nothing to please; their words are perverted, their actions misrepresented, and themselves looked upon as a burthen to their issue, and a rent charge upon those who came from their loins.'[10] Things might be all right as long as the old people kept hold of their money. But once let the children grasp the purse-strings and what happened? The old people were banished to a poorly furnished garret, sneered at, hidden from company lest they be an embarrassment to the smart friends of their children and, if they did escape to the tavern for a glass of wine and a smoke with an old friend, they were rebuked for their drunkenness.[11] It was lucky that it had never been possible for the young 'to bring in a Bill for the better trimming of mankind, i.e. to knock all ancient peple on the head'.[12] So wrote Defoe, in his sixty-seventh year, and still ready with a pat solution to the problem, a scheme for old people to avoid the insolence and ingratitude of their children by jointly investing in a private old people's home, complete with nurses, doctor and chaplain.[13]

Such a scheme, though possible, was probably unrealistic even for the old and rich in the days of Defoe. For the old and poor it could only be a fantasy. For them, bent double by a life of labour, living on bare floors in a damp house and just surviving on a dole unwillingly handed out by an uncharitable parish officer, old age

was not likely to bring much joy.[14] Many of the poor might think it
a privilege to die young and die fast. Nearly all foreigners com-
mented on the sangfroid, even gaiety, that Englishmen displayed
when they took their last journey from Newgate to the gallows at
Tyburn. They seemed to have a complete contempt for death. 'The
English are people that laugh at the delicacy of other nations who
make it such a mighty matter to be hang'd; their extraordinary
courage looks upon it as a trifle.'[15]

But were the English so extraordinary? Defoe was to point out
in *Applebee's Journal* that such a death was indeed a trifle.[16] Hanging
might be an unpleasant experience, especially since the drop was
not invented till 1760[17] and criminals were literally strangled by the
rope.[18] But, even if death took twenty minutes or longer, what
was that compared with the likely fate of the cheering, drunken
crowd who watched with delight the antics of the hanged man
dangling at the end of his rope? When Defoe saw four men making
their way in the cart to Tyburn, it was for those that ran after them
that he felt pity. 'Are they not all under an absolute indefeasible
sentence? . . . and with this difference too, that many of the rest
shall die in torture and terror, ten thousand times more grievous
than those four. Nay, perhaps few of the thousands who go to see
these four people die shall get so easy a passage out of life.'[19]

Defoe knew what he was talking about. As an old man he suffered
appalling agony from a stone in the kidney and underwent the
operation for its removal, an operation so terrible that 'the very
apparatus is enough to chill the blood, and sink a man's soul within
him'.[20] Did a man who suffered this suffer less than 'he that is
broken alive upon the wheel'?[21] Eighteenth-century man suffered
from our diseases and endured our pains without the advantages of
our medicines, our anaesthetics and our pain-killers to help him
bear them. In this respect he was however slightly better off than
medieval man. There was cheap gin and brandy to dull his senses
and cheap tobacco to steady his nerves. With a bit of luck they
might kill him before his pains became too great for even gin to
dull them. But few men had such luck.

Death, when it came, took many forms, as we are reminded if
we look at the Bills of Mortality, the weekly league table of deaths
and their causes, 'the diseases and casualties this week', which had
first been introduced to give the authorities an early warning of the
onset of plague, a warning which, when published, enabled the rich

to get out of town before it spread from the poor parishes to their own.[22] The causes of death have a certain alliterative fascination. They start, suitably enough, with the deaths of the very young and the very old, with abortive and aged, pass through ague, apoplexie, bleeding, and canker, through griping in the guts and stopping of the stomach, and end in vomiting, winde and wormes, a flurry of nastiness worthy of the purge-loving society in which they occurred.[23] Violent death was surprisingly rare in what at first seems such a violent society. Capt. John Graunt, in his *Observations upon the Bills of Mortality* of 1662, pointed out the low incidence of murder, far lower than in contemporary Paris.[24] By the 1720s the number of murders was even less.[25] The English criminal reflected the society in which he lived. He had already taken that important step from mindless violence to a concentration on crimes against property, a step which can be seen as a sure mark of progress, a harbinger of modern industrial society. And this despite the fact that stealing a silk handkerchief and strangling its owner with it carried the same penalty.[26]

Death might come in many forms, painful or peaceful, as a punishment or as a release, but few people, despite the bold show of indifference which they presented to foreigners, could think about it without fear.[27] 'Death is a calamity wherever it comes', wrote Defoe. 'How few bear it with patience, or think of it without horror.'[28] Defoe might have loved the world even more than did most of his worldly generation, but not many would have disagreed with this sentiment. Fear of death involved not only fear of the actual process of dying but fear of what lay beyond death, on the other side of time. Death was not a terminus, but a great junction where the saved and the damned who had journeyed together in life now parted for their different destinations. Deists and sceptics might deny futurity, but few people totally believed them. Even those who might have liked to believe in the finality of death were so affected by their upbringing and their passage through a generally religious society that they were bound to have doubts, even if they rarely rose to the surface of their minds. But, when they lay dying, those half-forgotten words of father, schoolmaster and preacher, which promised the judgment of God and eternal damnation for those whom God had not chosen, might be remembered with dread by the most confirmed sceptic. Then might the passage out of life be truly dreadful. Such a man might try to make up for an ill-spent life by a rapid repentance but this, even if successful, was likely to be a harrowing experience, 'a double terror to the dying person to have the work of dying and the work of repentance both upon his hands together'.[29]

What the dying man should have done, and what his sensible and religious fellows had been doing, was to prepare for death all his life. We should make 'a careful, and continual, and particular preparation for the time of our death and dissolution', preached Archbishop Tillotson, repenting every day or at least very frequently, so that 'we may keep our accounts in a good measure even, and not be in a hurry and confusion when we come to die, neither knowing where to begin our repentance, nor how to go through with so great a work in so short a time'.[30] The image of the good Christian who kept his accounts with God was a popular one with the shopkeepers and other members of the middle station who listened to such sermons. Thomas Gouge, in his *Christian Directions* of 1679, was another who recommended a daily auditing of the books of the soul to avoid the dangers of a spiritual bankruptcy. 'As he is the best tradesman that every day in the evening taketh an account of his worldly losses and gains; so he is the best Christian that every day in the evening taketh an account of his spiritual losses and gains, whether he go forward or backward in the ways of godliness.'[31] Many men in the world of Defoe followed Gouge's instructions, keeping a daily account of their spiritual and material transactions, often in the same book.

But, however stirring or homely their imagery might be, men like Gouge or Tillotson were for the most part preaching to the converted. It was those who slept through sermons or never went to church who needed to be convinced of the need for repentance. Man alone, even the most inspired of preachers, could do little to stir their apathy. It was necessary for God himself to step in, 'that mighty God that hangs this earth of ours upon nothing', and who, with a touch of his finger, can hurl it hither and thither.[32] Famine, pestilence, fire and earthquake were God's weapons to bring sinning man to a just repentance. Then might man pay attention, as in the plague of 1665, when the zeal which men showed in coming to church, 'and the earnestness and affection they shew'd in their attention to what they heard, made it manifest what a value people would all put upon the worship of God, if they thought every day they attended at the church that it would be their last'.[33]

Fear was a great agent of conversion, though it often came too
late or passed too quickly to do much lasting good. 'My soul was
all amazement and surprize', wrote the pirate, Captain Singleton,
of a storm in which he feared for his life:

> I thought my self just sinking into eternity, owning the divine
> justice of my punishment, but not at all feeling any of the moving,
> softning tokens of a sincere penitent; afflicted at the punishment,
> but not at the crime, alarmed at the vengeance, but not terrify'd
> at the guilt, having the same gust to the crime, tho' terrified to
> the last degree at the thought of the punishment which I con-
> cluded I was just now going to receive.[34]

Another storm had a greater effect on the souls of Amy and Roxana,
but not enough:

> The danger being over, the fears of death vanish'd with it; ay,
> and our fear of what was beyond death also; our sence of the
> life we had liv'd went off, and with our return to life, our wicked
> taste of life return'd, and we were both the same as before, if
> not worse. So certain is it that the repentance which is brought
> about by the meer apprehensions of death, wears off as those
> apprehensions wear off; and death-bed repentance, or storm-
> repentance, which is much the same, is seldom true.[35]

Fear of the gallows could be more effective, since there was more
time to think. Moll Flanders' repentance in the condemned cell at
Newgate was at first no better than that of Roxana, being based only
on the fear of death. But later she seemed to be more genuine. 'The
word eternity represented itself with all its incomprehensible
additions. . . . How absurd did every pleasant thing look! – I mean,
that we had counted pleasant before – when I reflected that these
sordid trifles were the things for which we forfeited eternal felicity.'[36]
This was better, though she still had a long way to go and people
did not spend all that long in the condemned hold. Perhaps it was
lucky that her death sentence was commuted to transportation.
This should give her long enough to repent properly, though her
highwayman husband did not think that much time was needed.
'A man was, in his opinion, as likely to repent sincerely in the last
fortnight of his life, under the agonies of a jail and the condemned
hole, as he would ever be in the woods and wildernesses of America.'[37]

Defoe accepted that last-minute repentance was possible. 'Many a criminal is accepted, even at the place of execution, which may be call'd driving as much as any thing.'[38] But it would be dangerous for a sinner to rely on God's willingness to accept him in the last moment of his life.

Some people needed far more than a moment of fear even to get them to think about repentance. They needed a whole programme of shocks. To convert Robinson Crusoe it was necessary to subject him to a startling progression of storms and other examples of divine providence and then cast him away alone on a desert island for twenty-eight years to think about them. Even then God had considerable trouble getting him to repent. It took a terrible dream, in which the fevered Crusoe saw a great black cloud from which a man descended, surrounded by a flame of fire and threatening to kill him with a spear, before he was persuaded of the need to consider his past sins, to pray and to say grace with his meals.[39] But Crusoe was a very stubborn man.

The need to sustain fear for a long time made plague the ideal agent of conversion. Defoe, a child in the plague year, was fascinated by this dreadful killer. Twice in his lifetime it seemed that plague would once again strike England.[40] During the war years he watched with apprehension and a certain excitement the great circuit of the plague which followed in the wake of the armies, from Bulgaria to Poland, from Poland to the Baltic and then, in 1712, to the Duchy of Bremen, only a short sea trip from a sinning and unready England.[41] Eight years later he was to report the last great western European plague which struck Marseilles in 1720, but then was held in check by the brutal efficiency of the French government.[42] Plague as a killer was an enemy of the commonwealth which needed every man it could get if the march towards progress was to continue. Defoe the economist recognized this and much of his journalistic effort is concentrated on advice to his countrymen on how to save themselves and their families if the plague should strike.[43] But for Defoe the moralist the plague had a different message.

Plague, although the greatest killer of all, gave man far more notice than other illnesses of its visitations. Man could see it coming as its inexorable progress was charted by the newswriters. This could only mean that God in his mercy was giving advance notice to a people to reform and repent. How different from an earth-quake, which might well 'make an heart-quake in every inpenitent sinner', but gave no warning of its arrival.[44] The threat of the plague spreading from France in the early 1720s gave Defoe the opportunity to develop this theme by drawing to his readers' attention the dangers that their usual irreligious attitude towards life was bringing them into. In 1722 he wrote two books on the subject; *A Journal of the Plague Year*, an imaginative reconstruction of the plague of 1665 which superbly demonstrates both the horror and the spiritual challenge of the disease, and *Due Preparations for the Plague*, a strictly practical book of instruction in the physical and spiritual preparations which the plague demanded.

Like most of his didactic works, this book takes the form of a series of dialogues, supposedly set in 1665, between a mother, her two sons and her daughter. The plague is rife on the continent and there is a general fear that it will soon cross over to England. The women take full advantage of the danger, seeing it as 'a messenger sent from God to scourge us from our crying sins'.[45] But the sons argue that their mother's concentration on preparation for death is morbid. They are also worried by the economic effects of a mass repentance. If everyone followed her advice there would be no business, as everyone from king to beggars fell on their knees together. News that the plague has abated seems to confirm their scepticism and they get on with the business of living. But then they hear that the plague really is going to come to England and begin to panic. Each man has his own particular fear and the brothers' dialogue perfectly sums up the central paradox of Defoe's thought:[46]

> 1ST. BRO. What shall we do, brother, what will become of us all, and what will become of the business?
> 2ND. BRO. Nay, what will become of our souls?

What did become of the souls of men when they left the world of Defoe? The theory was clear enough, though the details were vague. The saved went straight to an eternity of bliss in heaven and the damned went straight to an eternity of misery in hell. There was no intermediate state. William the Quaker makes the point when Captain Singleton threatens to commit suicide in a mood of despair:[47]

> 'I am past remedy already', says I.
> 'How do you know that?', says he.
> 'I am satisfied of it', said I.

'Well', says he, 'but you are not sure, so you will shoot your self to make it certain; for tho' on this side death you can't be sure you will be damned at all, yet the moment you step on the other side of time, you are sure of it: for when 'tis done, 'tis not to be said then that you will, but that you are damned'.

Not everyone was happy about this theory, clear though it was. There was, in particular, a growing body of opposition to the concept of eternal damnation.[48] It was such an excessive punishment that even the good found it difficult to believe that a merciful God could be so merciless. So excessive was it, indeed, that it did not always work as an effective deterrent. A lesser, finite, punishment might have been easier to bring home to sinners. What made it even worse was that a careful interpretation of the scriptures seemed to make it clear that the numbers of the damned were far greater than those of the elect. Was God justified in a creation which sent so many to Satan's kingdom? And if the poor were to get their reward in another world, as so many preachers told them, was there going to be room for all the god-fearing people of the middle station? Such fears could swell to a mind-destroying size in the heads of that now dwindling band who believed in the strict doctrine of predestination. For they knew they could do nothing about it. Such a doctrine worried sceptics and believers alike. Why did God go to all the trouble of creating man, knowing as he did so that the majority of his creation were already predestined to be damned? No wonder that the pious men and women of the middle station worried so much. Instinct told them they were saved, but logic and mathematics often led to terrifying doubts.

The Protestants had condemned themselves to these doubts. By abandoning purgatory they had abandoned the possibility of a second chance where those who had not achieved salvation in this life might still manage to redeem themselves. Some of Defoe's contemporaries regretted the disappearance of this intermediate state and would have welcomed the re-acceptance of purgatory by the Protestant divines. And many of those who were not prepared to swallow such a Papist heresy were ready to allow some mitigation of the horrors of hell. Some believed that hell was not eternal and that, after a period and an intensity of punishment adapted to the degree of their wickedness, the damned would eventually be saved or even reincarnated into a suitable earthly state. Others believed that there was no hell, that the souls of the wicked were annihilated at death. But few men dared to publish such thoughts. It was generally assumed that anyone who opposed the doctrine of eternal punishment must himself be a depraved and licentious man who only attacked the doctrine because he feared it. And, in any case, the very idea of hell was the best moral deterrent that existed, far better than the gallows. It would be very unwise to let the common people know that there were doubts about its existence. 'Death hath really no sting, and if it may be called an enemy, is a very harmless one, if there be no hell to follow it.'[49]

If there was a hell, where was it? This was a worrying question to a rational people who loved to look at maps. The easiest answer was to ignore it and follow those, perhaps the majority, who believed that hell was metaphorical. Defoe took this position, arguing that hell 'consists in the absence of him who is heaven'.[50] As for the hell of the poets, the artists and the more fanciful theologians, what nonsense it all was. 'I must own, that to me nothing can be more ridiculous than the notions that we entertain and fill our heads with about hell, and about the Devil's being there tormenting of souls, broiling them upon gridirons, hanging them up upon hooks ... with the several pictures of hell, represented by a great mouth with horrible teeth, gaping like a cave on the side of a mountain.'[51] None the less, many people worried about all that fire and brimstone. Where could it be? The ancients had thought that hell was a dark place under the earth, but exploration and a better understanding of geology had made such a location unlikely. In any case would the centre of the earth have been large enough 'to contain the lapsed angels and the infinite numbers of the damned'?[52] Most writers thought not, though the founder of political arithmetic proved to his own satisfaction that half the island of Ireland would provide enough room for all the bodies that must rise at the last day, 'not only footing to stand upon, but graves to lye down in, for that whole number: and that two mountains in that country were as weighty as all the bodies that had ever been from the beginning of the world to the year 1680, when this dispute happened'.[53]

The most ingenious solution to the location of hell came from the pen of a Kentish clergyman, Tobias Swinden, who managed to combine scriptural learning with an understanding of the cosmic geography of the Copernican universe.[54] He argued that, according to the scriptures, hell must be fiery, very large and in some sense beneath the earth. Where else could it be but the body of the sun? According to the Copernican system, the sun and not the earth was placed in the centre of the universe. It followed, therefore, that the two extremes were the sun below, a fiery hell 'capable of receiving vast, infinite numbers both of devils and also of the bodies of men', and the empyreum above, 'the region of angels and happy souls'.[55]

Few people disputed Swinden's location of heaven. Robinson Crusoe, his worldly travels at last finished, was to make an imaginative journey beyond the vestiges of the earth to the verge of the infinite. Here he found himself in the midst of that angelic world from whence were dispatched those good and bad spirits who had so important a role to play in the world of men. 'I found abundance of passengers going to and fro here, and particularly innumerable armies of good and evil spirits, who all seem'd busily employed, and continually upon the wing, as if some expresses pass'd between the earth, which in this part of my travels I place below me, and some country infinitely beyond all that I could reach the sight of.'[56] But he was not so foolish as to try to describe that far country to which the angels flew. It was enough for him to entertain the general notion that 'the favour of God is heaven and the loss of it the most dreadful of all hell'.[57]

Here, on the other side of time, we may leave the individual from the world of Defoe. He has made his linear progression from the womb to infinity. But when he died that world went on, fed by a never-ending stream of such individuals. Each one was unique. 'As there are not two faces, nor two voices alike, so not two men go through the world in the same track, or out of it by the same door.'[58] But when you looked at them together, now or in the broad sweep of history, they formed a pattern, a circular pattern infinitely repeated.

> One generation passeth away and another comes; we thrust our parents out, and our children serve us in the same manner; the world is a stage of life, where we come up in our turn, act our part, and move off to let the same follies be acted over again by our posterity.[59]

Daniel Defoe had seen it as his self-imposed role to demonstrate to the people of his world just how foolish their follies were. As a young man he had been optimistic that such preaching might be rewarded with at least a little success. But, as he too approached the day when he must pass away, he realized the hopelessness of his task. The follies of the world were too great for one man to cure. He could only hope that the follies of the future would not be even worse than those of his own beloved but extremely foolish generation.

NOTES

I. WORKS BY DEFOE. First edition in parentheses. Edition used, if different, in second parentheses.

AHJ   *An Appeal to Honour and Justice, tho' it be of his worst enemies* (1715)

AJ   *Applebee's Journal*

Alexander Ramkins   *The Memoirs of Maj^r Alexander Ramkins* (1719)

AM   *Atlas Maritimus and Commercialis; or, a General View of the World, so far as relates to Trade and Navigation* (1728)

AT   *Augusta Triumphans: or, the Way to make London the most flourishing City in the Universe* (1728)

BCD   *A Brief Case of the Distillers and of the Distilling Trade in England* (1726)

BD   *A Brief Deduction of the Original, Progress, and Immense Greatness of the British Woollen Manufacture* (1727)

Brief State (1730)   *A Brief State of the Inland or Home Trade of England* (1730)

CEG   *The Compleat English Gentleman* (ed. Karl D. Bülbring, 1890)

CET   *The Complete English Tradesman* 2 vols. (1726–7)

CJ   *The History and Remarkable Life of the Truly Honourable Col. Jacque* (1722) (OUP, 1970)

CL   *Conjugal Lewdness; or, Matrimonial Whoredom – a Treatise concerning the Use and Abuse of the Marriage Bed* (1727) (facsimile edition, Gainsville, Flo. 1967)

Considerations (1713)   *Considerations upon the Eighth and Ninth Articles of the Treaty of Commerce and Navigation* (1713)

Consolidator   *The Consolidator: or, Memoirs of Sundry Transactions from the World in the Moon* (1705)

Crusoe   *The Life and Strange Surprising Adventures of Robinson Crusoe of York, Mariner* (1719) (Everyman, 1972)

CS   *The Life, Adventures and Piracies of the Famous Captain Singleton* (1720) (Everyman, 1969)

Double Welcome   *The Double Welcome. A Poem to the Duke of Marlbro'* (1705)

DPP   *Due Preparations for the Plague, as well for Soul as Body* (1722)

EBNB   Every-Body's Business is No-Body's Business; or, Private Abuses, Publick Grievances (1725)

Englishman's Choice   The Englishman's Choice and True Interest in a Vigorous Prosecution of the War against France (1694)

E upon P An Essay upon Projects (1697) (Scolar reprint, 1969)

FARC   The Farther Adventures of Robinson Crusoe (1719) (Everyman, 1972)

FI   The Family Instructor (1715)

FI   The Family Instructor (1718)

GANC   Giving Alms no Charity, and Employing the Poor a Grievance to the Nation (1704)

GHDI   A General History of Discoveries and Improvements in useful Arts (1725-7)

GHP   A General History of the . . . Pyrates (1724)

GLS   The Great Law of Subordination consider'd; or, the Insolence and Unsufferable Behaviour of Servants in England duly enquir'd into (1724)

HA   An Essay on the History and Reality of Apparitions (1727)

Healey, *Letters*   G. H. Healey, *The Letters of Daniel Defoe* (Oxford, 1955)

HP   An Humble Proposal to the People of England, for the Encrease of their Trade, and Encouragement of their Manufactures (1729)

JPE   Journal of Political Economy

JPY   A Journal of the Plague Year (1722) (OUP, 1972)

KP   The King of Pirates: being an Account of the Famous Enterprises of Captain Avery (1720)

Lee   William Lee, *Daniel Defoe: his life, and recently discovered writings* 3 vols (1869)

MF   The Fortunes and Misfortunes of the Famous Moll Flanders (1722) (Everyman, 1972)

MJ   Mist's Journal

MOC   Memoirs of a Cavalier (1720) (OUP, 1972)

MM   Moderation Maintain'd, in Defence of a Compassionate Enquiry into the Causes of the Civil War (1704)

NFI   The New Family Instructor (1727)

NVRW   A New Voyage round the World by a Course never sailed before (1725)

PA   An Impartial History of the Life and Actions of Peter Alexowitz, the present Czar of Muscovy (1723)

PEC   A Plan of the English Commerce (1728)

PHD   The Political History of the Devil (1726)

PM   The Protestant Monastery: or, a complaint against the brutality of the present age, particularly the pertness and insolence of youth to aged persons (1727)

PMP   The Poor Man's Plea, in relation to all the Proclamations, Declarations . . . for a Reformation of Manners (1698)

PT   Parochial Tyranny: or, the House-keeper's Complaint against the insupportable exactions, and partial assessments of select vestries (1727)

QJE   Quarterly Journal of Economics

RC   *Religious Courtship: being Historical Discourses, on the Necessity of Marrying Religious Husbands and Wives only* (1722)

Reasons why (1711)   *Reasons why this Nation ought to put a speedy end to this expensive war* (1711)

Review   A Weekly Review of the Affairs of France and various similar titles, 9 vols (1704–13) (facsimile edition, 1938)

Roxana   Roxana, the Fortunate Mistress (1724) (OUP, 1969)

Short View   A Short View of the Present State of the Protestant Religion in Britain (Edinburgh, 1707)

SM   *A System of Magick* (1727)

Some Considerations (1728)   *Some Considerations on the reasonableness and necessity of encreasing and encouraging the seamen* (1728)

Some Reflections (1697)   *Some Reflections on a Pamphlet lately Publish'd Entituled, an Argument showing that a Standing Army is inconsistent with a Free Government* (1697)

SRRC   *Serious Reflections during the Life and Surprising Adventures of Robinson Crusoe* (1720)

SWWD   *The Shortest-Way with the Dissenters or Proposals for the Establishment of the Church* (1702)

TBE   *The True-Born Englishman. A Satyr* (1701)

Tour   A Tour through the Whole Island of Great Britain (1724–6) (Everyman, 1962)

True Collection (1703)   *A True Collection of the Writings of the Author of the True Born English-man* (1703)

VAW   *A Vision of the Angelick World* (1720), bound with *SRRC*

2. OTHER REFERENCES

AgHR   *Agricultural History Review*
EcHR   *Economic History Review*
HLQ   *Huntingdon Library Quarterly*
HMC   Historical Manuscripts Commission
JEGP   *Journal of English and Germanic Philology*
JEH   *Journal of Economic History*
JHI   *Journal of the History of Ideas*
JMH   *Journal of Modern History*
MP   *Modern Philology*
NCMH   *New Cambridge Modern History*
N & Q   *Notes and Queries*
PMLA   *Publications of the Modern Language Association of America*
P & P   *Past and Present*
PQ   *Philological Quarterly*
RES   *Review of English Studies*
SP   *Studies in Philology*
TRHS   *Transactions of the Royal Historical Society*

INTRODUCTION

1. For examples of the problems involved in the attribution of works to Defoe see William Lee, *Daniel Defoe: his life, and recently discovered writings* (1869), vol. 1; J. R. Moore, 'The Canon of Defoe's Writings', *The Library*, 5th ser. xi (1956); Rodney M. Baine, *Daniel Defoe and the Supernatural* (Athens Ga. 1968), esp. pt. 2, 'the spurious: the illusory Defoe'.

2. Indiana University Press (1960): BL copy corrected by the editor up to Nov. 1966.

3. 1704–13.

4. 1727.

5. 1728.

6. See Ian Watt, *The Rise of the Novel* (1957), pp. 40–59 for a discussion of the business side of writing in the early eighteenth century.

7. This was the assertion of the anonymous editor of the 1738 edition of the *Complete English Tradesman*. Quoted by Watt, *op. cit.*, p. 57.

8. *AJ*, 5.6.1725 (Lee iii, 390–3). A key to the abbreviations used in the notes will be found on p. 285–87.

9. *MJ*, 26.4.1718 (Lee ii, 36–7).

10. Bonamy Dobrée, *English Literature in the Early Eighteenth Century, 1700–1740* (Oxford 1959), p. 421.

CHAPTER I

1. In the engraving made from Eyre Crowe's painting. See the reproduction in J. R. Moore, *Daniel Defoe: Citizen of the Modern World* (1958), facing p. 97.

2. 1706.

3. *AHJ* (1715).

4. James Sutherland, 'Some early troubles of Daniel Defoe', *RES* ix (1933); *idem, Defoe* (1937), pp. 35–42.

5. *N & Q*, clxxv (1938), p. 44.

6. *Daniel Defoe: a study in conflict* (1954), p. 34.

7. p. 78; cf. pp. 41, 46, 52, 55, 84 etc.

8. *AHJ*, p. 28.

9. Fitzgerald, pp. 58–61.

10. Paul Dottin, *The Life and Strange and Surprising Adventures of Daniel Defoe* trans. Louise Regan (1928), p. 14, cf. *CJ*, pp. 9–10.

11. *Op. cit.*, p. 32.

12. For a discussion of Defoe's excellent and very modern education at Newington Green Academy see pp. 214–15.

13. Moore, *Defoe*, pp. 44–45. Defoe married Mary Tuffley on 1 January 1683–4.

14. p. 49.

15. Dottin, p. 40.

16. Sutherland, *Defoe*, p. 30.
17. Fitzgerald, p. 54.
18. For this see Sutherland, *Defoe*, p. 45.
19. For some indication of the expansion of English commerce between 1660 and 1700 see Ralph Davis, 'English Foreign Trade, 1660–1700', *EcHR* 2nd. Ser., vi, (1954). For the possibility that most of this expansion occurred after 1674 see W. R. Scott, *The Constitution and Finance of English, Scottish and Irish Joint-Stock Companies* (1912), i, 292. Defoe himself often emphasized the 1680s as a period of great expansion.
20. See Sutherland, *Defoe*, pp. 35–42, for more details on the evidence for Defoe's early business career.
21. *Idem*, p. 46.
22. Michael Shinagel, *Daniel Defoe and Middle-Class Gentility* (Harvard 1968).
23. See chapter 8.
24. *Review*, viii, Preface.
25. *Review*, vii, preface. 'For my part I have always thought the only true fundamental maxim of politicks that will ever make this nation happy is this – that the Government ought to be of no *party at all*.'
26. *Review*, vii, 297–98. For an analysis of contemporary politics see Geoffrey Holmes, *English Politics in the Age of Anne* (1967).
27. See pp. 19–22.
28. *AHJ*.
29. *Review*, ii, 498.
30. *Review*, viii, 614.
31. *AHJ*, p. 28.
32. See Defoe's comment on Monmouth, 'who really had not a great deal of personall merit', in Healey, *Letters*, p. 41.
33. John Oldmixon, *The History of England, during the Reign of King William and Queen Mary* ... (1735), p. 37. Defoe was plain Foe till 1695. Most writers accept the addition of the French particle as an indication of Defoe's urge to become a gentleman.
34. Defoe's finances remain a mystery. He later claimed that his tile-works employed a hundred poor families and made a profit of £600 p.a. (*Review*, ii, 33–34). One can also assume that much of his liabilities of £17,000 in 1692 were matched by assets abroad or on the high seas. But there still seems to have been a large gap in his income for him to have maintained the style he did in the late 1690s, whilst still satisfying his creditors. One can only assume he was in receipt of very considerable royal bounty.
35. e.g. *The Englishman's Choice and True Interest* ... (1694); *Some Reflections on a Pamphlet lately Publish'd* (1697); *The Two Great Questions Considered* (1700).

36. A. R. Humphreys, *The Augustan World* (1954), pp. 20–21.
37. 1698.
38. 1701.
39. 1702.
40. *Legion's Memorial* (1701), p. 2. See also *The Original Power of the Collective Body of the People of England* (1701). For a discussion of Defoe's political ideas see A. E. Levett, 'Daniel Defoe' in F. J. C. Hearnshaw (ed.), *The Social and Political Ideas of some English Thinkers of the Augustan Age* (1928).
41. 1702.
42. ix, 210.
43. It would have been very difficult to prove the libel had he pleaded not guilty. Sutherland, *Defoe*, pp. 92–94.
44. For Harley see the excellent recent biography by Angus McInnes, *Robert Harley Puritan Politician* (1970).
45. By means of William Paterson. See Healey, *Letters*, pp. 4–7.
46. In three parts 1714–15.
47. *AHJ*, p. 13.
48. For a good general discussion of the *Review* see A. W. Secord's introduction to the facsimile edition of 1938.
49. See Healey, *Letters*.
50. Defoe's usual pseudonym was Alexander Goldsmith and then, from 1710, Claude Guilot. Harley sometimes endorsed Defoe's letters with his pseudonym in Greek characters, though who that was supposed to fool is not quite clear.
51. Healey, *Letters*, pp. 124–5.
52. Especially in Scotland. See Moore, *Defoe*, p. 187 for references. cf. *Review*, viii, 495–6 for more information on Defoe's business interests.
53. Arthur W. Secord, 'Defoe in Stoke Newington', *PMLA*, lxiv (1951). In 1715 he acquired an even more expensive house.
54. e.g. Abel Boyer, *Political State* ... of June 1717 refers to the money that Defoe got from the Earl of Oxford to improve his house in Stoke Newington, 'his forge of politicks and scandal'. Quoted in Secord, *op. cit.*, p. 211.
55. Healey. *Letters*, pp. 29–50.
56. Healey, *Letters*, pp. 115–118. Addresses from Plymouth to Newcastle, Canterbury to Chester and even as far afield as Dublin.
57. Defoe often sent copy to the printers in advance when he was on his travels. This could of course lead to embarrassment, as on the famous occasion when he predicted that there would be no more battles in the campaign of 1706 in an issue which came out on the very day that the news of Ramillies reached London. *Review*, iii, 237–9. For the way in which the *Review* was written see Secord's introduction to the facsimile edition (1938).

58. Healey, *Letters*, p. 126.

59. H. M. C. Portland, iv, 333–6 quoted in Healey, *Letters*, p. 130, n. 2 and p. 131, n. 2.

60. Healey, *Letters*, p. 135; cf. p. 185.

61. *Idem*, p. 147.

62. See Christopher Smout, *Scottish Trade on the Eve of Union* (1963); Smout, 'The Anglo-Scottish Union of 1707. I. The Economic Background' and R. H. Campbell, 'The Anglo-Scottish Union of 1707. II. The Economic Consequences', *EcHR* 2nd. Ser. xvi (1964).

63. Healey, *Letters*, p. 13.

64. These appear in a number of places, but see in particular *Review* vols. iii and iv and his series of *Essays at Removing National Prejudices against a Union with Scotland* (1706–07).

65. E.g. the death of the emperor in 1711 could be seen as sufficient reason to change the *Review*'s policy towards the war in Spain. See p. 101. And Defoe rightly claimed that he had been consistent in his attitude towards the liberalization of trade with France. But the Tories forced him to be far more liberal than he would have liked to have been. See pp. 138–39.

66. E.g. *A Short Narrative of the Life and Actions of His Grace John, Duke of Marlborough by an Old Officer in the Army* (1711); *The Secret History of the October Club ... by a member* (1711); *Considerations upon the Eighth and Ninth Articles of the Treaty of Commerce and Navigation* (1713). Of course politics were so devious in the years 1710–14 that Defoe may well have written these pamphlets, too, on the orders of Harley.

67. *AHJ*, p. 24.

68. Healey, *Letters*, p. 379.

69. *Review*, viii, 693–96.

70. Healey, *Letters*, pp. 375–6.

71. The 'Restraining Orders' were issued secretly to the Duke of Ormonde, the general commanding in Flanders after Marlborough's dismissal.

72. *Review*, viii, 747–8. For Defoe's view on military dilatoriness see pp. 97–98.

73. *An Answer to a Question that no body thinks of, viz. But What if the Queen should die?*

74. *And what if the Pretender should come?* and *Reasons against the Succession of the House of Hanover.*

75. *AHJ*, pp. 26–9.

76. On this, see pp. 93–95.

77. *Journal to Stella*, ii, 568–9.

78. Healey, *Letters*, pp. 395, 446.

79. 6 Anne c. 7.

80. Anglesey was the leader of the 'Hanoverian' Tories in the Lords.

81. Healey, *Letters*, p. 446.
82. Healey, *Letters*, pp. 450–51. The object of the letter was to explain his role to the new Secretary of State for the Northern Department, Lord Stanhope. The letter was written to his Under-Secretary, Charles de la Faye.
83. Healey, *Letters*, p. 453.
84. For details see Sutherland, *Defoe*, pp. 269–74.
85. 'Source-hunters' have been thwarted to a certain extent by the fact that Defoe's library was sold jointly with that of Phillips Farewell and the two libraries were not listed separately. See *The Libraries of Daniel Defoe and Phillips Farewell: Oliver Payne's Sales Catalogue* (1731), ed. H. Heiderich (Berlin 1970).
86. Apart from the letters to de la Faye mentioned above, there is only one surviving letter between 1714 and 1728, when there survives a series of letters written by Defoe to his future son-in-law, Henry Baker.
87. The title of a chapter from Dottin, *op. cit.*
88. Sutherland, *Defoe*, p. 221. This must have meant that it reached quite a high proportion of the regular 'reading public'. See James Sutherland, 'The circulation of newspapers and literary periodicals, 1700–1730', *Library*, 4th ser. xv (1934) and Ian Watt, *The Rise of the Novel* (1957), pp. 36–37.
89. Sutherland, *Defoe*, p. 221.
90. Cf. the comments on Defoe's economic ideas as seen in the journal, *Mercator*, on p. 139.
91. See pp. 142–43.
92. Cf. Jacob Viner, 'Satire and economics in the Augustan age of satire', in Henry Knight Miller (ed.), *The Augustan Milieu* (Oxford 1970), pp. 90–91.

CHAPTER 2
1. 'Robinson Crusoe', *The Second Common Reader* (New York 1932).
2. *Review*, i, p. 291.
3. Bonamy Dobrée, *English Literature in the early eighteenth century, 1700–1740*, (Oxford 1959), p. 76.
4. *Review*, viii, p. 246.
5. The first volume of the *Family Instructor* (1715) went through ten editions in Defoe's lifetime and was still being reprinted in Victorian times.
6. *The Storm* (1704), preface, A 2.
7. Published in 1724.
8. Rudolf G. Stamm, 'Daniel Defoe: an Artist in the Puritan Tradition', *PQ*, xv (1936), pp. 236–7.
9. Michael Shinagel, *Daniel Defoe and Middle-Class Gentility* (Harvard

1968), p. 194, where he suggests 'that Defoe no longer was able to control his imagination or his material and being a good Puritan he decided not to tempt the devil any longer. He ceased writing imaginative biographies in which he identified with his creations not wisely but too well.'

10. *CL*, pp. 1–19.

11. 'By far the greatest single category of books published in the eighteenth century, as in previous centuries, was that composed of religious works.' Ian Watt, *The Rise of the Novel* (1957), pp. 49–50.

12. Such seems to be the view of Stamm, *op. cit.*; cf. Hans H. Andersen, 'The Paradox of Trade and Morality in Defoe', *MP*, xxxix (1941).

13. For a very good example of an intelligent man making this decision see Edmund Calamy, *An Historical Account of my own Life* (1829), i, p. 224 ff.

14. For more on Defoe's education see pp. 214–15.

15. H. T. Dickinson, *Bolingbroke* (1970), pp. 3–4, 159–60.

16. *Enquiry into the Occasional Conformity Bill* (1702), p. 5.

17. *A Short View.* pp. 24–25.

18. E.g. *FI* (1718), p. 55.

19. *FARC*, p. 300.

20. *Idem*, p. 303.

21. Charles Gildon, *The Life and strange surprizing adventures of Mr. D. . . . De F. . . . of London, Hosier* (1719), pp. viii–ix, pp. 41–45.

22. See above, p. 11.

23. *GLS*, p. 20. I am not trying to say that Defoe was pro-Papist. He attacks Catholics, just as did most of his contemporaries. But this is often for political reasons, especially during 1712–14 at the height of his attack on Jacobites. The point is that, despite these normal Protestant reactions, he is unusual in not sharing the almost pathological hatred of Papists shown by most religious writers of his day.

24. For a fascinating general discussion of the effects of the new thinking see Paul Hazard, *The European Mind, 1680–1715* (Eng. trans. 1953).

25. Dedication to Reason in *Jure Divino* (1706).

26. For a general discussion of Defoe's view of natural law see Maximilian E. Novak, *Defoe and the Nature of Man* (Oxford 1963).

27. Following Richard Cumberland, *De legibus naturae disquisitio philosophica* (1672). In this respect, though not in others, Defoe was of course following Thomas Hobbes, *Leviathan* (1651).

28. *Jure Divino*, bk. iv, 8.

29. *Jure Divino*, bk. iii, 10. Defoe was almost alone in the lengths to which he proclaimed self-preservation as an excuse for stepping outside the bounds of morality. See Novak, *op. cit.*, p. 67 and see

Richard Baxter, *A Christian Directory* (1673), ii, 109–110 for a contemporary casuist's views on this knotty problem.

30. *Review*, viii, 302.
31. (1722), p. 67.
32. E.g. *FI* (1715), pp. 24–25.
33. *JPY*, pp. 11–12.
34. *Review*, iv, 91.
35. *Jure Divino.*
36. William Shelton, *Divine Providence* (1680), p. 5 quoted in J. Paul Hunter, *The Reluctant Pilgrim* (Baltimore 1966), p. 52. For a general discussion of the doctrine of providence see Hunter, pp. 51–75 and Keith Thomas, *Religion and the Decline of Magic* (Penguin 1973), pp. 90–132.
37. Archbishop Tillotson, *Works*, Sermon XXXVI, p. 335; quoted by Hunter, *op. cit.*, pp. 57–58.
38. See the chapter, 'Miracles denied' in Hazard, *op. cit.*, pp. 185–212.
39. Thomas, *op. cit.*, pp. 93, 106.
40. For the identity of this rearguard see Hunter and Thomas, *op. cit.*; and Rodney M. Baine, *Daniel Defoe and the Supernatural* (Charlotte N.C. 1968).
41. A common metaphor; e.g. *History of the Union of Great Britain* (1709), pp. 55; cf. the 'secret hand', 'immediate finger' of providence.
42. For a summary of Defoe's general ideas on providence see *SRRC*, ch. 5. He was careful to point out the error of those who used the concept to deny individual responsibility, 'who determining the universal currency of events to providence, and that not the minutest thing occurs in the course of life, but by the particular destination of Heaven, by consequence entitle providence to the efficiency of their own follies.' (p. 209).
43. *Crusoe*, pp. 8–9, 69–70. Providence plays an important role in all Defoe's novels, but especially in *Robinson Crusoe*, who described his career as 'a life of providence's chequer-work' (p. 220); cf. Hunter, *op. cit.*
44. *FI* (1718), pp. 191–2.
45. See the saddler's comment on this problem in *JPY*, p. 68.
46. Gildon, *op. cit.*, pp. 8–9.
47. Hunter, *op. cit.*, pp. 59–60.
48. *FARC*, p. 355. St. Luke, xiii, 1–5.
49. *Review*, iii, 357.
50. *Review*, iii, 32.
51. *The Storm* (1704), p. 1.
52. *HA*, p. 55.
53. For contemporary views for and against angels see Baine, *op. cit.* pp. 12–36. Defoe was somewhat unorthodox in his angelology.

54. *Review*, viii, 95. Cf. *Review*, i, Suppl. No. 3, p. 6; *MJ* 13.2.1719/20 (Lee, ii, 195–8); *Crusoe*, p. 182; *FARC*, p. 258; *HA, passim* and many other instances.

55. *Review*, viii, 95.

56. *HA*, p. 34.

57. *HA*, pp. 32–43.

58. *PHD*, pp. 22–25.

59. *PHD*, 52, 97–98.

60. *PHD*, p. 52.

61. *PHD*, pp. 285–6.

62. *PHD*, pp. 354–5.

63. *PHD*, pp. 339–45.

64. Thomas, *op. cit.*, pp. 681–98.

65. *Review*, viii, 363.

66. *PHD*, p. 345; cf. Addison's essay on witches, *Spectator*, No. 117.

67. Many Protestants had never accepted the concept of angelic ministration, not wanting even a spiritual mediator between themselves and God.

68. Although Defoe was fairly orthodox in his history of the Devil he seems to go perilously close to the attractive, and contemporarily popular, heresy of Manichaeism in his description of the way the Devil operated on mankind. It is not too difficult to postulate the dual influence of a good God and an evil God working on the easily influenced Man from *PHD* and *HA*. Defoe would no doubt be horrified if he could see this note. On contemporary Manichaeism see D. P. Walker, *The Decline of Hell* (1964), pp. 53–58.

69. *The Little Review*, 14, p. 55. For opinion on fairies see K. M. Briggs, *The Anatomy of Puck* (1959), ch. 3.

70. *HA*, pp. 95–122. cf. Baine, *op. cit.*, pp. 85–86.

71. *Review*, i, Suppl. No. 3, p. 6.

72. *A True Relation of the Apparition of one Mrs Veal . . . to one Mrs Bargrave* (1706). For a detailed discussion of this see R. M. Baine, 'Defoe, Mrs Veal, and Mrs Bargrave', in his *Daniel Defoe and the Supernatural* (1968).

73. p. 3.

74. *HA*, p. 131.

75. *HA*, pp. 132–52.

76. William Lilly, *History of his Life* (1715), p. 88.

77. Defoe's most interesting work of casuistry is *The Complete English Tradesman*. Here he discusses a number of very difficult cases of conscience which a shopkeeper might be expected to have to face. See pp. 236–38. Probably the most widely read book on this subject in Defoe's time was Richard Baxter's *Christian Directory* (1673).

Reading this, it is easy to understand the difficulties faced by traditional morality when confronted with what was in many ways a very 'modern' business world. Baxter is sometimes represented as the apostle of a 'liberal' attitude towards such problems. This seems to be reading into Baxter more than is actually there. Baxter seems rather to represent the last-ditch defence of the traditional 'medieval' view of business ethics. Defoe, when wearing his moralistic hat, often follows Baxter but in his novels, and elsewhere, he transgresses.

CHAPTER 3

1. Frances Yates, *Giordano Bruno and the Hermetic Tradition* (1964), p. 198; see also *idem*, *The Art of Memory*.
2. *AJ*, 30.10.1725 (Lee, iii, 435).
3. 1726–7.
4. Started in 1723–4 and published in 1728.
5. For the bibliography of this work see J. R. Moore, 'The Canon of Defoe's Writings', *The Library*, 5th ser. XI (1956).
6. p. iii.
7. *CJ*, pp. 10–11.
8. See the introduction to the 1972 edition of *Memoirs of a Cavalier* for the historical research that Defoe had done in preparing this book.
9. For a discussion of such books see Geoffroy Atkinson, *The Extraordinary Voyage in French Literature before 1700* (New York 1920) and *The Extraordinary Voyage in French Literature from 1700 to 1720* (Paris 1922).
10. Atkinson (1922), pp. 15–16; [Gabriel Foigny], *A New Discovery of Terra Incognita Australis . . . by James Sadeur* (1693), pp. 63–72.
11. [François Misson], *A New Voyage to the East Indies by Francis Leguat* (1708), written in 1707.
12. *CEG*, p. 225.
13. Woodes Rogers, *A Cruising Voyage round the World* (ed. G. E. Manwaring, 1928); William Dampier, *Voyages* (ed. John Masefield, 1906).
14. *NVRW*, pp. 1–3.
15. *CJ*, pp. 292 ff; J. H. Parry, *The Spanish Seaborne Empire* (1966), pp. 292–8; Curtis Nettels, 'England and the Spanish-American Trade, 1680–1715'. *JMH*, iii (1931).
16. *GHDI*, p. 1.
17. *The Wisdom of God manifested in the Works of the Creation* (1691), p. 113.
18. *Review*, ix, 107.
19. *Review*, ix, 110.
20. No. 69.

21. *Review*, ix, 109–110.
22. *Review*, ix, 110. To be hunted by the Dutch and not the English, a matter of grave regret to Defoe.
23. *AM*, pp. 133–34.
24. For a summary of the great contemporary debate between the 'ancients' who believed that the world and man were undergoing a process of continuous decay from the golden age of the past and the 'moderns' who believed they were improving, see R. F. Jones, 'The Background of the *Battle of the Books*' reprinted in R. F. Jones *et al.*, *The Seventeenth Century* (1951). Defoe occasionally uses the terminology of the 'ancients'. e.g. *Good Advice to the Ladies* (1702), p. 15 where he uses the expression 'this iron age' and *Tour*, i, 54 where he writes of the inevitable rise and decay of 'towns, country, families, and persons'. But usually he was a modern. See *CEG*, p. 231 for his summary of the ways in which the 'moderns' have gained on the ancients.
25. *GHDI*, pp. 49–50.
26. *GHDI*, p. 50.
27. *GHDI*, p. iv.
28. *GHDI*, pp. 3–4. Cf. *AM*, p. 170 'the famous Arcadian plains, the Tempe, the Golden Groves, the flowry medes of the antients, lie now desolate'.
29. *PHD*, pp. 230–1.
30. *AM*, p. 170.
31. *GHDI*, p. 26.
32. *GHDI*, pp. 79–152; *PEC*, pp. 312–27. For an analysis of the Barbary corsairs and the reasons why the European nations never did what Defoe suggested see my *Corsairs of Malta and Barbary* (1970), esp. pp. 15–16, 265–7.
33. *GHDI*, pp. 61–65.
34. *GHDI*, pp. 76–78. He also supported the theory of immigration to the western parts of America from the Pacific islands, *AM*, p. 276, but opposed the third view that the American Indians had come by land from north-east Asia.
35. *The Sot-weed Factor* (1708), p. 11.
36. pp. 131–2.
37. *GHDI*, p. 239.
38. 1728.
39. J. H. Parry, *The Age of Reconnaissance* (1963), p. 324.
40. Parry, pp. 198, 201, 324; Dampier, 'Voyage to New Holland', *op. cit.*, vol. ii, pp. 423 ff. Dampier explains why he did not go south after reaching Western Australia in order to discover new land: 'I confess I was not for spending my time more than was necessary in the higher latitudes; as knowing that the land there could not be so

well worth the discovering, as the parts that lay nearer the line ...' (ii, 459). The whole expedition seems to have been singularly useless and when Dampier returned in 1702 he was found guilty by court martial of cruelty to his lieutenant.

41. *GHDI*, p. 269.
42. *CS*, pp. 57–168.
43. 'On Poetry' (1733) quoted in Wylie Sypher, *Guinea's Captive Kings* (New York 1969), p. 30. See pp. 27–37 for an interesting section on the 'Pseudo-Africa of Ignorance and Fancy'.
44. E. W. Bovill, *The Golden Trade of the Moors* (2nd. ed. 1968), p. 207.
45. *Idem*, p. 210.
46. *AM*, pp. 236–8.
47. *AM*, p. 276.
48. Bovill, *op. cit.*, pp. 23–4, 82.
49. 1725.
50. W. L. Schurz, *The Manila Galleon* (New York 1939).
51. Dampier, *op. cit.*, i, 356–7 for the suggestion that it might be profitable to sail south from Mindanao till you meet with a wind that will carry you over to Terra del Fuego. 'Returning you may probably touch somewhere on New Holland, and so make some profitable discovery in those places without going out of your way. And to speak my thoughts freely, I believe 'tis owing to the neglect of this easie way that all that vast tract of Terra Australis which bounds the South Sea is yet undiscovered.'
52. *NVRW*, i, 118.
53. *NVRW*, i, 119.
54. *A Treatise of the Scurvy* (1753).
55. *NVRW*, i, 192–208.
56. *Review*, viii, 165–92, 197–204, 233–35; *PEC*, p. 366–8; *AM*, p. 318, etc.
57. pp. 366–8.
58. For a description of the ferocity of the Araucanian Indians see 'Sir John Narborough's voyage to the Streights of Magellan' in John Harris, *Navigantium atque itinerantium Bibliotheca* (1705), ii, 801 ff (812 for Araucanian Indians). Narborough's account was one of Defoe's main sources for South America, though Narborough in fact gives little encouragement to the sort of scheme Defoe had in mind.
59. For more or less contemporary descriptions see Acarete du Biscay, *An Account of a voyage up the River de la Plata, and thence over land to Peru* (Eng. trans. 1698) and Woodes Rogers, *A Cruising Voyage round the World* ed. G. E. Manwaring (1928), pp. 54 ff.
60. Rogers, pp. 65–66.

61. William Pilling, *The Emancipation of South America* (1893), pp. 132 ff.
62. *NVRW*, ii, 143; actually Narborough was not very enthusiastic about Port Desire.
63. Woodes Rogers, *op. cit.*, pp. 248 ff.
64. *NVRW*, ii, 138–41. This seems to be a misquotation from Narborough, who compares the hinterland of Port St Julian with Cornwall, not Salisbury Plain – quite a difference.
65. Parry, *op. cit.*, p. 160.
66. A point well-made by Charles Gildon in his critique of *Robinson Crusoe*. Gildon, *op. cit.*, pp. viii–ix where Crusoe complains to Defoe for making him 'such a whimsical dog, to ramble over three parts of the world after I was sixty-five'.
67. *FARC*, p. 356.
68. Defoe wisely forgets to mention this in his works. The description of Selkirk's ordeal is in Woodes Rogers, *op. cit.*, pp. 91–96. There are quite a few similarities between his adaptation to his situation and that of Robinson Crusoe. Juan Fernandez is also described in Dampier, *op. cit.*, i, 112–119, together with an account of yet another castaway – a Moskito Indian. There is, however, no real evidence that Selkirk's adventures inspired *Robinson Crusoe*. Arthur W. Secord, 'Defoe in Stoke Newington', *PMLA*, lxvi (1951) suggests that the inspiration might have been the experience of Robert Drury, the son of one of Defoe's neighbours in Stoke Newington, who survived shipwreck in Madagascar and returned in 1717 after fourteen years among the natives. His experiences appear in *Robert Drury's Journal* (1729), which is also said to have been written by Defoe.
69. *KP*, p. 30. Both the penguins and the notice board seem to derive from Narborough, *op. cit.*
70. For provisions and health see Alan Villiers, *Captain Cook, the Seamen's Seaman* (1969), esp. pp. 29–33, 51, 123–6.
71. *Review*, i, 409.
72. *The Portuguese Seaborne Empire, 1415–1825* (1969), pp. 211–12.
73. Villiers, p. 107. It was not adopted by the conservative Admiralty till much later. On Harrison see Humphrey Quill, *John Harrison: the man who found longitude* (1966).
74. For the difficulty of finding Juan Fernandez see Woodes Rogers, p. 90.
75. Parry, *op. cit.*, p. 198.
76. *The Voyages, Dangerous Adventures and imminent escapes of Captain Richard Falconer* (1720). Some bibliographers attribute this book to Defoe.
77. J. S. Bromley, 'The French Privateering War, 1702–13', *Historical Essays 1600–1750, presented to David Ogg*, ed. H. E. Bell and R. L. Ollard (1964).
78. See Earle, *Corsairs*, for a full account of this activity.

79. *GHDI*, p. 148.
80. W. H. Lewis, *Levantine Adventurer, the travels and missions of the Chevalier d'Arvieux, 1652–1697* (1962), p. 114. See also d'Arvieux, *Mémoires* (Paris 1735).
81. Hubert Deschamps, *Les Pirates à Madagascar* (Paris 1949), p. 45.
82. Boxer, *Portuguese Empire*, pp. 136–7.
83. *GHP*, preface A 3.
84. The following section on piracy generalizes from several of Defoe's works, especially. *CJ, CS, FARC, GHP, KP* and *NVRW*.
85. *GHP*, p. 125.
86. The problems outlined above should be compared with those experienced by corsairs in the Mediterranean who had settled bases where they could sell or ransom their captives and sell the captured cargoes. The corsairs were rarely cruel to their captives, since they knew they could sell them and had no wish to damage such potentially valuable goods. See Earle, *Corsairs, op. cit.*
87. *GHP*, pp. 87–88.
88. *CS*, pp. 303–4.
89. *CS*, p. 244.
90. *KP*. p. 24.
91. *GHP*, pp. 169 ff.
92. See, for example, the discussion of such problems in *KP*, pp. 27–8.
93. See Deschamps, *op. cit.*
94. See G. E. Manwaring's introduction to Rogers, *op, cit.* and *GHP*, pp. 47–52.
95. *Review*, iv, 425–8.
96. Defoe denies the truth of this story in *KP*, pp. v–vi. Captain Avery wished it had been true, as they 'had money enough to have encourag'd us all to live honest,' pp. 63–64.
97. Deschamps, pp. 108–112 and 196 ff.
98. G. M. Walton, 'Sources of productivity change in American Colonial Shipping, 1675–1775', *EcHR*, 2nd. ser. xx (1967).
99. *E upon P*, p. 124.
100. See p. 73.
101. For a general discussion of attitudes towards negroes see Winthrop D. Jordan, *White over Black: American attitudes towards the Negro, 1550–1812* (1968) and Wylie Sypher, *Guinea's Captive Kings* (New York 1969).
102. *Crusoe*, p. 152.
103. *Crusoe*, p. 153.
104. *Crusoe*, pp. 125, 169–70.
105. *FARC*, p. 424.
106. *Op. cit.*, p. 14.
107. P. 559.

108. *Discourse of Trade* (1697), pp. 129-30.
109. *AM*, p. 237.
110. *AM*, p. 237.
111. Though competition amongst European slave traders was to educate the African middlemen in this respect. See p. 132. For good descriptions of the way in which the slave trade was carried on in Africa at this time see Elizabeth Donnan, *Documents Illustrative of the History of the Slave Trade to America* (New York 1965), vol. i.
112. 1702, p. 17.
113. *AM*, p. 237.
114. p. 95.
115. *AM*, p. 237.
116. *Genesis* 9-10.
117. See pp. 129-31.
118. *Review*, vi, 186. For a contemporary description of the sugar colonies see the book by Defoe's former employer, Dalby Thomas, *An Historical Account of the Rise and Growth of the West-India Collonies* (1690).
119. *E upon P*, p. 104. *Review*, i, 401-2.
120. Sypher, *op. cit.*, pp. 158-9.
121. *Review*, viii, 730.
122. *CJ*, p. 145.
123. A Committee of the Privy Council in 1789 investigated mortality in the slave trade and found that the average death-rate on the middle passage in 1680-88 was $23\frac{1}{2}$ per cent. Competition amongst slave-traders and increased demand were to force the price of slaves up in ensuing years so that the death-rate of the more valuable cargo was brought down to 10 per cent in 1734. K. G. Davies, *The Royal African Company* (1957), p. 292.
124. Defoe uses the word 'heaven' in this context in *AJ* 26.1.1722/3 (Lee, iii, pp. 95-96).
125. The theme of redemption and rebirth *via* transportation which plays an important part in several of Defoe's novels was a topical one. A new Act of Parliament of 1717 provided for the renewal of transportation to Virginia and Maryland after a lapse of some fifty years. Abbot E. Smith, *Colonists in Bondage* (Chapel Hill 1947) pp. 89-135. The new Act was thought to override the colonial laws prohibiting the import of convicts and in the summer of 1718 the flow of convicts began once again.
126. *AJ*, loc. cit.
127. Kai T. Erikson, *Wayward Puritans* (New York 1966); Alan Heinert, 'Puritanism, the Wilderness, and the Frontier', *New England Quarterly* xxvi (1953).
128. Parlicularly the northern mainland colonies. Defoe was in fact quite

worried about overproduction of tobacco and sugar (e.g. *Review*, vi, 1–2). He never recommended white emigration to the islands.

129. *Review*, i, 137–9, viii, 537–40, 569–72.
130. *Review*, i, 402.
131. For a more detailed analysis of Defoe's rationale of this see pp. 134–35.
132. For more on this see pp. 135–36.
133. See C. M. Cipolla, *Guns and Sails in the Early Phase of European Expansion, 1400–1700* (1965), pp. 145–7 for the effect of mobile light artillery in India during the Seven Years' War (1756–63).
134. See C. R. Boxer, *The Christian Century in Japan* (1951), pp. 248–307.
135. *The Consolidator* (1705), p. 5.
136. *AM*, p. 214.
137. *FARC*, p. 386. Cf. *SRRC*, pp. 133–42.
138. *FARC*, p. 395.
139. *PA*, p. 8. Cf. *CEG*, pp. 35–38. For Defoe on Russia see *PA, passim* and *AM*, pp. 127–32.
140. *Review*, ix, 156.

CHAPTER 4

1. *Review*, viii, 586.
2. *Religious Courtship*, p. 206.
3. *MOC*, pp. 31–32.
4. *Roxana*, p. 103.
5. *Review*, i, 121.
6. Roger North, 'The Life of the Hon. Sir Dudley North', *Lives of the Norths* (1826), ii, 329–330.
7. Especially Nicolini. See Colley Cibber, *Apology for his Life* (Everyman, 1914), pp. 198 ff. and the delightful mocking essays of Addison in the *Spectator*, e.g. Nos. 5 and 13.
8. *TBE*, p. 6.
9. *NVRW*, ii, 45.
10. *AM*, p. 152.
11. *CS*, p. 6.
12. *AM*, p. 155.
13. Boxer, *Portuguese Empire*, pp. 155–7.
14. For the classic account of the rise of English sea-power in the Mediterranean see Sir Julian Corbett, *England and the Mediterranean*, 2 vols. (1904).
15. *The Two Great Questions* (1700), p. 26.
16. No. 69.
17. *Review*, viii, 123.
18. *Review*, viii, 125.
19. *Review*, viii, 122.

20. *BD*, p. 10.
21. E.g. *GHDI*, pp. 46, 207.
22. *PEC*, p. 152–3; *GHDI*, p. 208; *BD*, pp. 8–20.
23. *PEC*, p. 48.
24. *PEC*, p. 186.
25. Economic historians are inclined to disagree with Defoe's account of the rise of the cloth industry. The commercial history of the reign of Elizabeth is brought down to earth in F. J. Fisher, 'Commercial trends and policy in sixteenth-century England', *EcHR*, x (1940); while a more accurate picture of the medieval growth of the cloth trade can be seen in E. M. Carus-Wilson and Olive Coleman, *England's Export Trade, 1275–1547* (Oxford 1963).
26. *GHDI*, pp. 213–14; *GANC*, pp. 4–8; *Review*, iv, 26; v, 573–5; *PEC*, p. 153.
27. *Review*, iv, 27.
28. *GANC*, pp. 4–8.
29. *PEC*, p. 153.
30. *BD*, pp. 20–30.
31. *PEC*, pp. 136–51.
32. *AM*, p. 143.
33. *PEC*, p. 173.
34. *BD*, pp. 30–32.
35. The best general expression of Defoe's views on the constitution, which are basically those of Locke, is in the preface to his poem *Jure Divino* (1706).
36. *Jure Divino*, p. iv.
37. *A Hymn to the Mob* (1715). In England the people govern but it is 'the people represented, not the people gather'd together; in short it is the Parliament in a House, not the rabble in the street.' p. ii.
38. *Review*, iii, 37–9.
39. *Review*, iii, 39.
40. *A Short View* (1707), p. 6.
41. *Review*, iv, 110.
42. *Review*, iv, 110.
43. *A Short View*, p. 7.
44. *A Short View*, p. 9.
45. *Moderation Maintain'd* (1704).
46. *MOC*, p. 166.
47. *MOC*, p. 270.
48. *Review*, vi, 18.
49. *Review*, iv, 632.
50. *AJ*, 9.9.1721 (Lee, ii, 425).
51. *GLS*, p. 40.
52. The theme of ingratitude reoccurs frequently in Defoe's works. See

in particular *TBE*, pp. 41–2; *The Mock Mourners* (1702) and *The Double Welcome* (1705). Defoe was in the habit of writing a panegyric on William in the *Review* once a year to remind Englishmen of the debt they owed him, e.g. vi, 365–8.

53. *TBE*, p. 8.
54. *FARC*, p. 235.
55. *Review*, ix, 198.
56. Dr. John Arbuthnot's *History of John Bull* was published in 1712.
57. *Review*, ix, 198.
58. *FARC*, p. 293.
59. *AJ*, 24.7.1725 (Lee, iii, 407–9); cf. B. L. de Muralt, *Letters describing the Character and Customs of the English and French Nations* (1726).
60. *Review*, vi, 23.
61. *Review*, iii, 418.
62. *Review*, iv, 250.
63. Pierre Goubert, 'Recent theories and research in French population between 1500 and 1700', in D. V. Glass and D. E. C. Eversley, *Population in History* (1968); Peter Laslett, *The World We Have Lost* (1965), p. 134; for a debate on the effect of continence and late marriage on the frustrated French see *Annales*, (1972).
64. Attributed to the French by Defoe in *TBE*, p. 8.
65. *Op. cit.*, p. 36.
66. *Review*, ix, 198.
67. *CET*, i, 386.
68. *And what if the Pretender should come?*, p. 18; cf. John Gay on Paris 'where slav'ry treads the streets in wooden shoes', C. F. Burgess (ed.), *The Letters of John Gay* (Oxford 1966), p. 15.
69. For useful summaries in English of the immense output of work on French agriculture see Pierre Goubert, *L'ancien Régime; French Society 1600–1750* (1973) and Jean Jacquart, 'French agriculture in the seventeenth century', in Peter Earle (ed.), *Essays in European Economic History, 1500–1800* (1973).
70. *AM*, p. 150. A similar contrast could be made in more modern times. In 1914, French consumption of wheat at $7\frac{1}{2}$ bushels per head per annum was the highest in the world, two bushels per head more than in the British Isles. Wilfred Malenbaum, *The World Wheat Economy, 1885–1939* (Harvard 1953), pp. 244–5.
71. de Muralt, p. 11; cf. *AM*, p. 150.
72. *Mercator*, No. 53.
73. For estimates of grain yields in various countries see B. H. Slicher van Bath, *The Agrarian History of Western Europe, 500–1850* (1963), pp. 330–333. For the very low yields in France see Jacquart, *op. cit.*, p. 171.
74. For subsistence crises see Goubert, *L'ancien Régime*, pp. 36–42.

75. *Review*, vi, 339.
76. *Review*, vi, 339. Cf. *AM*, p. 150.
77. *AM*, p. 143.
78. *Mercator*, No. 105.
79. *Mercator*, No. 106.
80. *AM*, p. 145.
81. *Considerations* (1713), p. 35.
82. e.g. *Review*, i, 385; *And what if the Pretender should come?*, p. 18; *AJ*, 17.2.1721/2 (Lee, ii. 487–8).
83. *Review*, i, 385.
84. *Considerations* (1713), pp. 16–17; for the wool-smugglers or owlers see *Tour* i, 112, 123 and elsewhere.
85. *AJ*, 17.2.1721/2 (Lee, ii, 487); cf. Ralph Davis, *Aleppo and Devonshire Square* (1967), pp. 28–29.
86. *AM*, p. 143.
87. *AM*, p. 143.
88. *Project d'une dixme royale*.
89. *Review*, i, 49–51. For a recent summary of the literature on the structure of French absolutism see Pierre Goubert, *L'ancien régime* vol. ii, *Les Pouvoirs* (Paris 1973).
90. *E upon P*, p. 7.
91. For some very pertinent remarks about the clash between liberty and authority in the Puritan mind see Christopher Hill, 'The Spiritualization of the Household', in *Society and Puritanism in Pre-Revolutionary England* (1964).
92. 1705 election takes up much of vol. ii of the *Review*; 1708 election in vol. v; 1710 election in vol. vii.
93. *Review*, vii, 332.
94. *And what if the Pretender should come?*, p. 32.
95. *AJ*, 16.9.1721 (Lee, ii, 428–9); cf. *DPP*, pp. 9–12, where he criticizes French methods.
96. *Review*, i, 57–59. Of course a high proportion of them then deserted. For French recruiting see Goubert, *L'ancien Régime: les pouvoirs* (Paris 1973), pp. 114–119.
97. *Review*, i, 59 cf. George Farquhar, *The Recruiting Officer* (1706).
98. *GANC*, p. 24. For English recruiting see J. W. Stoye, 'Soldiers and civilians', *NCMH*, vi, 770. The possibility of regular conscription was considered but dropped early in 1708. Defoe wrote two interesting papers on this, *Review*, v, 509–16, which are considered on pp. 162–63.
99. *Review*, v, 166; cf. *Reasons why* (1711), p. 14.
100. *PEC*, pp. 94–98.
101. *Review*, ii, 45–46.
102. *GANC*, p. 24. Stoye, *op' cit.*, states that recruitment was much easier

in the war of the 1690s, when there was much economic hardship and a smaller army than in the comparatively prosperous times of the War of Spanish Succession.

103. *Review*, iii, 54.
104. *Crusoe*, p. 5, 7; cf., *FI* (1715) where the eldest son joins the army after quarrelling with his father. He, too, comes to a sticky end.
105. *CJ*, p. 183.
106. *MOC*, pp. 48–58, quotation from p. 56.
107. *Double Welcome* (1705).
108. *Review*, i, 44.
109. *Review*, v, 405–7.
110. Defoe exaggerates a bit. Many younger sons fought in the English army. But the Scots were vital. A quarter of all regimental officers in the British army, 1714–63, were Scotsmen. Stoye, *op. cit.*, p. 783.
111. *The Mock-Mourners* (1702), p. 50.
112. Quoted in David G. Chandler, 'The Art of War on Land', *NCMH*, vi, 747–8; most of this discussion of changes in warfare is drawn from this article.
113. *A View of the Scots Rebellion* (1715), pp. 25–26.
114. Chandler, p. 749.
115. *Review*, i, 130.
116. *E upon P*, pp. 176–77.
117. *Anatomy of Exchange-Alley* (1719), p. 16; *E upon P*, pp. 176–77 for some rather doubtful arithmetic showing how jobbers could alter the odds 'by bringing down the vogue of the siege'.
118. *E upon P*, pp. 256–7.
119. *Review*, vi, 2.
120. Andrew Lossky, 'International relations in Europe', *NCMH*, vi, 151.
121. *Two Great Questions* (1700), p. 15. Cf. *E upon P*, p. 123 where the idea of a permanent international peace-keeping organization is outlined.
122. *The Memoirs of Major Alexander Ramkins* (1719), p. 50. Written by Defoe.
123. *Review*, vi, 17–18; *MOC*, p. 15.
124. *Review*, iii, 454.
125. *Review*, vi, 19.
126. *Two Great Questions* (1700), *passim*.
127. *Review*, iv, 186, 256, 299.
128. *Review*, vii, 210.
129. *Review*, viii, 573–6 and similar references in this volume.
130. *Review*, i, 221–23. Much of vol. i concerns the Hungarian revolt.
131. *Review*, i, 229–30.
132. *Review*, iv, 13–15.
133. *Review*, i, 202.
134. *Review*, vi, 261–72, 277–9. Quotation from p. 279.

135. *Review*, iii, 341–2.
136. *Review*, iii, 261–4.
137. *Review*, viii, 57–9, 353–60, 365–76 etc.
138. *Review*, iv, 421–3; v, 169–170, 245–7; viii, 345–8.
139. *Review*, v, 170.
140. e.g. *Review*, viii, 233–35. See above pp. 55–57.
141. *HP*, p. 44.
142. *Englishman's Choice* (1694), pp. 10–12.
143. *Englishman's Choice*, pp. 26–7.
144. *Some Reflections* (1697); *E upon P*, pp. 252–81; *Review*, v, 5–11.
145. *Review*, i, 341–7, 357–86; iv, 217–20. See pp. 137–39 for a more detailed discussion of Defoe's views on Anglo-French trade.
146. R. Ashton, *The Crown and the Money Market, 1603–1640* (1960); C. D. Chandaman, *The English Public Revenue, 1660–1688* (Oxford 1975).
147. *Essay upon Loans* (1710), pp. 6–7.
148. *Review*, vi, 7–8. For Defoe's general views on English public finance see *Essay upon Loans* (1710); *Review*, vi, 122–8; vii, 229–44, 534–71 etc.; *Reasons why this Nation* (1711); *Fair Payment No Spunge* (1717). For modern comparisons of French and English public finance see Roland Mousnier, 'L'évolution des finances publiques en France et en Angleterre pendant les guerres de la ligue d'Augsbourg et de la succession d'Espagne', *Revue Historique* ccv (1951) and P. G. M. Dickson and John Sperling, 'War Finance, 1689–1714', *NCMH*, vi, 285 ff.

CHAPTER 5

1. Part of this chapter has already appeared in my article, 'The Economics of Stability: the views of Daniel Defoe' in D. C. Coleman and A. H. John (eds.) *Trade, Government and Economy in Pre-Industrial England* (1976). For a very thorough study of all Defoe's economic ideas see the massive work by Edgar Illingworth, 'The Economic Ideas of Daniel Defoe', Ph.D. Leeds (1974). See also Maximilian E. Novak, *Economics and the Fiction of Daniel Defoe* (Los Angeles, 1962). Both these works have a rather different viewpoint and use a different type of analysis than is attempted in this chapter.
2. 1724–26.
3. See the brief appraisal of Defoe by Joseph Schumpeter in his *History of Economic Analysis* (1954), p. 372. Most historians of economic thought either ignore Defoe completely or at the most mention him in a footnote as one among several proponents of high rather than low wages. Heckscher, who praises Defoe, bases his praise on a total misconception of his economic ideas. Cf. *Mercantilism* (1955 ed.), ii, 171–2 with the argument of this chapter.

4. All four of these decades have problems in common; in particular they were periods when, for one reason or another, there were difficulties facing the producers of woollen cloth, England's major industry, and simultaneous and often causally connected problems of money supply and general liquidity. As a result the economic literature tended to emphasize the need for measures to protect exports and reduce imports, policies which were expected both to help the cloth industry and, *via* a surplus on the balance of trade, to increase the money supply. Arguments developed in such periods of crisis tended to become the economic orthodoxy of the age and were later to be given the rather unsatisfactory label of 'mercantilism'.

5. *Review*, ii, 45–70; iv, 35–36; vi, 138; *GANC*, pp. 10–11; *Mercator*, No. 143; *CET*, i, 384–7; ii, 124–5; *PEC*, pp. 59–62.

6. For a general study of the high wages *v.* low wages debate see Richard C. Wiles, 'The Theory of Wages in Later English Mercantilism', *EcHR*, 2nd. ser. xx (1968) and Edgar S. Furniss, *The Position of the Laborer in a System of Nationalism* (New York 1920), ch. 7. See also pp. 119–21.

7. I agree with William D. Grampp that the most important economic objective of the mercantilists was to maintain a high level of employment. See 'The Liberal Elements in English Mercantilism', *QJE* lxvi (1952), reprinted in J. J. Spengler and W. R. Allen, *Essays in Economic Thought* (1960), pp. 61–91. This was certainly Defoe's view and much of his economics rests on his fear that the level of employment might be reduced through under-consumption. This was a view he shared with many of his contemporaries, such as Petty, Barbon, North, Cary, Mandeville and Berkeley, though neither his analysis nor his recommendations for dealing with the problem were identical with the views of any one of them. For a discussion of the 'underconsumptionists' which treats them as forerunners of Keynes see T. W. Hutchison, 'Berkeley's *Querist* and its place in the economic thought of the eighteenth century', *The British Journal for the Philosophy of Science*, iv (1953) and *Idem, A Review of Economic Doctrines, 1870–1929* (Oxford 1953), pp. 346–7. Hutchison's analysis of Berkeley is attacked by Ian D. S. Ward, 'George Berkeley: Precursor of Keynes or Moral Economist on Underdevelopment?', *JPE*, lxvii (1959).

8. Defoe's argument for high wages is very similar to that of John Cary, *An Essay on the State of England* (Bristol 1695), pp. 143–50.

9. Grampp, *op. cit.*, p. 70. discusses Defoe's desire that both prices and wages should be high and writes, 'the difficulty of having both does not seem to have troubled him'. This is probably true. Defoe never seems to have worked this one out. He simply saw the

spending of wages as a dynamic process which pulled everything else along.

10. *Review*, ii, 37–8; *GANC*, pp. 17–18; *CET*, ii, 108–28. The best descriptions of circulation and distribution are in *Tour, passim*; *CET*, i, 388–407; ii, ii, 25–99; *PEC*, pp. 75–108, 152–244, 287–98.

11. *A Brief State* (1730), p. 7.

12. *Review*, iv, 31–36.

13. Other writers argued in a similar way. A more satisfactory explanation would be to argue that the greater density led to an improvement in productivity which in turn led to higher real wages or at least to higher real income per head. Productivity would have been raised by an increase in the territorial and occupational division of labour and by the fact that under the current conditions of a very low total population the application of more labour to the existing stock of land would have led to increasing, not decreasing, returns to scale in agriculture as well as industry. Schumpeter, *op. cit.*, pp. 251–2, argues that this was the implicit and correct assumption behind the almost universal contemporary desire for a larger population, a fact, if it is one, which singles out the world of Defoe from the Malthusian world of the early nineteenth century and most developing countries today.

14. Not to mention India and China.

15. *Review*, ii, 53–54, 69; *GANC*, p. 11.

16. A large literature exists on this but see the summary in Ralph Davis, *The Rise of the Atlantic Economies* (1973), pp. 194–211.

17. Eric Kerridge, *The Agricultural Revolution* (1967); Joan Thirsk, 'Farming Techniques' in Thirsk (ed.), *The Agrarian History of England and Wales*, vol. iv *1500–1640* (1967); Joan Thirsk, 'Seventeenth-century agriculture and social change', *AgHR*, xviii (1970), supplement; E. L. Jones, 'Agriculture and economic growth in England, 1660–1750: agricultural change', *JEH*, xxv (1965) reprinted in Jones (ed.), *Agriculture and economic growth in England, 1650–1815* (1967).

18. For wages and food prices see E. H. Phelps Brown and Sheila V. Hopkins, 'Seven centuries of the price of consumables compared with builders' wage-rates', *Economica*, xxiii (1956); M. W. Flinn, 'Agricultural productivity and economic growth: a comment', *JEH*, xxvi (1966). For the harvests see W. A. Hoskins, 'Harvest fluctuations and English economic history, 1620–1759', *AgHR*, xvi (1968).

19. *Review*, ix, 185–6; *CET*, ii, 118.

20. *Review*, ix, 186.

21. The distribution effects of low or high food prices have interested many historians. For a summary of the conditions thought necessary if low food prices were to lead to increased economic activity see

J. D. Gould, 'Agricultural fluctuations and the English economy in the eighteenth century', *JEH*, xxii (1962). For an optimistic view of the effect of low food prices see A. H. John, 'Aspects of English economic growth in the first half of the eighteenth century', *Economica* (1961).

22. *Review*, vi, 325–6. He was proved right when corn prices did collapse shortly after his death. See G. E. Mingay, 'The Agricultural Depression', *EcHR*, 2nd. ser., viii (1956).

23. First introduced experimentally in 1673. See D. G. Barnes, *A History of the English Corn Laws, 1660–1896* (1930).

24. *Review*, ix, 186; *CET*, ii, ii, 82–98; *AJ*, 10.7.1725 (Lee, iii, 404–5).

25. *A Brief Case of the Distillers* (1726). For a similar approach to the economic advantages of gin see Bernard de Mandeville, *The Fable of the Bees* (1723 ed.), pp. 86–91.

26. For the price of grain see J. E. Thorold Rogers, *A History of Agriculture and Prices in England*, vols. v–vi (1887), vol. vii (1902); B. R. Mitchell and Phyllis Deane, *Abstract of British Historical Statistics* (Cambridge 1962). For rents and the land market generally see H. J. Habakkuk, 'The English Land Market in the Eighteenth Century' in J. S. Bromley and E. H. Kossmann (eds.), *Britain and the Netherlands*, vol. i (1960); *idem*, 'English Landownership, 1680–1740', *EcHR*, x (1939–40) and Christopher Clay, 'The price of freehold land in the later seventeenth and eighteenth centuries', *EcHR*, 2nd. ser., xxvii (1974).

27. *Review*, vi, 143. For a somewhat more realistic estimate of the difference in the rent of arable and pasture land see Gregory King's figures in Charles Davenant, *An Essay upon the Probable Methods of making a People Gainers in the Balance of Trade* (1699) in Sir Charles Whitworth, *The Political and Commercial Works of Charles D'Avenant* (1771), ii, 216. The rent of pasture was about 50 per cent higher than that of arable.

28. *Review*, vi, 141–144.

29. cf. Jan de Vries, *The Dutch Rural Economy in the Golden Age* (1974).

30. *Review*, vi, 143; cf. William Petty, *Political Arithmetic* (1690) in C. H. Hull, *The Economic Writings of Sir William Petty* (1899), i, 268.

31. For a general discussion of agricultural change see Joan Thirsk, 'Seventeenth-century agriculture and social change', *AgHR*, xviii (1970), supplement; E. L. Jones, 'Agriculture and Economic Growth in England, 1660–1750: Agricultural Change' in Jones, *Agriculture and Economic Growth in England, 1650–1815* (1967).

32. *Tour*, i, 61–63, 222–23; ii, 193–211.

33. *Tour*, ii, 197.

34. *Tour*, ii, 203.

35. *Tour*, ii, 199.

36. For a general discussion of provincial towns see the introduction by

the editors in Peter Clark and Paul Slack (eds.), *Crisis and Order in English Towns, 1500–1700* (1972).

37. For the growth of amenities, such as street-lighting and theatres, see Malcolm Falkus, 'Lighting in the Dark Ages of English Economic History' in Coleman and John, *op. cit.*

38. *Tour*, i, 49–52; cf. Maidstone (i, 114–115), Winchester (i, 186–7), Shrewsbury (ii, 75), Derby (ii, 157), York (ii, 230–1) and several others.

39. E.g. Bury (*Tour*, i, 52); York (*Tour*, ii, 230–1).

40. For the importance of London's function in the economy see F. J. Fisher, 'London as an "Engine of Economic Growth"', in J. S. Bromley and E. H. Kossmann (eds.), *Britain and the Netherlands* vol. iv (1974).

41. This was true of nearly all towns.

42. E. Wrigley, 'A simple model of London's importance in changing English society and economy, 1650–1750', *P & P*, 37 (1967). For contemporary comments on London's vital statistics see Captain John Graunt, *Natural and Political observations upon the Bills of Mortality* (5th ed. 1676) in Hull, *op. cit.*, ii, 314–435.

43. *Review*, ix, 85–86.

44. *CJ*, p. 15.

45. *Tour*, i, 12.

46. *Tour*, i, 123.

47. *Tour*, i, 12.

48. *Tour*, ii, 275.

49. *Tour*, i, 142.

50. *Tour*, i, 157.

51. *Tour*, i, 342–6.

52. *Review*, iv, 15; *CET*, i, 399; ii, ii, 122–47; *Tour passim.*

53. *GANC*, pp. 17–18.

54. *A Brief State* (1730), pp. 17–18.

55. *CET*, ii, ii, 122–47.

56. Some contemporary writers did foreshadow twentieth-century employment policies in suggesting that the government had an important role to play in this respect: William Petty, 'A Treatise of Taxes and Contributions', in Hull, *op. cit.*, i, 29–31; George Berkeley, *The Querist* (1735–7) (1910 ed.), p. 72. For a general discussion of the Keynesian elements in the late seventeenth-century and eighteenth-century underconsumptionists see the two works by Hutchison cited in note 7 of this chapter.

57. Such arguments were very common. For a well-argued example see John Pollexfen, *A Discourse of Trade, Coyn and Paper Credit* (1697), p. 54. And see Wiles and Furniss, *op. cit.* for a general discussion of the works of the low wage advocates.

58. *PEC*, p. 60.

59. The reader may detect some inconsistency in Defoe's thought here. Whose side was he on? He seems to be arguing for high wages to increase the level of consumption and simultaneously agreeing with the majority of his fellows that high wages would lead to a withdrawal of labour and therefore would *not* increase the level of consumption. This is confusing, but the reason for the confusion is that Defoe never (wisely) defined exactly what he meant by a high wage. What he is really doing is arguing in the same way as the other writers, i.e. that an increase of wages above the level of subsistence will lead to a withdrawal of labour, *but* that the level of subsistence should be high enough to start with to allow the workman to buy far more than what other writers would have defined as subsistence. In other words, the supply curve of labour is still backward-sloping *but* it does not bend backwards at as low wages as others thought. Defoe was not the only writer of his time who argued this way. See Gardner, *Some Reflections on a pamphlet intituled 'England and East India Inconsistent in their Manufactures'* (1697) and for a modern interpretation agreeing in principle with my own see Wiles, *op. cit.*, p. 119. For a general discussion of the concept of the backward-sloping supply curve of labour see D. C. Coleman, 'Labour in the English Economy of the Seventeenth Century', *EcHR*, 2nd ser., viii (1956).

60. *GLS passim*; *EBNB passim*; *Augusta Triumphans* (1728), pp. 23–26; *PEC*, pp. 255–61. Defoe sees three main explanations of this further increase in wages, of which there is a hint but little more in E. W. Gilboy, *Wages in Eighteenth-Century England* (Cambridge Mass. 1934). The loss of men in the wars and emigration to the plantations had reduced the supply of labour. An increase in ostentation rather than wealth had increased the demand for servants. And the removal of French competition during the plague of 1720–22 had led to a boom in the cloth industry. For Defoe's criticism of servants see pp. 174–79.

61. *GLS*, pp. 82–86.

62. For an explanation of the ambiguous concept of a 'fairly high' wage see note 59 above.

63. Quote from *PEC*, pp. 62–63; see also *Review*, ii, 61–62; ix, 175–80, 198; *CET*, i, 391–2.

64. See Charles Wilson, 'Cloth production and international competition in the seventeenth century', *EcHR*, 2nd ser., xiii (1960).

65. There is an enormous literature on the English cloth industry. For some indication of the changes outlined here see J. de L. Mann, *The Cloth Industry in the West of England from 1640 to 1880* (1971); G. D. Ramsay, *The Wiltshire Woollen Industry* (1943) and D. C.

Coleman, 'Textile Growth' in N. B. Harte and K. G. Ponting (eds.), *Textile History and Economic History* (Manchester 1973).

66. e.g. in *Tour*, i, 61–63, 222–23; ii, 193–211.

67. *Review*, ix, 175–80, 200.

68. *Review*, ii, 85–86; *AM*, pp. 113–14. The argument in favour of this legislation is developed much more fully in Davenant, *An Essay . . . Balance of Trade* in Whitworth, *Works*, ii, 251 ff.

69. *Review*, ii, 14.

70. See the authorities listed above, note 65 and D. C. Coleman, 'An Innovation and its Diffusion: the "New Draperies"', *EcHR*, 2nd. ser., xxii (1969).

71. e.g. Joan Thirsk and J. P. Cooper (eds.), *Seventeenth-Century Economic Documents* (1972), p. 305; Simon Smith, *The Fleece* (1736).

72. P. J. Bowden, 'Wool supply and the woollen industry', *EcHR*, 2nd. ser., ix (1956).

73. See pp. 90–92. For French success in the Levantine market see Ralph Davis, *Aleppo and Devonshire Square* (1967), pp. 28–29 and A. C. Wood, *A History of the Levant Company* (1935), pp. 106–8, 119–20, 141–4.

74. *Review*, ii, 13–14; *BD*, pp. 44–52.

75. Defoe's comments on this are rather vague but see *Review*, ix, 198; *PEC*, pp. 35–37, 44. Most writers assumed that work was always unpleasant but Defoe realized that at least some tasks were in themselves enjoyable and that a workman might get considerable satisfaction from his skill and from the thought of having done a job well. For a much more confident exponent of the pleasure of work one needs to move forward to David Hume. See Eugene Rotwein, *David Hume: writings on economics* (1955), pp. xlii–xliv.

76. Cf. Cary's argument that low wages lead to poor-quality work. *An Account of the Proceedings of the Corporation of Bristol* (1700), pp. 13–14; quoted by Wiles, *op. cit.*, p. 123.

77. Cf. E. H. Hunt, 'Labour productivity in English agriculture, 1850–1914', *EcHR*, 2nd. ser., xx (1967), 285–88 and the references therein.

78. *PEC*, pp. 65–7. Cf. *CET*, i, 385 for estimate of English wages. A commoner estimate was that English wages were six times Indian wages. E.g. [Henry Martin?], *Considerations on the East India Trade* (1701) in J. R. McCulloch, *Early English Tracts on Commerce* (1886), pp. 549–50.

79. Acts of 1701 and 1721. For details see Audrey W. Douglas, 'Cotton textiles in England: the East India Company's attempt to exploit developments in fashion, 1660–1721', *Journal of British Studies*, viii (1969). For a well-argued defence of the East India Company see [Henry Martin?], *op. cit.*

80. Perhaps the best discussion of the concept which is described as

'order and regularity' is in [Henry Martin?], *Considerations . . . op. cit.*, pp. 580–93, cf. *Spectator*, No. 232 and John Cary, *An Essay . . . op. cit.*, pp. 145–7.

81. There exists a very considerable literature on individual industries. For a general survey see Charles Singer et al. (eds.) *A History of Technology*, vol. iii, *From the Renaissance to the Industrial Revolution, c. 1500–c. 1750* (Oxford 1957).

82. Joan Thirsk, 'The Fantastical Folly of Fashion' in Harte and Ponting *op. cit.*, pp. 66–73. For change in one part of the cloth industry see Ramsay, *op. cit.*, chapters 7 and 8.

83. *PEC*, p. 299; *GHDI*, p. 213.

84. D. C. Coleman, 'An Innovation and its Diffusion: the "New Draperies"', *EcHR*, 2nd. ser., xxii (1969).

85. J. U. Nef, 'The progress of technology and the growth of large-scale industry in Great Britain, 1540–1640', *EcHR* (1934).

86. See Thomas Sprat, *The History of the Royal Society* (1667) and Paul H. Maty, *General Index to the Philosophical Transactions* (1787) for an idea of the range of topics discussed. For different views on the relationship between science and technology in this period see Robert K. Merton, 'Science, technology, and society in the seventeenth century', *Osiris*, iv (1938) and A. R. Hall, 'Scientific Method and the progress of techniques', *Cambridge Economic History of Europe*, vol. iv (1967).

87. Defoe himself called the 1690s the 'Projecting Age', *E upon P*, p. 1.

88. *Tour*, ii, p. 47. A short reference covers nearly all mention of non-textile industry in this region.

89. *Tour*, ii, p. 47. Birmingham is not even in the index of the Everyman edition.

90. *Tour*. ii, p. 250.

91. Note that even in agriculture it is sheep-grazing which gets the most attention.

92. In his introduction to the *Tour*, p. xii.

93. See pp. 150–52.

94. *Mercator*, No. 8.

95. *CET*, ii, ii, 19–22.

96. *Mercator*, Nos. 49, 50, 52. Making and provisioning the ships also provided a demand for the products of agriculture.

97. *Review*, ix, 113.

98. *Treatise of Taxes* (1662), in Hull, *op. cit.*, pp. 55–6.

99. F. J. Fisher, 'London as an "Engine of Economic Growth"', *op. cit.*, p. 8.

100. Whether they were low-wage or high-wage advocates, most contemporary writers saw the inflow of cash as essential for the stimula-

tion (quickening) of trade at home. They thought that an increase in the quality of money would have more effect on the level of transactions than on the level of prices and so would not have the inflationary effects that a Ricardian specie-flow mechanism would suggest.

101. There was a very considerable increase in substitutes for money, such as bills and banknotes, in Defoe's time but their use was almost entirely confined to the wealthy and especially the mercantile community. In the long run cash was essential, both for wages and for retail transactions. Cf. Pollexfen, *op. cit.*, pp. 68–78.

102. There was however a growing criticism of the emphasis on the need for a positive balance of trade in Defoe's time, the usual argument being that gold and silver were commodities like any others and therefore there must automatically always be a balance. See, for instance, Nicholas Barbon, *A Discourse concerning coining the new money lighter in answer to Mr. Lock's Considerations* ... (1696), pp. 35–57; *idem*, *Discourse of Trade* (1690), p. 37 and Dudley North, *Discourses upon Trade* (1691), p. 13. For a more sophisticated approach see Isaac Gervaise, *The System or Theory of the Trade of the World* (1720) (reprint Baltimore 1954 with intro. by J. M. Letiche).

103. For details see Lawrence A. Harper, *The English Navigation Laws* (New York 1939).

104. G. L. Beer, *The Old Colonial System, 1660–1754* (New York 1912), vol. i, ch. 4.

105. Harper, ch. 23; Sven-Erik Aström, 'The English Navigation Laws and the Baltic Trade, 1660–1700', *Scandinavian Economic History Review*, viii (1960); John H. Andrews, 'Anglo-American Trade in the early eighteenth century', *Geographical Review*, xiv (1955). The weakest links were probably within the Empire and between the British and French colonial empires in America.

106. Ralph Davis, 'The rise of protection in England, 1669–1786', *EcHR*, 2nd. ser. xix (1966). These improvements were foreshadowed by the revision of the customs tariff in 1660. See C. D. Chandaman, *The English Public Revenue 1660–1688* (1975), pp. 12–13. For some doubts on Davis' thesis see N. B. Harte, 'The rise of protection and the linen industry' in Harte and Ponting, *op. cit.*

107. *Review*, ix, 89.

108. Defoe wrote a vast amount on the African trade. For what follows see *An Essay upon the Trade to Africa* (1711) and *Review*, v, 557–60, 565–71, 585–8, 621–4, 629–30; vi, 562–3; vii, 121–232; viii, 1–4; ix, 79–80, 89–90.

109. For a similar line of argument see Charles Davenant, *Reflections upon the Constitution and Management of the Trade to Africa* (1709) in Whitworth, *Works* v, 73–343.

110. For an excellent modern study see K. G. Davies, *The Royal African Company* (1957).

111. *Review*, i, 397–398. Defoe includes Norway in his analysis of Baltic trade.

112. Though she underwent some difficulty. See W. S. Unger, 'Trade through the Sound in the Seventeenth and Eighteenth Centuries', *EcHR*, 2nd. ser. xii (1959) and J. A. Faber, 'The decline of the Baltic grain trade in the second half of the seventeenth century', *Acta Historiae Neerlandica*, i (1966). For a more optimistic view see J. G. van Dillen, 'Economic fluctuations and trade in the Netherlands, 1650–1750' in Peter Earle, *Essays in European Economic History* (1974).

113. *PEC*, p. 75; cf. Pollexen, *op. cit.*, pp. 6–7 on 'storekeeper nations'.

114. See Jan de Vries, *The Dutch Rural Economy in the Golden Age* (Yale 1974), pp. 214–24.

115. *Review*, i, 401–2; cf. iv, 535–6, 548; vi, 181–4.

116. *Review*, iv, 539–40.

117. *PEC*, pp. 353–4.

118. See Jacob M. Price, 'The Map of Commerce, 1683–1721', *NCMH*, vi, for the progress made in the development of new sources of supply of naval goods.

119. See p. 71. For a more cautious view of the development of the colonies see Davenant, 'On the plantation trade', Whitworth, *Works*, ii, 8–9.

120. *Review*, iv, 504, 543–56, 563–8; *PEC*, pp. 354–58.

121. For a discussion of the differing gold/silver ratios between England and India see K. N. Chaudhuri, 'Treasure and Trade Balances: the East India Company's Export Trade, 1660–1720', *EcHR*, 2nd. ser. xxi (1968). The position was much more complex than I have described.

122. See [Henry Martin?], *Considerations . . .*, for a good statement of the pro-East India Company case. For Defoe's opinion see *Review*, i, 389–94.

123. *Review*, iv, 601–6; 613–5, 621–30; ix, 114; *MJ*, 27.6.1719 (Lee, ii, 136–9).

124. Bal Krishna, *Commercial Relations between India and England, 1601–1757* (1924).

125. See pp. 124–25 for a discussion of this prohibition.

126. *Review*, vii, 574–5.

127. Margaret Priestley, 'Anglo-French trade and the "Unfavourable Balance" controversy', *EcHR*, 2nd. ser. iv (1951–52); D. C. Coleman, 'Anglo-French Economic Relations, 1660–1714' in Coleman and John, *op. cit.* The best contemporary estimate is that of Charles Davenant, *Report to the Commissioners for stating the Public Accounts*

(1712) in Whitworth, *Works*, v, 347–63. Estimates are given for the Anglo-French balance from the 1660s onwards but they have a marked Tory bias, in other words they almost certainly make the trade look more advantageous to England than it really was.

128. *Review*, vii, 589–91.

129. *Review*, i, 337–47, 357–86; iii, 283; iv, 217–20; vii, 578–9, 597–600; viii, 13–14.

130. *Review*, i, 366.

131. *Review*, i, 366; vii, 577–82; viii, 37–40.

132. *Mercator, passim*; *Review*, ix, 173–6, 179–80, 185–6, 189–200.

133. e.g. *Review*, i, 341–3.

134. See especially *Mercator*, No. 65.

135. *Considerations upon the Eighth and Ninth Articles of the Treaty of Commerce and Navigation* (1713).

136. For a general discussion of the proposed treaty see D. A. E. Harkness, 'The opposition to the 8th and 9th articles of the Commercial Treaty of Utrecht', *Scottish Historical Review*, xxi (1924).

137. Stanley Gray and V. J. Wyckoff, 'The international tobacco trade in the seventeenth century', *Southern Economic Journal*, vii (1960).

138. For this see Curtis Nettels, 'England and the Spanish-American Trade, 1680–1715', *JMH*, ii (1931); and J. MacLachlan, *Trade and Peace with Old Spain, 1667–1750* (Cambridge 1940).

139. Between 1699–1701 and 1722–24 the total value of exports of English woollens fell from an average of £3·04m to £2·99m. The fall was steepest in exports to the traditional markets of northern Europe, whilst there was a considerable increase in sales to Spain and Portugal. Otherwise the most buoyant element in foreign earnings was in re-exports, especially of Asian products such as cottons, silks and tea which between them doubled in value in the same period from just over £$\frac{1}{2}$m to just over £1m. Ralph Davis, 'English foreign trade, 1700–1774', *EcHR*, 2nd. ser. xv (1962), p. 302.

140. *Review*, iv, 34.

141. *PEC*, pp. 343–48.

142. *PEC*, pp. x–xiii.

143. *GHDI*, pp. 149–152; *PEC*, pp. 312–30, 337–43.

144. See pp. 101–102.

145. *Review*, i, 385–6; viii, 177–9, 181–4.

146. *Review*, viii, 189–92.

147. *An Essay on the South-Sea Trade* (1711).

148. See pp. 55–57.

149. *BD*, pp. 41–52; *HP*, pp. 1–59; cf. the optimistic *PEC*, pp. 248–58. But even here there is an undercurrent of desperation.

150. *HP*, p. 6.

151. *PEC*, p. 181.

152. *BD*, pp. 49–52; *PEC*, pp. 252–5; *CET*, ii, ii, 171–6.

153. *HP*, p. 54.

154. *HP*, p. 56; cf. *PEC*, pp. 186–90.

155. see p. 108.

156. *BD*, p. 7.

157. *PEC*, pp. 84–92; cf. descriptions of such employed counties in *Tour*, e.g. Norfolk (i, 62–63), Devonshire (i, 221, 264); West Riding (ii, 193–4, 203–4).

158. *PEC*, pp. 91–92.

159. *PEC*, pp. 88–89. Cf. description of Cambridgeshire in *Tour*, i, 78.

160. *BD*, p. 7.

161. *Review*, ii, 26. Cf. Schumpeter's comments on the effect of the competition of children on their parents' income, *Op. cit.*, p. 274.

162. *GANC*, pp. 14–18; *Review*, i, 349–51; ii, 33–42; iv, 11–19; ix, 109. For a discussion of the background to the Workhouse Bill see p. 189.

163. Cf. Graunt, *op. cit.* ii, 353–4, 'that if there be but a certain proportion of work to be done, and that the same be already done by the non-beggars, then to imploy the beggars about it, will but transfer the want from one hand to another.'

164. *Review*, ii, 34.

165. *Review*, iv, 59.

166. *PEC*, pp. 287–90; cf. bone-lace at Blandford *Tour*, i, 217.

167. *PEC*, p. 289.

168. Cf. the grumbles of Sir Josiah Child: 'Not one justice of twenty (through pitty or other cause) will order delinquents to be whipt and sent from parish to parish, to the place of her birth or last abode', *A New Discourse of Trade* (1693), p. 62. For the effectiveness of the Act of Settlement of 1662 and the extent to which its provisions were qualified by the certificate system see S. & B. Webb, *English Poor Law History: Part I. The Old Poor Law* (1963), pp. 321–40; G. W. Oxley, *Poor Relief in England and Wales, 1601–1834* (1974), pp. 41–55; Ethel M. Hampson, 'Settlement and removal in Cambridgeshire, 1662–1834', *Cambridge Historical Journal*, ii (1928). The overall opinion is that the bark of the Settlement Laws was worse than their bite.

169. See, for example, J. Cornwall, 'Evidence of population mobility in the seventeenth century', *BIHR*, xi (1967); Peter Clark, 'The migrant in Kentish towns, 1580–1640' in Peter Clark and Paul Slack (eds.), *Crisis and Order in English Towns, 1500–1700* (1972).

170. *Some Considerations* (1728), p. 21.

171. *Review*, vi, 150.

172. *Review*, ii, 69.
173. And probably output per head. See Schumpeter, *op. cit.*, pp. 261–2 and note 8 of this chapter.
174. A general argument against a small population was that people would be able to live too easily by grazing animals to feel any need to do anything else. The usual example was Ireland. Cf. Petty, *Treatise of Taxes* (1662) in Hull, *op. cit.*, p. 34; Davenant, *Ways and Means* (1695) in Whitworth, *Works*, i, 73–74; *Spectator*, No. 200.
175. *TBE, passim*; *GANC*, pp. 4–8; *Review*, v, 571–8; *PEC*, 299–311 and see p. 82.
176. See note 13 above.
177. *Review*, iv, 31–36. See pp. 110–111 for an expansion of this argument.
178. *Review*, vi, 149–71, especially pp. 161–4. *Tour*, i, 200–206; cf. *PEC*, p. 18.
179. *Review*, vi, 162.
180. *Review*, vi, 169–171; *Tour*, i, 206. Defoe's schemes for settling immigrants were very similar to various contemporary utopian schemes for settling the poor. See pp. 191–92.
181. *GANC*, pp. 18–19; cf. *Review*, ii, 25–27; vi, 149–50.
182. *Review*, ii, 26.
183. *GANC*, pp. 18–19. This is another example of Defoe's tendency to anachronism. He implies that the knitting-frame is a recent innovation. Cf. Thirsk, 'Fantastical Folly of Fashion', *op. cit.*
184. *Idem.* It is in his opposition to labour-saving devices that we find the most important difference between Defoe and the other contemporary high-wage advocate, John Cary of Bristol. Cary's analysis of high wages depends on an increase in productivity through the use of labour-saving improvements enabling England to compete in foreign markets. *Essay on the State of England* (1695), pp. 145–6.
185. *Review*, ii, 38.
186. *CET*, ii, ii, 43–46.
187. *Review*, vi, 167; cf. *CET*, ii, 109.
188. *Review*, ix, 101.
189. *A Brief State* (1730), p. 27.
190. *PEC*, p. 227; cf. *PEC*, pp. 56–59. Defoe does praise developments in inland waterways in various places (e.g. *Tour*, ii, 48, 141, 207–8). New waterways which compete with existing routes of land transport are likely to be condemned. Those which open up the areas which previously had no transport at all are likely to be praised.
191. *E upon P*, pp. 68–112; *CET*, i, 395–7.
192. *CET*, ii, 109. Although cf. *Tour*, ii, 127 and in general ii, 117–32 where Defoe makes the conventional cost-cutting case for the improvement of roads. The economic observations in the *Tour* are

much more conventional and optimistic than those in most of
Defoe's economic writings, a fact which should be considered more
carefully by those who quote the *Tour* as typical of Defoe.

193. *Review*, ix, 84.

194. *Discourse of Trade* (1690), p. 32.

195. *Fable of the Bees* (1714). The original poem, *The Grumbling Hive*,
from which the much longer *Fable* was developed was published in
1705; Mandeville's work naturally attracted many critics, but their
arguments are generally very feeble. See, for instance, George
Blewitt, *An Enquiry whether a general practice of virtue tends to the wealth
or poverty, benefit or disadvantage of a people* (1725). For the conventional
anti-consumption view see Davenant, *Ways and Means, op. cit.*, p. 71
and Pollexfen, *op. cit.*, p. 158.

196. *BCD*.

197. *AT*, pp. 45–47; *AJ*, 18.12.1725 in Lee, iii, 450–52. So was Mandeville, *op. cit.*, pp. 86–91.

198. *CET*, ii, ii, 94–8. Cf. for English consumption of drink, *TBE*, p. 28:
> An Englishman will fairly drink as much
> As will maintain two families of Dutch

199. e.g. Hans H. Andersen, 'The Paradox of Trade and Morality in
Defoe', *MP*, xxxix (1941), pp. 23–46, and see pp. 32–34.

200. *GHDI*, p. 8; *CET*, ii, ii, 111–117.

201. *CET*, ii, ii, 99–122.

202. *E upon P*, pp. 246–8.

203. *FI* (1715), p. 121.

204. *AT*, pp. 38–41.

205. *Review*, vi, 254–60, quotation from p. 257.

206. *Review*, iii, 379.

207. *Review*, vi, 257–60.

208. *PMP*, p. 3.

209. *PMP*, p. 4.

210. *GLS*, p. 52.

211. *PMP*, p. 5.

212. *BCD*, p. 17.

213. *GLS*, pp. 61–2.

214. Mitchell and Deane, *op. cit.* give 1689 as the peak when the beer
assessed for excise reached a figure of 5·1m barrels of strong beer
and 2·7m barrels of small beer. Each barrel held 36 gallons and the
population was about 5½m. Actual consumption would have been
much higher, since home-brewed beer was not assessed.

215. *PMP*, p. 5.

216. For a general discussion of this strange movement see Dudley W. R.
Bahlman, *The Moral Revolution of 1688* (Yale 1957). For an enthusiastic contemporary account by one of the Societies' main propa-

gandists see Josiah Woodward, *An Account of the Progress of the Reformation of Manners* (1704). Defoe attacked the Societies for their double standards towards rich and poor, and for their hypocrisy. This is the theme of *PMP* (1698) and *Reformation of Manners* (1702).

217. Woodward was a prolific author of these.
218. Woodward, *op. cit.*, p. 20.
219. *BCD*, pp. 46–47.
220. *BCD*, pp. 24–31.
221. Mitchell and Deane, *op. cit.*
222. *CET*, ii, ii, 101.
223. *DPP*, pp. 55–56; *AJ*, 28.9.1723 and 13.11.1725 (Lee, iii, 186–9, 439–41); *CET*, ii, ii, 147–71; *CL*, pp. 394–97.

CHAPTER 6

1. These examples are all taken from B. L. de Muralt, *Letters describing the characters and customs of the English and French nations* (1726).
2. Theoretically, the right to bear arms was the sign of the true gentleman, a right which could be assessed by occasional heraldic visitation. But, perhaps significantly, the whole century from 1670 to 1770 was characterized by a collapse in heraldic authority with the result that arms were widely assumed without right or grant. A. R. Wagner, *English Genealogy* (2nd. ed. Oxford 1972), pp. 119–32.
3. For the 'pseudo-gentry' see Alan Everitt, 'Social mobility in early modern England', *P & P*, 33 (1966), pp. 70–71.
4. Guy Miege, *The Present State of Great Britain and Ireland* (1715), p. 169.
5. Letters and diaries provide amusing illustrations of this. Pepys is an obvious example, as is Jonathan Swift, *Journal to Stella*.
6. *The Present State of the Arts in England* (1755) quoted in Wagner, *op. cit.*, p. 96.
7. For an interesting attempt to systematize the changes in English social structure see Lawrence Stone, 'Social mobility in England, 1500–1700', *P & P* 33 (1966).
8. About half in London and half in provincial towns. The latter were growing fastest.
9. Gregory King estimated that four per cent of heads of families in 1688 were professionals, nearly as many as the commercial middle classes. See Charles Davenant, *An Essay for making the people gainers in the balance of trade* (1699) in Whitworth, *Works*, ii, 184. I include officers, placemen, clergymen, lawyers, and persons in liberal arts and sciences in this four per cent. The proportion would have grown considerably after 1688 as a result of the expansion of the armed forces and the government service.
10. Guy Miege, *The New State of England* (1691), p. 226. Cf. *Review*, i, 44.

11. For the various gradations of the law and the difficulties of succeeding in most of them see R. Campbell, *The London Tradesman* (1747), pp. 72ff.

12. Campbell, *op. cit.*, is a fascinating guide to the crafts of London. For the gold and silver lace-man see pp. 147–54. See also D. V. Glass, 'Socio-economic status and occupations in the City of London at the end of the seventeenth century' in A. E. J. Hollaender and William Kellaway (eds.), *Studies in London History* (1969), pp. 382–3 for the range of trades and crafts in London in the 1690s.

13. Campbell, pp. 2–22; cf. Samuel Richardson, *Familiar Letters on Important Occasions* (1741), Letter I.

14. Campbell, p. 4.

15. For France see Pierre Goubert, *L'ancien Régime* (1973). For England see Alan Everitt, 'Farm labourers' in Joan Thirsk (ed.), *Agrarian History of England and Wales*, vol. iv (1967), p. 339 where he estimates that by the end of the seventeenth century nearly half the population were landless or nearly landless labourers. Gregory King puts 56 per cent of his heads of families into the two groups, 'labourers and out-servants' and 'cottagers and paupers'. But it is necessary to add something for in-servants, whom he does not distinguish separately. Judging by the size of families he assigns to the wealthier members of society it seems clear that King thought there must be well over half a million in-servants, in other words well over 10 per cent of the population. Whitworth, *Works*, ii, 184.

16. *Review*, v, 513–516.

17. *Review*, v, 512. 'And without doubt, the appointing the parishes to pick out from among them the most useless and unprofitable of their own number to supply the want of men for the necessary defence of the whole, is the tenderest and the most considerate method, with respect to the people and liberty, that can be.'

18. This was a very high estimate. Most contemporary estimates were in the range from 5 to 7 millions. King estimated $5\frac{1}{2}$ millions, *op. cit.* Sir William Petty estimated 7 millions, 'Another Essay in Political Arithmetick' (1682) in Hull, *op. cit.*, ii, 460. Malachy Postlethwayt estimated 6 millions in 1750, *The Universal Dictionary of Trade and Commerce* (1751), s.v. 'People', ii, 430. Modern estimates suggest that King and Postlethwayt were the most accurate, King being slightly too high and Postlethwayt slightly too low. For a discussion of the literature see M. W. Flinn, *British Population Growth 1700–1850* (1970).

19. $27\frac{1}{2}$ per cent of King's heads of families roughly coincide with Defoe's second group, i.e. eminent merchants, lesser merchants, freeholders, farmers and shopkeepers, of whom farmers and freeholders made up 23 per cent. But if servants were excluded this

would be a considerably lower proportion of the male population.

20. *CET*, ii, ii, 78.

21. *Review*, vi, 142.

22. The most ambiguous group is the fifth who are distinguished by location as much as by consumption. Defoe sometimes lumped farmers with the middle sort and sometimes not. See p. 167.

23. *Review*, vi, 142. Note the equation between the 'gentleman' and the 'rich man'.

24. *Op. cit.*

25. The wage *rate* of the labourer seems to have been about two-thirds that of the artisan, and in fact the differential between the two rates seems to have narrowed in this period. See E. H. Phelps Brown and Sheila V. Hopkins, 'Seven centuries of building wages', *Economica* (1955). King's low estimate for the labourers reflects among other things their chronic underemployment. See pp. 182–86.

26. Needless to say, Defoe thought London had far more than the half million inhabitants estimated by Gregory King. Such a great city could not possibly have less than one and a half million inhabitants; *Tour*, i, 322.

27. *Tour*, ii, 159–65, 204–8.

28. *Review*, vi, 142.

29. *Crusoe*, p. 6.

30. Books were not cheap. The first edition of *Robinson Crusoe* cost 5 shillings, two days' wages for a skilled workman. Ian Watt, *The Rise of the Novel* (1957), p. 41. For a general discussion of the new middle class reading public and the books which were written for them see Watt and Bonamy Dobrée, *English Literature in the early eighteenth century, 1700–1740* (Oxford 1959), esp. pp. 1–15.

31. *Review*, v, 515.

32. *MJ*, 31.10.1719 (Lee, ii, 156–61); cf. *Spectator* No. 21: 'We may lay it down as a maxim that when a nation abounds in physicians it grows thin of people.'

33. e.g. *The Villainy of Stock-Jobbers Detected* (1701); *Review*, v, 425–8; vi, 117–121; viii, 242–3; *Anatomy of Exchange-Alley* (1719). Their main crime was to manipulate the market, for political reasons as well as for their own personal profit.

34. *Review*, iii, 6.

35. *Treatise of Taxes* in Hull, *op. cit.*, i, 28.

36. *England's Treasure by Forraign Trade* (1664), p. 2. Written in the 1620s.

37. This is a very common theme. For an interesting example of changing attitudes see Helen Sard Hughes' analysis of successive editions of Chamberlayne's *Angliae Notitia* in 'The Middle-Class Reader and the English Novel', *JEGH*, xxv (1926), pp. 366–68.

38. The best account of the rise of shopkeeping is Dorothy Davis, *A History of Shopping* (1966); see also R. B. Westerfield, *Middlemen in English Business* (Yale 1915).

39. 'Those little retailing shops are the life of all our trade; by these the bulk of the business is carried on to the last consumer': *A Brief State* (1730), p. 21. Two excellent autobiographies provide fascinating insights into the life of the provincial shopkeeper. J. Harland (ed.), *Autobiography of William Stout* (1851) and William L. Sachse, *The Diary of Roger Lowe* (1938).

40. *N.H., The Compleat Tradesman: or, the exact dealer's daily companion* (1684), p. 20.

41. *N.H., op. cit.*, p. 18. Cf. Campbell, *op. cit.*, pp. 188–9 on the trade of the grocer, 'the mystery of which he may learn in a month or two'.

42. Davis, *op. cit.*, p. 152.

43. R. Grassby, 'The personal wealth of the business community in seventeenth-century England', *EcHR*, 2nd. ser. xxiii (1970), pp. 223–4.

44. *N.H., op. cit.*, p. 20.

45. I will consider this in some detail in chapter 8.

46. *Review*, ix, 85–86.

47. *CET*, ii, 128–42.

48. *CET*, ii, 133–34.

49. For virtually identical attitudes to business in nineteenth-century France see David S. Landes, 'French entrepreneurship and industrial growth in the nineteenth century', *JEH*, ix (1949).

50. *AJ*, 13.7.1723 (Lee, iii, 159). The passage forms part of an attack on Mandeville and other opponents of education for the poor.

51. *GLS*, p. 17.

52. *Jure Divino*, ii, 10.

53. For a summary of these see *GLS*, pp. 8–9.

54. D. V. Glass, *op. cit.*, p. 386 estimates that there were a minimum of 11,000 apprentices in the City of London in the 1690s. I know of no estimate for the country as a whole. Apprenticeship was declining. See Glass p. 385 and J. R. Kellett, 'The Breakdown of Gild and Corporation Control over the handicraft and retail trade in London', *EcHR*, 2nd. ser. x (1958).

55. It also included the sons of paupers, though pauper-apprentices form a rather special group which I will not discuss here.

56. Gregory King estimated there to be 560,000 servants in 1696. See Chalmers (1810), *op. cit.*, p. 89; cf. J. Jean Hecht, *The Domestic Servant Class in Eighteenth-Century England* (1956), pp. 33–34. Some indoor servants stayed for life but for most it was a transitional period of uncertain length before marriage. Apprenticeship was normally

for either seven or eight years. Starting ages varied but were usually between 14 and 18.

57. *PEC*, pp. 101–2.
58. Richard Burton. *The Apprentices' Companion* (1681), p. 2.
59. R. Campbell, *The London Tradesman* (1747), pp. 188–9, 196–8.
60. *FI* (1715), pp. 260–1; *GLS*, pp. 10–11. Defoe estimated that premiums had doubled or trebled in his lifetime. O. Jocelyn Dunlop, *English Apprenticeship and Child Labour* (1912), pp. 199–204 accepts Defoe's view.
61. Dunlop, *op. cit.*, pp. 196ff. Guild control over apprentices was becoming very weak and wages were partly an attempt to retain apprentices who had a disconcerting habit of deserting once they thought they had learned enough (p. 194). The premium also gave the parent an interest in getting his money's worth.
62. *FI* (1715), pp. 260–1.
63. *GLS*, p. 13.
64. By Richard Burton, pseudonym of Nathaniel Crouch.
65. Burton, *op. cit.*, p. 44. Cf. Richard Baxter, *A Christian Directory* (1673), p. 133 for similar sentiments.
66. *FI* (1715), pp. 261–3.
67. *GLS*, pp. 12–13.
68. *EBNB*, pp. 9–10, 12.
69. Robert Dodsley, *Servitude: a poem* (1729), p. 29. Andrew Moreton Esq. was a pseudonym much used by Defoe in the 1720s when he was writing on social or moral problems. Dodsley has a good point but it has to be accepted that Defoe was by no means alone in making this comment about servants' clothes.
70. *GLS*, pp. 14–15, 53, 78–81; *EBNB*, 4–5.
71. *GLS*, p. 78.
72. *EBNB*, p. 14.
73. See pp. 120–21.
74. For a summary of the rather limited information see Hecht, *op. cit.*, pp. 141–76.
75. *GLS*, pp. 139–40. Defoe suggests a loss through emigration and warfare of 700,000 people.
76. Batista Angeloni, *Letters on the English Nation* (1756), letter xxxi; Hecht, pp. 158–68; Dorothy Marshall, 'The Domestic Servants of the Eighteenth century', *Economica*, ix (1929), p. 25 quotes P. J. Grosley, *A Tour to London* (1772), p. 75 for tips doubling servants' wages. For Defoe's views see *EBNB*, pp. 10–11.
77. *EBNB*, pp. 7–9. For a defence of servants' rights see Dodsley, *Servitude*, pp. 30–31.
78. *GLS*, pp. 270–1.
79. Dodsley, *op. cit.*, p. 27.

80. *EBNB*, p. 5.
81. *London Chronical*, iii (1758), p. 116c.
82. In London at least. Conditions of service in the country could be rather different.
83. *EBNB*, pp. 11–12.
84. *Servitude* (1729), p. 19.
85. John Beresford (ed.), *Memoirs of an eighteenth-century footman* (1927). The calculation is from Dorothy Marshall, 'The domestic servants of the eighteenth century', *Economica*, ix (1929), p. 32.
86. A fairly common theme. E.g. *EBNB*, pp. 5–7 and the early part of *Moll Flanders*.
87. Marshall, *op. cit.*, p. 38.
88. *EBNB*, pp. 19–21 and cf. *Moll Flanders* where it is a little difficult to see just who is making the running.
89. *GLS*, p. 261, cf. p. 293.
90. The fullest discussion of this is in *RC*. See the preface for the general observations above.
91. *RC*, p. 343.
92. *GLS*, pp. 78–89; *TBE*, p. 27.
93. 'The poor are too low to keep a servant, yet they are generally too high to be servants themselves', *GLS*, p. 260.
94. Richard Baxter, *A Christian Directory* (1673), pp. 627–9.
95. *RC*, pp. 60–83.
96. p. 80. The information is repeated and elaborated on p. 152. This is not the only place in Defoe where a strict attention to religious duties earns an immediate material reward. Cf. the old lady in the *Family Instructor* who reforms a child. 'Sometimes she would persuade me, otherwhiles give me money, and other good things', *FI* (1715), p. 138.
97. For a useful discussion of these limitations see D. C. Coleman, 'Labour in the English economy of the seventeenth century', *EcHR*, 2nd. ser. viii (1956).
98. For a general discussion of attitudes to time see E. P. Thompson, 'Time, work-discipline, and industrial capitalism', *P & P*, 38 (1967). He suggests that the attitude to time discussed here is something that develops in the seventeenth century.
99. *GLS*, p. 211.
100. *GLS*, pp. 211–19; quotation from p. 219.
101. *GLS*, p. 71.
102. *GLS*, pp. 82–4.
103. *GLS*, pp. 91–3.
104. For a discussion of the changes that such a realization brought into economic thinking see A. W. Coats, 'Changing attitudes to labour in the mid-eighteenth century', *EcHR*, 2nd. ser. xi (1958–9). For

the effect of new products and the spirit of emulation on the home market see D. E. C. Eversley, 'The Home Market and Economic Growth in England, 1750–80', in E. L. Jones and G. E. Mingay, *Land, Labour and Population in the Industrial Revolution* (1967). Harold Perkin, *The Origins of Modern English Society, 1780–1880* (1969), thinks that this attitude was the driving force which led to the industrialization of England.

105. George Berkeley, *The Querist* (1735–7) (1910 ed.), p. 11.

106. W. A. Lewis, *The Theory of Economic Growth* (1955), ch. 2.

107. *Review*, vi, 142.

108. *GANC*, p. 11; *Review*, ii, 53–59.

109. *Review*, ii, 53.

110. *Review*, ii, 54.

111. S. and B. Webb, *English Poor Law History: Part I. The Old Poor Law* (1963), pp. 114–116.

112. For this see p. 145 and p. 189.

113. *Review*, iv, 91. Cf. *PT*, pp. 33–34.

114. *Review*, iv, 91.

115. R. Campbell, *The London Tradesman* (1747), pp. 159–60.

116. Campbell, p. 192; cf. Swift on August in London: 'It is a scurvy empty town this melancholy season of the year.' 'May my enemies live here in summer! and yet I am so unlucky that I cannot possibly be out of the way at this juncture. People leave the town so late in summer, and return so late in winter that they have almost inverted the seasons', *Journal to Stella*, i, 338, 345.

117. *JPY*, pp. 94–95.

118. *Review*, ii, 69.

119. *Review*, iv, 613–15, 621–3, 625–7.

120. *FARC*, p. 275.

121. *Review*, iv, 19.

122. Though Defoe accepts that a man in want 'by accident' has a right to relief. Indeed even a man in want 'by slothfulness and idleness' should be relieved, 'for no man ought to starve, let his crime be what it will.' But before he is relieved he should be punished. *E upon P*, p. 143.

123. See Defoe's criticism of the clothworkers who did not take advantage of the high wages in the early 1720s to save for the inevitable rainy day, *GLS*, pp. 82–4.

124. *E upon P*, pp. 145–71. Quote from p. 148.

125. *E upon P.*, p. 169.

126. For a discussion of this literature see S. and B. Webb, *op. cit.*, pp. 102 ff.

127. Michel Foucault, *Madness and Civilization* (Eng. trans. 1967), ch. 2. 'The Great Confinement'.

128. Cf. W. L. Parry-Jones, *The Trade in Lunacy* (1972). Defoe attacked private mad-houses and argued that lunatics should be confined in public institutions under strict regulation. *Review*, iii, 277–80, 327, 353–6; *AT*, pp. 30–38 for husbands shutting up their wives and then spending their dowries on a riotous life.

129. Bernard de Mandeville, *Fable of the Bees* (1723 ed.), pp. 94–99; *A Modest Defence of Publick Stews* (1724). Mandeville anticipated the Victorian defence of regulated prostitution as the best way of defending middle–class female virtue from the incorrigible lust of their menfolk. For the public laundries see *London Chronicle*, iii (1758), p. 149. This was a plan of Fielding's to absorb reformed prostitutes and the daughters of the poor, suitably distinguished by the severity of their work and the families they would be sent to once they had done their time. The reformed prostitutes would be sent to 'more inferior families'. For Defoe's views see *AT*, pp. 27–8.

130. *EBNB*, p. 24–32. They would be replaced as shoe-blacks by 'great numbers of ancient persons, poor widows and others, who have not enough from their respective parishes to maintain 'em', all licensed by the JPs and each with her own stand (p. 32).

131. For a general discussion of the proposals and the actual evolution of the workhouse see S. and B. Webb, *op. cit.*, pp. 102–21 and pp. 215–72. For a summary of more recent research see Geoffrey W. Oxley, *Poor Relief in England and Wales, 1601–1834* (1974), ch. 5.

132. See notes 162–165 of Chapter 5 for references.

133. S. and B. Webb, *op. cit.*, pp. 113–114.

134. S. and B. Webb, *op. cit.*, p. 266.

135. *Account of Several Workhouses* (1725), p. iv.

136. *Idem*, p. v.

137. Quoted in *idem*, p. 108.

138. *PT*, pp. 33–34.

139. See pp. 148–49.

140. *Proposals for raising a college of industry* (1696) reprinted in A. Ruth Fry, *John Bellers (1654–1725); Quaker, economist and social reformer* (1935).

141. Cf. Sir William Petty, *Treatise of Taxes* (1662) where he discusses a hypothetical society in which ten per cent of the population 'can raise necessary food and raiment' for the whole. Few writers were as optimistic as this. Hull, *op. cit.*, i, 30.

142. *The Miseries of the Poor* (1717); *Particular Answers to the more material objections made to the proposal . . . for relieving . . . the poor* (1722).

143. *E upon P.*, p. 143.

144. *PT*, pp. 30–2. Taking 5 people to the house this is only 2 per cent,

a very optimistic estimate. Cf. Petty who estimated that of the 1,000 inhabitants of a hypothetical territory, 100 or 10 per cent would be 'supernumerary', i.e. poor. *Treatise of Taxes* (1662) in Hull, *op. cit.*, i, 30. What the real figure was is unknown, but Petty's estimate seems more realistic than that of Defoe.

145. This is the main theme of *Parochial Tyranny* (1727). Most of the poor rate was spent on parish feasts or over a 'bird and a bottle' in a tavern. The watchmen ran a protection racket. The vestry took bastards off the harlot's hands for a down payment etc. etc.

146. *An Essay on Charity and Charity-Schools* (1723), p. 285.

147. *Roxana*, pp. 22–23.

148. *AJ*, 3.7.1725 (Lee, iii, 400–3).

149. Cf. the suspicion voiced in *Roxana*, pp. 5–6 that the generous reception given in London to the Huguenot refugees who fled from France after the revocation of the Edict of Nantes in 1685 had led to their numbers being swollen by droves of European beggars who had made their way over to England to share in the good times.

150. *CS*, p. 148.

151. *TBE*, p. 19. The main theme of this poem is the questionable ancestry of the apparently well-born.

152. *CEG*, p. 13.

153. Much of *CEG* is on this theme. The idea that virtue, not birth, makes the gentleman is a very old one. Cf. George McGill Vogt, 'Gleanings for the history of a sentiment: generositas virtus, non sanguis', *JEGP* xxiv (1925). But only a middle-class writer like Defoe would really take it seriously.

154. For a discussion of this literature see George C. Brauer, jr., *The Education of a Gentleman: theories of gentlemanly education in England, 1660–1775* (New York 1959).

155. *FARC*, p. 229.

156. *Review*, vi, 135.

157. For Sir Roger de Coverley see the *Spectator*, especially Nos. 106 ff.

158. *Journal to Stella* (1711), i, 326.

159. See G. E. Mingay, 'The Agricultural Depression', *EcHR*, 2nd. ser. viii (1956) for a discussion of landlords' relationships with tenants.

160. [William Darrell], *A Gentleman instructed in the conduct of a virtuous and happy life* (1704), p. 29.

161. *CEG*, *passim* but esp. pp. 43–57.

162. 'The perfeccion of a fool, namely to be proud of his ignorance', *CEG*, p. 40.

163. *Review*, v, 407. The historical truth of this sort of criticism is a little difficult to assess. The most famous piece on gentlemen agrees with Defoe and his contemporaries. T. B. Macaulay, *History of England*, i,

318 ff. But Macaulay was as prejudiced as Defoe. But there does seem to have been a decline in upper-class educational standards. See pp. 212–14.

164. *The Gentleman's Library* (1722), p. 48.

165. Whitworth, *Works, op. cit.*, ii, 184.

166. King suggests that the landed classes were net savers. But this does not preclude large numbers of them from being dis-savers. Strangely enough some commentators assume that, because King thought the poor were net dis-savers as a group, all of them were, which is just as much nonsense as suggesting that all the gentry earned more than they spent.

167. *Roxana*, p. 167.

168. For landed incomes see the authorities listed above, note 26, chapter 5.

169. *CET*, ii, 162.

170. *Review*, iii, 27. Though some people thought it was actually cheaper to live in London and thus avoid the expenses of housekeeping and hospitality in the country.

171. *CL*, pp. 256–7.

172. For a loving documentation of many sensational cases see *Tour, passim*.

173. *Review*, ii, 10.

174. *Tour*, i, 158 cf. i, 168.

175. *Tour*, ii, 2.

176. *Tour*, i, 336.

177. For the actual development of these standards in the seventeenth century see F. J. Fisher, 'The development of London as a centre for conspicuous consumption', *TRHS*, 4th ser. xxx (1948).

CHAPTER 7

1. For Defoe's extreme views on self-preservation see above, p. 36.

2. *A Christian Directory* (1673), p. 630.

3. *The Commentator*, xl (20.5.1720) quoted in G. A. Starr, *Defoe and Casuistry* (Princeton 1971), p. 92.

4. *FI* (1715).

5. James Janeway, *A Token for Children: being an exact account of the conversion, holy and exemplary lives, and joyful deaths of several young children* (1671 and numerous further editions into the first half of the eighteenth century). William Sloane, *Children's Books in England and America in the Seventeenth Century* (New York 1955), p. 44, describes *A Token for Children* as 'a book more often recommended to seventeenth-century children than any other except the Bible'.

6. Janeway, *op. cit.* (1720 ed.), preface A3–A4.

7. *FI* (1715), p. 78.

8. *The well-ordered Family* (Boston 1712), p. 63 quoted by Edmund S. Morgan, *The Puritan Family* (1944), p. 53.

9. Wadsworth, 'The Nature of Early Piety', p. 10 quoted by Morgan, *op. cit.*, p. 51.

10. James McMath, *The Expert Mid-wife* (1694), pp. 11–12. Cf. John Dunton, *The Athenian Oracle* (1703), i, 30, 41.

11. *Tatler* No. 15 quoted by J. Ashton, *Social Life in the Reign of Queen Anne* (1904), p. 3.

12. Archbishop Tillotson, *Six Sermons on Education* etc. (1694), pp. 110–111; cf. William Ames, *Conscience*, p. 157 who held 'that it is a sinne in that mother, that without some just cause hindring, doth not nurse her children with her own breasts'.

13. *CEG*, pp. 73–74.

14. For general evidence of this see J. H. Plumb, 'The New World of Children in Eighteenth-Century England', *P & P*, 67 (1975); Philippe Ariès, *Centuries of Childhood* (Eng. trans. 1962); Rosamond Bayne-Powell, *The English Child in the Eighteenth Century* (1939).

15. Sloane, *op. cit.*, ch. 4; Victor E. Neuburg, *Popular Education in Eighteenth-Century England* (1971), ch. 5.

16. ed. James L. Axtell, *The Educational Writings of John Locke* (Cambridge 1968), pp. 114–137, quotation from p. 137. For the influence of stoic ideas, especially those of Seneca, see W. Lee Ustick, 'Changing Ideals of Aristocratic Character and Conduct in Seventeenth-Century England', *MP*, xxx (1932).

17. Axtell, pp. 216–17.

18. Axtell, pp. 152–3.

19. Quoted in Morgan, *op. cit.*, p. 57.

20. e.g. it was used by Defoe in *PM*, p. 21.

21. Tillotson, *Six Sermons*, *op. cit.*, p. 155.

22. *Idem*, pp. 117–18.

23. *Idem.*, p. 206.

24. *FI* (1715), pp. 372–3.

25. *FI* (1718), pp. 175–212.

26. *FI* (1718), p. v.

27. For a discussion of earlier conduct books see Chilton Latham Powell, *English Domestic Relations 1487–1653* (New York 1917) and Levin L. Schücking, *The Puritan Family* (Eng. trans. 1969).

28. For a discussion of the growth and importance of the institution of family worship see Christopher Hill's article, 'The Spiritualization of the Household' in his *Society and Puritanism in Pre-Revolutionary England* (1964).

29. *FI* (1715), pp. 126–8.

30. Neuburg, *op. cit.*, ch. 3 'The Art of Reading'; Sloane *op. cit.*, pp. 48–49. He discusses the 'Thumb Bible, less than 2 inches square,

in which John Taylor, the water-poet, had summarized the Old and New Testaments in verse.'

31. For attempts to estimate the ability to write, or rather to sign one's name, see Lawrence Stone, 'Literacy and education in England, 1640–1900', *P & P*, 42 (1969); Roger Schofield, 'Measurement of literacy in pre-industrial England' in Jack Goody, *Literacy in Traditional Societies* (Cambridge 1968); for an optimistic assessment of the ability of the English poor to read see Neuburg, *op. cit.*, ch. 7.

32. Lawrence Stone, 'Literacy and education in England 1640–1900', *P & P* 42 (1969); W. A. L. Vincent, *The Grammar Schools: their continuing tradition, 1660–1714* (1969). For a more optimistic view see Nicholas Hans, *New Trends in Education in the Eighteenth Century* (1951) pp. 38–41 where he points out that some city grammar-schools such as Christ's Hospital and Manchester Grammar School were in the forefront of progress.

33. White Kennett, *The Charity of Schools for Poor Children* (1706).

34. Entry was normally at the age of seven or eight. Children left school between fourteen and sixteen. Vincent, *op. cit.*, p. 58.

35. Hans, *op. cit.*, pp. 19–23.

36. Axtell, *Locke, op. cit.*, p. 167. For the contemporary debate on the relative value of education at school and education at home see George C. Brauer, *The Education of a Gentleman* (New York 1959), pp. 195–228.

37. Hans, pp. 41–54.

38. *AT*, p. 4.

39. See Margaret James, *Social Problems and Policy during the Puritan Revolution, 1640–1660* (1930), ch. 7; Irene Parker, *Dissenting Academies in England* (Cambridge 1914), ch. 1.

40. There is a considerable literature on Newington Green Academy which was the subject of a debate between Samuel Wesley, a former pupil who later conformed to the Church of England and attacked the Dissenting academies, and Samuel Palmer. Defoe also replied to Wesley's criticisms in *More Short-Ways with the Dissenters* (1704). For references and a discussion of the education offered at Newington Green see Lew Girdler, 'Defoe's education at Newington Green Academy', *SP* l (1953); see also the valuable discussion of Morton's innovations in Joe W. Ashley Smith, *The Birth of Modern Education* (1954), pp. 56–61.

41. *Examiner*, No. 15. Quoted by Michael Shinagel, *Daniel Defoe and Middle-Class Gentility* (Harvard 1968), p. 82. Cf. pp. 81–86 for a general discussion of Swift's low opinion of Defoe, 'the fellow that was pilloryed, I have forgot his name'.

42. *AJ*, 30.10.1725 (Lee, iii, 435–6); cf. *CEG*, pp. 199–200.

43. *AJ*, 6.11.1725 (Lee, iii, 438–9).

44. For general studies of the Dissenting academies see Parker, *op. cit.*; Smith, *op. cit.* and H. M. Maclachlan, *English Education under the Test Acts* (1931).

45. Parker, pp. 59–63. Entrance to Oxford and Cambridge was often as young as this.

46. Hans, pp. 117–35.

47. For a general study of these schools see Hans, *op. cit.*, pp. 61–135.

48. For a general study of the charity schools see M. G. Jones, *The Charity School Movement* (Cambridge 1938) and Neuburg, *op. cit.*

49. This expression for the children of the poor, 'without shoes and stockings, perhaps half naked, or in tattered rags, cursing and swearing at one another, almost before they can speak', appears in *A Memorial concerning the Erecting . . . Orphanotrophy* (c. 1728), quoted by Ivy Pinchbeck and Margaret Hewitt, *Children in English Society* vol. i (1969), pp. 292–3.

50. Quoted by Pinchbeck and Hewitt, p. 288.

51. A phrase used by Bishop Joseph Butler of Bristol in 1745. Quoted by Neuburg, p. 6.

52. A point made in particular by Bernard de Mandeville, *An Essay on Charity and Charity Schools* (1723), pp. 312–25.

53. White Kennett, *The Charity of Schools for Poor Children* (1706), p. 15.

54. This was a serious problem which led to a not very successful attempt to provide boarding charity schools. See Jones, *op. cit.*, pp. 47–8.

55. For similar reasons charity schools had little success in industrial areas. The children's labour was too valuable to allow them to go to school.

56. *Essay on Charity-Schools* (1723), p. 328.

57. In *AJ*, 13.7.1723 (Lee, iii, 157–9); see also his earlier *Charity still a Christian Virtue* (1719) where he defends charity-school fund-raising activities. Some charity-school children had been accused of begging when they were raising funds.

58. *AJ, loc. cit.*

59. *MOC*, p. 8. He also 'passed through the proper exercises of the house', i.e. classics. The cavalier was of course lucky to go to Oxford in the good years before the Civil War. See above, p. 213.

60. *MOC*, p. 10.

61. *Crusoe*, p. 5.

62. *Roxana*, p. 6.

63. *MF*, p. 16.

64. *CS*, pp. 3–5.

65. *CJ*, p. 1.

66. *CJ*, p. 160.

67. *CS*, pp. 68–9.

68. *CEG*, pp. 184–231.
69. *CEG*, pp. 137–141, 154–5.
70. *CET*, ii, 53–85.
71. *CET*, ii, 55.
72. Wadsworth, *Well-Ordered Family*, p. 58 quoted in Morgan, *op. cit.*, p. 39.
73. This will be considered in Chapter 9.
74. Jeremy Taylor, *The Rule and Exercises of Holy Living* (1650), p. 200.
75. For a discussion of the calling or vocation in Massachusetts see Morgan, *op. cit.*, pp. 29–39.
76. *Essays upon Several Moral Subjects* (3rd. ed. 1720), iii, 82.
77. *CET*, i, 50.
78. Alan D. McKillop, 'Samuel Richardson's advice to an apprentice', *JEGP*, xlii (1943).

CHAPTER 8

1. *The Commentator*, xl (20.5.1720).
2. *Idem.*
3. *Tour*, i, 72.
4. *MF*, p. 52.
5. *CET*, ii, 190–1.
6. *CET*, ii, 184–5.
7. Some good examples of the workings of patronage can be seen in Swift's *Journal to Stella*.
8. *CET*, ii, 105.
9. *CET*, ii, 28–52.
10. *CS*, p. 168.
11. *CS*, pp. 309–10.
12. *CS*, p. 322.
13. For an interesting study of *Roxana* as a novel of moral decay see Maximilian E. Novak, 'Crime and punishment in Defoe's *Roxana*', *JEGP* lxv (1966).
14. Cf. Bonamy Dobrée, *English Literature in the early eighteenth century, 1700–1740* (Oxford 1959), p. 414, where he suggests that Defoe's main personages were 'outside the general structure of society'.
15. *Review*, viii, 302–3.
16. *CS*, p. 329.
17. *CEG*, p. 257. For a classification of different methods of social mobility in the order of speed of elevation see Lawrence Stone, 'Social mobility in England, 1500–1700', *P & P* 33 (1966).
18. For Defoe on marriage see below ch. 9. Marriage could lead to extremely rapid elevation. See Stone, *op. cit.*
19. At least it was unlikely for a pirate to succeed *qua* pirate. On the other hand the skills of piracy could well be adapted to a successful

Notes

335

privateering or naval career and hence lead to acceptance by
society.

20. For 'trade-pyrates' see *Review*, iv, 425–6.
21. *MF*, pp. 9–12.
22. *Roxana*, pp. 9–11.
23. *CET*, ii, 56.
24. See above, pp. 169–70.
25. *CET*, i, 61–7.
26. For the puritan sabbath and the institution of family worship see
above p. 210.
27. Defoe did not think that a good master should keep his apprentices
completely away from his customers. Introduction to customers and
suppliers was part of the apprentice's instruction and was necessary
if there was to be continuity in the world of shopkeeping. The old
should constantly give away to the new. But this did not mean that
the shopkeeper should simply hand over all his business to the
apprentice by never being in the shop when the customers came to
make a purchase.
28. *CET*, i, 120.
29. *CET*, i, 53–55.
30. *CET*, i, 312–21. See especially the description of the fittings in a
new pastrycook's shop, pp. 314–15.
31. *CET*, i, 319.
32. *A Christian Directory* (1673), ii, 121.
33. *CET*, i, 274–9. Cf. Dorothy Davis, *A History of Shopping* (1966), pp.
181–3 for an imaginative passage describing what a gullible shopper
of the twentieth century might have faced in an eighteenth-century
shop.
34. *CET*, i, 406. For a good example of the relationship between capital
and credit in the case of a real shopkeeper see *The Autobiography of
William Stout, op. cit.*
35. *CET*, i, 410.
36. The dangers of retail credit play an important part in the discussions
of trade in the *Review*, e.g. iii, 21–27, 33–35; v, 519–20; vi, 129–32.
But he was forced to change his tune.
37. *CET*, i, 412–13.
38. *Review*, iii, 17.
39. *CET*, i, 416–23.
40. *CET*, i, 241.
41. *CET*, i, 225–57.
42. For a more extended discussion of commercial casuistry see Baxter,
op. cit., vol. ii. This section and other parts of Baxter's *Christian
Directory* have been reprinted in Jeannette Tawney (ed.), *Chapters
from a Christian Directory* (1925).

43. Window-shopping and 'tumbling' goods were favourite occupations of the idle wives of the wealthy which were often condemned or satirized in contemporary literature. For some examples see J. Ashton, *Social Life in the Reign of Queen Anne* (1904), pp. 73–75. For Defoe on this see *CET*, i, 103–116.

44. *CET*, ii, 282.

45. *Conscience* (1639), p. 236.

46. *CET*, ii, 128.

47. *CET*, ii, 133–34.

48. Especially since the middle classes were likely to ape the court and wear mourning, too. See *Review*, ii, 7–8.

49. Defoe naturally attacks ostentation and extravagance but accepts the fact that if a tradesman lives too meanly people will suspect his credit, *CET*, i, 133–48.

50. *CET*, i, 88.

51. *CET*, i, 89–97. Defoe, a former bankrupt himself, wrote voluminously on bankruptcy in his career. He criticized the stupidity and cruelty of creditors who, by refusing a composition, wasted what was left of the bankrupt's estate and forced the bankrupt either to act dishonestly by fleeing abroad or to the places of sanctuary in London or else to be condemned to a pitiful life and a slow but sure death in a debtor's prison. He also criticized the venality of both lawyers and commissioners of bankruptcy whose fees and entertainments took money from debtor and creditor alike. He was at least partly responsible for the successful passage of the *Act for preventing frauds committed by bankrupts* of 1706, which improved the position of debtors by making it far more difficult for creditors to refuse to make a composition with a bankrupt who made an open and unreserved surrender. While Defoe naturally opposed the often savage treatment of bankrupts, he was the first to admit the difficulty of distinguishing between the honest and the fraudulent and also the need for creditors to have the power to have a debtor arrested. Without such powers the whole system of personal credit on which Defoe's trading world rested would have collapsed. For Defoe on bankruptcy see *E upon P.*, pp. 191–227; *Review*, iii, 69–148; 397–400; iv, 95–100, 107–31; v, 523–44, 579–83, 590–2, 603–4; vi, 519–63; *Remarks on the Bill to Prevent Frauds Committed by Bankrupts* (1706); *The Unreasonableness and ill consequences of Imprisoning the Body for Debt* (1729); as well as the reference to *CET* cited above.

52. *CET*, ii, 198–199.

53. *Review*, iii, 145–8. Defoe himself claimed to have done this.

54. *1 Corinthians* X, 12, quoted *CET*, ii, 195–6.

55. *CET*, ii, 21.

56. *CET*, ii, 233.

57. *CET*, ii, 92.
58. *CET*, ii, 159–82.
59. *CET*, ii, 150. Defoe names £20,000 as a suitable acquisition before retirement, *CET*, ii, 160. This would be a fairly considerable fortune for a businessman. See R. Grassby, 'The Personal wealth of the business community in seventeenth-century England', *EcHR*, 2nd. ser. xxiii (1970), pp. 228–9. Defoe even suggested that there should be a law to oblige the really rich businessman, with a fortune of £40,000–£60,000, to leave off trade, *CET*, ii, 148.
60. *CET*, ii, 239–40.

CHAPTER 9

1. For a general discussion of women's rights see Rebecca Scott, 'Women in the Stuart economy' (unpublished London M.Phil. 1973); Roger Thompson, *Women in Stuart England and America* (1974), ch. 8. Cf. for the situation in Victorian times, which had changed very little, Leonore Davidoff, 'Mastered for life: servant and wife in Victorian and Edwardian England', *Journal of Social History*, vii (1974).
2. For a general discussion of the double standard, especially in terms of the different treatment accorded to male and female adultery, see Keith Thomas, 'The Double Standard', *JHI* xx (1959).
3. *PHD*, p. 62.
4. *A Christian Directory* (1673), p. 480.
5. Alice Clark, *Working Life of Women in the Seventeenth Century* (1919), pp. 35–36; Robert P. Utter and Gwendolyn B. Needham, *Pamela's Daughters* (1937), p. 21; cf. B. L. de Muralt, *Letters describing the character and customs of the English and French nations* (1726), p. 12 states that 'among the common people, the husbands seldom make their wives work', which would certainly have seemed astonishing to any foreigner if it was true.
6. *Roxana*, p. 148.
7. Some of the most savage invective comes from the pen of Swift. See, for example, *The Progress of Marriage* (1722); *The Journal of a Modern Lady* (1729).
8. On this whole subject see Utter and Needham, *op. cit.*
9. *RC*, p. 92.
10. *CL*, pp. 25–26.
11. For Defoe's views on the education of women see *E upon P*, pp. 282–304. Shortly before Defoe published this, Mary Astell had written *A Serious Proposal to the Ladies* (1695) which was also a plea for better education for women, so that they could serve God better and also fulfil their important function as educators of children. In *Some Reflections upon Marriage* (1700) she advocated better

education to enable women to make a wiser choice of husband. See Florence M. Smith, *Mary Astell* (New York 1916). There was a fairly widespread attack on feminine inequality in the 1690s but it was short-lived. See Maximilian Novak's introduction to the 1967 facsimile edition of Defoe's *CL* for bibliography.

12. *E upon P*, pp. 294–6.

13. E.g. Defoe's attack on men as slanderers of women in *Tour*, i, 128 and his observation that man as the pursuer is the more guilty: "'Tis a pretty way we have got, to seek the temptation, and then blame the tempter', *Review*, iii, 527.

14. *EBNB*, p. 6.

15. As did Roxana's first husband.

16. *GLS*, pp. 6–7.

17. *AT*, pp. 31–38; quotation from p. 31.

18. Defoe expressly repudiates this description in *GLS*, p. 3.

19. *Angliae Notitia* (15th ed. 1684), p. 356.

20. *The English Lady's Catechism* (1703), quoted by J. Ashton, *Social Life in the Reign of Queen Anne* (1904), p.69. de Muralt said that the English thought that they had the best wives in the world because they did not mind them bringing their mistresses home, *op. cit.*, p. 37.

21. *Angliae Notitia*, p. 354.

22. Spiro Petersen, 'The matrimonial theme of Defoe's *Roxana*', *PMLA* lxx (1955), p. 88. See also on married women's rights Gellert Spencer Alleman, *Matrimonial Law and the Materials of Restoration Comedy* (Wallingford Pa. 1942); Thompson, *op. cit.* and Scott, *op. cit.*

23. Quoted by Thompson, *op. cit.*, p. 162.

24. *RC*, p. 263.

25. Quoted in Ashton, *op. cit.*, p. 26. Cf. *Spectator* No. 295.

26. Petersen, pp. 187–90; Thompson, pp. 163–4. Very often such settlements were made by means of a trust. Roxana's Dutch merchant agreed that her estate be 'all settl'd in trustee's hands, for your own use, and the management wholly your own.' (p. 259). See the long and very interesting discussion between them on the general subject of married women's property rights, pp. 135 ff.

27. *Roxana*, p. 148.

28. *Roxana*, p. 132.

29. Mary Astell pointed out sensibly enough that women were under no obligation to marry and should not do so unless they could love and respect their husbands. Most women, of course, did feel that they were obliged to marry. *Some Reflections upon Marriage* (1700).

30. L. L. Schueckling, *The Puritan Family* (1969), p. 53.

31. *A Christian Directory* (1673), p. 481.

32. For details see the introduction to Brian Frith (ed.), *Gloucestershire Marriage Allegations 1637–1680* (1954).

33. One major reason for avoiding a public marriage may have been the enormous expense involved in the customary presents and entertainments. Ashton, *op. cit.*, pp. 32–3. The cost would almost certainly outweigh the price of a special licence.

34. W. E. H. Lecky, *History of England in the Eighteenth Century* (1897), ii, 115–16.

35. *CL*, pp. 366–78.

36. *Review*, ix, 84.

37. Thompson, *op. cit.*, p. 113.

38. *Review*, i, supplement No. 3, pp. 19–20. The promise in this case was exacted from a man by a woman who threatened to shoot herself if he did not promise to marry her! The story is in *Review*, i, supplement No. 2, pp. 12–13.

39. *FARC*, p. 305.

40. P. 205, 'in the case of Jesson and Collins, Easter Term, 2 Annae'.

41. *CJ*, pp. 221–222. Actually this happened in Italy but it certainly could have happened in England.

42. Defoe pinched this idea from John Dunton, who had introduced it in the *Athenian Mercury* in the 1690s. He was far from pleased by Defoe's piracy. See the *Life and Errors of John Dunton* (1818 ed.), pp. 423–6 and see *The Athenian Oracle* 3 vols. (1703) for the collected letters from the *Athenian Mercury*.

43. Gregory King, *Natural and Political Observations 1696*, ed. George Chalmers (1810), p. 89. See also D. V. Glass, 'Notes on the demography of London at the end of the Seventeenth Century', *Daedalus* xcvii (spring 1968).

44. *MJ*, 11.6.1720 (Lee, ii, 247). Cf. King, *loc. cit.*

45. Or as Moll Flanders put it, 'the wars, and the sea, and trade, and other incidents have carried the men so much away', p. 63. The surplus of male emigrants to America led to a female shortage in the colonies. Roger Thompson sees this as the main reason for the much superior treatment of women in America, *op. cit.*

46. H. J. Habakkuk, 'Marriage settlements in the eighteenth century', *TRHS*, 4th. ser. xxxii (1950), finds an increase in bachelorhood among males in the middle and upper classes, p. 24.

47. *MF*, p. 18.

48. *MF*, p. 25. Cf. Utter and Needham, *op. cit.*. p. 31, 'Chastity was priceless because it was the only thing God had given to woman which commanded a price.'

49. *MF*, p. 23.

50. (1709), p. 25.

51. *The Rule and Exercises of Holy Living* (1650). p. 90.

52. *Review*, i, 227; cf. *CL*, p. 282: 'He's a rogue, say they, that gets a woman with child before marriage; and he's a fool that marries her afterwards. He's a knave that promises to marry her; but he's a fool that performs it.'

53. *Review*, i, 227.

54. *Roxana*, p. 152.

55. e.g. by making sure her husband is drunk on his wedding night, cf. *MF*, p. 49.

56. Jeremy Taylor, *Doctor Dubitantium* in Reginald Heber (ed.), *Whole Works* (1850), x, 113. '*Nemo tenetur infamare se*, is a rule universally admitted among the casuists, "no man is bound to discover his own shame"', quoted in G. A. Starr, *Defoe and Casuistry* (Princeton 1971), p. 117, n. 11.

57. *Review*, i, suppl. no. 2 (Oct. 1704), p. 13.

58. *The Virgin Unmask'd* (1709). p. 30.

59. *CJ*, p. 189.

60. *MF*, p. 65.

61. p. 6.

62. *Roxana*, p. 256.

63. Thompson, *op. cit.*, p. 118; Habakkuk, 'Marriage settlements . . .', *op. cit.*, pp. 24–25.

64. Habakkuk, p. 21. The portion or dowry was what the wife brought. The jointure was the annual income settled by the husband on the wife in case she survived him. By the late seventeenth century the normal relationship was £1,000 of portion to £100 of jointure. Earlier it had only been 5 or 6 to 1.

65. *MF*, p. 52.

66. *Review*, ix, 84.

67. *MF*, p. 64.

68. *Roxana*, p. 166. Cf. the analysis of 'the healing action of a city marriage' in just such a gentleman's family in *CEG*, pp. 250–2.

69. *Review*, iv, 403–404; cf. *Roxana*, pp. 7–10.

70. *Well-ordered Family*, p. 42, quoted in Morgan *op. cit.*, p. 19. Cf. Thompson, *op. cit.*, pp. 116–118 for other references on this subject.

71. *CL*, p. 101.

72. *CL*, p. 59. To marry one man and to love another was to run the risk of committing 'adultery and incest with him every day in my desires', as did Moll Flanders with the brother of her first husband, p. 51.

73. *Review*, i, Suppl. no. 1 (Sept. 1704), p. 9.

74. *Review*, i, Suppl. No. 2 (Oct. 1704), p. 14.

75. *A Christian Directory* (1673), pp. 481–2.

76. *The Little Review*, no. 6, p. 22.

77. *FARC*, p. 273.

78. *RC*, pp. 142–5.
79. *FI* (1715), p. 126.
80. *RC*, p. 206.
81. *RC*, pp. 183–287.
82. *RC*, pp. 5–36. Later the suitor is converted by one of his poor tenants, convinces the girl of his sincerity and they all live happily ever after.
83. *FI* (1718), pp. 9–11.
84. *FI* (1718), pp. 1–95.
85. Defoe warns such young men that they may be taking on more than they bargained for by telling the story of a woman of 65 who married a boy of 10. She did not release him for sixty-two years when he was 72 and she 127! *CL*, pp. 362–3.
86. *CL*, pp. 229–51.
87. *CL*, pp. 229–30.
88. *CL*, p. 239.
89. Quoted by Brian Frith, *op. cit.*, p. xxv.
90. See, for instance, Salmon, *op. cit.*, p. 67; Jeremy Taylor, *Holy Living*, *op. cit.*, p. 201; Morgan, p. 42.
91. Which is what Sir Edward Coke is supposed to have done when his daughter refused to marry John Villiers; quoted by Thompson, *op. cit.*, p. 119.
92. *RC*, p. 30.
93. *Review*, i, 272.
94. *RC*, p. 133.
95. *RC*, p. 99.
96. Such calculations are based on the analysis of parish registers, an occupation which has now become a full-time profession in its own right. Publications in this field have as a result become legion but see E. A. Wrigley, 'Family limitation in Pre-Industrial England', *EcHR*, 2nd. ser. xix (1966); J. D. Chambers, *Population, Economy and Society in Pre-Industrial England* (1972), ch. 2; Pierre Goubert, 'Recent Theories and Research in French Population between 1500 and 1700' in D. V. Glass and D. E. C. Eversley, *Population in History* (1965) and the interesting article by J. Hajnal, who converts the fact of late marriage and the high proportion of people never married into a generalized European marriage pattern which he compares with the differing patterns in the rest of the world, 'European Marriage Patterns in Perspective' in Glass and Eversley, *op. cit.*
97. Cf. Defoe, 'a married apprentice will always make a repenting tradesman', *CET*, i, 155.
98. The expression used by the book-seller, John Dunton, *The Life and Errors of John Dunton* (1818 ed.), p. 61. Defoe thought that a father whose son married before he was well-enough established to have

a proper household with servants would have 'a dishclout for a daughter in law', *CET*, i, 156. The only trouble with late marriage was that it encouraged prostitution. *Some Considerations upon Street-walkers* (1726), pp. 6-7.

99. Goubert estimates that in France, where there was practically no evidence of contraception in the seventeenth century, the interval between births was about 25 to 30 months, *op. cit.* This long interval is sometimes explained by the contemporary custom of breast-feeding children until they were in their second year. However, the contraceptive effects of breast-feeding are by no means conclusively proved. Wrigley found that the mean age at which women bore their last child was 40, and that the fecundity of women was less in their thirties than in their twenties. Goubert found that it took two births in France to produce one adult. Child mortality was not quite so high on the average in England, but it was particularly high in Defoe's lifetime because of the new virulence of smallpox, a child-killer. This was very severe in the 1670s and 1680s and was one reason for the slow population growth of the time.

100. *AJ*, 20.3.1724/5 (Lee, iii, 367-69).

101. King, *Natural and Political Observations 1696*. ed. George Chalmers (1810), p. 89, quoted by Scott, *op. cit.* There were 950,000 wives, 240,000 widows, 300,000 female servants and 110,000 female sojourners and single persons. The three latter groups outnumbered their male equivalents by over 200,000, some indication of the poor market for women which might well have been much worse by 1720 after another twelve years of war.

102. P. E. H. Hair, 'Bridal pregnancy in rural England in earlier centuries', *Population Studies* xx (1966) estimates that between a third and a sixth of all brides must have been pregnant at marriage between 1540 and 1835, with the proportion increasing after 1700.

103. Hair's sample *was* rural but in any case there are technical problems in analysing urban parish registers.

104. Cf. Chambers, *op. cit.*, pp. 49-50.

105. See for example E. M. Leroy Ladurie, *The Peasants of Languedoc* (1974), p. 302.

106. J. L. Flandrin, 'Contraception, mariage et relations amoureuses dans l'Occident chrétien', *Annales* xxiv (1969); *idem*, 'Mariage tardif et vie sexuelle', *Annales* xxvii (1972); J. Depauw, 'Amour illégitime et société à Nantes au XVIIIe siècle', *Annales* xxvii (1972).

107. See above pp. 248-49.

108. *CL*, p. 26.

109. *CET*, i, 348-68.

110. *CET*, i, 115.

111. See above pp. 169-70.

112. Or soon found out. Cf. *CJ*, pp. 193–4; Alexander Ramkins, pp. 161–3 and see Baxter, *Christian Directory*, p. 479, 'your wants in a married state are hardlier supplied than in a single life. You will want so many things which before you never wanted ... that all will seem little enough, if you had never so much.'

113. *FI* (1718), p. 173.

114. *FI* (1718), pp. 17–19.

115. *The Lady's New Year's-Gift: or, Advice to a Daughter* first published in 1688. There were numerous editions in Defoe's lifetime. I quote from the 7th of 1701.

116. p. 26.

117. pp. 36–37.

118. pp. 58–59.

119. Morgan, *op. cit.*, ch. 1; L. L. Schueckling, *The Puritan Family* (1969), ch. 1; James T. Johnson, 'English puritan thought on the ends of marriage', *Church History* xxxviii (1969); W. and M. Haller, 'The puritan art of love', *HLQ*, v (1940–1) and the conduct-books of the first half of the seventeenth century, especially William Gouge, *Of Domesticall Duties* (1622) and Daniel Rogers, *Matrimoniall Honor* (1642). Milton was in some ways the most liberal of the puritan writers on marriage. He placed 'the apt and cheerful conversation of man with woman, to comfort and refresh him against the evil of solitary life' before procreation as the end of marriage. But his arguments are bent towards the man's comfort, as in this quotation; 'The Doctrine and Discipline of Divorce' in *Prose Works* (1848), iii, 181.

120. *Holy Living, op. cit.*, pp. 80–81.

121. *Idem*, p. 92.

122. *CL*, pp. 54–56.

123. *CL*, pp. 61–63.

124. *CL*, p. 303.

125. *CL*, p. 318.

126. e.g. Gouge, *op. cit.*, pp. 223–4.

127. *CL*, p. 303; it is not clear what theory of conception Defoe did hold. He confined himself to the remark that 'the work of conception is hit off at once', i.e. was not continuous (*CL*, p. 303). The commonest seems to have been the Galenic theory of double emission, a theory which gave women some important rights since it held that they could not conceive until they had attained their pleasure. A-C. Kliszowski, in an unpublished study of seventeenth-century French theologians, wrote that 'all the theologians of this time permit the woman to excite herself before conjugal relations – *se excitare tactibus* – and most of them also allow her to do the same after the man's withdrawal, if she has not yet attained her pleasure', quoted in

The World of Defoe

344

Flandrin, 'Marriage tardif . . .', *op. cit.*, p. 1369; cf. James McMath, *The Expert Mid-Wife* (1694), pp. 10–11. It is probable that Defoe, who seemed to object to anyone getting pleasure from sex, would have rejected this for the established modern view of single emission.

128. *CL*, pp. 239–42.

129. Cf. Baxter, *op. cit.*, p. 479. 'Q. May the aged marry that are frigid, impotent and uncapable of procreation? A. Yes, God hath not forbidden them: And there are other lawful ends of marriage, as mutual help and comfort . . .'

130. E.g. Wrigley, *op. cit.*

131. *CL*, p. 55.

132. *CL*, pp. 134–36; abstinence was the least blameworthy way of preventing conception.

133. *CL*, pp. 150–158.

134. Cf. N. E. Himes, *Medical History of Contraception* (1936).

135. *CL*, p. 161–65; quotation from p. 161.

136. *CL*, p. 163.

137. *MF*, pp. 138–46, quotations from pp. 144, 146.

138. *Review*, i, Suppl. no. 5 (Jan. 1705), pp. 14–15.

139. *CL*, p. 133.

140. On this subject see Petersen, *op. cit.*; Alleman, *op. cit.* and the learned works quoted by them. For a simple summary of the position see O. R. McGregor, *Divorce in England* (1957), ch. 1.

141. Separation was *divortium a mensa et thoro*. Only annulment, *divortium a vinculo matrimonii*, was what we call divorce, i.e. where the parties were free to remarry.

142. *The Little Review*, 7, p. 27.

143. I quote this from Thompson, *op. cit.*, p. 171, but it is so apt that it is quoted in virtually every work on the subject.

144. *AJ*, 15.8.1724 (Lee, iii, 291–3).

145. *Op. cit.*, pp. 65–6.

146. *AJ*, 22.8.1724 (Lee, iii, 293–5), cf. *CJ*, p. 198.

147. *AJ*, 16.1.1724/5 (Lee, iii, 355).

148. Quoted by Alleman, *op. cit.*, pp. 117–119.

149. *Roxana*, pp. 41–2; cf. Petersen, pp. 176–7.

150. *CJ*, p. 198.

151. For the law in Massachusetts see Thompson, *op. cit.*, pp. 174–78.

152. *Conscience* (1639), pp. 209–10; cf. Baxter, *op. cit.*, pp. 536–9, Gouge, *op. cit.*, p. 215.

153. 'The Doctrine and Discipline of Divorce', *Prose Works*, iii, 183. See also 'The Judgement of Martin Bucer concerning Divorce', 'Tetrachordon' and 'Colasterion' in the same volume.

154. *AJ*, 24.4.1725 (Lee, iii, 379–80).

155. *CL*, pp. 118–19.

CHAPTER 10

1. *AJ*, 23.5.1724 (Lee, iii, 266).

2. See above Ch. 9, note 99.

3. Peter Laslett, *The World We Have Lost* (1965), pp. 93–94 suggests that the expectation of life of a person of twenty-one would be about a further thirty years.

4. For an interesting comparison of the effect of death in a modern society where the dead have completed their obligations to the living and in a society like that of Defoe where they often 'die with unfinished business', see Robert Blauner, 'Death and social structure', *Psychiatry* xxix (1966).

5. See above pp. 262–63.

6. *E upon P*, pp. 132–42.

7. This was the purpose of the jointure. See above p. 247. See also H. J. Habbakkuk 'Marriage settlements . . .', *loc. cit.*

8. John Gay, *The Beggars' Opera* (1728), Act I, Sc. x.

9. ed. Chalmers (1810 ed.), p. 89.

10. *Chickens feed Capons* (1731), p. 1.

11. *PM*, pp. 6–15.

12. *PM*, p. 4.

13. *PM*, pp. 24–31.

14. *AJ*, 7.7.1722 (Lee, iii, 23–24).

15. H. Misson, *Memoirs and observations in his travels over England* (1719), pp. 123–4.

16. *AJ*, 25.9.1725 (Lee, iii, 431).

17. Leon Radzinowicz, *A History of English Criminal Law* (1948), i, 203. First used in the execution of Earl Ferrers.

18. The victims' relatives often pulled on their legs to shorten their agony.

19. *AJ*, 25.9.1725 (Lee, iii, 431).

20. Lee, iii, 430.

21. *Loc. cit.*

22. For a contemporary discussion of the Bills of Mortality and their history see Capt. John Graunt, *Natural and Political Observations upon the Bills of Mortality* (5th. ed. 1676) in C. H. Hull, *Economic Writings of Sir William Petty* (Cambridge 1899), ii, 314–435.

23. See the Bill inserted as an illustration in *JPY* between pp. 113–14.

24. *Op. cit.*, p. 354.

25. J. M. Beattie, 'The pattern of crime in England, 1660–1800', *P & P*, 62 (1974), p. 61.

26. For a discussion of the increase of offences carrying the death penalty, nearly all offences against property, see Radzinowicz, *op. cit.*, p. 4 and Appendix A. The number of such offences rose from about fifty in 1688 to about two hundred and fifty in 1820.

27. Although the combination of Stoic and Christian philosophy helped Englishmen, even in Defoe's time, to keep their upper lips stiff. Seneca, in particular, was very popular. There can be few better expositions of the trifling nature of death than in the chapter, 'The contempt of death makes all the miseries of life easy to us', in the best-selling *Seneca's Morals* translated by Sir Roger L'Estrange (1678).

28. *AJ*, 25.9.1725 (Lee, iii, 430).

29. *DPP*, p. 130.

30. Archbishop Tillotson, *The Usefulness of Considering our Latter End* in the *Family Chaplain* (1775), vol. i, 100–122.

31. P. 84. Quoted in G. A. Starr, *Defoe and Spiritual Autobiography* (Princeton 1965), p. 11.

32. Samuel Doolittle, *A Sermon occasion'd by the late earthquake* (1692), p. 12. This sermon is an excellent exposition of the relationship between divine providence and natural disaster. Defoe's best piece on this subject is the preface to *The Storm* (1704).

33. *JPY*, p. 175.

34. *CS*, p. 237.

35. *Roxana*, p. 128.

36. *MF*, p. 248.

37. *MF*, p. 260.

38. *DPP*, p. 189.

39. *Crusoe*, pp. 65–68.

40. It never did. The great killer during most of Defoe's lifetime was smallpox.

41. *Review*, viii, 297–300; ix, 13–14.

42. *AJ*, 10.9.1720 and 1.10.1720 (Lee, ii, 277–8, 284–5). For French methods see above, pp. 93–94.

43. See especially the first part of *DPP*.

44. Doolittle, *op. cit.*, p. 23.

45. *DPP*, p. 147.

46. *DPP*, pp. 181–2.

47. *CS*, p. 325.

48. For much of what follows I am indebted to D. P. Walker's fascinating book, *The Decline of Hell* (1964).

49. Timothy Cruso, *Discourses upon the Rich Man and Lazarus* (1697), p. 56. Cruso, a well-known Nonconformist preacher, was a schoolmate of Defoe and it is generally assumed that Defoe borrowed the name for Robinson Crusoe.

50. *PHD*, p. 212; *VAW*, p. 45.

51. *PHD*, p. 212.

52. Tobias Swinden, *An Enquiry into the Nature and Place of Hell* (1714), pp. 72–77.

53. Sir William Petty, *Another Essay in Political Arithmetic* (1682), in Hull, *op. cit.*, ii, 467–8.
54. *Op. cit.*
55. Swinden, pp. 107–37.
56. *VAW*, pp. 31–32.
57. *VAW*, p. 45.
58. *AJ*, 25.9.1725 (Lee, iii, 430).
59. *Review*, iv, 320.

INDEX

PETER EARLE

Peter Earle was born in 1937 and educated at University
College, London, and at the London School of Economics, where he has been a lecturer in economic history
since 1966. He started his academic career as a specialist
in the economic and social history of the Mediterranean
(his first published book was *Corsairs of Malta and
Barbary*), but now works mainly on English history,
having currently in preparation a book on Monmouth's
Rebellion.